Children's Writing and Reading

Analysing Classroom Language

KATHARINE PERERA

Basil Blackwell
in association with
André Deutsch

First published 1984
Reprinted 1986, 1988

Basil Blackwell Ltd
108 Cowley Road, Oxford OX4 1JF, UK
in association with André Deutsch Limited, 105 Great Russell
Street, London WC1B 3LJ, England

Basil Blackwell Inc.
432 Park Avenue South, Suite 1503
New York 10016, USA

British Library Cataloguing in Publication Data

Perera, Katharine
  Children's writing and reading.—(The
  Language library)
  1. Language arts (Elementary)   2. Language
  and education   3. Written communications
  ——Study and teaching (Elementary)
  I. Title   II. Series
  372.6'23   LB1576
  ISBN 0–631–13653–3
  ISBN 0–631–13654–1 Pbk

Library of Congress Cataloging in Publication Data

Perera, Katharine
  Children's writing and reading.
  (The Language Library)
  Bibliography: p.
  Includes indexes.
  1. Children—Language.   2. Language acquisition.
    3. English language—Composition and
  exercises.   4. Reading.   5. English language—
  Grammar.
  I. Title.   II. Series.
  LB1139.L3P375   1984   372.6   84-8857
  ISBN 0–631–13653–3
  ISBN 0–631–13654–1 (pbk)

Typeset by Santype International Ltd., Salisbury, Wilts.
Printed in Great Britain by Page Bros (Norwich) Ltd

For Suria

Contents

Acknowledgements

One theme of this book is the need to consider drafting and revision as an essential part of the writing process. It is, therefore, a particular pleasure to be able to acknowledge the help I have had in this task. The original idea for the book came from David Crystal. From the initial stages of planning the outline to the finished work, he has offered both detailed, perceptive criticisms and invaluable encouragement. My colleague, Alan Cruttenden, has helped me greatly by discussing the overall development of the book and particular problematic issues; he has also provided thoughtful comments on chapters 3 and 4. I have received stimulating reactions to the draft of the whole book from Frank Skitt, a wise and gifted primary headteacher, who welcomed me over a period of several years into his school, where I learnt a great deal about assisting language development in young children.

Writing this book has reminded me of the extent to which scholarship is a shared endeavour. Barry Kroll and Gordon Wells of the Child Language Development Project at Bristol University and Robin Fawcett and Michael Perkins of the Polytechnic of Wales have been very generous in allowing me to use corpora of material collected by their research projects; in addition, Robin Fawcett has given me useful criticisms of chapter 3. John Harris, Jeffrey Wilkinson and Kenneth Yerrill have been kind enough to allow me to make use of material in their unpublished theses.

To Joy Munro and Patricia Bowden I am most grateful for meticulous and dependable secretarial help.

On a personal level, I have been blessed by the support and encouragement of family and friends. Above all, I want to thank my husband, Suria, who, as well as providing valuable ideas and sensitive criticisms, has sustained me with his care, concern and understanding throughout the long and sometimes daunting process of writing.

Figures and tables

FIGURES

TABLES

Abbreviations used in grammatical description

Brackets indicate that the additional symbols are optional; the full form is used only when specificity is required.

A	clause element: adverbial
adj	adjective
Adj P	multi-word adjectival phrase
adv	adverb
AP	multi-word adverbial phrase
aux	auxiliary verb
Aux VP	auxiliary verb phrase
C_o	clause element: object complement
$C_{(s)}$	clause element: (subject) complement
c	co-ordinator
Cat VP	catenative verb phrase
cop	copula
d	determiner
int	intensifier
n	noun
n	(subscript) any number, e.g. adj_n = any number of adjectives
no.	cardinal number
NP	multi-word noun phrase
$O_{(d)}$	clause element: direct object
$O_{(i)}$	clause element: indirect object
o	ordinal
op	operator
part	particle
pre-d	pre-determiner
prep	preposition
post-d	post-determiner
q	quantifier
S	clause element: subject

s	subordinator
V	clause element: verb
v	member of word-class 'verb'
VP	multi-word verb phrase

Symbols

*	grammatically unacceptable form, e.g. *this boys
?	unlikely but not impossible form, e.g. ?red tall chimneys
!	semantically unlikely or impossible utterance, !Goliath killed a stone.
( )	within an example, the bracketed element is optional, e.g. Jim knew (that) Bill would come.
[ ]	within an example, square brackets mark the position where ellipsis has occurred, e.g. Bob swept the room and [ ] lit the fire.
/ /	slant brackets enclose phonemic transcription
⟨ ⟩	angle brackets enclose a written form as opposed to a spoken one, e.g. 'The plural is formed with ⟨-s⟩ or ⟨-es⟩.'
.../	slant lines mark tone-unit boundaries
— —	pause (length indicated by the number of dashes)
`	falling intonation nucleus
´	rising intonation nucleus
ˇ	fall-rise intonation nucleus
^	rise-fall intonation nucleus
'	stressed syllable

Phonemic symbols used in transcription

CONSONANTS

p	pet	/pet/	s	sit	/sɪt/
b	bed	/bed/	z	zoo	/zu/
t	tub	/tʌb/	ʃ	ship	/ʃɪp/
d	do	/du/	ʒ	measure	/meʒə/
k	cat	/kæt/	h	hat	/hæt/
g	gap	/gæp/	m	men	/men/
tʃ	chin	/tʃɪn/	n	nag	/næg/
dʒ	jam	/dʒæm/	ŋ	sing	/sɪŋ/
f	fell	/fel/	l	let	/let/
v	vat	/væt/	r	red	/red/
θ	thin	/θɪn/	j	yes	/jes/
ð	then	/ðen/	w	wet	/wet/

VOWELS

i	read	/rid/	ɜ	bird	/bɜd/
ɪ	rid	/rɪd/	ə	the	/ðə/
e	bed	/bed/	eɪ	say	/seɪ/
æ	bad	/bæd/	əʊ	so	/səʊ/
ɑ	calm	/kɑm/	aɪ	high	/haɪ/
ɒ	cot	/kɒt/	aʊ	how	/haʊ/
ɔ	caught	/kɔt/	ɒɪ	toy	/tɒɪ/
ʊ	good	/gʊd/	ɪə	here	/hɪə/
u	mood	/mud/	ɛə	there	/ðɛə/
ʌ	hut	/hʌt/	aɪə	fire	/faɪə/

CHAPTER 1

Introduction

Experienced teacher witnesses were of one mind in their concern for recognizable progress in a child's command of language. As one head of department put it: 'I would quarrel with the philosophy that problems sort themselves out by continued and increased exposure to books and good English.'

(DES, 1975, pp. 172–3)

When children start school they have already acquired a great deal of oral language and within two or three years most of them have mastered the initial stages of learning to read and write. This does not mean, however, that subsequently these language abilities can be left to look after themselves. The quotation that begins this book comes from a chapter in the Bullock Report entitled 'Language in the Middle and Secondary Years': it suggests that teachers throughout much of the school age-range feel that they should take deliberate steps to extend their pupils' linguistic resources. This positive approach is endorsed by the Bullock Committee: 'We advocate, in short, planned intervention in the child's language development' (DES, 1975, p. 67).

In order for such intervention to succeed, it has to work in harmony with the natural sequence of language acquisition, since simply to teach some aspect of language without knowing whether the child is at an appropriate stage to respond to it is to invite failure for the pupil and disillusion for the teacher. Therefore, if teachers are going to plan activities to improve their pupils' command of language, they need a clear understanding of the normal course of language development. In addition, because reading and writing are so important in our education system and so much language work is concerned with these two modes, teachers also need to be aware of the rather complex relationships between oral and written language; not only class teachers in primary schools and English teachers in secondary schools, but also all those who use reading and writing as a means of teaching and testing their subject.

The chief focus of this book is on the grammatical structures of written language – the structures of children's own writing and of material written for them in books, workcards, instructions and examination questions. Its main aim is to provide teachers (and others, such as speech therapists and educational psychologists) with the framework of knowledge that they need in order to be able, first, to assess their pupils' grammatical abilities, and then to intervene appropriately to extend them. Accordingly, chapter 3 outlines children's grammatical development from about eighteen months to fourteen years or so, and chapter 4 illustrates some of the differences between speech and writing. To describe the structures of a language comprehensibly, it is necessary to use an agreed system of grammatical analysis. For this reason, chapter 2 presents a grammatical framework for the description of English, so that all those who use this book share not only the same terminology but also an awareness of the grammatical principles that underlie the analysis. With this tripartite foundation of a grammatical description of English, knowledge of children's grammatical development, and an understanding of some of the differences between speech and writing, it becomes possible to examine some structural aspects of written language in the classroom: chapter 5 studies children's own writing and chapter 6 focuses on their reading materials.

The next two sections outline some of the ways in which the subject matter of chapters 5 and 6 can be of use to teachers in their routine classroom activities.

Children's writing

With regard to children's writing, there are many tasks which teachers have to undertake which can be carried out more confidently and consistently if there is some understanding of the stages that children pass through in their development as writers. The first such task to consider is the setting of written work. Here, an awareness of the different demands that are made by different kinds of writing can enable teachers to set assignments that are appropriate for the age and ability of their pupils, so that the ablest are stretched and the weakest supported. For example, in a mixed-ability history class, the ablest writers might tackle an essay entitled 'Florence Nightingale's contribution to nursing' while those who are struggling could attempt 'A letter from Scutari', or 'Extracts from Florence Nightingale's diary'. A developmental perspective also allows teachers to set work that will focus their pupils' attention on precise aspects of the craft of writing. Occasionally, student teachers' lesson plans give, as the objective of a writing lesson, 'To improve creative writing'. Such vagueness can be replaced by a more specific and realizable goal. For instance, pupils might be encouraged to describe a series of events out of chronological order, so that they begin to learn some of the special effects that can be achieved; they might be advised to take particular care over the links between sentences; they might experiment with different ways of beginning their sentences; or they might start learning to handle structures other than the story. In this connection it is worth noting the results of a survey of children's writing carried out by the Bullock Committee: although over eighty per cent of their sample of nine-year-olds wrote original stories during the week in question, less than half wrote factual accounts based on 'personal investigations in connection with science and mathematics' (DES, 1975, p. 472).

Another task is the correction of written work. Teachers spend a great deal of time and effort in marking errors. It is therefore particularly important that they recognize that there are many kinds of mistake which, because they arise from a variety of causes, require different remedies. Although all the sentences from (1) to (4) contain grammatical errors, they cannot all be dealt with appropriately by some blanket comment like 'Be more careful' or 'Read through your work before you give it in':

1 In this particular rockpool that I looked in was so crammed with all kinds of marine life.
2 Children which had to work in the coal mines I feel bad about this.
3 His dog came with him to get the birds what the man killed.
4 Although they tried hard but they didn't win the match.

A closely related task is the assessment of writing. Whether teachers award a grade or write a comment such as 'You can do better than this', they are, inescapably, making judgements about the worth of each piece. They may be relating each one to the others in the set; or they may be comparing an individual's performance on this occasion and this topic with his performance on earlier occasions and other topics; or they may be considering his writing in relation to his oral response. In every case, such judgements involve assessment, comparison and evaluation. The clearer the criteria for making the judgements, the more reliable they are likely to be. Some of the criteria will be non-linguistic, of course. Depending on the nature of the particular assignment, they may include any of the following factors: liveliness, humour, imagination, factual accuracy, length, neatness, and so on. But at least some of the factors which influence the assessment will be purely linguistic ones, such as the range and appropriateness of the vocabulary, the maturity of sentence structures, and the cohesiveness of paragraphs.

Given that this book concentrates chiefly on grammatical features, it is encouraging to note that there is some evidence of a correlation between teachers' impressionistic assessments of children's writing and the level of occurrence of mature syntactic structures. In 1965, the London Association of Teachers of English selected twenty-eight pieces of writing from a corpus by fifteen-year-old pupils. A team of examiners assessed the essays impressionistically, assigning each one a grade on the scale A to E. Later, Yerrill (1977) made a grammatical analysis of these graded essays, noting particularly the occurrence of constructions which he had previously found to be indicators of linguistic maturity. His results showed that (with differences in length taken into account) the essays that had been graded A and B on overall impression contained two and a half times as many of these mature constructions as those graded C, D and E.

An advantage of the ability to recognize mature syntax is that it can help teachers to avoid underestimating their pupils' linguistic abilities and, consequently, forming expectations that are damagingly low. Sometimes writing can be scrappy and lacking interesting ideas, untidily presented in poor handwriting with bad spelling and weak punctuation, and yet still provide evidence of a certain linguistic maturity. It is understandably very difficult for teachers to see through all the weaknesses to the underlying strengths. Nevertheless, in order to build on what children can do and to make appropriate demands on them, it is essential to be aware of the good features that are buried beneath the dismal surface of the writing.

The last teaching task to mention is the provision of advice and guidance which will help pupils to improve their written work. That this is, in practice, very demanding is suggested by the following comment in the Bullock Report:

> Most [secondary teachers of English] suggested that whatever direct instruction in how to write might be needed by pupils could be presented by teachers during classroom writing lessons and could be based on actual experience in written communication. *Yet hour after hour of classroom observation failed to reveal many efforts to provide such direct help.* (DES, 1975, p. 172, my italics)

A pupil may produce a sentence like this:

5 I gave my brother a present that to my great relief and delight he very much liked it.

It is obviously easiest just to cross out *it* and, perhaps, to write a comment such as 'Use simpler sentences'. However, it would be more helpful (though admittedly more time-consuming) to demonstrate that the sentence is built up from two simpler ones:

5a I gave my brother a present.
5b To my great relief and delight, he very much liked it.

The structure becomes clearer if *to my great relief and delight* is temporarily omitted. Then, when (5a) and (5b) are joined, it is apparent that *a present* is referred to by *that*, so *it* is no longer needed:

5c I gave my brother a present *that* he very much liked.

Now, *to my great relief and delight* can be re-inserted:

5d I gave my brother a present that, to my great relief and delight, he very much liked.

Children's reading materials

It is important for teachers to be able to make an accurate assessment of the readability level of books and workcards, both when selecting materials for purchase in the first instance and when choosing books from the stock-room that will match as closely as possible the reading levels of the various groups within a class. Teachers habitually take into account such factors as presentation, interest level, vocabulary difficulty and conceptual demands, but they need also to be aware of the comprehension problems that can be caused by grammatical complexity and by certain types of discourse structure. Such an awareness is particularly valuable in those cases where the physical presentation of the book does not accurately reflect its level of linguistic difficulty. It is not uncommon, for example, for books with large print and full colour illustrations to contain language that is more suitable for secondary pupils than for the juniors that the publishers have apparently had in mind. Similarly, it sometimes happens that books marketed for CSE classes are linguistically more demanding than those aimed at HNC or 'A' level groups. (See, for example, Whitcombe, 1973.)

A sensitivity to grammatical complexity can also alert teachers to potential sources of misunderstanding in instructions and examination questions; hence, it provides a principled rather than a random basis for simplifying such materials. For instance, if pupils are given the following written instruction:

6a Do not write the results on the diagrams that you have drawn or colour the bar graphs.

and several of them do colour the bar graphs, it is clear that they are not just being perverse or disobedient. Rather, they have been unable to hold the negative in mind for the eleven words between *not* and *colour*. Nor have they recognized the force of *or*. Since skilled readers know that *or* after a negative means 'and ... not', this suggests an obvious way to revise the instructions:

6b Do not write the results on the diagrams that you have drawn *and do not* colour the bar graphs.

Perhaps the most important reason of all for teachers to be able to analyse the language structure of reading materials is that, having pinpointed linguistic difficulties, they are then in a position to provide explicit teaching to help children tackle them. After all, the teacher's aim should not be always to present pupils with the simplest language available. Books which contain vocabulary and grammatical constructions not commonly used in everyday speech are a potent source of language enrichment. To choose only simply-written books, or to simplify more demanding ones, would deprive children of this vital stimulus to their linguistic development. The skilful teacher, who knows precisely which aspects of a text the pupils will find difficult, can afford to present linguistically demanding material on occasions, so long as appropriate support is provided to help them master the new constructions.

Other approaches to text assessment

In order to make assessments of text difficulty, many teachers use either a readability formula or the cloze procedure. Both of these measures have their place and both have the advantage of yielding a score, which makes comparison between texts straightforward, but they have disadvantages too.

There are many published readability formulae (see Harrison, 1980, for an overview); the most widely used combine a measure of vocabulary difficulty with a calculation of sentence length in an arithmetical formula that produces an approximate reading age. Their most obvious weakness is that sentence length is used to assess grammatical difficulty. Long sentences may be difficult (although length in itself is not the main cause of their difficulty) but that does not mean that short ones are always easy. Indeed there are many instances where a sentence can be made easier to understand by lengthening it rather than shortening it. For example, Reid (1972, p. 398) presented two matched groups of seven-year-olds with one sentence each from the following pair:

7a The girl standing beside the lady had a blue dress.
7b The girl had a blue dress and she was standing beside the lady.

All the children then had to answer this question:

7c Who had a blue dress? (The girl/the lady)

Those who read the ten-word sentence (7a) achieved a score of 41.4 per cent, while those who read the longer sentence, the thirteen-word (7b), gained the substantially higher score of 88.6 per cent. Therefore, the formulae can be dangerously misleading if the inclusion of the sentence-length measure encourages users to think of length as a CAUSE of reading difficulty.

Another disadvantage is that the formulae can only assign a global score to passages – which have to be at least one hundred words long – and cannot pinpoint specific sources of difficulty. Thus they can indicate that a particular book will be too demanding for children of a given reading age but they cannot reveal what has caused the difficulty, or provide suggestions either for supportive teaching or for text simplification.

The second type of readability measure to consider, the cloze procedure, uses specially prepared passages from the text which is to be assessed: words are omitted at regular intervals and replaced by a standard-length line, e.g.:

8 The badger is a _____ animal. It lives at _____ end of a
  long _____ in the earth called _____ set.

Subjects are then asked to fill in the blank spaces. (In this case, the omitted words are *shy, the, tunnel* and *a*.) The percentage of insertions that match the author's original words is said to be a measure of the reader's ability to understand the passage as a whole. The distinctive advantage of the procedure is that the scores are derived from readers' responses to the structure of the text and so take their knowledge and ability into account. Like readability formulae, however, cloze passages cannot show where reading difficulty lies or how it might be overcome.

Grammatical analysis

A study of the grammatical structures of written language forms the core of this book. The sections on 'Children's writing' and 'Children's reading materials' have outlined some of the ways in which knowledge of these structures can be applied in the classroom. This section gives reasons for the focus on grammar and for the choice of grammatical framework that is used throughout the book.

An approach to children's writing can look broadly at such aspects as the initial stimulus to write, the pupils' response to different kinds of topic, their imaginativeness, commitment and originality, the teacher's reaction to the finished product, and so on; or it can look more narrowly at the actual language children use – at the linguistic strengths they reveal and the difficulties they experience. The broader approach is already well represented in stimulating work by such writers as Burgess *et al.* (1973), Clegg (1964) and Holbrook (1961), but there is rather less material available with a specifically linguistic orientation.

Within a linguistic framework, it is possible either to examine all aspects of language, including vocabulary, or to study structure alone. I have chosen to concentrate on structure because, without some explicit formal knowledge, it is hard for teachers to respond appropriately and helpfully to children's use of grammar, whereas it is rather easier to depend on common sense and intuition in responding to their choice of vocabulary. For instance, if a pupil writes:

9 During the nineteenth century, British seamen had to live and work
  in grotty conditions.

it is immediately apparent that the colloquial word *grotty* – which might be very telling in other circumstances – is unsuitable in a piece of writing about a fairly formal topic. However, if a pupil writes:

10 The most deadly snake it is the boa constrictor.

where the occurrence of the pronoun *it* after the noun phrase *the most deadly snake* seems awkward, it is perhaps less obvious that this is an example of a construction that is quite common in speech but not generally used in writing. Then, in sentence (11), teachers are certain to notice the non-standard grammar of *done* – though they might not recognize it as a dialect form:

11 Standing in the shop doorway was the man who done the burglary.

But it is rather less certain that they will notice the unusual structure of the sentence (which begins, untypically, with a verb) and see it as an indicator of a certain level of linguistic maturity.

Similarly, in books written for children, difficult vocabulary is often conspicuous but difficult grammar may not be so readily identifiable. For example, teachers will recognize that some of the words in the following sentence may cause comprehension problems for junior children:

12a The herds are preyed on by carnivores, or meat-eating animals like the wolves.

They may not realize that the lexical difficulty is compounded by the grammatical structure of the sentence. In order to test this particular example, I presented it, typewritten, to thirty children aged 8;11 to 10;10, with a mean age of 10;0. Below it, on the same page, were sentences (12b) and (12c):

12b The herds prey on the carnivores.
12c The carnivores prey on the herds.

The children were asked to tick the sentence which best expressed the meaning of (12a). Since seventeen of them (57 per cent) chose (12b), it is clear that the grammatical relationships between the parts of the sentence, signalled by words like *are* and *by*, were widely misunderstood.

We have already seen that there is no simple relationship between sentence length and grammatical difficulty. This means that when teachers have to compare texts in order to assess their readability, the straightforward measurement of length is not a reliable guide to the relative difficulty of sentences like (13) and (14):

13 His was a simple form of worship.
14 In those days men thought that religion was the most important thing in their lives and they fought and died for it.

In fact, a study of children's grammatical development suggests that the shorter sentence, (13), contains a construction that is likely to cause more reading problems than anything in (14). A less demanding version of (13) would be:

15 His form of worship was a simple one.

The revision highlights the fact that, in the original, the subject, *his form of worship*, has been split into two parts, with the result that readers have to reach the end of the sentence before they know what *his* refers to.

Teachers need to be sensitive to different kinds of grammatical complexity because not all writers and publishers who produce books for primary and middle schools pay specific and systematic attention to grammatical structures.[1] Vocabulary, on the other hand, tends to be rather carefully scrutinized. The mistaken assumption that vocabulary is the most important linguistic factor in readability seems to underlie the following sentence, from the preface to a series of information books widely used in primary schools:[2] 'The subject matter and vocabulary have been selected with expert assistance, and the brief and simple text is printed in large, clear type.'

The emphasis on grammar in this book is not intended, however, to deny or underrate the importance of other factors. There is not much point in a pupil's essay containing mature patterns of sentence structures if the writing is turgid, pompous or irrelevant; or in a textbook being clearly written if it is boring, poorly presented or factually inaccurate. So the grammatical analyses that will be presented in chapters 5 and 6 are seen as being just one part of a total assessment of written language.

Having suggested why the study of grammatical structure is central to this book, it is now necessary to explain the choice of grammatical framework. It is easy to talk (and write) as if there is just one grammatical description that can be unerringly applied to any samples of a language. This is far from the truth. At a fairly trivial level, grammarians often differ in the terminology they use to label a particular element or structure. For example, Halliday's Systemic Grammar (see Berry, 1975) uses **predicator** where Quirk *et al.* (1972) use **verb**; Halliday uses **group** where Quirk *et al.* use **phrase**; and Halliday labels as **complement** elements that are separated by Quirk *et al.* into the two classes of **object** and **complement**. This is initially confusing but not fundamentally serious. More importantly, grammarians differ in what they intend their grammars to achieve.

Broadly speaking, descriptive grammars, such as Quirk *et al.* (1972), aim to give a comprehensive and systematic account of the patterns of a specific language by labelling the component parts and by showing where they occur and how they function. In contrast, generative grammars are more ambitious. First, they aim to provide insights not just into

---

1 An exception is *Databank* (Crystal & Foster, 1979) – a series of information books in which the grammatical structures are deliberately selected from those that are well established in the speech of nine-year-old children.
2 *Ladybird Leaders*. Loughborough: Ladybird Books.

individual languages but also into language in general. Second, they attempt to formulate grammatical rules so precisely that, if a computer were to be programmed to follow them and equipped with a carefully specified list of vocabulary, it could produce all the grammatical sentences of a language without, in the process, printing out any impossible or ungrammatical sequences. (As yet, no generative grammar has fully accomplished that aim.) Generative grammars are more powerful and more theoretically interesting than descriptive ones. However, generative grammarians write and rewrite grammatical rules in order to achieve economy and elegance of presentation: generally, for instance, one complex rule is preferred to three simpler ones. The result is that such rules are an academic construct. They do not represent, and are not intended to represent, the way in which the human brain produces or interprets sentences. For this reason, it seems preferable in a book of this kind to use a descriptive grammar of English as a framework for analysis. Such grammars are simpler and more familiar to most people than generative grammars and they are less likely to give the misleading impression that they are specifying the steps and processes by which we actually construct the sentences we use, and understand those that we hear or read.

From the various descriptive grammars of English that are available, the one by Quirk *et al.* (1972) has been chosen for this book because it is up-to-date, relatively comprehensive (it is published in both a full and an abridged version), and uses terminology that is, on the whole, fairly well known. In addition, it has been used as the basis for large-scale projects that include among their aims the analysis and evaluation of children's language (e.g. Crystal *et al.*, 1976). Nevertheless, it should still be remembered that this grammar provides just one analysis of the data – not the only possible analysis. An outline of the grammar is presented in chapter 2; readers already familiar with it could go straight to chapter 3 after this introduction.

To carry out a complete grammatical analysis of, say, a paragraph is undeniably a time-consuming task, so it is important to emphasize that it is not being suggested that teachers need to do such analyses routinely; rather, that they should have the ability to do them when the need arises. This might be when a pupil seems to be making no progress in his writing, or when the language of a textbook is causing a class unexpected difficulties. An advantage of learning to do a systematic analysis is that it heightens overall sensitivity to language structure. Once teachers have become aware, for example, of some of the constructions that provide evidence of maturity in children's writing, or of those that may cause difficulty in reading, they are likely to recognize them whenever they occur, without necessarily carrying out a full grammatical analysis of the whole passage.

Grammatical structure and grammatical complexity

If an analysis of grammatical structures is to contribute to judgements of the relative maturity of two pieces of children's writing, or of the relative difficulty of two textbooks, then there must be a principled basis for ordering these structures on a scale of complexity. It is not enough to analyse the language – it is also necessary to evaluate it. At an intuitive level it is probably reasonably apparent that (17) is grammatically more advanced (or complex) than (16):

16 The boys were playing football in the park.
17 The fact that they were beaten was surprising.

But it is not immediately obvious which of the two following sentences is the harder (either to produce or to process):

18 The girl who has won the squash championship is speaking to reporters.
19 Reporters are speaking to the girl who has won the squash championship.

The problem, therefore, is how to rank grammatical structures according to their intrinsic complexity. A comment by Crystal *et al.* (1976, p. 26) is pertinent here:

> Current psycholinguistic theory has no coherent explanation for syntactic complexity, and any attempts to assert that some structures are 'more basic' or 'more complex' than others, on intuitive grounds, soon land one in difficulty, if anything other than the most elementary of sentence-building processes are being investigated. Differences of opinion rapidly arise.

A solution sometimes advocated is to turn to the rules of a generative grammar. It is argued that the more complex the rules are for producing a particular structure, then the harder that structure must be for the language user. Thus, all the grammatical structures of the language could be ranked according to the complexity of the rules that specify their derivation. This view is known as the Derivational Theory of Complexity. However, the theory would only work if the rules of a generative grammar reflected the speaker's own production and comprehension processes, and it has already been explained that they do not. An example may help to clarify the point. A generative grammar might derive a sentence such as (20a) by the series of steps outlined in (20b) to (20e):

20a The red car hit the tree.
    Informal derivation
    20b The car hit the tree.
        The car was red.

20c The car which was red hit the tree.
20d The car red hit the tree.
20e The red car hit the tree.
(= 20a)

This is obviously a long and complex derivation which does not accord with our intuition that (20a) is quite a simple structure. It also suggests, improbably, that (20c) is easier in some way than (20e). Therefore this approach to grammatical complexity is not what is needed in this book.[3]

Another way of tackling the problem is to consider the sequence in which grammatical constructions are acquired by children. This approach rests on two assumptions. The first is that those constructions which are part of the adult language and which occur early and frequently in children's speech and writing will be easier for children to read than those constructions which appear later and more rarely. The second assumption is that the adult constructions that appear late and rarely in children's language are likely to be indicators of linguistic maturity. This is the approach adopted in this book, since it seems particularly appropriate where the language users in question are children who are still in the process of acquiring their mother tongue. The information from language acquisition studies will be supplemented by data from experiments that seek to assess children's comprehension of specific grammatical patterns. Judgements about relative grammatical complexity that are derived from language acquisition studies have to be fairly tentative. Knowledge about the later stages of acquisition is slight in comparison with the considerable amount of information that has been accumulated about the first three years. This means that, as new studies are completed, aspects of the ordering suggested in this book may have to be revised.

Grammar in the classroom

To suggest that a framework of grammatical knowledge can be of benefit to teachers is not to suggest that it should be formally taught to children. Since the beginning of the century, a body of research has accumulated that indicates that grammatical instruction, unrelated to pupils' other language work, does not lead to an improvement in the quality of their own writing or in the level of their comprehension. Furthermore, the majority of children under about fourteen seem to become confused by grammatical labels and descriptions. It is obviously harmful for children to be made to feel that they 'can't do English' because they cannot label, say, an auxiliary verb, when they are perfectly capable of using a wide range of auxiliary verbs accurately and appropriately. There is a brief summary of this research evidence in Wilkinson (1971, pp. 32–5).

3 For a fuller account of the Derivational Theory of Complexity see Foss & Hakes (1978, pp. 125–6).

Although some teachers of older secondary pupils may want to introduce a systematic study of grammar, generally speaking, the 'planned intervention in the child's language development' that is advocated in this book can be implemented by means of demonstration and example, without the use of technical terminology or batteries of exercises. What matters is that teachers themselves understand the nature of the structures their pupils are trying to master, so that they can be confident that any advice they offer is both appropriate and revealing. A quotation from the Bullock Report (DES, 1975, pp. 7–8) sums up the approach:

> We are not suggesting that the answer to improved standards is to be found in . . . more grammar exercises, more formal speech training, more comprehension extracts. We believe that language competence grows incrementally, through an interaction of writing, talk, reading, and experience, the body of resulting work forming an organic whole. But this does not mean that it can be taken for granted, that the teacher does not exercise a conscious influence on the nature and quality of this growth.

Summary

The next five chapters aim to do the following things:

(i) to provide a description of English grammar which teachers will be able to apply in the analysis of both oral and written language.

(ii) To provide an outline of children's acquisition of grammar so that (a) it becomes clear both how much has been acquired and what remains to be mastered when they start school, and (b) their development in writing and reading can be related to the development of their oral language.

(iii) To describe the differences between speech and writing in order to make clear that the demands and the resources of written language are different from those of speech. Since writing is not merely speech written down, learning to write makes new linguistic demands on children and learning to read provides them with new linguistic resources.

(iv) To show how grammatical development in children's writing builds on their oral language and is fostered by their reading; and how, in turn, written language contributes to general language development.

(v) To suggest why certain grammatical constructions may contribute to reading difficulty so that (a) teachers can take linguistic factors into account when selecting books; (b) they have a principled basis for simplifying texts when appropriate; and (c) they can devise ways of helping children to cope with grammatical difficulty.

A practical linguistic problem that arises in a book such as this is how to refer to people in the singular without specifying their sex. English has no sex-neutral pronoun that can be used to refer to nouns such as *teacher* and *pupil*: *he* is discriminatory, *s/he* is unpronounceable, *he or she* is clumsy.[4] Whenever possible I have avoided the issue by using a plural noun and *they*. Sometimes, however, a singular form is essential. On these occasions, I have adopted the convention of referring to the teacher as *she* and the pupil as *he* – naturally, this should not be taken to mean that male teachers and female pupils are discounted.

4 For a fuller account of this problem see p. 38 below.

CHAPTER 2

A descriptive framework for grammatical analysis

2.1 THE AIMS AND METHODS OF GRAMMATICAL DESCRIPTION

I believe that it is valuable for teachers to be able to make a grammatical analysis of pieces of written language. If samples of pupils' writing are analysed, the process reveals which structures have been mastered, which are in the process of being acquired and which are apparently not yet in active use. The information so gained can contribute to the assessment of the pupils' linguistic maturity and to the teacher's plans for the development of their writing abilities. Similarly, if extracts from books which are in use in the classroom are analysed, the exercise can highlight grammatical constructions which may contribute to children's failure to understand the text. With this knowledge, the teacher is in a better position both to select books at an appropriate level and to provide detailed help with the more advanced stages of reading. In order to make such a grammatical analysis, we need to have an agreed system of grammatical description. This chapter outlines a descriptive approach to English based on the grammars by Quirk *et al.* (1972) and Quirk and Greenbaum (1973). Where the description or terminology differs significantly from Quirk's usage, this will be indicated in the text.

A grammatical description consists of identifying regularly-occurring patterns in the language and assigning labels to them. This identification entails recognizing those stretches of language that function grammatically in the same way and distinguishing them from stretches of language that have different grammatical characteristics. A grammatical description must be manageable, revealing and principled. For the description to be manageable, the number of grammatical categories has to be kept small; this requires generalizations to be made which inevitably involve compromises between accuracy and economy. On the other hand, if the description is to be genuinely revealing the categories must not be too broad, otherwise important structural differences will be hidden. A description is principled when it results from the application of clear criteria to the process of identifying and comparing language patterns. It is necessary for these criteria to be made explicit so that different people, working independently on the grammatical analysis of a given passage, can turn to the criteria when in doubt, rather than to their own intuitions. Only by this means will they be able to arrive at closely similar analyses.

Deciding when two groups of words have the same structure and when they differ grammatically is not so straightforward as it sounds because their physical appearance is not a good guide. For instance, the following two sentences look very different because they contain different numbers and types of words:

1 John is fit.
2 The tall man in blue shorts was a good athlete.

Despite the obvious differences, there are some important grammatical similarities between sentences (1) and (2). On the other hand, sentences (3) and (4) look very similar since they differ by only one word:

3 Jean turned off the tap.
4 Jean turned off the road.

However, surprisingly perhaps, there are important structural differences between them.

Grammatical tests

Since simply looking at language does not reveal grammatical patterns, linguists use various operations to make structural comparisons. The first to consider is the test of **reduction**. If a group of words can be reduced to simpler forms while retaining the overall structure and acceptability of the sentence, then the full and reduced constructions will generally have the same grammatical function, e.g.:

5a The tall man in blue shorts

5b The man   was a good athlete.

5c John

Each of the underlined items in (5) has the same grammatical function. Not all of the words in (5a), however, can accept reduction in this way, e.g.:

5d *The tall   was a good athlete.
5e *In blue shorts

(5d) and (5e) are ungrammatical (and therefore, following standard linguistic practice, are marked with an asterisk). This shows that *the tall* and *in blue shorts* do not have the same grammatical function as *the man* in (5b) or *John* in (5c).

Then there is the **omission** test; this shows whether an element is an optional or obligatory part of language structure, e.g.:

6a   The patient collapsed in the bath.
6b   The patient collapsed.
7a   The patient was in the bath.
7b   *The patient was.

Omission of *in the bath* reveals that it is an optional part of sentence (6) but an obligatory part of sentence (7).

A third test is **transposition**. Changing the position of the word *off* in the following sentences (which were first introduced as examples (3) and (4)) provides evidence that they are structurally different, since the transposition is successful in (8b) but not in (9b):

8a   Jean turned *off* the tap.
8b   Jean turned the tap *off*.
9a   Jean turned *off* the road.
9b   *Jean turned the road *off*.

The transposition test also distinguishes between those sentence elements that are generally movable and those that are relatively fixed in their position. For example, in sentence (10) *sometimes* can be moved but all the other words have to stay in the same order:

10a *Sometimes* George buys sweets.
10b George *sometimes* buys sweets.
10c George buys sweets *sometimes*.

Another test is **substitution**. Substituting words at a given place in a sentence is the first step in deciding whether items belong to the same or different word classes, e.g.:

11a   Their neighbours were *kind*.
11b   Their neighbours were *helpful*.
11c   *Their neighbours were *busily*.

The fact that *busily* cannot be substituted for *kind* strongly suggests that it does not belong to the same word class. In contrast, *helpful* can acceptably substitute for *kind* and so may belong to the same class. The substitution test has to be used with circumspection though, since, in some sentence patterns, words of different classes may substitute for each other, e.g.:

12 Their neighbours were *kind*/helpful.
13 Their neighbours were *teachers*.

In order to show that *kind* and *helpful* belong to a different class from *teachers* it is possible to use the **expansion** test, as the two constructions can be expanded in different ways:

14a   Their neighbours were *very kind*/helpful.
14b   *Their neighbours were *very teachers.*
15a   Their neighbours were *good teachers.*
15b   *Their neighbours were *good kind*/helpful.

Sentences (14) and (15) show that constructions with words from the *kind* class (**adjectives**) can be expanded by *very*, unlike words from the *teachers* class (**nouns**); and that noun constructions can be expanded by *good* but adjective constructions cannot.

So far, the tests we have used have affected only one part of the sentence. The final group of tests to consider, the **transformation** tests, are more far-reaching in that they characteristically involve more than just the operation of one process such as substitution or omission. **Transformation** is a term from generative grammar. Broadly, it applies to the grammatical processes which operate on a basic structure to produce sets of sentences that native speakers intuitively feel to be related. Commonly-occurring transformations are **negation, question formation** and **passivization**, as exemplified in (16b)–(16d):

16a   The juggler broke some plates.
16b   The juggler didn't break any plates.
16c   Did the juggler break any plates?
16d   Some plates were broken by the juggler.

The negative transformation in (16b) will illustrate the point that transformations usually involve more than one change to the basic structure: not only is *didn't* inserted but also the form of the verb is changed from *broke* to *break* and *some* is replaced by *any*. Transformations are systematic and rule-governed. This can be demonstrated by showing a transformationally related pair of sentences to a number of native speakers of English, e.g.:

17a   The dog chewed the slipper.
17b   The slipper was chewed by the dog.

and then asking them to create a similar pair from a basic structure like *The cat ate the envelope*. The result will be that they all produce an identical passive version (without necessarily knowing the name of the transformation that they have just applied). Such uniformity is possible only when behaviour is being (unconsciously) governed by rules.

Like the other tests we have examined, transformations can be used to reveal structural differences between sentences that look superficially similar, e.g.:

18a   Andrea is dancing.
19a   Andrea likes dancing.

These sentences can be differentiated by applying the question-forming transformation, which works differently in (18) and (19):

18b Is Andrea dancing?
19b *Likes Andrea dancing?
19c Does Andrea like dancing?
18c *Does Andrea be dancing?

Sometimes the passive transformation can be successfully applied to one sentence but not to another that looks much the same, e.g.:

20a Sarah ran the home.
20b The home was run by Sarah.
21a Sarah ran home.
21b *Home was run by Sarah.

Throughout this chapter, these grammatical tests, along with a more intuitive consideration of meaning, will be used to identify recurring structural patterns in the language.

2.2 SENTENCE TYPES

Major and minor utterances[1]

There is an important distinction to be made between the utterances grouped at (I) below and those grouped at (II):

I Thank you very much.
   Good morning.
   I beg your pardon.

II I am going to London next week.
   Does Lorraine play squash?
   The delegates hadn't finished their coffee.

Those in group I are social expressions, used in clearly defined situations, and are characterized by having very limited possibilities for the substitution of any of the elements. For example, *morning* in *Good morning* can be substituted by *day, afternoon, evening* and *night* but not, with the same intonation and in the same linguistic context, by *lunchtime* or *week*, e.g. *Good lunchtime*. And *Good* cannot be substituted at all, e.g. *Bad morning*. Expressions like those in group I can be called minor utterances: they are important socially but unimportant grammatically because they are **unproductive**, that is they cannot serve as the blueprint for the creation of new utterances. In contrast, the expressions in group II are highly **productive** because the substitution of different words will

1 These labels are taken from Crystal *et al.* (1976, pp. 44, 49). Quirk *et al.* (1972, pp. 411–14) distinguish 'major classes of utterance' from 'formulaic utterances, greetings etc.'.

generate a very large number of new acceptable sentences. They form the bulk of the language and – in opposition to minor utterances – can be labelled **major** utterances. They are the subject of study in this chapter.

Full and elliptical utterances

Any major utterance can be either **full** or **elliptical**. Broadly speaking, a full utterance can be used at the start of a conversation, e.g.:

22 My bus was ten minutes late.
23 Have you ever been to America?

Elliptical utterances, on the other hand, characteristically occur as responses to questions, e.g.:

24 *A*: How do you travel?
    B: By bus.

25 *A*: What is Margaret doing next week?
    B: Going to London.

Although *by bus* and *going to London* could not be used to initiate a conversation, it is worth emphasizing that such elliptical responses are an essential part of normal speech. The use of a full sentence as a response where an elliptical one would have been possible may sound unnatural, pedantic or even hostile, e.g.:

26 *A*: Do you travel to work by car?
    B: Yes I do travel to work by car.

In an elliptical utterance, words are omitted which can be mentally supplied by the listener or reader using information from the linguistic context. Responses to questions provide the most obvious examples but ellipsis can also occur in continuous discourse, e.g.:

27 They are called spinnerets. Some spiders have six as shown in the picture.

The second sentence in (27) is elliptical, as the word *spinnerets* has to be mentally inserted by the reader after *six*.

Sentence functions

All major utterances can also be classified according to their function. There are four sentence functions that have a regular correlation with grammatical form: these are statements, questions, commands and exclamations. We can consider the statement as the basic type from which the others are derived by the operation of grammatical rules, e.g.:

28a You are discreet.
28b Are you discreet?
28c Be discreet!
28d How discreet you are!

A grammatical description usually begins with a study of full statements because the other sentence functions – questions, commands and exclamations – and all elliptical utterances can most easily and economically be handled as transformations of the statement.

Sentence complexity

Sentences can consist of just one independent clause, in which case they are called **simple**, or they can consist of two or more clauses.[2] If these clauses are joined by the process of **co-ordination** (which most often uses *and*), the resulting sentence is **compound**; if they are joined by the process of **subordination**, the result is a **complex** sentence. The terms 'independent clause' and 'simple sentence' are synonymous. (Indeed, some grammarians do not use the word 'clause' at all, preferring to describe a complex sentence as a collection of **embedded** sentences.) The structure of simple sentences is described in section 2.3, compound sentences in 2.4 and complex sentences in 2.5.

2.3 THE STRUCTURE OF SIMPLE SENTENCES

Most of this section is concerned with the structure of statements, with just a brief examination of questions and commands.

Clause structure of statements

Consider the following statements:

29 They argued.
30 She complained.
31 He muttered.

We can discover the structural properties of these sentences by applying some of the tests described in 2.1. Omitting a word shows that what remains is not an acceptable, non-elliptical statement, e.g. (29) *They*, (30) *complained*. Transposing the words in each sentence also produces

---

2 For a full account of the use of the terms *clause* and *sentence* in *A Grammar of Contemporary English*, see Greenbaum (1980).

an unacceptable sequence, e.g. (31) *muttered he. Then, the substitution test shows that the first word in each sentence can be substituted for other first words; similarly, the second words can all substitute for each other – for example:

32 They/she/he argued.
33 They argued/complained/muttered.

But substituting first words for second words, and vice versa, is not possible, e.g. *They she, *argued complained. What this shows is that in these examples there are words from two different classes which have different grammatical functions. Already it is becoming necessary to use labels in order to keep the description manageable. The two indispensable elements of clause structure in sentences (29)–(31) will be labelled **subject** and **verb**. This means that the structure of these sentences (and all others like them) can be economically denoted by the letters **SV**.

The grammatical tests have shown that the simplest possible statement must have both a subject and a verb; that these elements occur in a fixed order; and that they are drawn from two different word classes.

As the subject and verb are such important elements of clause structure, it is worth considering their grammatical roles. Traditionally, verbs have been defined as 'doing' words, and there is much truth in the definition, since many verbs do indeed refer to actions, e.g. eat, carry, write, build. However, the definition is not adequate, as many verbs refer to states or processes that do not have any obvious 'doing' component, e.g. seem, forget, be. In addition, there are many words which, although they refer to actions, are not verbs, e.g. movement, explosion, arrival. So it is more revealing and more accurate to use grammatical function to define the verb.

A very important function is the expression of **tense**. The tense of the verb marks (among other things) the contrast between past and present time, e.g.:

34 Many people watched bear-baiting.
35 Many people watch horse-racing.

Here, the difference between past time reference in (34) and present in (35) is signalled solely by the different tense forms of the verb, watched and watch.

Another function of the verb is to mark the **person** and **number** of the subject. An illustration may help to explain this: if you were to find a torn scrap of paper with just the words . . . succeeds in reaching a high standard . . . you would know from the form of the verb succeeds that the missing subject must be he, she or it (or one of the words they can refer to, e.g. John, the student, the report). He, she and it are **singular** forms, contrasting with **plural** they. They are also **third person** forms, contrasting with **first person** I and **second person** you. After a third person singular subject, a verb in the present tense has the form **stem** + s (e.g. succeeds);

after all other subjects, a present tense verb has the form **stem** (e.g. *succeed*). (An exception is the verb *to be*, which has three different present tense forms, unrelated to the stem, viz. *I am, you/we/they are, he/she/it is*.) This relationship between the person and number of the subject and the form of the verb is known as **concord**. The relationship is not generally apparent when the verb is in the past tense, e.g. *he/they succeeded*. Once again, the verb *to be* is an exception, since there is a contrast between the form used after both first and third person singular subjects – *I/he was* – and the form used after all other subjects – *you/we/they were*.

A finite verb, then, can be defined as a word which changes its form to mark tense, and concord of person and number. (The distinction between finite and non-finite verbs will be made later; in simple statements the verb is always finite.) We can use this definition to identify a verb even when it is not obviously a 'doing' word, e.g.:

36a The explosion seemed astonishingly violent.

If we change the time-reference of this sentence from past to present, we get:

36b The explosion *seems* astonishingly violent.

If the third person singular subject *the explosion* is made plural, we have:

36c The explosions *seem* astonishingly violent.

The three different forms *seemed, seems* and *seem* expressing tense and number contrasts are proof that, in each sentence, *seem* is the finite verb, although its meaning is less 'eventful' than that of the non-verbs *explosion, astonishingly* and *violent*.

Having established a usable definition of the verb, we can now turn to the subject. Traditionally, the subject has been defined as 'the word that does the action of the verb'. This is certainly true of many sentences but it does not express the whole truth. In the following sentences, the subjects experience the action of the verb rather than initiating it:

37a John Kennedy was assassinated.
38a The new shop has been opened.

It is more helpful to use the grammatical notion of concord in identifying the subject, since a third person singular subject will have to be followed by a singular verb form, and a plural subject by a plural verb form, regardless of who 'does the action'. So, when the singular subjects of (37a) and (38a) are made plural, the verbs have to change accordingly:

37b John and Robert Kennedy *were assassinated*.
38b The new shops *have been opened*.

So far we have seen that, in full statements, there has to be a subject and a verb occurring in a fixed order; the subject has a concord relationship with the verb; and the verb changes its form to mark tense, and the person and number of the subject. We can now consider sentences that consist of three clause elements, e.g.:

39a The policeman broke the vase.
40a The dog bit the postman.
41a The waiter ate the biscuits.

Each sentence consists of a subject and verb followed by one more element: *the vase, the postman* and *the biscuits*. If we apply the passive transformation to these sentences, the result is:

39b The vase was broken by the policeman.
40b The postman was bitten by the dog.
41b The biscuits were eaten by the waiter.

The (b) versions of sentences (39)–(41) have the same meaning as the (a) versions but a different form – they are passive whereas the (a) sentences are active. Whenever the passive transformation can be successfully applied, the active sentence must contain an **object**, since it is the object of the active sentence that becomes the subject of the passive sentence. If there is only one object in a sentence it is called the **direct object**. Therefore, we can label the third element in sentences (39a)–(41a) the direct object and the clause pattern itself can be abbreviated to **SVO**. As we shall regularly use the passive transformation to identify grammatical objects, it is worth listing the components of the process:

i) The object of the active sentence becomes the subject of the passive sentence.
ii) The form of the verb changes. It has to consist of the appropriate part of the verb *to be*, plus the **past participle** of the active verb. For example, in (41) the active verb *ate* becomes *were eaten* in the passive. (The past participle is the form of the verb that regularly occurs after *have*; in irregular verbs it frequently ends, in writing, in ⟨*-en*⟩, e.g. *they have **eaten**, they have **spoken***; in regular verbs it ends in ⟨*-ed*⟩, e.g. *they have **arrived**.*)
iii) The subject of the active sentence follows the passive verb and is introduced by *by*, e.g. in (41b) *by the waiter*. It is now called the **agent phrase** and may be omitted, e.g. *The biscuits were eaten.*

Sentences (39a)–(41a) can be compared with another, superficially similar, set.

42a The first prize was a vase.
43a John became a postman.
44a The best entries were the biscuits.

Again, each sentence consists of a subject and a verb followed by one more element. These elements look like the objects in sentences (39)–(41) because the same nouns are used: *vase, postman* and *biscuits*. In order to discover whether they really are objects we can attempt to apply the passive transformation:

42b *A vase was been by the first prize.
43b *A postman was become by John.
44b *The biscuits were been by the best entries.

Clearly, the transformation cannot be successfully applied to these sentences, which means that they do not have the SVO structure. The substitution test reveals that they can accept adjectives after the verb, e.g.:

42c The first prize was *beautiful*.
43c John became *angry*.
44c The best entries were *delicious*.

This further differentiates them from the SVO sentences, since adjectives cannot substitute for nouns that are functioning as objects:

39c *The policeman broke beautiful.
40c *The dog bit angry.

The clause element that can be either a noun or an adjective is called the **complement**, so sentences (42)–(44) can be labelled **SVC**. Another difference between the SVO and the SVC clause pattern becomes apparent if the substitution test is applied to their verbs. In the SVO sentence (40a), a very large number of verbs could be substituted for *bit*, e.g.:

40a The dog bit/chased/followed/harassed/ . . . the postman.

In contrast, in the SVC sentence (43a) there are strictly limited substitution possibilities for the verb *became*, e.g.:

43a John became/was/remained/looked(?) a postman.

The most typical verb in an SVC clause is the verb *to be*. There is no such thing as a typical verb in an SVO clause because the choice is too wide. A final difference between the SVO and SVC patterns is a semantic one. Characteristically, the object is quite distinct from the subject, whereas the complement either describes or refers to the subject. Thus, in the SVO sentence *John chased the postman*, John and the postman are obviously two different people but in the SVC sentence *John became a postman*, John and the postman are the same person. This relationship where two separate constituents in a sentence refer to the same person or thing is known as **co-reference**. (The co-referentiality is emphasized in the precise label for the clause element: **subject complement**. Although the term 'complement' is often used alone, the fuller label is useful when differentiating it from another type of complement that will be introduced later.)

To sum up the differences between the SVO and SVC structures: an SVO clause can be passivized, an SVC cannot; the complement can be expressed by an adjective, the object cannot; the verb in an SVC clause is typically *be* but there is no typical SVO verb; the complement has a co-reference relationship with the subject, the object does not.[3]

Having considered the three-element sentence patterns SVO and SVC, we can now examine sentences that consist of four clause elements, e.g.:

45a The teacher gave the children a prize.
46a The director offered John a new job.
47a The judge sent the winners a message.

If we make the first noun after the verb the subject of a passive sentence, we get:

45b The children were given a prize by the teacher.
46b John was offered a new job by the director.
47b The winners were sent a message by the judge.

As this transformation is successful, these nouns must be objects in the active sentences. If we then take the second noun after the verb and make it the subject of a passive sentence the result is:

45c A prize was given *to* the children by the teacher.
46c A new job was offered *to* John by the director.
47c A message was sent *to* the winners by the judge.

Again the transformation is successful, so sentences (45a)–(47a) must have two objects and can be labelled **SVOO**. There are some grammatical differences between the two objects in each sentence, however, so they are given different names; the first element after the verb is called the **indirect object** and the second one the direct object (which we have already seen in the SVO pattern). The indirect object can be identified by the fact that it can undergo a transformation which allows it to occur AFTER the direct object, so long as it is introduced by a preposition (which is usually *to* but can also be *for*):[4]

---

3 There are a very few verbs that regularly occur in three-element clauses that do not fit neatly into this classification; examples are *have, possess, cost, resemble*. These verbs generally fail the passivization test so – by the above definition – would not be followed by objects, but they do not take complements either. The best solution is probably to analyse sentences like *Bill has a cold* or *The book costs £7* as SVO but to notice that, exceptionally, they cannot be passivized.

4 Quirk *et al.* do not consider that the prepositional construction is an indirect object; rather they treat it as an adverbial, so they would label *The teacher gave the children a prize* as SVOO and *The teacher gave a prize to the children* as SVOA. I prefer to follow Crystal *et al.* (1976), who label both constructions as SVOO. This is semantically satisfying as the change in form does not involve any change of meaning, and it is particularly useful when children's language development is being described because their earliest expression of the notion of **recipient** (which is the characteristic semantic role of the indirect object) tends to involve the prepositional construction – except when *me* is the indirect object.

45d The teacher gave a prize *to the children.*
46d The director offered a new job *to John.*
47d The judge sent a message *to the winners.*

The omission test shows that the indirect object can usually be omitted, with the only change of meaning being a loss of specificity, e.g.:

47e The judge sent a message.

In contrast, the direct object cannot usually be omitted without a radical change of meaning (symbolized by an introductory exclamation mark), e.g.:

47f !The judge sent the winners.

There is another, rather rare, sentence pattern that has four elements, e.g.:

48a The teacher considered the prize an extravagance.
49a The director made John manager.
50a The judge declared the best entries the winners.

If these sentences had the same structure as the SVOO sentences (45a)–(47a), they would have two passive versions, but in fact they have only one, with the first element after the verb becoming the subject of the passive sentence, e.g.:

48b The prize was considered an extravagance by the teacher.
49b John was made manager by the director.
50b The best entries were declared the winners by the judge.

The second element after the verb in each sentence cannot become the subject of a passive version, e.g.:

*An extravagance was considered the prize by the teacher.

So the first element after the verb is a direct object and it only remains to identify the second. The substitution test shows that adjectives as well as nouns can occur in this position (unlike SVOO sentences):

48c The teacher considered the prize *beautiful.*
49c The director made John *angry.*
50c The judge declared the best entries *delicious.*

(Contrast:

45e *The teacher gave the children *beautiful.*)

This operation reveals the likeness between sentences (48c)–(50c) and sentences (42c)–(44c), where the subject complement was expressed by an adjective. We noticed in sentences (42a)–(44a) (where the subject complement was expressed by a noun) that there was a co-reference relationship between the subject and the complement. There is also co-reference in sentences (48a)–(50a) – for example, *John* and *manager* are the same person. Therefore, the fourth element in these sentences, which can be expressed by a noun or an adjective and which has a co-reference relationship with the object, is called an **object complement** and the sentence is labelled **SVOC**.

So far we have identified the following clause elements: subject, verb, direct object, indirect object, subject complement and object complement. We have seen that they occur in the following clause patterns: SV, SVO, SVC, SVOO and SVOC. Some generalizations about English grammar can be made from an examination of these patterns. First, the order of the elements is relatively fixed. There can be occasional slight variation for stylistic purposes (examples will be given in chapters 4, 5 and 6), but, apart from that, the only regular flexibility is found in the two positions that can be occupied by the indirect object, e.g.:

51a The headteacher showed *the parents* the report.
51b The headteacher showed the report *to the parents*.

Second, the subject and verb are always obligatory; and frequently the direct object and subject complement are constrained to occur because of the grammatical requirements of the verb. For instance, some verbs, such as *carry, borrow, welcome*, are normally followed by a direct object, while others, e.g. *become, seem*, have to be followed by a subject complement. The omission test demonstrates this:

52a   John carried the suitcase.
52b   *John carried.
53a   Margaret seemed happy.
53b   *Margaret seemed.

Third, each of the six clause elements only ever occurs once in any one clause. (Although there are two objects in the SVOO pattern they are of different types, one direct and the other indirect.) It is necessary to notice, in this connection, that any of the clause elements may have a complex expression and yet fill only a single grammatical function, e.g.:

54 <u>John</u> <u>carried</u> <u>*the suitcase and an umbrella.*</u>
     s   v   o

In (54) the object is *the suitcase and an umbrella*; although there are two nouns, there is only one object. Grammatically, the expression could be reduced to a simpler form, e.g. *the luggage*, and still fulfil the same function.

Now it is possible to introduce the seventh clause element and to show how it differs from the other six:

55a *Sometimes* Paul makes wine.
55b Paul *sometimes* makes wine.
55c Paul makes wine *sometimes*.

Sometimes is an **adverbial** (A) and the sentences at (55) show that it can occur in a variety of positions, unlike all the other clause elements.[5] Not all adverbials have such a wide freedom of occurrence but, generally, they are characterized by their movability. Next, it is also nearly always the case that adverbials are grammatically optional; the sentences at (55) would be perfectly acceptable without the adverbial. The third distinctive characteristic of this clause element is that there is no theoretical limit on the number of adverbials that can occur in any one clause. Stylistic considerations impose some restriction, of course, but four or five can seem quite natural, e.g.:

56 <u>On Saturdays, Pauline often jogs briskly round the park</u>
    A   S   A   V   A   A

    <u>for an hour.</u>
     A

The structure of this sentence is ASAVAAA. For economy of labelling – on charts, in summaries and so forth – adverbials are often listed at the end of the 'basic' clause pattern, regardless of their position, so (56) might appear as SVAAAAA and all three sentences at (55) could be recorded as SVOA. The most common semantic roles of the adverbial are to describe the temporal or locative features associated with the verb, or the manner in which an action was performed. These roles can be demonstrated by asking questions related to sentence (56), e.g.:

When does Pauline jog round the park?   On Saturdays.
Where does Pauline jog on Saturdays?   Round the park.
How does Pauline jog?   Briskly.

Although adverbials are usually optional elements of structure, there are a very few verbs which generally require one, e.g.:

57 The children stepped *on the wet cement.*
58 Shakespeare lived *from 1564 to 1616.*

Neither of these sentences would be acceptable without an adverbial, so there is a clause pattern **SVA** (where the adverbial is obligatory). A handful of verbs require both an object and an adverbial, e.g.:

59 <u>Alan put *the car in the garage.*</u>
   S   V   O   A

As neither the object nor the adverbial in (59) could be omitted, there is also a clause pattern **SVOA**.

---

5 Quirk *et al.* subdivide adverbials into adjuncts, disjuncts and conjuncts. These distinctions will not be made and these terms not used in this book.

We have now considered all the major clause patterns of English statements and can summarize them like this:

SV
SVO
SVC
SVA $(+A_n)$
SVOO
SVOC
SVOA

Here, the brackets round A show that it is optional and the subscript n indicates that there is no theoretical limit on the number of adverbials that can occur. This formulation shows that every full statement consists of a subject and verb, and that verbs may be followed by objects, complements or adverbials. (Quirk *et al.* (1972, p. 344) use the term **complementation** as a collective label for all clause elements that are REQUIRED to follow the verb; this allows us to say that a full statement consists of a subject, a verb and any complementation.) Such apparently rigid and restricted clause structure is given flexibility and a wealth of variety by the addition of any number of optional adverbials at various points in the clause.

'There' transformation

All of the basic clause patterns have a variant form introduced by **existential** *there*, e.g.:

60a There's a pen on the table.

This use of *there* is called existential because it refers to the existence of a person or thing rather than to the place where it can be found. (In its locative use, *there* is an adverb.) Sentence (60a) is structurally related to (60b):

60b <u>A pen</u> <u>is</u> <u>on the table.</u>
     S   V   A

Two grammatical features are necessary if the *there* transformation is to be applied:

i) the subject must be **indefinite** (i.e. **a** *pen*, rather than **the** *pen*);
ii) the clause will normally contain part of the verb *to be*.

Existential *there* contrasts with adverbial *there* in three ways: first, its pronunciation is always unstressed (sounding like *the* -/ðə/); second, it has no reference to place; and third, it fulfils the role of the grammatical subject of the clause; so, when the question transformation is applied, existential *there*, as subject, changes places with the verb, e.g.:

60c Is *there* a pen on the table?

This can be contrasted with the sentences at (61), where *there* is a stressed adverbial and the subject (moved from its habitual position before the verb) is *my pen*:

61a *There'* s my pen – on the table.
    A   V   S   A

61b Is *my pen* there, on the table?

The inversion of subject and verb in the question at (61b) proves that here *my pen* is the grammatical subject. The following labelled pairs of sentences show that each of the remaining six clause patterns can undergo the *there* transformation if the two necessary conditions are fulfilled:

62a Someone was shouting.
    S   V

62b There was someone shouting.

63a A man is selling balloons.
    S   V   O

63b There is a man selling balloons.

64a No-one can be so stupid.
    S   V   C

64b There can be no-one so stupid.

65a Plenty of people have been giving him advice.
    S   V   O   O

65b There have been plenty of people giving him advice.

66a Something has been making her unhappy.
    S   V   O   C

66b There has been something making her unhappy.

67a Nobody was putting the toys away.
    S   V   O   A

67b There was nobody putting the toys away.

A stylistic tendency of English explains why the 'there' transformation is often preferred to the basic structure when the subject is indefinite. This tendency is for **given** information to occur at the beginning of a clause and for **new** information to appear after the verb. It is very often the case that the grammatical subject is also the topic of conversation and has already been mentioned in the preceding discourse; therefore it is 'given'. When the subject is 'given', it has definite expression (e.g. **the** *pen*). Indefinite forms are always used to express 'new' information. Therefore, a subject that is indefinite (e.g. **a** *pen*) must be introducing new material into the discourse: the 'there' transformation has the effect of delaying this new expression until after the verb, while filling the subject position in the clause with *there*, which is empty of meaning.

Clause structure of questions

All seven statement clause patterns (and their *there* transforms) can be used to ask questions if, in speech, they are said in a questioning tone of voice with an appropriate facial expression and, in writing, they are punctuated with a question mark, e.g.:

68 You're going already?

But, from a grammatical point of view, there are three types of questions which are characterized by a structure which systematically contrasts with that of statements. They are called **Yes/No** questions, **Wh-** questions and **Tag** questions.

Yes/No *questions*

Yes/No questions are so called because it is GRAMMATICALLY possible to answer them with the single word *yes* (or *no*). Nevertheless, in real life it does not often happen that one-word answers are given, since they would frequently sound abrupt or even rude, e.g.:

69 Do you know the time?   No.

We can discover the structure of these questions by comparing them with their related statements, as in the following examples:

70a <u>The children</u> <u>are fighting.</u>
         s   v

70b Are the children fighting?

71a <u>Carol</u> <u>has got</u> <u>a new car.</u>
        s   v   o

71b Has Carol got a new car?

72a <u>The bill</u> <u>will have been paid.</u>
         s   v

72b Will the bill have been paid?

In each case, the verb element consists of more than one word: there is a **lexical** verb (e.g. *fight*) preceded by one or more **auxiliaries** (e.g. *be*, *have*, *will*). To make a question, the order of the subject and the first auxiliary is inverted. If the lexical verb is part of *to be* (or, occasionally, *to have*), then subject and lexical verb can be inverted in a question, e.g.:

73a Sarah is a teacher.
    S   V   C

73b Is Sarah a teacher?

Otherwise, it is not possible to invert the order of the subject and the lexical verb, e.g.:

74a Sarah likes the teacher.
    S   V   O

74b *Likes Sarah the teacher?

75a Sarah went to London.
    S   V   A

75b *Went Sarah to London?

But obviously it is possible to make questions from statements like (74a) and (75a); it is done by 'importing' the auxiliary *do*, e.g.:

74c *Does* Sarah like the teacher?
75c *Did* Sarah go to London?

The auxiliary verb precedes the subject and carries the markers for number (e.g. 74) and tense (e.g. 75) which, in the statements, are carried by the lexical verbs *likes* and *went*.

Wh- *questions*

Wh- questions are introduced by the following words: *who, whom, whose, which, what, when, where, why* and *how*. It is clearly impossible to answer them with *yes* or *no*, e.g.:

76 Where are you going?   *No.

The *wh-* word focuses the question on a particular grammatical element in the related statement, e.g.:

77a *What* did you buy?

77b You bought something.
     S   V   O

Thus, in (77a), *what* has the function of object, which is expressed in (77b) by *something*. The *wh-* word is placed at the beginning of the sentence; after that the structure is generally the same as in *yes/no* questions, with subject-auxiliary inversion (as in (76)) and the importation of auxiliary *do* when necessary (as in (77a)). The only exception is when the *wh-* word functions as the subject of the sentence. In that case, the need to keep the *wh-* word at the beginning 'overrides' subject-auxiliary inversion, e.g.:

78a <u>Who</u> <u>is making</u> <u>that noise?</u>
      s   v   o

78b *Is who making that noise?

This also means that, when the question-word is subject, there does not have to be an auxiliary in the question, e.g.:

79 <u>What</u> <u>kept</u> <u>you?</u>
     s   v   o

Tag questions

Tag questions occur predominantly in speech, because they are a means of inviting agreement from the listener, or at least of verbally prodding him to make a response, e.g.:

80 The children are behaving well, *aren't they?*
81 You liked your job, *didn't you?*

The examples show that the question (italicized) is 'tagged on' to the end of a statement. A tag always consists of an auxiliary verb which copies the person, number and tense of the verb in the statement, followed by a pronoun which refers to the subject of the statement. If the statement does not contain an auxiliary, the appropriate form of *do* is used in the tag, as in sentence (81). The other feature to notice is what is called the **reversal of polarity**. That means, if the statement is positive, the tag is usually negative, as in (80) and (81); if the statement is negative, the tag has to be positive, e.g.:

82 The children can't open that gate, *can they?*

Occasionally positive statements are followed by positive tags – they tend to sound aggressive or challenging, e.g.:

83 You've already met him, *have you?*

Clause structure of commands

All seven statement clause patterns (but not their *there* transforms) can, transformationally, become commands. Generally, this entails omitting the subject and using the stem form of the verb, e.g.:

84 Shut the door!   (VO)
85 Be careful!   (VC)
86 Go away!   (VA)

Very occasionally the subject is included, e.g.:

87 You be good!   (SVC)

Notice that (87) is differentiated from the statement at (88) by the form of the verb:

88 You are good.

Sometimes the auxiliary *do* is used in commands, with a persuasive function, e.g.:

89 Do sit down.

Phrase structure

Before we can examine the structure of different types of phrase there are three introductory points that need to be made. The first concerns the nature of the clause elements that we have studied. It is important to realize that the labels subject, object, complement, and so on, refer to abstractions; that is, 'subject' says something about the grammatical role of the element within the clause rather than specifying the kinds of words that can actually be used to fulfil that role. This means that when we meet descriptions such as SVC, SVOO, etc., we know quite a lot about the grammatical relationships that will exist between the different parts of the clause and about the kinds of transformation that can be applied, but rather little about the physical appearance of the utterance, its length, complexity and so forth. An example may help to clarify this point. Consider sentences (90) and (91):

90 <u>She</u> <u>buys</u> <u>jewellery.</u>
    s   v   o

91 <u>The tall elegant woman in front of me</u> <u>was buying</u>
                s   v

<u>several very expensive silver rings.</u>
                 o

Both sentences have the structure SVO; the characteristics of these three clause elements are manifested in both sentences: the subject has a concord relationship with the verb, the verb carries tense and number markers, the object follows the verb and can become the subject of a passive sentence. But there the similarity ends because in (90) each clause element is expressed by a single word whereas in (91) each element is expressed by a group of words. Therefore, in order to achieve a revealing description of a piece of language, it is necessary not only to identify the clause elements and the pattern they form together but also to analyse the internal structure of each element so that sentences like (90) and (91) can be differentiated as well as compared. So, in studying phrase structure we shall be studying the range of concrete expressions that can be used for each of the abstract clause elements. Subjects, objects and complements are expressed by **noun phrases**, verbs by **verb phrases**, adverbials by **adverbial phrases** and complements also by **adjective phrases**. Each phrase type will be described in turn.

The second introductory point is that the word 'phrase' can cause misunderstanding. In everyday usage it is generally held to refer to a group of words that does not contain a verb – one of the definitions in *The Shorter Oxford English Dictionary*, for example, is: 'A group of words . . . having no finite verb of its own'. In grammatical description, however, the term 'phrase' is applied to any words which express a single clause element. As the verb is one of the clause elements, it means that the words which express the verb constitute a verb phrase (a contradiction in terms for the dictionary definition), e.g.:

92 <u>The children</u> <u>have been fighting.</u>
       s   v

   noun phrase   verb phrase

A rather more confusing aspect of the technical use of the word 'phrase' is that it does not always even refer to a GROUP of words but is used by many grammarians, including Quirk *et al.*, to refer to a single word, when that word is the sole expression of a clause element. So grammarians say that the subject, object and complement are expressed by a noun phrase and (as we shall see in more detail later) that the noun phrase may be a single noun, a pronoun or a noun phrase – that is, a group of words with a noun as its **head**, or most important member, e.g.:

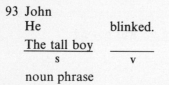

93 John
   He   blinked.
   <u>The tall boy</u> <u>   </u>
      s   v
   noun phrase

In (93) the subject is expressed by a noun phrase which may be a single noun (*John*), a pronoun (*he*) or an 'obvious' noun phrase (*the tall boy*, where *boy* is the head noun). This example shows that the term 'noun phrase' is being used with two different meanings: (1) to label anything that can function as subject, object and complement; and (2) to label a GROUP of words that has a noun as its head and that can function as subject, object and complement. It is tempting to use another term altogether for one of these meanings, but idiosyncratic terminology creates fresh problems, so I shall basically follow Quirk *et al.* but use the full forms 'noun phrase', 'verb phrase' and so on as the labels for any items that express the appropriate clause element, and the abbreviated forms

'NP', 'VP', etc. to refer specifically to a GROUP of words. This enables us to say that a noun phrase may consist of a single noun, a pronoun or an NP.

The essential characteristic of any multi-word phrase is that, if it is reduced to a single word, its grammatical function within the sentence is unchanged. Sentence (94) has the clause structure SVAA:

94 His sister was living in London at that time.
     S   V   A   A

If each multi-word phrase is reduced, the resulting sentence (95) still has the structure SVAA:

95 She lived there then.
    S   V   A   A

It is this reduction test that enables us to decide, for example, that *his sister* is a phrase but *sister was* is not because *sister was* contains words from two different clause elements and cannot be reduced to a simpler construction while still retaining the structure of the original sentence. The maintenance of the original structure is an important part of this operation because it is frequently possible to reduce two different clause elements to one and still have an acceptable sentence, e.g.:

96 She was reading a book.
    S   V   O

97 She was reading.
    S   V

Example (97) is grammatically acceptable but the SVO structure of (96) has been changed to an SV pattern so we shall NOT consider *was reading a book* as a phrase, even though it is reducible.[6] On the other hand, sentence (98) shows that *was reading* and *a book* in (96) can each be considered as phrases, since each can be reduced without altering the SVO pattern:

98 She reads books.
    S   V   O

---

6 This operational definition of the word 'phrase' reveals a sharp contrast between Quirk *et al.*'s analysis and the hierarchical phrase structure grammar of transformational generative approaches where the verb phrase subsumes objects, complements and adverbials. Thus, in

She was reading a book, She was reading quietly,
S   V   O   S   V   A

She was reading the children a story,
S   V   O   O

the elements VO, VA and VOO would all ultimately be reduced to 'verb phrase' so each sentence would be labelled, at the highest level, NP + VP.

The third introductory point is that a study of phrase structure is made easier by the understanding that words can usefully be considered as belonging to one of two large groups: there are **open-class** words and **closed-system** words. The open word-classes are nouns, verbs, adjectives and adverbs (although there are sub-sets of verbs and adverbs that belong to closed systems). These classes are called 'open' because they are already very large and can accept new items without any difficulty. Examples of fairly recent additions to these classes are the noun *supergrass*, the verb *gazump* and the adjective *grotty* with its related adverb *grottily*. The words in open classes carry a great deal of information; they have meanings that can be defined and given in dictionaries. In contrast, closed-system words belong to very small sets that are highly resistant to the addition of new members. Examples are the set of personal pronouns (*I, me, you, he, him, she, her, it, we, us, they, them*) and the set of primary auxiliary verbs (*be, have, do*). It is noticeable how easy it is to list exhaustively the members of each set, whereas it is quite impossible to do this with an open class, such as nouns. Even where speakers feel the need for a new closed-system word, it is rare for one to find acceptance. A topical illustration of this point is to be found in the area of the personal pronouns: English lacks a third person singular pronoun that can refer to people without specifying their sex. Consider, for instance, how you would complete the gaps in the following sentence:

99a If anyone has lost _____ ticket _____ should report to a stewardess, who will do her best to help _____ .

There are three possible solutions, none completely satisfactory:

99b If anyone has lost *his* ticket *he* should report to a stewardess, who will do her best to help *him*.

This suggests that *anyone* is male, ruling out the equally plausible female interpretation.

99c If anyone has lost *his or her* ticket *he or she* should report to a stewardess, who will do her best to help *him or her*.

No-one could accuse the speaker of (99c) of sexism but the sentence is hardly elegant.

99d If anyone has lost *their* ticket *they* should report to a stewardess, who will do her best to help *them*.

For most people this is probably the preferred solution, although it means using plural pronouns to refer to a singular subject. Aware of this gap in the pronoun system, the Equal Opportunities Commission commissioned Dr David Firnberg to create a new pronoun. He has suggested two possibilities: *ist, ist, ists*; and *hey, hem, heir, heirs*, e.g.:

99e If anyone has lost *heir* ticket *hey* should report to a stewardess who will do her best to help *hem*.

Despite the clear need for such an item, there is no sign of its being adopted.

Closed-system words are generally rather difficult to define; frequently it is easiest to contrast them with another word in the system, e.g., *this* contrasts with *that*, *the* contrasts with *a*. The information they carry is usually more grammatical than lexical. For this reason, they can often be omitted from telegrams or newspaper headlines with little loss of meaning, e.g.:

100 Plane arrives Tuesday 1800.

If the closed-system words were retained and the open-class words omitted, however, no meaning would be recoverable at all:

101 *The on at.

The very large group of open-class words are referred to as **lexical** words, or **content** words; the much smaller group of closed-system words are usually known as **grammatical** words or **function** words. Any full major sentence will contain lexical words (and may or may not have any function words); only elliptical sentences in responses can consist of function words alone, e.g.:

102 **A**: Who's bringing the sandwiches?
     B: We are.

Fries (1952, p. 104) identifies 154 function words (in comparison with dictionary entries of well over half a million lexical words). He comments that their structural importance is so great that, although they are few in number, they constitute about one-third of the words in any written or spoken text.

Each of the four phrase types we shall study has as its head a word from one of the four open classes, i.e. a noun, verb, adverb or adjective. In addition, it may also have one or more closed-system words which help to indicate the grammatical identity of the phrase; for example, a word ending in *-ing*, like *ironing*, may be a constituent of either a noun or a verb phrase. If it is preceded by *the*, it is functioning as a noun; if it is introduced by part of the verb *to be*, then it will be identified as a verb, e.g.:

103 David did the ironing.
      s   v   o

             NP

104 David was ironing.
      s   v

             VP

In order to keep the labelling for the phrase level of analysis as distinct as possible from the clause level, constituents of phrases will be labelled with lower-case letters rather than capitals. So, while the clause element 'adverbial' is represented by **A**, the phrase constituent 'adverb' will be denoted by **adv**.

The noun phrase

The noun phrase regularly expresses the clause elements subject and object and frequently expresses the complement. It may be a **noun**, a **pronoun** or an **NP** (see p. 37).

Nouns. The class of **nouns** is very large and not all members of the class have identical grammatical characteristics. This means we can distinguish sub-classes of nouns, using grammatical criteria. Consider the italicized nouns in the following sentences:

105a A *pear* is a valuable source of vitamins.
106a *Milk* is a valuable source of protein.

Both nouns are singular, being followed by the singular verb *is*. They differ in two important ways: *pear* has to be preceded by a closed-system word such as *a*; *milk* cannot occur with *a*, e.g.:

105b **Pear* is a valuable source of vitamins.
106b **A milk* is a valuable source of protein.

Secondly, only *pear* can be made plural:

105c *Pears* are a valuable source of vitamins.
106c **Milks* are a valuable source of protein.

Nouns like *pear*, which have both singular and plural forms, are called **count nouns** because they refer to separable, countable entities, e.g. *three pears, six ideas, several suggestions*. Nouns like *milk*, which normally have only a singular form, are called **mass nouns**, because they refer to substances that are not generally thought of as separable or countable, e.g. **three milks, *six musics, *several informations*. However, the division of nouns into these two sub-clauses is not a hard-and-fast matter. There are many words which regularly function as mass nouns which can on occasion also be used as count nouns. For instance, in (107a) *beer* is a mass noun as it occurs in the singular without a function word but in (107b) it is a plural count noun:

107a *Beer* is fattening.
107b He drank *six beers*.

More rarely, a count noun (like *slipper*) can be used as a mass noun, e.g.:

108 The cat had fish for dinner, the dog had *slipper*.

Both mass and count nouns are **common nouns** and, as such, can be contrasted with **proper nouns**, which refer uniquely to a particular person, place or thing, e.g.:

109 *Bjorn Borg* is an outstanding tennis player.
110 Our neighbours visited *Jodrell Bank* last week.

There are both similarities and differences between common and proper nouns. Like common nouns (both mass and count), proper nouns have a possessive form, expressed in writing by ⟨'s⟩, or ⟨s'⟩, e.g. ***The Guardian's staff***, ***The Netherlands'*** *coastline*. Like mass nouns, proper nouns are not normally preceded by *a* and are not generally made plural, e.g.:

111 *They visited *a France*.
112 **Susans* came to see me.

(There are some exceptions to this, however, e.g.:

113   *A Mr Smith* has called to see you.
114   There are *six Susans* in this class.

In addition, there are some proper nouns which are always plural, e.g. *The Pennines*, *The Hebrides*.) The major contrast between proper nouns and all common nouns is that, whereas both mass and count nouns can occur with function words, proper nouns usually do not, e.g.:

115   I bought *the/some* milk.
116   He ate *the/some* pears.
117   **The/some* Bjorn Borg won the match.

Where a function word does regularly occur with a proper noun, e.g. *The Pennines*, it is a fixed part of the name, so there is no possibility of substituting another function word, e.g.:

118 *We visited *some Pennines*.

The various sub-types of noun are shown in figure 1. Proper nouns, mass nouns and plural count nouns can all stand alone as subject, object or complement. Singular count nouns have to follow a function word and therefore form the head of an NP – except in newspaper headlines, e.g. *Man bites dog*.

Traditionally, nouns have been defined as 'naming words'. Although this description applies to the earliest nouns that children use, e.g. *mummy, garden, cup*, it is less obviously applicable to nouns such as *speed, decision, idea*. In addition, the semantic definition is no help in revealing the differences between the different sub-classes of nouns. A grammatical description focuses on the function and form of the various sub-classes of noun and also notes which function words regularly occur with each type. Though more cumbersome than a semantic definition, this kind of description is more revealing and more accurate. Drawing together the characteristics we have already noted, we can say:

   i) Nouns can function as the subject, object or complement of a clause.
  ii) They have a possessive form, expressed in writing by ⟨'s⟩ or ⟨s'⟩.

iii) Common nouns occur with *the*.

iv) Common count nouns (by far the largest sub-class of nouns in a speaker's vocabulary) usually have a singular and a plural form. The plural of regular nouns is formed by the addition, in writing, of ⟨-s⟩ or ⟨-es⟩. Singular count nouns occur with *a*.

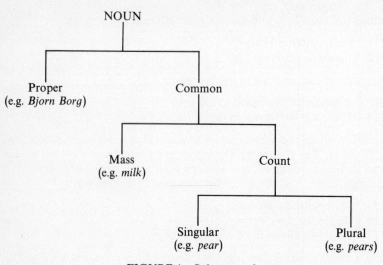

FIGURE 1   Sub-types of noun

Pronouns.   The class of **pronouns** too can serve to express the subject, object or complement of a clause. Their characteristic (though not their only) function is to stand for a noun or NP. So *David, the boy, his father*, can all be replaced by *he*; *Rosemary, your grandmother, the actress*, can all be replaced by *she*; and so on. Although pronouns frequently substitute for nouns, they differ from them grammatically in several important ways, just four of which will be mentioned here:

1 They belong to a closed system, not an open class (see p. 38). This means there are very few of them: roughly sixty, compared with the scores of thousands of nouns.

2 Whereas nouns have the same form regardless of the clause element they are expressing, the personal pronouns have different forms for subject and object roles (these forms are generally called **subjective** and **objective cases**), e.g.:

119 The boy/*He* ran home.
120 Jane saw the boy/*him*.

3 Like proper nouns, but unlike common nouns, pronouns do not normally occur as the head of an NP after a closed-system word, e.g. **the she, *that him*.

4 In the third person singular, the personal pronouns necessarily

specify gender. So, while we can refer to *a teacher, a nurse, a friend*, without specifying whether they are male or female, as soon as we use a pronoun to replace these nouns we have to choose between *he* and *she*, *him* and *her*.

NP. An **NP** may be simple or complex. We have seen already that a singular count noun (e.g. *pear*) has to be preceded by a closed-system word, such as *the*. The other kinds of common noun can also follow *the*; this gives the most basic and the most common NP – a common noun as head of the phrase, preceded by a closed-system word. This group of words that includes *the* is known as the class of **determiners** because, to some extent, they 'determine' the kind of noun that can follow. That is, not all determiners can be followed by all nouns but rather there are **co-occurrence restrictions** between groups of determiners and sub-classes of noun. We can group determiners according to the types of noun they can precede: the co-occurrence restrictions between the six groups of determiners and three sub-classes of noun are shown in table 1.

TABLE 1   Co-occurrence restrictions between determiners and sub-classes of noun

	Sub-classes of noun		
Determiner groups	*Count singular* (*e.g.* pear)	*Count plural* (*e.g.* pears)	*Mass* (*e.g.* milk)
a) the; my, your, his, her, its, our, their; no; whose	✓	✓	✓
b) this, that	✓		✓
c) some, any		✓	✓
d) a(n); each, every; either, neither	✓		
e) these, those		✓	
f) (not) much			✓

This grouping shows that the determiners listed at (a) can occur with all types of common noun; those listed at (b) and (c) can occur with two out of the three sub-classes; and those listed at (d), (e) and (f) are restricted to one sub-class only. In addition to their co-occurrence restrictions, another important grammatical characteristic of determiners is that they are mutually exclusive. In other words, no more than one can occur before each head noun, so sequences like **my this pen* are impossible. The simplest NP, then, consists of a determiner and a noun; it can be labelled **dn**.

The head noun in an NP can accept both **pre-modification** and **post-modification**. Pre-modification includes the determiners, other closed-system words that can optionally occur with the determiner, and various kinds of adjectives.

The other closed-system words that may occur with the determiner are **pre-determiners** and **post-determiners**. These are small sets of words that, like determiners, have co-occurrence restrictions with the head noun. Pre-determiners are words like *all, half* and *both*, which may be followed by *of*, e.g. **all *(of)*** *the mile,* **half *(of)*** *the pear,* **both *(of)*** *the pears.* Post-determiners include **ordinals** – o (e.g. *first, second, next, last*); **cardinal numbers** – **no**. (e.g. *one, two, three*); and **quantifiers** – **q** (e.g. *many, few, more, most, several*). These closed-system words combine together before a head noun like this:

<u>both</u> of <u>my</u> <u>last</u> <u>two</u> <u>essays</u>
pre-d   d   o   no   n

<u>half</u> <u>the</u> <u>next</u> <u>few</u> <u>attempts</u>
pre-d   d   o   q   n

The order of these pre-modifying closed-system words is firmly fixed; rearrangements are not possible, e.g. **the half few next attempts.*

Between the closed-system words and the head noun there can occur, theoretically, any number of **adjectives.** In practice, it is rather rare to find more than three or so, e.g. *some **big, red, juicy** apples.* Advertising language is the exception here, since it is not uncommon to find adjectival pre-modification as extensive as this:

121 Look at our *large, roomy, elegant, practical, monogrammed leather* suitcase.

Unlike the closed-system pre-modifiers, adjectives are not rigidly restricted to an inflexible order. The NP in (121), for example, could be rewritten as *our elegant, practical, large, roomy, monogrammed, leather suitcase.* Nevertheless, the order is not random. Some verb forms can have an adjectival function, e.g. *monogrammed*, and some nouns can also be used adjectivally, e.g. *leather.* Such verbal and nominal forms usually appear closer to the head noun than the 'true' adjectives, such as *large* and *elegant.* Then, considering semantic categories, there is a tendency for general adjectives to precede more specific ones and for adjectives of size and shape to come before those of age and colour; so *attractive antique furniture* and *tall red chimneys* are more normal than *?antique attractive furniture* and *?red tall chimneys.* (The initial question mark indicates that a sequence is unlikely but not impossible.) Many adjectives can themselves be modified by an **intensifier** such as *very.* Those that can be so modified generally occur before those that cannot, e.g. *very large* but not **very monogrammed.* Other frequently-used intensifiers are *rather, quite, terribly, so, especially*, e.g.:

122 <u>The very fierce dog was making a quite appalling noise.</u>

        S   V   O

d   int   adj   n   d   int   adj   n

The structural relationships within NPs of the kind illustrated in (122) are quite complex. The omission test shows which items are dependent on each other. Taking *the very fierce dog* as an example, there are at *A* all the NPs that result from permissible omissions, while at *B* there are sequences that are either impossible, or possible only in restricted uses of language, such as newspaper headlines. (Omissions are shown by gaps, to make the structure clear.)

A	*the very fierce dog*	**B**	*the very fierce dog*	
	the fierce dog		*the very fierce	
	the dog		* very fierce dog	
			*the very dog	

This shows that the adjective *fierce* has to occur with a noun; that the singular count noun *dog* must have a determiner; and that the intensifier *very* cannot occur without an adjective.

A variety of structures can post-modify the head noun in an NP. Rarely, in set phrases that show their French origins, adjectives can follow a noun, e.g. *heir* **apparent**, *court* **martial**. (In formal usage, the plurals of *court martial* and *heir apparent* are *courts martial* and *heirs apparent*, showing that *court* and *heir* are the head nouns in the phrases and *martial* and *apparent* are adjectives.) More frequently, adjectives follow indefinite pronouns, e.g. *someone* **else**, *something* **surprising**, *somewhere* **cheap**. In a rather literary style, two or more adjectives may be co-ordinated after the head noun, e.g. *a young girl*, **shy and hesitant**, which is less prosaic than *a shy, hesitant young girl*. Adverbs that refer to direction or location can also follow a head noun, e.g. *the way* **back**, *the people* **nearby**. Apart from these rather restricted uses of adjectives and adverbs, post-modification is by phrases and clauses. Post-modifying clauses will be dealt with in the section on the complex sentence, so here we shall simply consider the prepositional phrase.

The prepositional phrase is a common post-modifying construction. It consists of a preposition followed usually by a noun phrase but occasionally by an adverb, e.g. *(the jug)* *on the shelf*, *(the jug)* *on there*. Here, the head noun *jug* is post-modified by a prepositional phrase consisting of the preposition *on* and either the NP *the shelf* or the adverb *there*. Prepositions are closed-system items. Examples are: *at, in, on, of, with, by, from, about*. They are always dependent on a noun phrase (or an adverb); that is, they occur as part of a phrase, not as independent structural elements. When the noun phrase is a pronoun, it has to be in the objective case; e.g. *(the man)* *with* **her**, not *(the man)* *with* **she**. In normal speech, prepositions are unstressed – but there is a noticeable tendency for broadcasters to stress them, e.g.

123 Our man WITH the results is Frank Bough.

As a prepositional phrase generally consists of a preposition plus a noun phrase, it is possible for that noun phrase to be post-modified by a prepositional phrase, and so on (theoretically) indefinitely. This means that **NPprepNP** can be described as a **recursive** structure, because it is one of those constructions where the same grammatical process can be repeatedly applied. Here is an example of an NP that illustrates repeated post-modification by prepositional phrases: *the man in the shop on the corner of the street*. The head noun *man* is post-modified by the prepositional phrase *in the shop*; the head of this phrase, *shop*, is post-modified by *on the corner*; and *corner* is modified by *of the street* – which could, of course, be further post-modified.

We have seen that the label NP can be applied to very simple **dn** constructions, e.g. *the boy*. It can also refer to highly complex phrases which combine both pre-modification and multiple post-modification of the head noun, e.g.:

124 <u>Both</u> <u>of</u> <u>those</u> <u>first</u> <u>two</u> <u>feeble</u> <u>faint-hearted</u> <u>attempts</u>

				s			
pre-d	d	o	no.	adj		adj	n

<u>at</u> <u>the</u> <u>essay</u> <u>on</u> <u>Chaucer</u> <u>were</u> <u>hopeless.</u>

					v	c

		prep. phrase	
prep	d	n	prep.	phrase

prep	n

Even such a complex NP as the subject of (124) can, grammatically, be reduced to **dn** – *those attempts*. We can be sure that this is the right reduction, and that it is *attempts* rather than *essay* or *Chaucer* that is the head noun, because it has a co-occurrence restriction with the determiner *those* and a concord relationship with the verb *were*. It would not be possible for *essay* or *Chaucer* to be the head noun in this sentence frame, e.g.:

125a Those attempts were hopeless.
125b *Those essay were hopeless.

Noun phrases in apposition.   Sometimes two noun phrases, both expressing the same clause element, can be placed side by side, e.g.:

126 *The President of the Trust, the Prince of Wales,* welcomed the guests.

Here, the subject of the sentence is the two noun phrases, *the President of the Trust* and *the Prince of Wales*. In this type of construction, the second noun phrase is said to be **in apposition** to the first. There are many different types of appositive relationship but the most typical kind has the following two characteristics: first, there is co-reference between the two noun phrases; and, second, the omission of either phrase leaves an acceptable sentence. These features are exemplified in (126), where the President of the Trust and the Prince of Wales are (in this case) the same person, and where either phrase alone could function as subject, e.g.:

127a The President of the Trust welcomed the guests.
127b The Prince of Wales welcomed the guests.

Co-ordinated noun phrases. Any of the noun phrases outlined above can be joined to another noun phrase (provided the two are semantically appropriate) by means of a **co-ordinator**, such as *and* or *or*. So simple forms can be co-ordinated, e.g. *John and Jeff, he or she, the boys and the girls*; but so can complex NPs, e.g. *car passengers with travel documents and foot passengers with passports.* In addition, simple forms can be joined to complex ones, e.g. *you and all your companions on the back row.* The process of co-ordination is recursive; theoretically, there is no limit to the number of noun phrases that can be joined together to form a subject, object or complement. Generally, when more than two noun phrases are co-ordinated, the co-ordinator is included only between the last two; the others are linked by intonation in speech and commas in writing e.g.:

128 They saw *lions, tigers, elephants, and lots of monkeys.*

We have spent a considerable amount of time on the structure of the noun phrase because it has such a variety of constituents, which contract complex grammatical relationships. It will become clear in chapter 6 that different types of writing are to a substantial extent differentiated by the kinds of noun phrase they contain.

The verb phrase

The verb phrase regularly expresses the clause element verb. Immediately it is obvious that the terminology is rather unhelpful, since the same name is used both for the abstract clause element and for the class of words that give concrete expression to that element. This undifferentiated labelling contrasts with, say, the clause element subject, whose associated word class is the noun. Although the use of the same term for two different aspects of structure can cause problems, it does serve to highlight the fact that there is a closer relationship between the clause element verb and the word class verb than there is between any other elements and word classes. That is to say, the clause element verb has to be expressed by a member of the verb word class, whereas the clause elements subject, object and adverbial can each be expressed by a range of items; and finite verbs can only express the element verb – unlike nouns, for example, which can function as subjects, objects and complements. In order to distinguish between the two uses of the word verb, the clause element is symbolized in this book by a capital letter – **V** – and members of the word class by a lower-case letter – **v**.

The verb phrase can be a single-word finite verb or a multi-word phrase – a VP. There are three basic types of VP: the **auxiliary VP**, the **catenative VP**, and the **verb + particle VP**.

Verbs. The verbs which can stand alone in full sentences are finite **lexical verbs**. They constitute an open class with many thousands of members. We have seen already (p. 22) that they carry markers of number and tense. The form of the verb that follows *to* can be called the **stem**, and the form that occurs after a third person singular subject in the present tense can be called **stem + s**, e.g. *arrive* and *arrives*. All lexical verbs have a stem + s form; just four are irregular: *be, have, do* and *say.* Instead of **bes* we have *is*, and instead of **haves* we find *has. Does* and *says* are regular in their written forms but irregular in their pronunciation, where we would expect them to rhyme with *shoes* and *pays.*

There are two tenses expressed by the various forms of the lexical verb: present and past. In regular verbs, the past tense is formed by the addition, in writing, of ⟨-ed⟩ to the stem, e.g. *arrived.* Irregular verbs generally make the past tense by changing the vowel, e.g. *sing, sang; ride, rode.* The major function of the two tenses is the expression of the time when an action took place. However, there is not a completely straightforward relationship between tense and time. Consider the following examples:

129 The sun *rises* in the east.
130 It's time he *bought* a new coat.
131 The play *starts* at 8 o'clock tomorrow night.

Rises is in the present tense but refers to all time, past, present and future; *bought* is in the past tense but does not refer to a past action, rather to a hypothetical future one; and *starts* is in the present tense but refers unequivocally to future time. For this reason, some grammarians refer not to present and past forms but to stem + s and stem + ed forms. In this case, it is necessary to remember that stem + ed also includes those irregular verbs that change the vowel rather than adding ⟨-ed⟩.

When we looked at nouns, we saw that they did not all share the same grammatical characteristics and could not all substitute for each other in every construction. The same is true of verbs, so we can establish subclasses. Some verbs can occur in the sentence patterns that contain objects, i.e. SVO, SVOO, SVOC and SVOA. Examples are *recommend, give, elect* and *put.* These verbs are called **transitive**. A much smaller group of verbs function in SVC sentences, e.g. *be, become, seem.* These are known as **copulas**. Finally, there are the verbs which do not require either an object or a complement. They occur in the sentence patterns SV and SVA and are called **intransitive**, e.g. *arrive, live.* It is worth adding that many verbs belong to more than one of these sub-classes, so a verb like *eat* can be either transitive or intransitive, and a verb like *look* can be either intransitive or a copula.

The auxiliary VP. Unlike lexical verbs, auxiliary verbs belong to closed systems. There are three **primary** auxiliaries (*be, have* and *do*) and about a dozen **modal** auxiliaries (e.g. *can, could, will, would*). In full sentences, auxiliaries always occur with a lexical verb, e.g.:

132 John *will arrive* on Saturday.

They occur alone only in elliptical clauses, e.g.:

133 John won't go but I *will*.

Auxiliaries can be differentiated from lexical verbs by the grammatical functions they perform. We have seen already (pp. 32–4) that they are essential for the formation of questions. They are also required in most negatives. In the following negative sentences, the negative element comes between the auxiliary and the lexical verb:

134 The parcels *have* **not** *arrived*.
135 They *weren't talking*.
136 The police *couldn't* help.

In speech and informal writing the negative *not* is normally reduced to *-n't*, which is never written as a separate word but attached to the auxiliary. It is not possible to follow a lexical verb (except *be* and *have*) with *not* or *-n't*, e.g.:

137 *He knowsn't the answer.

In order to make such a sentence negative, the auxiliary *do* has to be imported, e.g.:

138 He *does*n't know the answer.

The lexical verbs *be* and *have* are exceptions to the general rule. Even when they are not functioning in a VP as auxiliaries, they still have the grammatical privileges of auxiliaries, e.g.:

139 Helen *isn't* a doctor.
140 Brian *hasn't* a clue.

Quirk uses the term **operator** to cover all the auxiliary verbs and the lexical verbs *have* and *be*. So, more accurately, we can say that questions and negatives require an operator in the verb phrase. When there are several auxiliaries in the phrase, it is always the first that acts as operator and carries the markers of number and tense, e.g.:

141 The girl **hasn't been arrested** yet.

Another important function of the operator is as a **pro-form**. A pro-form is an item that stands for another sentence constituent in order to prevent repetition. A verbal pro-form can stand for the verb element and any complementation it may have, e.g.:

142 *A*: Who can mend a puncture?
       B: I *can*.
143 The builders will leave tomorrow. I expect the decorators *will* too.

In (142) *can* is a pro-form for *can mend a puncture* and in (143) *will* substitutes for *will leave tomorrow*. If there is not an operator present, then *do* is introduced, e.g.:

144 She lives in Hertford and so *does* Jane.

All auxiliaries function as operators in questions, negatives and pro-forms. Having noted what they have in common, we can now consider the differences between the two sub-classes, both in form and function. The primary auxiliaries, *be*, *have* and *do*, all have a stem + *s* form, albeit somewhat irregular. They also show a straightforward contrast between past and present forms, e.g. *is/was*, *has/had*, *does/did*. On the other hand, the modal auxiliaries (e.g. *can*, *must*) have no stem + *s* form, e.g.:

145 I/he *can* go.

In addition, there is not always a straightforward relationship between past and present forms; for example, *shall* and *should* do not express a contrast in time but rather in degree of certainty, e.g.:

146a I *shall* clean the windows.
146b I *should* clean the windows.

Both actions are in the future, but one is more likely to be fulfilled than the other.

Within the VP, the two sub-classes of auxiliary have sharply different functions. The primary auxiliaries express the grammatical categories of **aspect** and **voice** whereas the modals have an important semantic role in the expression of **modality**, i.e. notions such as certainty, possibility, necessity and obligation. We have seen that the primary auxiliary *do* is used as an operator when there is not one present already. It has no other role than to fulfil the grammatical functions of the operator. For this reason, it is frequently described as a 'dummy' auxiliary. *Be* and *have*, however, are both needed for the expression of aspect, and *be* is also used in the formation of the passive voice.

Broadly, aspect has to do with the time-span of an action: whether it has duration or not, whether it is complete or not, and so on. The past and present tenses are not marked for such aspectual features and are generally referred to as **simple**, in contrast with the **progressive** and **perfective** aspects. The progressive aspect, which may be in the past or present, is formed with part of the verb *to be* followed by the stem + *ing* form of the lexical verb. (All lexical verbs, even *be*, have a regular stem + ing form, which is sometimes called the **present participle**.) The progressive aspect has three major uses:

i) To refer to something that is (or was) happening currently, often with a sense of temporariness, e.g.:

147 Tom *was watching* TV at the time.

ii) To refer to action in progress – but not necessarily happening at the moment of speaking, e.g.:

148 Jean *is writing* a book about butterflies.

iii) It can also refer to action in the future, so long as the time is either contextually or linguistically specified, e.g.:

149 Richard *is playing* Macbeth in the school play next week.

The perfective aspect, past or present, is formed with part of the verb *to have* followed by the **stem + en** form of the lexical verb, e.g. *he has eaten, they had written*. The stem + *en* form is often called the **past participle** (see p. 24). This name is useful because there is a range of different forms for this part of the verb and, in fact, only a small minority of lexical verbs have a past participle that actually ends in -*en*. All regular verbs have a past participle ending in -*ed*, which is indistinguishable from the simple past, e.g. *he has **talked**, they had **arrived***. Irregular verbs demonstrate a variety of past participle forms, e.g. *he has **spoken**, they had **drunk**, she had **gone***. There are two major uses of the perfective aspect:

i) To refer to some indefinite, unspecified time in the past, e.g.:

150 Damian has visited Nigeria many times.

ii) To refer to an action in the past that is relevant to the present. Compare the use of the present perfective and the simple past in the following examples, where the act of baking is in the past in both cases but where in (151) the emphasis is on the cakes' current availability:

151 I *have baked* some cakes. Would you like one?
152 I *baked* some cakes yesterday but there are none left now.

The progressive and perfective aspects can be combined, using *have* plus *be* plus stem + *ing*, giving both the sense of duration conveyed by the progressive and of 'past with current relevance' associated with the perfective, e.g.

153 They *have been talking* for hours.

As well as occurring in progressive VPs, the verb *to be* is also required for the formation of the passive voice. This is made with part of *to be* followed by the stem + *en* (i.e. past participle) of the lexical verb, e.g. *is taken, was eaten*. We have seen already (p. 24) that, in the passive transformation, the object of the active sentence becomes the subject of the passive one and the active subject becomes the agent phrase, which may be omitted. In fact, Quirk *et al.* (1972, p. 807) point out that in roughly four out of every five passive sentences in English, the agent is not expressed. This is one of the major reasons for the use of the passive: it means that the active subject can be omitted when, for example, it is unknown, unimportant, or not to be divulged, e.g.:

154 My car *was stolen* last week (by whom is unknown).
155 The road *has been dug up* again (by whom is unimportant).
156 I *have been told* that your work is unsatisfactory (by whom is confidential).

Such avoidance of the active subject is particularly favoured in impersonal writing because it removes the need to use personal pronouns, e.g.:

157 The bunsen burner *was lit*.
     (NOT: **I** lit the bunsen burner.)

Both tenses and all three aspect forms can be made passive, so long as the lexical verb is transitive. The full range of primary auxiliary VP constructions is presented in table 2. (They are given in the third person singular form only; there are changes to the first auxiliary in the VP according to the person and number of the subject, of course.) An examination of the table reveals that there are rigid restrictions on the combination and ordering of the primary auxiliaries: there are never more than three in one VP and they have to occur in the order (*have*) + (*be*) + (*be*).

The clear-cut modal auxiliaries are *can, may, will, shall, could, might, would, should, must* and *ought to*. (There are a few borderline cases, such as *dare, need* and *used to*, which have some characteristics of lexical verbs and some of auxiliaries.[7]) The modals allow the speaker either to make a judgement of the likelihood of an event or state – e.g.:

158 John *may* come later.
159 There *must* be a hundred people here.

– or to express such notions as obligation, permission, ability, willingness or futurity – e.g.:

160 He *should* work harder.
161 I *will* meet you at the station.

---

7 For example, *dare* is like an auxiliary in its ability to combine with the negative *n't*, e.g. *I daren't let go*, but it is like a lexical verb in its ability to occur with the auxiliary *do*, e.g. *I didn't dare let go*.

TABLE 2   The forms and functions of finite VPs with primary auxiliaries

Auxiliary verb	Form of lexical verb	
	Stem+*ing*	Stem+*en*
be	*is riding* *was riding* PROGRESSIVE ASPECT	*is ridden* *was ridden* PASSIVE VOICE SIMPLE ASPECT
have		*has ridden* *had ridden* PERFECTIVE ASPECT
have + be	*has been riding* *had been riding* PROGRESSIVE-PERFECTIVE ASPECT	*has been ridden* *had been ridden* PASSIVE VOICE PERFECTIVE ASPECT
be + be		*is being ridden* *was being ridden* PASSIVE VOICE PROGRESSIVE ASPECT
have + be + be		*has been being ridden* *had been being ridden* PASSIVE VOICE PROGRESSIVE-PERFECTIVE ASPECT

There is only ever one modal in a VP and it always precedes any other auxiliaries. The verb which follows the modal (whether a lexical verb or a primary auxiliary) is in the stem form. All the verb phrases in table 2 can be introduced by a modal auxiliary if the appropriate changes are made, e.g. *is riding* can become *will be riding, has been being ridden* can become *must have been being ridden,* and so on. This last example illustrates the maximum possible size of an auxiliary VP, i.e. one modal plus three primary auxiliaries plus a lexical verb. Thus we can see that, in terms of length, the auxiliary VP does not have the potential for expansion that we have seen in the NP.

The catenative VP.   Some lexical verbs can be followed by other lexical verbs to form a chain; these are known as **catenative** verbs ('catenate'

means 'to link in a chain').[8] Examples are:

162 The children *want to go* home.
163 Mike *helped mend* the television.
164 Bernard *likes watching* football.

In each italicized VP the first verb is the catenative, the second the **catenated** verb. Catenated verbs usually take one of three forms: they can be in the infinitive (e.g. *to go*), in the stem form (e.g. *mend*) or in the stem + *ing* form (e.g. *watching*). There is no theoretical limit on the number of verbs that can be catenated within one phrase (though, stylistically, too many would be unacceptable), e.g.:

165 Gerald *meant to try to remember to promise to help to repair* the bicycle.

And there is no grammatical constraint on the order in which they appear, e.g.:

166 Gerald *promised to remember to help to try to repair* the bicycle.

The verb + particle VP.   The lexical verbs that have been used in examples so far have all been single-word verbs, e.g. *ride, swim*. There are, however, lexical verbs that consist of a verb and one (or occasionally two) particles, e.g. *blow up, look for, approve of, do away with, look down on*. In some of these combinations both parts retain at least some of their independent meaning, e.g.:

167 George *cared for* his mother.

where both *care* and *for* are readily interpretable.
   Often, the particle loses any literal meaning but serves to specialize the meaning of the lexical verb, e.g.:

168 They *washed up* the dishes.

Despite the presence of *up*, there is no question of *washing up* being done at a higher level than plain *washing*. Occasionally, both verb and particle

8 Quirk *et al.* do not use the term 'catenative'. They consider these verbs along with direct objects. (See *A Grammar of Contemporary English*, Sections 12.48–12.58). The grammar of these constructions is very complex and only an outline account will be given here. The simplest catenative constructions, e.g. *want to go*, are sensibly described as verb phrases. This analysis can be extended to cases where the catenated verb is followed by a direct object, e.g. *tried to help him.* (Such a description is given by Crystal *et al.*, 1976.) However, the situation becomes more complex when a noun phrase is introduced between the two verbs, functioning as subject of the second verb, e.g. *They expected **Jean** to make a cake.* There are (at least) two ways of analysing such constructions: Crystal *et al.* (1976) would treat *expect Jean to make* as the VP with *they* as subject and *a cake* as the object. Quirk *et al.* would consider *Jean to make a cake* as a subordinate non-finite clause functioning as the object of *expected.* The subordinate clause has its own subject – *Jean*; verb – *to make*; and object – *a cake.* I shall follow Quirk's analysis where there is an intervening noun phrase. For a fuller account, see Palmer (1974).

lose their literal meanings, being fused into a new idiom, e.g. *catch on* (meaning 'to understand') or *put up with* (meaning 'to tolerate'). Grammatically, these VPs can be divided into two sub-classes, called **phrasal** verbs and **prepositional** verbs. The simplest way to differentiate these types is to substitute a pronoun for the NP that follows the verb, e.g.:

169a Snow White looked for *her ring.*
169b Snow White looked for *it.*

There is no problem with this substitution; this means that *look for* is a prepositional verb. It can be contrasted with *eat up* where straightforward pronominal substitution will not work, e.g.:

170a   Goldilocks ate up *her porridge.*
170b *Goldilocks ate up *it.*

For the substitution to be successful, there has to be transposition of the particle as well, e.g.:

170c Goldilocks ate it up.

This transposition is characteristic of the sub-class of phrasal verbs.

The three types of VP we have considered can all be combined to produce a long and complex structure, e.g.:

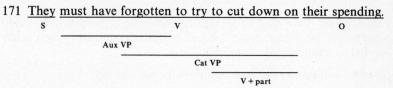

171 They must have forgotten to try to cut down on their spending.

In addition, any of the verb phrases can be co-ordinated, e.g.:

172 They *laughed and tried to dance.*

The adverbial phrase

The adverbial phrase expresses the adverbial clause element. It subsumes a number of different structures: a single-word adverb, and three types of phrase (AP) – the **adverb AP**, the **nominal AP** and the **prepositional AP**.

Adverbs.   Most adverbs belong to an open class; they are formed from adjectives by the addition of *-(al)ly*, e.g. *quickly, linguistically, silently.* Thus, when a new adjective is introduced, e.g. *bionic*, we can readily make a new adverb, e.g. *bionically.* But a group of frequently used adverbs that occur early in children's language development belong to a closed system. They are not formed from adjectives and do not admit new items, e.g. *up, down, here, there, now, then, yesterday, today, tomorrow.*

The adverb AP.   This phrase consists of an adverb as a head word preceded by an intensifier, e.g.:

173 She spoke *very quickly*.
174 The car runs *quite smoothly*.
175 I must leave *right now*.

The nominal AP.   We have seen that the NP and the VP always have a noun and a verb respectively as head word of the phrase. This is not the case with the AP, which does not always have an adverb as head of the phrase. When the adverbial refers to time, it is common to have a noun as head of the phrase, preceded by one or more closed-system words, e.g.:

176 Jane worked *all morning*.
177 Tom left *last week*.
178 They got it right *the second time*.

The prepositional AP.   These phrases have just the same structure as the prepositional phrases which post-modify nouns (p. 45), i.e. they consist of a preposition and either a noun phrase or, more rarely, an adverb, e.g.:

179 The guests arrived *at eight o'clock*.
180 The car stopped *with a jolt*.
181 Edna dropped her pen *down there*.

Occasionally there may be ambiguity about the grammatical function of a prepositional phrase, since it could be either post-modifying a noun or serving as an independent adverbial, e.g.:

182 I will talk to the sergeant at the police station.

This sentence has two different meanings which derive from the two possible roles of *at the police station*. If the prepositional phrase is post-modifying *sergeant* then the sentence is concerned with WHO I will talk to (the sergeant at the police station – and no one else). However, if the phrase has an adverbial function, then the sentence is about WHERE I will talk to the sergeant (at the police station – and nowhere else).

Like each of the other phrase types, adverbial phrases can be co-ordinated, e.g.:

183 She gutted the rabbit *quickly and efficiently*.
184 Neil walked *out of the house and down the road*.

The adjective phrase

The adjective phrase is one way of expressing the clause element complement. The verbs which occur in SVC clauses are copulas; some of them, e.g. *be, become*, can accept either a noun phrase or an adjective phrase as a complement; others, e.g. *smell, taste*, can be followed by a complement only if it is adjectival, e.g.:

185 The soup smelt *delicious*.

The adjective phrase may consist of a single-word **adjective** or of different types of Adj P: **intensifier + adjective** and **adjective + prepositional phrase**. In each Adj P the head word is an adjective.

TABLE 3   The expression of clause elements in simple sentences

Expression	Clause elements			
	Subject Direct object Indirect object	Subject complement Object complement	Verb	Adverbial
Noun phrase				
Noun				
Pronoun				
NP: d($+adj_n$)+n ($+prepNP_n$)	✓	✓		
Noun phrases in apposition				
Co-ordinated noun phrase				
Verb phrase				
Verb				
VP: aux($+aux_3$)+v				
cat.v($+cat.v_n$)+v			✓	
v+part				
Co-ordinated verb phrase				
Adverbial phrase				
Adverb				
AP: int+adv				
NP				✓
prep. phrase				
Co-ordinated adverbial phrase				
Adjective phrase				
Adjective				
Adj P: int+adj				
adj+prep.phrase		✓		
Co-ordinated adjectival phrase				

Adjectives. Most adjectives have two different possibilities of occurrence within the clause. They can be part of a noun phrase, pre-modifying the head noun (p. 44) – in this role they are referred to as **attributive** adjectives – or they can stand alone (or as the head of an Adj P) as the complement element, e.g. (185) above. This is referred to as their **predicative** function. A very few adjectives can fulfil one or other of these roles but not both. For example, the following adjectives can only be used attributively: *the **main** reason, the **mere** thought, his **utter** stupidity.* We do not say, **The reason was main*, etc. On the other hand, some, such as *afraid* and *unwell* have only a predicative function. So, while we can say, *The man was afraid*, we do not normally refer to *the afraid man.

The intensifier + adjective Adj P.   This is a straightforward construction, e.g.:

> 186 The tickets are *very expensive*.
> 187 The assistants looked *rather tired*.

The adjective + prepositional phrase Adj P.   Certain adjectives can be post-modified by a prepositional phrase. There is a close relationship between each adjective and its particular preposition, e.g. *good at, interested in, fond of, keen on, liable to, delighted with*, etc.

> 188 Those students are *good at linguistics*.
> 189 He was *delighted with the results*.

Any of the adjective phrases can be co-ordinated, e.g.:

> 190 Lorraine looked *well and happy*.
> 191 Gareth is *interested in sport and especially keen on rugby*.

There are two points to be made to conclude this section on phrase structure. First, any clause element can be analysed in terms of its phrase structure, using the descriptive labels outlined above, regardless of whether that element occurs in a full utterance or an elliptical one; and regardless of whether it is in a statement, a question or a command, a simple, compound or complex sentence. Second, it should be clear by now that even a 'simple' sentence that has one of the seven basic clause patterns can be remarkably complicated if several of the clause elements are expressed by multi-word phrases rather than by single words. This shows that, in order to give a revealing description of a piece of language, it is necessary to make an analysis at both clause and phrase levels, e.g.:

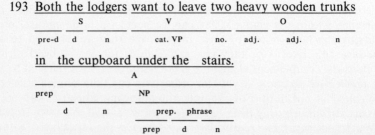

192 That noisy boy from Liverpool must have turned up.

193 Both the lodgers want to leave two heavy wooden trunks in the cupboard under the stairs.

An analysis that simply labelled these sentences as SV and SVOA without specifying their phrase structure would hide more than it revealed. A summary of the types of construction that can express each clause element is given in table 3.

2.4 THE STRUCTURE OF COMPOUND SENTENCES

A **compound** sentence is one where two or more clauses (or simple sentences) are joined together by the process of co-ordination. This means the clauses are linked, like sausages in a string. They may be joined by co-ordinating conjunctions, called more simply **co-ordinators**, or by intonation (in speech) or commas (in writing), e.g.:

194 The men whistled and the boys stamped.
　　　s　　　v　　　c　　　s　　　v

195 The men whistled, the boys stamped and the players jeered.
　　　s　　　v　　s　　v　　c　　s　　v

The commonest co-ordinator is *and*; others are *or* and *but*. Where the clauses to be joined have no lexical words in common, they are simply linked by the conjunction, as in (194) and (195) – the only restriction being that there must be a semantic relationship between the clauses otherwise there is no justification for joining them, as illustrated in the unlikely sentence at (196):

196 ?Two years ago our neighbours went to Holland and your shoes are dirty.

When the two clauses to be conjoined contain common elements, that is, either identical lexical items or words referring to the same person or thing – words with the same **referent** – two grammatical processes come into operation. These are **substitution** and **ellipsis**.

Substitution

In substitution a pro-form replaces the common element to avoid repetition. It always occurs in the second of two conjoined clauses. Nouns and NPs in subject, object and complement positions are replaced by pronouns, e.g.:

197 *John* fell over and **he** hurt himself.
198 Pam met *the architect* and Jane briefed **him**.
199 Helen met *an architect* and Paul talked to **one** too.
200 Martin bought *some sweets* and Alan bought **some** too.

These examples show that where the replaced word is identical to another in the sentence and also refers to the SAME person or thing, then the personal pronouns (e.g. *he, him*) are used. So in (198) *him* replaces *the architect* and we know that Pam and Jane spoke to the same person. In contrast, where the replaced word is identical to another in the sentence but refers to a DIFFERENT person or thing, then indefinite pronouns (e.g. *one, some*) have to be used. Thus, in (199) *one* replaces *an architect* but two different architects are involved.

Adverbial phrases can be replaced by pro-forms such as *there, then* and *like that*, e.g.:

201 Keith is *in the loft* and Geoff is **there** too.
202 Anthony will arrive *next Saturday morning* and Damian will leave **then**.
203 Anne walks *very vigorously* and she talks **like that** too.

Verb phrases are replaced by the pro-form *do*, e.g.:

204 Bill smokes and Jim *does* too.
205 The police arrived and the press *did* as well.

The first clauses in (204) and (205) each have an SV structure. In such cases the verbal pro-form simply replaces the verb. However, where there is complementation after the verb, the pro-form stands for both the verb and its complementation. These two components of clause structure can be jointly labelled the **predicate**; using this label enables us to say that the verbal pro-form replaces the predicate. For example:

206 The actors *waited very patiently* and so *did* the audience.

The predicate of the first clause consists of a verb and an adverbial. The pro-form *do* stands for both of these elements; therefore, the second clause has to mean that the audience waited very patiently. It cannot be interpreted as meaning that the audience waited but they were not patient.

The verbal pro-form is generally accompanied by *too, as well* or *so*. Word order remains the same when *too* and *as well* are used (e.g. sentences (204) and (205), but it is altered by *so*: example (206) shows that it causes subject-operator inversion. The choice of *so*, with resulting inversion, is particularly favoured when the subject noun phrase is very long. This is because there is a stylistic preference in English for ending a sentence with the longer of two clause elements. Therefore, (207) is rather more likely to occur – in careful writing – than (208):

207 The police arrived and so did hordes of reporters and photographers with masses of equipment.

208 The police arrived and hordes of reporters and photographers with masses of equipment did too.

(208) seems awkward because the short pro-form occurs at the end of the sentence, after a particularly long subject.

Ellipsis

In some circumstances it is possible for common elements to be omitted from a conjoined sentence to avoid repetition. Where the listener or reader can mentally replace the omitted words, without having to resort to guesswork, the omission is known as **ellipsis**.[9] So, in (209) the subject of the second clause is **ellipted** (or elided):

209 They went to the park and [ ] played rounders.

There is no difficulty in mentally inserting *they* in the square brackets. On the other hand, if someone started speaking and absent-mindedly trailed into silence, as in (210), it would NOT be accurate to refer to the incomplete sentence as an example of ellipsis:

210 I went shopping and bought a . . .

Here, the missing purchase could be any one of a thousand things so the listener could not fill the blank without guessing.

First of all, we can consider the ellipsis of a single clause element (or of part of one). In the examples, the position of the ellipted words is marked by square brackets and the 'common elements' (which could fill the brackets) are italicized. When the subjects of co-ordinate clauses are the same, it is normal for the second to be ellipted, e.g.:

211 *John* fell over and [ ] hurt himself.

This is a more frequent construction than (197), where the co-referential pronoun *he* was used as subject of the co-ordinate clause. The verb can be ellipted so long as it is followed by complementation. If an auxiliary is

9 It is necessary to distinguish ellipsis from the notion of **deletion** that features in transformational grammar. In order to explain relationships in sentences, transformational grammarians posit underlying structures – which are not acceptable English sentences – and construct obligatory deletion rules to remove the surplus items. For example, in the sentence *John wants to go home*, *John* is the subject of the finite verb *wants* and of the infinitive *to go*. Therefore, to make this structure explicit, in a transformational grammar this sentence would be given an underlying form something like this: *John wants John to go home*. Then an obligatory rule would delete the second *John*, to give an acceptable sentence. Thus, deletion is a process which can operate on underlying structures to produce acceptable 'surface' structures. Ellipsis, on the other hand, is applied to fully grammatical sentences in order to reduce repetition.

a common element but the lexical verbs are different, then the auxiliary alone is omitted, e.g.:

212 Eileen *has* drafted an agenda and Arnold [   ] written the minutes of the last meeting.

However, the whole VP can be left out if it is common to both clauses, e.g.:

213 The police *were photographing* the strikers and the press [   ] the onlookers.
214 Robert *must have walked* quickly and James [   ] slowly.

In the case of subject or verb ellipsis, the omission is always in the second clause. In contrast, when the direct object or complement is omitted, the ellipsis affects the first clause, e.g.:

215 Nina chopped [   ] and Richard fried *the onions*.
216 Margaret was [   ] and Michael became *a Catholic*.

When the head noun of an NP (functioning as subject, object or complement) is common to two clauses, it is sometimes possible for that noun to be ellipted, leaving the rest of the phrase intact, e.g.:

217 They invited twelve *people* and ten [   ] came.
218 Lorraine likes the blue [   ] but Sheila prefers the brown *shoes*.

Now we can have examples where two clause elements are ellipted. It is possible to ellipt the subject and verb together, e.g.:

219 *He has bought* Gareth a book and [   ] Alex a tractor.

Or it may be just the subject and auxiliary, e.g.:

220 *She can* check the tyres and [   ] change a wheel.

Finally, the lexical verb and direct object can be ellipted so long as an auxiliary remains, e.g.:

221 I haven't *eaten it* yet but I will [   ] later.
222 He couldn't have *bought the ring* yesterday but he might [   ] tomorrow.

These examples differ from the other illustrations of ellipsis because the italicized words cannot be mentally inserted in the square brackets without alteration: in (221) *eaten it* would have to become *eat it* and in (222) *bought the ring* would have to become *buy the ring*.

2.5 THE STRUCTURE OF COMPLEX SENTENCES

Sometimes, one clause is joined to another not by linking but by **embedding**. That is, one clause is included as part of another clause. As there is now a hierarchical relationship between the two clauses, rather than the egalitarian one that obtains in co-ordination, this process is known as **subordination**; the embedded clause is referred to as a **subordinate** (or **dependent**) clause, while the including clause is called a **main** (or **matrix**) clause. A sentence that contains one or more subordinate clauses is known as **complex**. Subordinate clauses may be finite, non-finite or, occasionally, verbless.

Finite, non-finite and verbless subordinate clauses

A **finite** subordinate clause is structurally complete, having a subject, a verb and any necessary complementation. The verb is always finite; that is, the form of the verb changes if number or tense is altered (see p. 22). The clause is usually introduced by a marker of subordination: *that*; or a *wh-* word – e.g. *who, which*; or a **subordinator – (s)** – e.g. *when, because, if, although*. These three features of finite subordinate clauses are illustrated in the following examples:

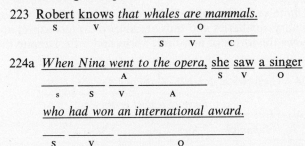

223 Robert knows *that whales are mammals.*

224a *When Nina went to the opera,* she saw a singer

who had won an international award.

First, each of the italicized subordinate clauses is structurally complete: there is an SVC subordinate clause in (223) while those in (224) have the structures SVA and SVO. Second, all the clauses have finite verbs: *are, went* and *had won*. (If the tense of the sentence is changed, the form of all finite verbs changes – not just those in the main clause, e.g.:

224b When Nina *goes* to the opera, she *will see* a singer who *has won* an international award.)

Finally, the clauses are all introduced by a function word that marks them as subordinate: *that, when* and *who*.

A **non-finite** subordinate clause, on the other hand, need not be structurally complete; indeed, it is common for the subject not to be included. The verb is non-finite. This means that a form of the verb is used which does not accept tense and number markers. These forms are the infinitive, the stem + *ing* (or present participle), and the stem + *en* (or past participle). In the following examples, the non-finite subordinate clauses are italicized:

225a The cat is watching *the mouse run round the cage.*
225b The cat is watching *the mice run round the cage.*

226a *Being a solicitor*, Tessa understands the legal position.
226b *Being a solicitor*, Tessa understood the legal position.
227a *Once frozen*, the turkeys are easier to store.
227b *Once frozen*, the turkeys were easier to store.

The subordinate clause in (225) is structurally complete, having a subject, *the mouse*, a verb, *run*, and an adverbial, *round the cage*. In (226) the subordinate clause has a verb, *being*, and a complement, *a solicitor*, but no expressed subject. (227) has just a subordinator, *once*, and a verb, *frozen*. Examples (225) and (226) show that non-finite clauses readily occur without a lexical marker of subordination (presumably because the non-finite verb itself shows that the clause must be subordinate). The three different non-finite forms of the verb are illustrated in these sentences: the infinitive *run*, the stem + *ing being*, and the stem + *en frozen*. The (a) and (b) versions of each sentence give proof that the italicized verb is non-finite, since it does not change its form, although in (225) the number of the subject is altered and in (226) and (227) the tense of the main verb is changed.

Although non-finite verbs do not indicate tense and number, they can combine with primary auxiliaries and thus are able to express aspect and voice. Table 4 shows the forms of non-finite verbs and VPs. Despite this

TABLE 4   The forms of non-finite verbs and auxiliary VPs

Auxiliary verb	Form of lexical verb		
	Infinitive	Stem + *ing*	Stem + *en*
	to ride	*riding*	*ridden*
be		*to be riding*	*to be ridden*
			being ridden
have			*to have ridden*
			having ridden
have + be		*to have been riding*	*to have been ridden*
		having been riding	*having been ridden*
be + be			*to be being ridden*
have + be + be			*to have been being ridden*
			having been being ridden

wide range of verb forms, a considerable amount of information may be lost when a non-finite subordinate clause is used, e.g.:

228 *When thawed*, the fish may be grilled or fried.

If we try to expand the clause, adding a subject and an auxiliary verb, it becomes clear that we cannot tell whether the subject should be singular, giving *when it is thawed* . . . , or plural – *when they are thawed* . . . The next example is inexplicit for a different reason:

229 *Picking up the big scissors carefully*, the students cut the cloth.

The main verb *cut* could be either present or past tense; the non-finite verb *picking up* may have any time reference so the sentence could mean either:

229b The students *picked up* the big scissors carefully and cut the cloth.

or:

229c The students *pick up* the big scissors carefully and cut the cloth.

The third type of subordinate structure to consider is the **verbless** clause. This seems like a contradiction in terms, since a clause is normally defined as a construction that consists of at least a subject and a verb. We have already seen structures – commands and non-finite clauses – where the subject of the clause is omitted. (Such omission is typical in commands, common in non-finite clauses.) There are some circumstances where the verb, too, may be understood from the context. In written English particularly, it is quite common for such a verb to be omitted. Generally, the verb will be part of *to be* but it may also be any of the auxiliaries. If the subject of a verbless clause is also omitted, it is normal to assume that it is co-referential with the subject of the main clause, e.g.:

230 *When in port*, ships must fly their national flags.

Here, the understood subject of the verbless clause is *they* (referring to *ships*, the subject of the main clause) and the understood verb is *are*.

Grammarians vary in the liberality with which they interpret the notion of a verbless clause. Because I believe that caution needs to be exercised in postulating 'understood' items which do not actually appear in the text, I shall label as verbless clauses only those constructions which fulfil both of the following conditions:

  i) The 'understood' verb is an operator (see p. 49).
  ii) The clause is EITHER introduced by a subordinator (s) OR it contains at least two clause elements.[10]

10 It should be noted, however, that this rather rigorous definition excludes some constructions which Quirk *et al.* (1972) label as verbless clauses. For example, in *He ran the shop single-handed*, Quirk (p. 351) considers that *single-handed* is best classified as a verbless adverbial clause; I should prefer to call it simply an adverbial.

These conditions are met by the following italicized examples (possible 'understood' items are shown in square brackets):

231 Steven has won more competitions *than* *Bill* [*has*].
         s   S   [op]

232 [*Once*] *The ordeal* [*was*] *behind them,*
       [s]   S   [op]   A

the Vietnamese refugees settled down well.

In both sentences the 'understood' verb is an operator; (231) has a subordinator and one clause element; (232) has no subordinator but two clause elements – a subject and an adverbial.

Before considering the grammatical functions that subordinate clauses can fulfil, it may be helpful to itemize some of the important differences between subordinate and co-ordinate clauses.

Some differences between subordinate and co-ordinate clauses

i) Co-ordinate clauses are joined side by side in a linking process, whereas a subordinate clause is included WITHIN a main clause.

ii) Co-ordination joins items at the same grammatical level, e.g. phrase with phrase or clause with clause, but subordination can join items from different levels, e.g. a phrase with a clause:

233 The belief *that the sun travelled round the earth*
                              s

lasted a long time.
  V   A

The subject of this sentence is *the belief that the sun travelled round the earth*; the head noun *belief* is post-modified by the italicized subordinate clause. So, here a clause is included as part of a noun phrase.

iii) A subordinate clause may precede or follow the clause it joins, while a co-ordinate clause has to follow its partner, e.g.:

234a We went to the park *although the weather was awful.*
234b *Although the weather was awful* we went to the park.
235a We went to the park *but the weather was awful.*
235b **But the weather was awful* we went to the park.*

iv) When two joined clauses contain common elements there can be ellipsis of the subject or verb of a co-ordinated clause but not of a subordinate clause, e.g.:

236 *The supporters* shouted and [   ] waved their scarves.
237 Margaret *bought* a new car and Ian [   ] a motorbike.

238 *The supporters shouted when [   ] waved their scarves.

239 *Margaret bought a new car because Ian [   ] a motorbike.

v) Replacement of an element within the sentence by a pronoun or pro-form can only occur in the second of two co-ordinated clauses. Such replacement can occur in the subordinate clause regardless of whether it is first or second clause in the sentence, e.g.:

240a I saw John and he looked well.

240b *I saw him and John looked well.

241a When I saw John, he looked well.

241b When I saw him, John looked well.

vi) A co-ordinator cannot be preceded by another conjunction but a subordinator can, e.g.:

242 The boys swam and although it was hot the girls played tennis.

243 *The boys swam and but it was hot the girls played tennis.

We can broadly divide all subordinate clauses into two classes: those that function as a clause element and those that form part of a phrase. The clause elements are subject, object (direct and indirect), complement (subject and object), adverbial and verb. So far, we have seen the subject, objects and complements expressed by a noun phrase; they can also be realized by a **nominal clause**. The adverbial can be expressed by an **adverbial clause**. The verb cannot be realized by a clause. This means that there are two types of clause that can themselves function as clause elements. Both can be finite or non-finite; adverbial clauses can be verb-less as well.

Subordinate clauses functioning as clause elements

The nominal clause

(a) *Finite.* Finite nominal clauses can function as subject, as both types of object and as both types of complement. Subject clauses are usually rather formal and are more common in writing than in speech. They can be introduced by a range of wh- words, e.g.:

244 <u>What Bernard predicted</u> <u>has happened.</u>
        s   v

245 <u>Whoever goes to the meeting</u> <u>could take</u> <u>notes.</u>
        s   v   o

246 <u>Why the secretary resigned</u> <u>is not</u> <u>clear.</u>
        s   v   c

They can also be introduced by *that* e.g.:

247a *That he will receive substantial compensation* is certain.
　　　 　　　　　　　　　　　s　　　　　　　　　　　　　v　 c

Such clauses can serve as subjects in any of the seven basic clause patterns. When they occur in an SVC sentence, like (247a), a transformation is often applied which moves the subject clause to the end of the sentence and fills the vacant subject position with the pronoun *it*, e.g.:

247b *It* is certain *that he will receive substantial compensation.*
　　　 s　v　 c　　　　　　　　　(extraposed subject)

This transformation, known as **extraposition**, is particularly favoured when the subject clause is long and the complement is short, because it allows the longer element to occur at the end of the sentence. We have seen already (p. 60) that there is a stylistic preference in English for this 'short-long' arrangement, which is referred to as **end-weight**.

Much more common than subject nominal clauses are object clauses. The most obvious instances are clauses that occur after verbs of speaking, when someone's words are reported either directly or indirectly, e.g.:

248 Jonathan said, *'I am ready.'*
　　 s　　　v　　　 o

249 Jonathan said *(that) he was ready.*
　　 s　　　v　　　　　o

In direct speech, e.g. (248), there is no marker of subordination; in indirect speech, e.g. (249), *that* is optional. Other verbs that can be followed by *that* clauses are *expect, hope, imagine* and *think*, e.g.:

250 Pauline thought *(that) John would win the prize.*
　　 s　　　v　　　　　　　o

Again, the clause-marker *that* is optional; when it is not used there is said to be a **zero** marker of subordination. Quirk *et al.* (1972, p. 734) suggest that such 'zero object clauses' are more common in informal than formal use. Some verbs, such as *believe, realize* and *learn*, can be followed both by *that* clauses and by clauses introduced by a range of *wh*- words, e.g.:

251 Mark believed *what Jonathan said.*
　　 s　　 v　　　　　 o

252 Laura realized *why Jonathan had gone.*
　　 s　　 v　　　　 o

These *wh*- words are not optional. Some verbs, such as *know, forget* and *decide*, can be followed by *that* clauses, *wh*- clauses, and clauses introduced by *if*, or *whether*, e.g.:

253 Jonathan did not know *if Mark had left.*
　　 s　　　 v　　　　 o

Rarely, a nominal clause can function as indirect object. It will usually be introduced by *whoever*, e.g.:

254 The stewards gave *whoever came early* a free programme.
       s   v   O$_i$ O$_d$

Nominal clauses functioning as subject complement can be introduced by *that* (or zero) or by a *wh-* word, e.g.:

255 The amazing thing is *(that) he knows all the answers.*
       s   v   C

256 Their response was *what we expected.*
       s   v   C

Very occasionally, a nominal clause will express the object complement, e.g.:

257 They will paint the banners *whatever colour they like.*
       s   v   O   C

In examples (244) to (257), the structure of each sentence has been labelled to highlight the grammatical role of the nominal clause it contains. Each subordinate clause can, of course, also be analysed in terms of its own clause structure. So, if we take sentences (254) and (255) as examples, the nominal clauses can be analysed like this:

254 The stewards gave *whoever came early* a free programme.
       s   v   O   O
                        s   v   A

255 The amazing thing is *that he knows all the answers.*
       s   v   C
                       s   v   O

Sometimes, the *wh-* word that introduces a nominal clause also functions as the object of the clause.[11] In such cases, the normal SVO order becomes OSV. This can be demonstrated by analysing the subordinate clause in sentence (256):

256 Their response was *what we expected.*
       s   v   C
                       O   s   v

(b) *Non-finite.* Non-finite nominal clauses contain a non-finite verb: either *to* + stem or stem + *ing*. These clauses occur freely in subject, object and complement positions. Examples of non-finite subject clauses are given at (258) to (260):

11 Some grammarians, e.g. Crystal *et al.* (1976), do not treat the *wh-* word as a clause element within the subordinate clause.

258 *Smoking ten cigarettes a day* can damage your health.
      S   V   O

259 *To attack a defenceless person* is unforgivable.
      S   V   C

260 *For a dog to attack its owner* is very rare.
      S   V   C

The subordinate clauses in (258) and (259) do not have a subject; the structure of the one in (259), for example, is VO:

To attack a defenceless person
  V   O

In contrast, the subordinate clause in (260) does have a subject – *a dog.* This example makes the point that such a clause, when its verb is the *to* + stem form (e.g. *to attack*), has to be introduced by *for*. The same contrast is found in non-finite clauses functioning as complements, e.g.:

261 The plan is *to attack the intruders.*
     S   V   C

262 The plan is *for the dogs to attack the intruders.*
     S   V   C

Because the subordinate clause in (262) has a subject and a *to* + stem verb, it has to be introduced by *for*. This is not true of non-finite clauses functioning as objects, e.g.:

263 The police expect *the dogs to attack the intruders.*
     S   V   O

The object clauses are quite often introduced by *wh-* words, e.g.:

264 They didn't understand *what to do.*
     S   V   O

265 They knew *where to go.*
     S   V   O

As with finite nominal clauses, it is possible to analyse the non-finite clauses not only in terms of their grammatical role in the sentence, but also in terms of their own clause structure. Taking sentences (263) and (264) as examples, we can make the following analyses:

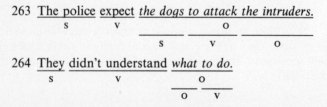

The subordinate clause in (264), like the earlier one in (256), shows the reversal of the normal verb-object order.

The adverbial clause

(a) *Finite.* It is very common for the adverbial clause element to be expressed by a clause. This is especially true of those that refer to time, reason (sometimes called 'cause'), result, condition and purpose. Rather rarer are adverbial clauses of concession, place (sometimes called 'location'), and manner. Sentences (266) to (273), in which the adverbial clauses are italicized, illustrate these various types:

Time

    266 Dave usually read the children a story *when he came home.*

Reason

    267 He was tired *because he had had a long journey.*

Result

    268 The children were already in bed, *so he went upstairs.*

Condition

    269 *If they were naughty,* he would be cross.

Purpose

    270 He read quietly *so that they would fall asleep.*

Concession

    271 *Although the children were tired,* they listened attentively.

Place

    272 He left the book *where they could find it easily.*

Manner

    273 They fell asleep quickly, *as they always did.*

Finite adverbial clauses are always introduced by a subordinator; common examples are *because, if, so, although, where, as.* It is clauses of time that have the widest range of subordinators – they include *when, while, as, after, before, until* and *as soon as.*

Adverbial clauses can occur either before or after the main clause, as examples (269) and (270) illustrate. Occasionally, they may interrupt a main clause, e.g.:

    274 She had, *before she opened the door,* listened intently.

(b) *Non-finite.* Non-finite adverbial clauses can contain any of the three non-finite verb forms – *to* + stem, stem + *ing* and stem + *en*. Commonly, they refer to time, reason, purpose and concession. In the following examples, the non-finite clauses are italicized:

Time

275 *Having eaten the jellies,* the children started on the crisps.
276 James joined the company *after leaving the navy.*

Reason

277 *Being a vegetarian,* Nigel ordered a nut rissole.

Purpose

278 Damian wore a tie *to please his mother.*
279 *In order to save time,* the bus driver ignored request stops.

Concession

280 *Though beaten in all his early races,* he refused to give up.

Sentences (276), (279) and (280) show that the non-finite adverbials can be introduced by a subordinator (e.g. *after, in order to, though*), but the remaining examples demonstrate that, unlike the finite adverbials, they do not have to have one.

(c) *Verbless.*   Verbless adverbial clauses are typically written language constructions. They are frequently introduced by a subordinator, e.g.:

281 *When alone,* he usually eats in the kitchen.
282 *Though an experienced sailor,* she still suffered from seasickness.

But they can also occur without a subordinator, e.g.:

283 *The dance over,* the band went home.
284 Jane looked radiant, *all her unhappy memories safely in the past.*

What all the subordinate clauses we have examined have in common is that they can generally be reduced to simpler, non-clausal expressions, which still play the same grammatical role in the overall sentence. We can illustrate this by means of two earlier examples, (245) and (266):

245 *Whoever goes to the meeting* could take notes.
$\downarrow$
The delegate   _____   ____
     s   v   o

266 Dave usually read the children a story *when he came home.*
$\downarrow$
                                       at night
____ ____ ____ _____ ____
  S   A   V O_i O_d A

This reduction test enables us to differentiate the functions of clauses that look very similar, e.g.:

285 John knows *where they live.*

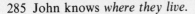

their address

   S   V   O

286 John waited *where three roads intersect.*

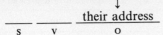

at the junction

   S   V   A

Although the subordinate clauses in both these sentences are introduced by *where*, the first is a nominal clause and the second an adverbial. This is demonstrated by the fact that the nominal reduces to a noun phrase and the adverbial to an adverbial phrase. It would not be possible, for example, to use an adverbial phrase in (285): **John knows at the junction.*

As nominal and adverbial clauses themselves function as clause elements, we can now revise table 3 (p. 57) and show in table 5 the full range of expression of clause elements.

Other subordinate clauses function at a lower level, as part of a phrase rather than as an independent clause element. We have seen already that there are verb phrases, noun phrases, adverbial phrases and adjectival phrases. All of these apart from the verb phrase can include a clause.

Subordinate clauses functioning as part of a phrase

The clause in the noun phrase: appositive and relative clauses

There are two kinds of clause that can post-modify the head noun in the noun phrase: these are the **appositive** clause and the **relative** clause. Both may be finite or non-finite. In the following examples, the head noun is printed in bold and the post-modifying clause in italics.

The appositive clause. Like a noun phrase in apposition (p. 46), the appositive clause re-expresses the idea contained in the head noun, e.g.:

287 The **suggestion** *that the lecture should be cancelled* was not well received.
288 They have heard a **rumour** *that a new motorway will cut across the park.*

When finite, these clauses have to be introduced by *that*. Non-finite appositive clauses are formed with the infinitive, e.g.:

289 The shareholders approved of the **decision** *to sell some assets.*

The finite relative clause. A relative clause gives additional information about the head noun of a noun phrase. This noun is usually referred to as the **antecedent**. Finite relative clauses are introduced by **relative pron-**

TABLE 5   The expression of clause elements in simple and complex sentences

Expression	Subject Direct object Indirect object	Subject complement Object complement	Verb	Adverbial
		Clause elements		
Noun phrase				
Noun				
Pronoun				
NP	✓	✓		
Noun phrases in apposition				
Nominal clause				
Co-ordinated noun phrase				
Verb phrase				
Verb				
VP			✓	
Co-ordinated verb phrase				
Adverbial phrase				
Adverb				
AP				
Adverbial clause				✓
Co-ordinated adverbial phrase				
Adjectival phrase[12]				
Adjective				
Adj P		✓		
Co-ordinated adjectival phrase				

ouns which do not simply function as markers of subordination but which also have a grammatical role within the subordinate clause. (But see footnote 11 on p. 69.) For example, in the following italicized relative clauses, the relative pronoun functions as the subject of the clause:

290   The **man** *who/that came to dinner* stayed a month.

291   John saw the **car** *that crashed.*

12 Some grammarians use the term 'adjectival clause'; this refers to the structure that, in this book, is called a relative clause. Such clauses function within the noun phrase and not at clause level, so they do not appear in this table.

292 That was a **decision** *which seemed sensible.*
     S   V   C
              _____
              S   V   C

These sentences show that a relative clause can occur in a noun phrase whether the phrase is functioning as subject (290), object (291) or complement (292) of the sentence. The role of the relative pronoun depends upon its function within its own clause, not on the function of the whole noun phrase within the sentence. The relative pronouns that can serve as subject of the relative clause are *who, that* and *which*: either *who* or *that* is used when the antecedent is human, as in (290); either *that* or *which* when it is non-human, as in (291) and (292).

In the next set of examples, the structure of each main clause is kept the same as in (290) to (292), but the internal structure of each relative clause is altered so that now the relative pronoun is not functioning as subject of its clause but as object:

293 The **man** *(that/who/whom)* *we* *invited* *to dinner* stayed a month.
              O   S   V   A

294 John saw the **car** *(that)* *his brother* *had crashed.*
                         O   S   V

295 That was a **decision** *(which)* *the directors* *considered* *sensible*
                          O   S   V   C

In this construction, the object occurs at the beginning of the clause, which means that the normal SVO order becomes OSV. When the relative pronoun functions as object in the relative clause, it can be omitted, as the brackets in the examples indicate. If the antecedent is human, as in (293), the relative pronoun can be *that* or *who* or, more formally, *whom*. Non-human antecedents are referred to by *that* or *which*, as in (294) and (295). Therefore, the markers of subordination when the relative pronoun is the object of the clause are *who, whom, that, which* and zero (i.e. an omitted pronoun).

The most frequent roles for relative pronouns are as subject or object of the relative clause. However, in addition, they can occur in a prepositional construction, e.g.:

296 The **politician** *to whom the demonstrators spoke* seemed very sympathetic.

297 The scientists examined the **equipment** *with which the experiment was performed.*

The only relative pronouns that can occur in this construction are *whom* and *which*. It is noticeably formal; in informal writing and most speech it is common to find the preposition at the end of the relative clause. Then, more markers of subordination are permissible, including zero, e.g.:

298 The **politician** *(who/whom/that) the demonstrators spoke to* seemed very sympathetic.

The relative pronoun *whose* is a determiner which has to form part of an NP. This NP (not just the pronoun) functions as subject or object of the relative clause it introduces, e.g.:

299 Tessa looked after the **children** *whose mother was in hospital*
                                s   v   a

300 I saw the **footballer** *whose brother you know.*
                       o   s   v

There is a possessive relationship between the noun in the *whose*+n phrase and the antecedent noun. For example, in (299) *mother* is the noun in the *whose*+n phrase, and *children* is the antecedent noun; therefore there is a possessive relationship between these two nouns. The underlying structure of the sentence can be expressed in a way which reveals this relationship:

Tessa looked after the children.
The children's mother was in hospital.

In the examples that we have had so far, the relative clause has immediately followed its antecedent. This is the most normal usage, but instances do occur where the two are separated, e.g.:

301 Several other unions will vote against a **resolution**, supported by a number of moderate unions, *that deals with incomes and the return of a Labour government.*

The non-finite relative clause. Non-finite relative clauses can be made with the stem+*ing*, the stem+*en* and the *to*+stem forms of the verb. The most straightforward are those with the stem+*ing* form, e.g.:

302 **People** *wearing leather shoes* will not be allowed on these courts.
303 The interviewer spoke to the **policeman** *directing the enquiry.*

These can be seen as instances of ellipsis; for example, in (302) *people wearing leather shoes* is a reduced version of *people **who are** wearing leather shoes*, and in (303) *the policeman directing the enquiry* is shortened from *the policeman **who was** directing the enquiry*. Here, the auxiliary (which carries tense and number markers) and the relative pronoun have been ellipted. This can only happen when the relative pronoun is the SUBJECT of the relative clause, so there is no non-finite version of the relative clause in (304):

304a The **man** *that the policeman was following* quickened his pace.
304b *The **man** *the policeman following* quickened his pace.

The stem+*en* form of the verb too can occur in clauses that have had the subject relative pronoun and the auxiliary ellipted, e.g.:

305 The **food** *eaten in India* is generally highly seasoned.
306 They admired the exotic **flowers** *being grown in the greenhouse.*

If these clauses are expanded into finite constructions, it becomes apparent that the verb phrases consist of part of the verb *to be* plus the stem + *en* form, e.g. *which is eaten* and *which were being grown*. These are passive verb phrases. Therefore, this construction can be used only when the verb is transitive (p. 48). So there can be no non-finite version of the relative clause in (307) because *fall* is an intransitive verb:

307a The **children** *who had fallen over* started to cry.
307b *The **children** *fallen over* started to cry.

Non-finite relative clauses with *to* + stem (the **infinitive**) are rather more complex. Consider the following example:

308 The last **people** *to arrive* were obviously exhausted.

It is possible to expand this to a full relative clause – *the last people who arrived* – but it has involved not only the insertion of the relative pronoun *who* but also the alteration of the lexical verb. Sometimes more extensive changes have to be made, e.g.:

309 Lager is the **drink** *to have in hot weather*.

To make a finite relative clause from this it is necessary to insert a relative pronoun, a subject and a modal auxiliary – *the drink which one should have in hot weather*. The problem is that there is no sure way of knowing what subject and modal should be chosen; it would certainly be possible in this example to have also *the drink which you ought to have in hot weather*. This means that there is not always a straightforward relationship of ellipsis between post-modifying infinitive clauses and finite relative clauses. (On p. 61 it was emphasized that the replacement of ellipted items should not involve guesswork.) So, although these clauses clearly have much in common with relatives, they are perhaps better considered simply as non-finite post-modifiers of a noun phrase.

A final point to note about all relative clauses is that they can be divided into two types according to the semantic relationship between the clause and its antecedent. Any relative clause will be either **restrictive** or **nonrestrictive**. A restrictive relative clause is closely tied to its antecedent. It restricts the reference of the head noun by differentiating it from all other members of the class; for instance, *the man who came to dinner* is set apart from all other men. For this reason, restrictive relative clauses are hardly ever used after proper nouns, as these already have unique reference. From a grammatical point of view, restrictive clauses are characterized by being able to accept the full range of relative pronouns; and, in appropriate circumstances, they can have a zero marker of subordination. In speech, a restrictive clause is spoken together with its antecedent noun in one pronunciation unit; in writing, this unity is reflected in the absence of any punctuation mark separating the clause from its antecedent.

Non-restrictive clauses, on the other hand, have a more parenthetical function and status. Semantically, they add some incidental information about the antecedent (which is already fully specified). They can readily be used with proper nouns, e.g.:

310 **Hilary,** *who is a keen climber*, went to the Lakes yesterday.

This relative clause is not specifying a particular *Hilary* but rather providing more information about someone who is already known to both speaker and listener. Grammatically, non-restrictive clauses are more limited in the ways they can be introduced, since *that* and zero are not possible. For example, in the following sentences, only *which* can be used, when the relative clause is non-restrictive:

311a   Wholemeal **bread,** *which many people prefer*, is more expensive than white.
311b   *Wholemeal **bread,** *that many people prefer*, is more expensive than white.
311c   *Wholemeal **bread,** *many people prefer*, is more expensive than white.

In speech, non-restrictive relative clauses are said in a separate pronunciation unit from the antecedent – often they are spoken in a lower pitch. In writing, they are separated from the antecedent by punctuation, either a pair of commas or dashes, e.g.:

312 Our **neighbours** – *who are very keen gardeners* – have just got an allotment.

Significant differences of meaning can arise from this distinction between restrictive and non-restrictive clauses, e.g.:

313a Joan has three **sons** *who are doctors*.
313b Joan has three **sons**, *who are doctors*.

In the restrictive example, (313a), we learn that three of Joan's sons are doctors but we do not know how many sons she has altogether or what the others do. (The sentence could continue, *and one who is a vet*.) By contrast, in the non-restrictive example, (313b), we learn that Joan has only three sons and that they all happen to be doctors.

The clause in the adverbial phrase

The adverbial is frequently expressed by a prepositional phrase which consists of a preposition followed by a noun phrase. The head noun of the phrase can be modified by a relative clause, e.g.:

314 The children ran along the **path** *that led to the sea*.
       S   V   A

                      prep   d   n   relative clause

315 She sang in a piercing **voice** *that made the windows vibrate.*
   S   V ———————————————— A
        prep d   adj   n   relative clause

The adverbial phrase may also include a **comparative** clause, e.g.:

316 Ted walks *more* **quickly** *than Tom runs.*
    S   V   A

317 Breathe *as* **slowly** *as you can.*
    V   A

The subordinators that introduce these clauses, *more . . . than* and *as . . . as*, are discontinuous, being separated by the adverb that functions as head of the phrase. Comparative clauses are very often verbless. (As two activities are being compared it is not surprising that there are common elements in the two clauses, providing the right conditions for ellipsis.) For example:

318 Roy was working *more* **energetically** *than Craig* [*was*].
    S   V   A

319 Andrew speaks French *more* **fluently** *than Martin* [*does*].
    S   V   O   A

The clause in the adjective phrase

Like adverbs, adjectives readily accept comparative clauses, e.g.:

320 Fred will be **tall**er *than his father was.*
    S   V   C

321 Young people today are *more* **sophisticated** *than they were*
              S   V   C

in the old days.
      C

322 The new aeroplanes are *as* **noisy** *as the old ones used to be.*
        S   V   C

The comparison may serve either to equate two things, as in (322), or to differentiate them, as in (320) and (321). We have already seen the discontinuous subordinators *more . . . than* and *as . . . as*. When an adjective is short it is made comparative by the addition of *-er* (e.g. *taller* in (320)) rather than by the preposing of *more*. But *-er* and *more* have the same grammatical role; both function as part of the comparative clause, even though *-er* is not an independent word.

Some adjectives can be followed by a *that* clause, e.g.:

323 He was **confident** *that he would win.*
324 Elaine is **afraid** *that Michael will catch chicken-pox.*
325 Colin was **sure** *that Elizabeth would be successful.*

In each of these clauses, *that* is optional.

It is very common for an adjective to be post-modified by a non-finite clause consisting of an infinitive and any complementation it may have, e.g.:

326 The relief organizations were **eager** *to help the refugees.*

In this sentence, the subject of the main verb – *the relief organizations* – is also the subject of the infinitive. In other words, it is the relief organizations who are eager and it is they who will do any helping. This is the most usual grammatical structure in this type of sentence. With a few adjectives, however, there is a different pattern of relationships, e.g.:

327 The victims of the war are **difficult** *to help.*

Here, *the victims of the war* are the subject of the main verb but not of the infinitive; they are not going to do any helping, rather someone (unspecified) is trying to help THEM. The adjectives that occur in this rather unusual construction include *difficult*, *hard*, *easy* and *simple*. It has been described here because it has featured prominently in experiments to assess the later stages of children's language development and will, therefore, be referred to again in the next chapter.

The major types of subordinate clause are summarized in table 6.

Other subordinate clauses

There are three constructions which occur in complex sentences and which do not fit neatly into the clause level and phrase level scheme that I have been following so far. They are not especially frequent constructions but they do occur, particularly in written language, so they must be briefly mentioned.

Comparatives

We have seen comparative clauses modifying adverbs and adjectives. In addition, there are constructions like this:

328 Bernard smokes *fewer* cigarettes a day *than his father did.*
329 *More* people buy books now *than used to borrow them in the past.*

These subordinate clauses are semantically linked to noun phrases but they are discontinuous constructions and seem better treated separately from the noun phrase.

TABLE 6 Major types of finite subordinate clause

Functioning at clause level			Functioning at phrase level		
Type	*Introductory words*	*Function*	*Type*	*Introductory words*	*Function*
Nominal clause	*that* *wh-* words *if, whether*	subject direct object indirect object subject complement object complement	Appositive clause	*that*	modifying NP
			Relative clause	*that, who, which, whom, whose*	modifying NP
			Comparative clause	*more . . . than* *as . . . as*	modifying AP, Adj P
Adverbial clause	*when, while, if, because, although, since, where,* etc.	adverbial	'That' clause	*that*	modifying Adj P

Sentential relatives

The relative clauses that we have studied so far have had a noun as their antecedent and have been part of a noun phrase. It is possible, however, for a whole clause or sentence to be the antecedent, e.g.:

330 Our friends said that they were planning to emigrate, *which surprised us very much.*

331 Judith was able to speak to the trade union delegate, *which delighted her.*

In examples like these, where the relative clause modifies the preceding clause or sentence, it is not accurate to think of the relative as part of a noun phrase.

Clefts

When a speaker wants to emphasize a particular word, he can do it by giving it extra stress or loudness. Writers sometimes attempt to imitate this by using such devices as underlining, italicization or capitals. There are also grammatical constructions which enable a writer to place the emphasis unambiguously on the word of his choosing (as the speaker always can). One of these is the **cleft** construction which cuts (or 'cleaves') one clause into two, putting the word to be emphasized at the end of the first clause. In the following examples, the word to be emphasized is italicized in the untransformed version (a) and then occurs at the end of the first clause in the cleft construction (b):

332a *Ian* proposed to Tina in the pub.
332b It was Ian who proposed to Tina in the pub.
333a Ian proposed to *Tina* in the pub.
333b It was Tina that Ian proposed to in the pub.
334a Ian proposed to Tina in the *pub.*
334b It was in the pub that Ian proposed to Tina.

These examples show that clefts are always introduced by *it* and part of the verb *to be*; and that they usually have a contrastive flavour, e.g.:

334c It was in the pub that Ian proposed to Tina, not in the park.

To conclude the examination of sentence structure, we can note that there is no limit to the number of clauses that can be joined by the processes of co-ordination and subordination within one sentence. This means that, although we started with only seven clause elements and seven basic clause structures, there is infinite variety in the patterns of sentences that can be created. If we take the simple structure SVO and realize each clause element simply, we can make a sentence like:

335 The waiter ate the biscuits.
        s   v   o

But by using a more complex realization of each element, we can have:

336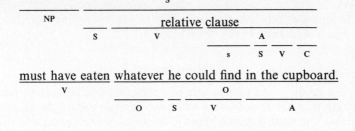

2.6 CONNECTED SENTENCES IN DISCOURSE[13]

The chief function of a grammatical description is to specify the structures that occur WITHIN a sentence; when sentences are joined together in extended stretches of speech or writing, the most important links between them are semantic rather than grammatical. That is, the sentences together build up a coherent, unified meaning. This is largely achieved by lexical means, since key lexical items are repeated, or replaced by semantically related words. Nevertheless, even at this level – beyond the individual sentence – there are grammatical features which serve to hold the discourse together.

Quirk *et al.* (1972, chapter 10) describe these connective features chiefly under the headings of substitution, ellipsis, time and place relaters, and logical connecters. (The categories of substitution and ellipsis were used in the examination of compound sentences in 2.4 above.) Instead of following their description, I shall outline here the slightly different framework presented by Halliday and Hasan (1976). The reason for this change of approach is that most researchers who have studied discourse patterns in children's speech and writing have based their work on Halliday and Hasan, so an understanding of their terminology will be helpful in the later chapters in this book. They posit four different cate-

13 **Discourse** is used here to mean a group of sentences that are perceived as belonging together because (a) they have a common topic and (b) there are formal links between them; that is, words are repeated across sentences, or replaced by pronouns etc., and sentences are joined together by items like *therefore* and *on the other hand*. Both these criteria are necessary because it would, for example, be possible to select sentences about football matches at random from different newspapers and put them together; they would be on the same topic but, even so, they would not form a discourse. A discourse may be spoken or written; it may be short or long; it may be by one speaker or more than one. (NB. Some linguists use the term 'text' for what I am describing as discourse. For them, the label 'discourse' applies only to linguistic interaction between speakers.)

gories of grammatical **cohesion** between sentences: **reference, substitution, ellipsis** and **conjunction**. Their term 'conjunction' will be replaced in this book by the label **sentence connectives**, in order to avoid confusion with the processes of co-ordinate and subordinate conjunction that we have seen to operate between clauses within a sentence. Each of the four categories will be very briefly described.

Reference

There are small, closed-system sets of words that can be used to refer to something that has already been mentioned and so reduce the amount of repetition. The most common types of reference are to people and things, and to time and place. People and things can be referred to by personal pronouns (*I, you, he*, etc.), possessive pronouns (*mine, yours, his*, etc.), and possessive determiners (*my, your, his*, etc.). These forms are illustrated in the following sentences:

337 I bought a dress in the sales last week. *It* still had *its* original price ticket on the sleeve.
338 Jane met Peter last Saturday. *She* asked *him* for *his* address and *she* gave *him hers*.

In these examples, the personal pronoun *it* refers to *a dress*, *she* refers to *Jane* and *him* refers to *Peter*. The possessive pronoun *hers* refers to *Jane*, while the possessive determiners *its* and *his* refer to *a dress* and *Peter* respectively. The examples show that these reference items refer to specific, identifiable entities – a particular dress, a unique Jane and Peter.

The words that refer to time and place are the pro-forms *then, here* and *there*, e.g.:

339 Shakespeare lived in the sixteenth century. Life was particularly dangerous *then*.
340 The waste products are kept in a special warehouse. Any inflammable or dangerous substances are stored *there* too.

In (339), *then* refers to *the sixteenth century* and in (340), *there* refers to *a special warehouse*.

Substitution

Substitution is in many ways very similar to reference (indeed, Quirk *et al.* subsume both processes under the same heading). It differs from it in that the substitute replaces a word (or phrase or clause) in the discourse without implying an identical referent, e.g.:

341 I have broken the teapot. I must buy a new *one*.

Here *one* replaces the word *teapot* in the first sentence but does not refer to the actual teapot; in other words, the new teapot may differ in size, shape, colour and so on from the one that was broken – and even if it is physically identical, it is still a different teapot.

There are three types of substitution: nominal, verbal and clausal. The commonest nominal substitutes are *one* and *ones*, e.g.:

342 Jean bought a skirt and a suede jacket. Lesley preferred the leather *one*.
343 Keith has broken all the decorations. I must buy some new *ones*.

One in (342) substitutes for the singular noun *jacket*; *ones* in (343) for the plural noun *decorations*. The only verbal substitute is *do*, e.g.:

344 The noise grew louder so Joy left. Neil *did* too.

Here, *did* substitutes for the verb *left*. There are two clausal substitutes, *so* and *not*, e.g.:

345 There could be some tickets left. Richard thinks *so*.
346 **A** Is his leg broken?
    B I hope *not*.

In (345), *so* stands for the clause *there could be some tickets left* and in (346) *not* both stands for the first clause and negates it, i.e. *I hope that his leg is not broken*.

Ellipsis

Ellipsis can be thought of as substitution by zero. We have already seen this process at work in compound sentences (p. 61), in adverbial clauses (p. 72), in reduced relative clauses (p. 76) and in comparative clauses (p. 79). It can also operate across sentences, so that a listener or reader has to 'track back' to an earlier sentence to replace the missing item. In speech, the most frequent use of ellipsis is in dialogue, e.g.:

347 *A*: What are they doing at the weekend?
    B: [They are] decorating the kitchen [at the weekend].

In normal conversation the words in square brackets would not be spoken because they can be understood from the preceding linguistic context. Ellipsis is also common in writing; here are some examples from novels – the place where the ellipsis occurs is marked by empty square brackets, the omitted words are given in italics at the end of each example:

348 The guests at the party all looked very attractive. Most [ ] came in fancy dress.   *of the guests*
349 We tired of that and explored further into the truck. Up near the front [ ] we found several cardboard boxes.   *of the truck*
350 When she thought of the danger she would face in just a few more hours she wanted to kiss them all goodbye. But knowing

that Timothy, at least, was already suspicious, she did not dare
[   ] but told them only that they should not worry if she was a
little late getting home for supper.   *to kiss them all goodbye*

Sentence connectives

The processes of reference, substitution and ellipsis all serve to eliminate
unnecessary repetition from a discourse. Sentence connectives are different in that their function is to make a semantic link between adjacent
sentences. Because of this role, they cannot be used at the beginning of a
discourse, where there is nothing for them to connect with; so, a sentence
like *Therefore my parents will be arriving soon* cannot appropriately be
used to initiate a conversation, though it would be quite acceptable
without *therefore*.

Halliday and Hasan present sentence connectives in four groups,
established on semantic grounds. Acknowledging that other groupings
would be possible, they label theirs **additive**, **adversative**, **causal** and **temporal**. The following are some of the commonest in each group:

Additive: and, also, or, in addition, besides, furthermore.
Adversative: but, yet, though, however, nevertheless, on the other hand,
                   in contrast.
Causal: so, then, therefore, consequently, as a result, for this
                   reason.
Temporal: first, then, next, previously, after that, meanwhile, finally,
                   in conclusion.

The additive connectives indicate that an additional argument or idea is
about to be presented, e.g.:

351 I can't go to the cinema because I haven't finished my essay.
Besides, I haven't got any money.

The adversative connectives show that a contrasting point of view is
going to be expressed, e.g.:

352 I should finish my essay this evening. *However*, I would very
much like to see the film.

Causal connectives highlight the link between cause and effect, action
and result, e.g.:

353 I haven't finished my essay yet. *Therefore*, I should stay in this
evening.

Temporal connectives order events or ideas in a sequence, e.g.:

354 I'll finish my essay as quickly as I can. *After that*, I'll go to the
cinema.

Conclusion

The purpose of this chapter has been to provide a shared framework of grammatical description that can be used as an analytical tool in the rest of the book. It has involved introducing many technical terms and a considerable amount of grammatical detail. The terms and the techniques of analysis should gradually become familiar as they are applied and further exemplified in the following chapters. It will become clear, I believe, that it is only with an explicit, systematic foundation of grammatical knowledge that it is possible to identify and understand some of the strengths and weaknesses in children's developing mastery of their language. The length of this chapter (which provides only an outline of English grammar, with much detail ignored) perhaps helps to make tangible the enormous feat of learning that is undertaken by young children as they acquire competence in understanding and speaking their mother tongue. It is to that subject that we turn in the next chapter.

CHAPTER 3

The acquisition of grammar

... there should be planned attention to the children's language development. It should be the school's conscious policy to develop in all children the ability to use increasingly complex forms.

(DES, 1975, p. 520)

3.1 INTRODUCTION

When children learn their mother tongue they have to learn the sound system, the vocabulary and the grammar of the language, as well as social conventions of language use – for example, that people take it in turns to speak, that elderly strangers have to be addressed in rather different ways from one's schoolfriends, and so on. Because the main concern of this book is with grammatical structure, only grammatical aspects of language development are outlined in this chapter. (There are several excellent accounts that cover all the areas of language acquisition; see, for example, Cruttenden (1979), Dale (1976), de Villiers & de Villiers (1978).) More precisely, it is the acquisition of grammar in speech that is covered; grammatical development in writing will be considered in chapter 5. The account is descriptive rather than explanatory because there is not enough room in one chapter both to present developmental data and to discuss competing theories of language acquisition; also, it concentrates on the acquisition of English as a mother tongue, rather than ranging over cross-linguistic studies and universal features of the language-learning process. Even after imposing all these restrictions it is still necessary to be selective, because the area of study that remains is vast. The principle of selection I have followed is to give more weight to those aspects of grammar that are still developing when the child starts school. Particularly, the focus is on structures that cause children to struggle in their comprehension or production of speech, since an awareness of these difficulties contributes to a fuller understanding of some of the problems children face in reading and writing.

The organization of the chapter requires explanation. It would seem logical to begin with the first two-word combinations that appear sometime during the child's second year and to follow a smooth chronological sequence until language acquisition is complete. Unfortunately, this is not practicable. A description of the child's language, say at the age of three, entails an account of some grammatical structures that are just beginning, others that are in process of change, and yet others that are firmly established. It is more revealing from a grammatical point of view to see how each construction develops from its embryonic beginnings to full maturity. The chapter is arranged so that, broadly, the order of sections 3.2 to 3.5 matches the order of the onset of the constructions they describe (e.g. simple sentences (3.2) appear before compound ones (3.3)), and so that, within each section, the sub-sections are roughly in order of onset time (e.g. negatives (p. 115) precede passives (p. 124)). This plan generally matches the organization of the grammatical framework presented in the previous chapter. Similarly, the grammatical terminology established in that chapter is used here.

Because child language studies are conducted all over the world, by researchers working in different linguistic traditions, there is considerable variation in the terms used in published reports. For example, one writer may refer to superordinate clauses, another to main clauses and a third to matrix clauses. Wherever the choice of particular terms is not essential to a theoretical viewpoint, I have standardized them in this chapter, as far as possible. There is not always information available in the language acquisition literature about both the production and the comprehension of a particular construction; where there is, an account of the development of productive ability generally precedes any comments about comprehension.

Chronological ages are suggested for particular levels of development, but these need to be treated with great caution. Averages and norms can be very misleading when applied to individual children. It is generally agreed that most children pass through all the major stages of acquisition in the same order but that they do so at different rates. For example, in a study by Miller (1973, p. 384), all the five children went through the same steps in acquiring *yes/no* questions. The average age of acquisition was 2;11 – but that average did not apply to any individual child: for example, Susan mastered the questions at 2;5, Harlan at 2;10 and Carl at 3;4. As for the presentation of ages in this chapter, precise ages are given in years and months, e.g. 6;11; the vaguer expression 'six-year-olds' has its everyday meaning of children aged 6;0 to 6;11 (with one exception, to be noted below). In American studies, it is standard practice for school grade levels to be given. Normally, I have converted a grade level to its equivalent age range; as American children enter grade 1 at age six, this can be done by adding five to the grade level. So we could expect children in grade six to be aged 11;0 to 11;11. However, it is worth noting that American classes frequently span a wider age-range than is common in British classrooms: in a study by Strickland (1962), the children in grade 6 actually ranged in age from 10;6 to 14;11.

In interpreting the results of acquisition studies it is important to remember not only that children develop at different rates but also that researchers have various methods of obtaining their data. Broadly, there are naturalistic studies and experimental studies. The collection of naturalistic data can be longitudinal: this may involve keeping detailed records of one or two children over a period of months or years ('diary' studies), or it may mean collecting tape-recorded samples of speech from a larger group of children at regular intervals over a year or so; this is the method used by Wells (1974) in the Bristol Child Language Project. Or the collection can be cross-sectional: this involves recording the language of a number of children of the same age, and possibly comparing it with the language of matched subjects of another age; this is the procedure followed by Fawcett and Perkins (1980) in their study of the language of English-speaking Welsh children aged six to twelve.

Naturalistic studies have certain limitations: they may not capture any instances of some rare but interesting constructions, even though many hours of spontaneous speech are recorded; and they do not lend themselves easily to the study of comprehension. To fill these gaps, researchers turn to experimental studies. The methods used include acting out instructions with toys, imitating the experimenter's utterances, and describing or selecting pictures. Sometimes the test sentences or situations used may seem rather unnatural. Nevertheless, the advantage of such experiments is that they focus attention on the child's ability to produce or process decontextualized language, without support from his general knowledge or immediate surroundings. It is worth bearing in mind that this decontextualization has direct relevance to some of the reading that children do in school. This is because, when they read non-fiction, they may meet unfamiliar grammatical constructions and new subject matter at the same time. In this situation, they get no help from the context in their interpretation of the language.

Different techniques of data collection can, not surprisingly, produce different results. In addition, researchers vary in the way they interpret their data. Some, for example, give credit for the earliest appearance of a particular structure; others, more cautious, wait until it has become firmly established in the child's grammatical repertoire, and so on. In all cases, it should be remembered that whenever researchers refer to a child's knowledge of a construction or mastery of a grammatical rule, they always mean that the child knows how to USE that form, not that he has the explicit knowledge that would enable him to talk about it in grammatical terms.

In order to illustrate the kinds of construction that children use at different ages, I have taken examples from some of the many published studies of children's language acquisition. In addition, I have found it particularly helpful to be able to draw extensively on the raw data contained in *Child Language Transcripts 6–12, Volumes I–IV*, published in mimeographed format by Fawcett and Perkins (1980).[1] At a time when the great majority of acquisition studies concentrate on the pre-school period, their large-scale project is unusual – and valuable – in focusing on the language development of school-age children. The transcripts record the spontaneous speech of four groups of thirty children, each child being within three months of 6;0, 8;0, 10;0 or 12;0 when studied. (So a reference to the six-year-olds, for example, in this study encompasses children aged 5;9 to 6;3 – not 6;0 to 6;11 as elsewhere in this chapter.) The children were recorded in two different situations: first, in peer groups of three, as they built a house using a large set of Lego; and second, in an individual interview with an unknown adult. The suggestions I make about various linguistic features in the transcripts should be regarded as provisional until the project's own computer-processing of the data is complete; the publication of the results of this analysis is awaited with interest.

A final introductory point is that the oral language of young school-children often differs from that of mature speakers not so much in the constructions that are chosen but in the errors that are made in their use. This chapter therefore makes fairly frequent mention of children's errors. However, identifying errors in transcripts of children's speech is not so straightforward as it might seem. The spontaneous speech of adults is not error-free, and it is important not to apply to children standards which would not be met by adults in similar circumstances. So, in pinpointing errors, I have made every effort to avoid including slips of the tongue, non-standard expressions and so on, that will be lifelong features of the speaker's language, and to present only those forms that children will grow out of. In other words, the errors referred to are seen as immaturities in the language system rather than as 'mistakes' in a prescriptive sense. It must be acknowledged, though, that the distinction is not always an easy one to make.

3.2 THE ACQUISITION OF SIMPLE SENTENCES

Clause structure of statements

Children begin using single words, such as *mama* and *more*, between about 1;0 and 1;6, but we shall not consider their linguistic ability to be specifically GRAMMATICAL until two or more words are combined in one utterance – usually at some time between 1;6 and 2;0. At the one-word

1 I am very grateful to Robin Fawcett and Michael Perkins for their generous permission to quote from their transcripts, and to Robin Fawcett for his helpful comments on an earlier draft of this chapter.

stage, more nouns are used than any other type of word (Garman, 1979), and nouns also feature prominently at the two-word stage; two nouns may occur together, with a variety of grammatical functions and semantic roles, or one noun may be used with a verb, adverb or adjective. A two-word combination can, of course, be either a phrase or a clause. Because children's early utterances are so fragmentary, a knowledge both of the context and of the child is often needed for an accurate interpretation of structure and meaning. For example, *daddy car* may be an early noun phrase, meaning 'daddy's car' or it may be an embryonic clause, with two possible patterns: SA – 'daddy [is in the] car' or SO – 'daddy [is cleaning the] car'. In her study of three children from the age of 1;8, Bloom (1971) found that their earliest and most productive two-word combinations were analysable as clauses rather than as phrases. Therefore, in this chapter the development of clause structure will be described before phrase structure, but it is necessary to remember two things: first, that children vary – some, like Jonathan (Braine, 1976), using a large number of phrases such as *red car* and *old carrot* before clause patterns are established – and, second, that in any case the development of both clause and phrase structure generally goes on side by side.

The following examples, taken from Braine's (1976) data, illustrate the most frequently occurring types of two-word clause. Where necessary, additional words are given in square brackets to clarify structure and meaning:

SO	1 daddy [is brushing] teeth	(Kendall, 1;11)
	2 Melissa [is drawing] eye	(Kendall, 1;11)
SA	3 sand [is in] eye	(Jonathan, 2;0)
	4 Mommy [is in] bathroom	(Kendall, 1;11)
OA	5 [put] back raisin	(Jonathan, 2;0)
VO	6 want car	(David, 1;9)
	7 eat banana	(Jonathan, 1;11)
VA	8 go home	(Kendall, 1;11)
	9 sit down	(David, 1;9)
SV	10 daddy write	(Kendall, 1;11)
	11 Elliot sleep	(Jonathan, 2;0)
SC	12 Kendall [is a] monkey	(Kendall, 2;0)
	13 hair [is] wet	(Kendall, 2;0)

Many researchers who concentrate entirely on the earliest stages of language acquisition label these combinations in terms of the semantic relationships they express, such as location, identification, etc., rather than in terms of putative grammatical functions. Such labelling emphasizes the meaningful, communicative nature of the child's language and, at the same time, avoids the danger of seeming to credit him with an early awareness of grammatical categories. The grammatical labels are used here for descriptive convenience because, in an account that has a developmental perspective, it is useful to be able to apply the same labels throughout the whole course of language development.

When children first start combining words, they frequently express an idea in a sequence of two-word clauses, e.g.:

14 baby block
    baby throw
    throw block

As they clearly have the communicative need for a three-word clause (*baby throw block*), their use of several shorter clauses instead suggests that they do not yet have the language-processing capacity to produce one.

The two-word clauses above from Kendall, Jonathan and David illustrate the well-known fact that children's utterances almost always follow adult word-order. At this early stage, when different word classes are not marked either by endings (e.g. *-ed*, *-ing*) or by function words such as determiners and auxiliaries, the only way that grammatical relationships can be expressed is by linear order. As examples (1) to (13) show, subjects come before verbs and both regularly precede objects and adverbials. There are very occasional exceptions, e.g. (from Braine, 1976):

15 hug Mommy (i.e. VS – 'Mommy hugs')   (Kendall, 2;0)
16 doggy slipper (i.e. AS – 'slipper on doggy')   (Kendal, 1;11)

But, as Brown *et al.* (1969, p. 42) say of their data, 'these are the only exceptions in thousands of well-ordered sentences'.

From her language samples, Menyuk (1969) suggests that clauses without a subject are the most common type in the earliest months, with more subjects being used after about 2;0. Bloom (1971) on the other hand says that SO, SV and VO clauses are the ones most frequently used by the children she studied. Differences of this kind between data collections partly reflect differences in children's personalities. For instance, Miller and Ervin (1964), commenting on the linguistic differences between their subjects, Susan and Christy, point out that Susan is an active busy child, always talking about what she is doing, so she produces many verb structures, e.g. *chair fall, tear paper*. In contrast, Christy is a more passive child who waits to be entertained: her earliest word combinations have a labelling function, e.g. *that [is a] truck*.

Once the joining of two clause elements is established, the child can progress to three- and four-element sentences. (As phrase structure is also developing, clause elements may now be expressed by a phrase rather than by a single word.) Crystal *et al.* (1976) suggest 2;0 to 2;6 for the onset of three-element structures such as:

SVO 17 Kimmy ride bike
SVA 18 Kristin sit chair

and 2;6 to 3;0 for four-element expressions like:

SVOA 19 mummy spill juice on the floor
SVAA 20 dolly go to bed now

The most common errors at clause level up to about age three are omission of the subject (particularly when it is obvious from the context) and omission of the copula verb *to be*.

When the four-element pattern with an indirect object is first used, it is generally in the form SVO_d *to* O_i, e.g.:

21a Daddy gave the ball to Billy.

rather than in the more condensed $SVO_i O_d$ form:

21b Daddy gave Billy the ball.

Osgood and Zehler (1981) tested children aged 3;0 to 5;10 and found that, when they were shown toys performing giving and receiving actions, the children preferred to use the *to* construction to describe what they had seen. This preference seems to be a continuing one. Strickland (1962) recorded the spontaneous speech of 575 children aged six to fourteen and she found that the pupils in the oldest group (aged 10;6 to 14;11) used SVO_d *to* O_i; more than twice as often as they used $SVO_i O_d$. Studies have also shown that comprehension of the *to* form is superior. Gourley and Catlin (1978), testing children aged four to seven, reported that only 24 per cent of their seven-year-olds understood the $SVO_i O_d$ form while 90 per cent were successful with SVO_d *to* O_i. Cook (1976) found that, by the age of eight, children had completely mastered the *to* construction but even at ten only half of his subjects could interpret $SVO_i O_d$ sentences accurately.

The earliest adverbials used by children refer to place; they appear when two-word combinations first begin. Adverbials of time and manner come slightly later – not before 2;6, according to Brown *et al.* (1969). During the primary school years the number of adverbials used increases and, in addition, children become more flexible in their use of them, placing them in a wider range of positions within the clause. For example, Strickland (1962, p. 38) points out that eleven-year-old children quite often include an adverbial within the verb phrase, e.g. *have been always trying*, but that this is rare among six-year-olds. Her results also suggest that twelve-year-olds use 30 per cent more adverbials than six-year-olds but that the proportion of each type remains closely similar; the figures are given in table 7.

Once the basic clause elements and clause patterns have been acquired, which normally happens before children start school, they form a relatively unvarying background to the rest of language acquisition.

TABLE 7 Number and type of adverbials used in speech at 6 and 12[3]
(based on Strickland (1962) p. 44.)

Type of adverbial	Grade 1 (N = 100)		Grade 6 (N = 100)	
	6;0 to 8;5 mean = 6;11[2]		10;6 to 14;11 mean = 12;0[2]	
	Number	Percentage of all adverbials	Number	Percentage of all adverbials
Place	830	35.5	1048	33.9
Time	799	34.3	1055	34.1
Manner	572	24.5	837	27.0
Cause/Purpose/ Condition	132	5.7	154	5.0
TOTAL	2333	100	3094	100

Large-scale studies by Strickland (1962) and O'Donnell *et al.* (1967) have established the frequencies of the most common clause patterns in the speech of primary school children, and these are presented in table 8. The figures in table 8 show no consistent developmental trends. The differences in the results from the two studies probably derive from the type of language that was sampled: Strickland recorded fairly general conversation while O'Donnell *et al.* asked their subjects to tell the story of a silent cartoon film that they had just watched, so the language was predominantly narrative. These and other studies (e.g. Loban (1963) and Menyuk (1969)) show that almost all children are capable of producing quite a wide range of clause patterns by the time they start school but that they use just a few – SVO, SVOA, SVA, SVC – 80–90 per cent of the time and use the remaining patterns much more rarely. Apart from SVAA and SVOO, some of the clause patterns that are used very infrequently are:

SVOC 22 That made him happy.
AVS   23 Here comes a hunter.

and those with existential *there* in subject position (see p. 30), e.g.:

24 There was a bird in the tree.

This picture does not change significantly during the primary school years. Loban (1963, p. 84) comments that evidence of language maturity

2 Strickland does not give mean ages for the hundred children at each grade level; the approximate means given in the table have been derived from the age-ranges she gives on p. 8.
3 Strickland analyses the indirect object with a preposition as an adverbial; in this table the SVO_d *to* O_i construction has been removed from the list of adverbials and the percentages of each remaining type reworked accordingly.

TABLE 8   Percentages of most frequently occurring clause patterns in two studies of children's speech
(based on Strickland (1962) pp. 29, 30, 33 and 44, and O'Donnell et al. (1967) p. 72)

	Strickland		O'Donnell et al.	
	Grade 1 (N = 100)	Grade 6 (N = 100)	Grade 1 (N = 30)	Grade 7 (N = 30)
Clause pattern	6;0 to 8;5 mean = 6;11^2	10;6 to 14;11 mean = 12;0^2	6;3 to 7;4 mean = 6;8	12;2 to 14;6 mean = 13;0
SVO ⎫	34.2	38.7		
SVOA ⎭	14.8	16.3		
	49.0	55.0	46.5	41.6
SVA ⎫	15.4	14.1		
SV ⎬	5.8	8.3		
SVAA ⎭	2.8	0.5		
	24.0	22.9	33.0	44.7
SVC	10.7	15.8	6.6	5.8
SVO$_d$ to O$_i$	3.0	3.7	n.a.	n.a.
SVO$_i$O$_d$	1.9	1.8	0.8	0.5
Other structures	11.4	0.8	13.1	7.4
TOTAL	100	100	100	100

is not to be found at clause level but rather at phrase level, where clause elements can be realized in a variety of ways: 'Not pattern but what is done to achieve flexibility within the pattern proves to be a measure of effectiveness and control of language at this level of language development.'

However, there is one clause pattern that was not mentioned in the large-scale acquisition studies of the Sixties which has recently had some attention and which may possibly show developmental trends. It is the clause with a **recapitulatory** pronoun, e.g.:

25a   These people with big cars *they* should pay more tax.

This construction begins with a noun phrase (*These people with big cars*) which is then left outside the structure of the clause, where its place is taken by a co-referential pronoun (*they*). It occurs chiefly in speech – in writing we would more normally find:

25b   These people with big cars should pay more tax.

It has been suggested that it is more common in the speech of children than of adults and that its use decreases as linguistic maturity increases. For example, Cotton (1978) recorded occurrences in the speech of children between the ages of 7;9 and 9;9 and found a significant decrease with age. However, an analysis of spontaneous speech made by Yerrill (1977) suggests that nine-year-olds still use the construction quite frequently but that twelve-year-olds restrict its use to clauses with a particularly long subject, e.g.:

26 Mr Griffiths, the one maths teacher I used to have in the first year, oh dear, *he* used to sort of frighten you to death.

(12 years, p. 234)

In Fawcett and Perkins' (1980) transcripts of ten-year-olds there are half a dozen or so instances,[4] e.g.:

27 my 'father and my friend's father/*they* 'own a 'garage up in Bèdlinog/ (III, p. 85)
28 my 'leg *it*'s 'gone to slèep/ (III, p. 284)

There are roughly the same number in the transcripts of the twelve-year-olds, e.g.:

29 'Ironground the báron/*he* 'gives them rîfles you know/ (IV, p. 14)
30 my bróther/ *he*'s 'only thrée/ (IV, p. 214)

Examples (28) and (30) reveal that these children do not use the recapitulatory pronoun only when the subject NP is long. From the evidence available, it does not seem possible to draw firm conclusions about the relationship between the use of this construction and linguistic maturity. In any case, it is never a frequent pattern. Its interest lies in the fact that, because it is essentially colloquial, it is one of the structures that children have to learn to forgo in their writing. We shall return to that point in chapter 5.

Leaving the recapitulatory pronoun structure aside, we can say that, apart from the increased and more varied use of adverbials, children do not show major differences in the clause patterns they choose as they grow older. Nevertheless, they do gradually display greater control and fluency in their handling of them. For instance, infant children still sometimes make the clause-level error of lack of concord between the subject and the verb, but it becomes less frequent during the junior school years. Fawcett and Perkins' (1980) six- and eight-year-olds occasionally use the stem form of the verb after a third person singular subject in the present tense, e.g.:

31 one of them '*catch* a màn/ (6 years; I, p. 134)
32 my 'daddy *like* cartóons/ (6 years; I, p. 259)
33 'someone '*roll* it óut/ (8 years; II, p. 145)

4 A particularly helpful feature of these transcripts is that prosodic features are marked: tone unit boundaries are indicated by /, stressed syllables by ', and the pitch movement on the intonation nucleus by / \ ^ and ᵛ. For an account of these features, see pp. 168–70 and pp. 173–8 below.

They may also use the stem + s form inappropriately, e.g.:

34 you '*hides* from sómeone/   (6 years; I, p. 101)
35 'some of them *is* náughty/   (8 years; II, p. 264)

Such errors are much rarer in the older children's speech; where they do
occur, it sometimes seems likely that it is the overall complexity of the
sentence that is responsible for the failure of concord, e.g.:

36 he 'uses 'something called an 'osmic projéctor/ that '*beam* himself
     in time/   (12 years; IV, p. 14)

As far as fluency is concerned, Loban (1963, pp. 32–3) demonstrates
that the period between five and twelve is characterized (at least for abler
children) by the steady reduction in the number of incomplete utterances
and **mazes** that occur in speech. ('Maze' is a term coined by Loban (1963,
p. 8) to label false starts, voiced hesitations and meaningless repetitions.)

Phrase structure

The noun phrase

The NP[5].   Many children start using two-word NPs around the age of
two, shortly after the first two-word clauses have appeared. Initially,
these phrases have a labelling function as the child draws attention to
something he sees or wants. Often, an adjective plus a noun is the commonest early combination. The first closed-system words to occur are the
post-determiners (p. 44), namely, the quantifiers (e.g. *more*), the ordinals
(e.g. *other*) and the cardinal numbers. The earliest determiners are usually
the demonstratives (e.g. *this*) and the possessives (e.g. *my*). The determiners *a* and *the* appear any time up to a year later: Brown (1973)
judged that their use was firmly established in his subjects between 3;0
and 3;5. Here are some examples, from children aged about two, of the
commonest types of two-word NP. The data are from Braine (1976) and
I have adapted the analysis made by Garman (1979) to give a rough
order of frequency, with the most frequent first:

    i) adj n   hot pipe   (Jonathan, 1;11)
                  big bed   (Kendall, 2;0)

   ii) post-d n   more lotion   (Kendall, 2;0)
                  two spoon   (Jonathan, 2;0)
                  other hand   (Jonathan, 2;0)

5 As the term 'NP' is used slightly idiosyncratically in this book, readers who have not
read chapter 2 may like to turn to p. 37 for an explanation.

iii) n['s]n   Kimmy house   (Kendall, 1;11)
               daddy shoe   (Jonathan, 1;11)

iv) dn   this book   (David, 1;10)
               my penny   (Kendall, 1;11)

In Braine's data collection, types (i)–(iii) are all used four to five times as often as (iv).

From about 2;6 the noun may have two pre-modifiers and, from around the third birthday, three or even more, e.g. *that red car, my new velvet skirt, this very bumpy old train*. Another structure that may occur before the fourth birthday is the noun with a pre-determiner, e.g. *all my friends, both of the kittens*. By pairing sentences taken from children of different ages, Menyuk (1969, p. 39) shows how the mastery of pre-modification enables the speaker to express information more concisely:

37a I see a house. It's made of wood.   (3;11)
37b I see a wooden house.   (5;11)

38a I see a house and another and another.   (4;11)
38b I see three houses.   (6;0)

In O'Donnell *et al.*'s (1967) samples of children's speech, the use of open-class pre-modification increased by a third between the ages of six and thirteen.

Crystal *et al.* (1976) suggest that nouns post-modified by prepositional phrases begin to appear about the age of three. There is remarkably little published data on children's acquisition and use of the NP prep NP construction but it seems not to be extensively used in the early years. Loban (1963, pp. 48–50) shows that it is rare between the ages of five and twelve and draws attention to the fact that it occurred nearly twice as often in the speech of his high-ability group as in his low group. Figures given in O'Donnell *et al.* (p. 59) show that, on average, the six-year-olds in the study used prepositional post-modification only one tenth as often as they used adjectival pre-modification; the thirteen-year-olds displayed a marked increase in the use of post-modifying prepositional phrases. The following examples from the speech of six-year-old children are taken from Fawcett & Perkins (1980, vol. I); page numbers are given in brackets:

a picture *of Legotown*   (3)
the front *of the bus*   (79)
the end *of the runway*   (84)
the island *of King Kong*   (142)
the back *of the school*   (206)
the ghosts *with the hoods over*   (48)

a little box *with press buttons*	(207)
the man *on the roof*	(53)
the roofs *on the houses*	(99)
a wolf *from the forest*	(251)

In this data collection there are more examples of *of* in the NP prep NP construction than of all the other prepositions put together.

In a large-scale unpublished study, described by Rosenberg and Koplin (1968, p. 48), children, aged six to eighteen, and adults were asked to join semantically-related simple sentences together. The youngest children characteristically co-ordinated the sentences, e.g. *I have a coat and it is red*, whereas older children made more use of adjectival modification, e.g. *I have a red coat*. The ability to handle a range of modifiers, both before and after the head noun, developed gradually, not reaching adult norms until the age of fifteen or sixteen.

In terms of the USE of NPs, an important development takes place when the child uses a phrase not simply as an isolated label but rather as the realization of a clause element within a larger utterance, e.g. (from Braine, 1976):

39 [I] want *more cookie*   (David, 1;10)
40 that [is] *Kimmy ball*   (Kendall, 2;0)

Many studies have shown that children first use such phrases in post-verbal positions, as objects or complements. Phrases expressing the subject are a later acquisition – and when they do occur they tend to be restricted to **dn**. Loban notes that, even at twelve, the pupils in his study predominantly used the simplest noun phrases as subjects. He considers that complex NPs in subject position provide evidence of linguistic maturity, since the ablest children in his study used eight times as many expanded subject NPs as the weakest group. Strickland (1962) shares this view because she found a significant increase in the use of complex subject NPs between the ages of six and eleven. In the language of both children and adults, complex subject NPs are very much more common in writing than in speech, as will become apparent in chapters 5 and 6.

So far in this section the use of the determiner in the NP has been taken for granted. It is worth having a look at it in a little more detail, however, as it is a complicated area of English grammar and errors are still apparent at the age of eight. In order to use determiners correctly the child has to learn that they are mutually exclusive; that they are (generally) required before common nouns but not proper nouns; that some determiners occur with mass nouns, others with count nouns and that some occur with singular nouns, others with plurals. Clearly, this requires an awareness of the different sub-classes of noun as well as a knowledge of the co-occurrence possibilities of all the determiners (see table 1 on p. 43). Studies with young children have shown that they are sensitive to noun sub-classes surprisingly early. Brown (1957), for example, working with children aged three to five, tested awareness of the difference between mass and count nouns. He used a set of pictures, each of which portrayed an action, a mass substance, and an object; for example, a pair of hands kneading confetti-like material in a container. There were also small cards which depicted the three components of the main picture separately. The children were shown a picture and told, for example, 'This is a sib' or 'Here is some latt'. Depending on which sentence they heard, they then had to select the small card which illustrated either the count noun (*sib*) or the mass noun (*latt*). Roughly 70 per cent of the children responded appropriately to the grammatical and semantic information conveyed entirely by the determiners *a* and *some*.

Despite evidence of success in such comprehension tasks, mistakes in production continue to occur for some years. The examples in table 9, which have been taken from Fawcett & Perkins (1980), show that errors are still fairly common at age six and, though considerably reduced, have not been completely eradicated even by twelve.

Apart from learning the co-occurrence restrictions that hold between determiners and sub-classes of noun, the child has to learn how to use definite and indefinite NPs appropriately, and that is more complex than it appears at first. Consider the following examples of definite NPs:

41 I bought some apples and pears – *the pears* were very expensive.
42 I was riding my bike yesterday when *the chain* came off.
43 *The moon* will be full next Saturday.

In each italicized NP the definite article *the* is used because there is a sense in which the noun is known to both speaker and listener: in (41) this is because *pears* have already been mentioned; in (42) it is because it is common knowledge that a bicycle not only has a chain but also has only one – the whole bicycle **entails** its parts, including the chain. Thus the mention of *bicycle* allows reference to *the* chain although *chain* has not occurred before. In (43) definite reference is possible because, although there are many moons – Jupiter has twelve, for example – we share the cultural assumption that *the* moon is the one that circles the earth. When the referent is not already specific for both speaker and listener by virtue of one of these three processes, then generally the indefinite articles *a* or *some* are used,[6] e.g.:

44 I haven't got *a pen*.
45 I want to buy *some shoes*.

6 For a fuller account of this complex area of grammar see Brown (1973) pp. 340–56.

TABLE 9   Mistakes in determiner usage
(data from Fawcett and Perkins (1980, vols. I to IV); page numbers in brackets)

Type of error	Age 6 (vol. I)	Age 8 (vol. II)	Age 10 (vol. III)	Age 12 (vol. IV)
'a' before a vowel	a eight (7) a ordinary house (124)	a advert (230)	a accident (169)	a arcade (44) a estuary (75) a accountant (210)
singular/plural confusion	one people (91)		these family (59) these person (138)	this friends (306)
mass/count confusion	much gates (28) much roofs (180)	much blues (124) a dynamite (231)	much bricks (44) a grass (131)	
omission	in car park (192) I got indian suit (18)	have been nice job (207)		
wrong determiner after negative[7]	I haven't got none doors (222)			

Two particular problems arise. The first relates to NPs like *the chain* in (42) that are specific by entailment. As Brown (1973, p. 347) says:

> specificity by entailment depends upon knowledge of the parts making up all kinds of wholes. This is knowledge that can continue to grow through a lifetime though, no doubt, at some point at a decelerating rate.

Thus, in the following sentence, the correct choice between *a* and *the* depends upon the speaker knowing whether a car has one or more pistons:

46   My car is out of action because _____ piston has seized.

7 There are examples from children in all four age-groups of non-standard determiner use in negative sentences, e.g. *they haven't got no chimney things* (IV, p. 7), but it is likely that at least some of these are dialect expressions rather than linguistic immaturities; *none doors*, on the other hand, is clearly immature.

The second problem is that *the* can only be appropriately used when the noun is specific for both speaker and listener; it is very often specific for the speaker alone but he has to put himself in the position of his listener when he selects a determiner. Not surprisingly, this is something that young children find very hard to do, for it involves an awareness of the extent to which their knowledge and experience is shared by others.

Experimental studies by Maratsos (1976) and Emslie and Stevenson (1981) show that children are aware of the needs of the listener, and can use indefinite reference appropriately, by the age of four. However, Warden (1976), who used a more demanding experimental task, says that even seven-year-old children overuse definite reference. He placed pairs of children on either side of a screen and gave one child a sequence of cartoon pictures, with the instruction to tell his partner the story they depicted. For example:

47 A dog is chasing a hen. A cow stops the dog and the hen is hiding behind the cow. The hen has laid an egg.

The younger subjects (aged 3;0 to 7;11) were quite likely to say, 'A dog is chasing *the* hen', whereas the nine-year-olds largely avoided this overuse of definite reference.

The spontaneous speech samples of Fawcett and Perkins (1980) demonstrate convincingly that at eight, and even, to a lesser extent, at ten and twelve, children make the error of using definite reference for something that is still unspecified for the listener. This is most noticeable in their accounts of films they have seen and games that they play. They are obviously aware of the need for indefinite reference, because they start with *a* – or, very often, *this* (or *these*), which is a common colloquial way, both for children and adults, of indicating that a noun is specific for the speaker though not for the listener. But as the account continues, inappropriate definite reference creeps in. Example (48) illustrates the use of all three forms: *a*, *these*, and inappropriate *the*:

48 *Int.:* what's Cross Fire?
  J: sèe/you 'got *a gún*/ and 'then there's all *these . . . mârbles* on it/ . . . and 'then you 'try to 'get the 'one with the 'blue ring around it/ 'into *the bòx*/
  Int.: you shoot something into a box.

(8 years; II, p. 130)

Here, the interviewer's response emphasizes that 'the box' is not part of the shared knowledge in this conversation. The next example shows a twelve-year-old still occasionally using definite reference inappropriately:

49 *Int.:* what's Willy Wheelers?
  M: it's a 'game you 'put some bátteries in/ and you 'turn *the díal*/ for *the láp*/ and 'little men on mòtor cycles/ pèdal round/

(12 years; IV, p. 80)

A comment by de Villiers and de Villiers (1979, p. 89) is pertinent here:

> a difficult lesson that the child learns over the first ten or more years of life is that others do not have the same privileged access that he does to his thoughts and past experience, and that to be skilful in conversation he must share that knowledge explicitly.

To sum up this section on the NP, we can say that evidence of linguistic maturity can be found in increasing use of adjectival pre-modification; in the development of prepositional post-modification; in the use of expanded NPs in subject position; in the correct choice of determiners, and in the appropriate use of definite and indefinite reference. O'Donnell *et al.* (1967) believe that the greatest advances in the mastery of nominal constructions during the primary/middle school years are made between the ages of six and seven, and eleven and thirteen.

Pronouns. The first pronouns to be used are generally *it*, *this* and *that*, e.g. *tie it, what's that*? They appear sometime after the earliest two-word NPs and they function as objects or complements. The full system of personal pronouns, with its complex set of contrasts involving person (*I/he*), number (*I/we*), gender (*he/she*) and case (*I/me*), begins to be established by about 2;6 but may take another two or more years to be fully mastered. The first person pronouns (*I/me*) are usually acquired before the third person (*he/she*), which precede the second person (*you*); the singular forms are used before the plurals (Cruttenden, 1979). Young children very often use objective case pronouns in subject position, particularly when referring to themselves, e.g. *me want it*.

Learning to use *I* and *you* correctly poses problems because the child must refer to himself as 'I' although he is addressed as 'you' and must say 'you' to his mother, who calls herself 'I'. It is noticeable that many parents use names rather than pronouns with young children, presumably to overcome this difficulty, e.g. *Mummy will put Lindsey to bed* rather than *I will put you to bed*. Some mothers continue to say 'mummy' rather than 'I' even after their children have started school.

There is some evidence that during the first year or so of pronoun acquisition, children may use a full NP where a pronoun serves for more mature speakers. Thieman (1975, p. 266) showed pictures to children aged 3;8 to 5;2, describing each one in a sentence. The subjects were then asked to talk about the pictures themselves. The older children tended to use pronouns in the same way as the experimenter, while the youngest child, Lloyd, 3;8, preferred NPs, e.g.:

50 *Exp.:* The boy told his mother a funny story and *she* laughed.
   Lloyd: The boy told the story to his mummy and *the mummy* laughed.
51 *Exp.:* The bird sat in the tree and *it* sang a song.
   Lloyd: The bird sat in the tree and *the bird* sang a song.

Once the pronouns are acquired, they are used very extensively, especially in subject position. Maratsos (1979) says that it is common for 80 per cent of young children's subject noun phrases to consist of pronouns. In Loban's (1963) study, pronouns occupied the subject position 81 per cent of the time with five-year-olds, and 76 per cent with twelve-year-olds. These figures for children's use of pronouns in subject position are closely matched by Crystal's (1980) figure of 77 per cent in informal conversation among adults.

By the time the child starts school, any mistakes in the form of the personal pronouns are likely to be confined to the expression of gender and case. Menyuk (1969, p. 43) gives examples of gender errors made by five-year-olds: *he's a big train, she's a nice daddy.* As far as case is concerned, the biggest difficulty occurs when a first person pronoun is coordinated with a proper noun or an NP in subject position; here, there is an enduring tendency to say, *me and X,* or *X and me.* In fact, such expressions are probably only marginally errors, as they certainly occur from time to time in the speech of educated adults. Nevertheless, in careful speech or formal situations they would be avoided. The following examples come from Fawcett and Perkins:

52 'sometímes/ *'me and my móther/* 'make a hoùse/   (6 years; I, p. 35)
53 *me and Ándrea/ and Jénnifer/* . . . 'had to wrìte something/
(8 years; II, p. 267)
54 *'me and Gareth* will make the 'house and the gárage/
(10 years; III, p. 69)

As well as learning the forms of pronouns, children have to learn how to use them appropriately. Like the definite determiners, pronouns should refer to a noun that is specific for both speaker and listener. Primary school children tend to overuse them, assuming that their listener knows as much as they do. In 1926, Piaget reported a series of experiments in which children aged six to eight were told stories or given explanations and then had to pass on what they had heard to other children. Commenting on the inexplicitness of their language, he wrote:

Pronouns . . . are used right and left without any indication of what they refer to. The other person is supposed to understand. (p. 102)

The speech samples collected by Fawcett and Perkins provide ample evidence of this pronominal vagueness in six-year-olds; it decreases noticeably after that but still occurs occasionally in the speech of the older children. In the following examples from the transcripts, the italicized pronouns cannot be interpreted from the preceding context:

55 *C:*   'somebody was going to 'kill one of the 'Charlie's Ángels/
but *it* 'hit the tyrè/ of the 'Charlie's 'Angels' càr/
Int.:   what did – the bullet?
(6 years; I, p. 13)

56 *Int.:* 'Stretch out Strong' – what's that?
    P: you 'pull *them* and *he* strètches/   (6 years; I, p. 64)
57 *Int.:* how d'you play chess . . . ?
    M: you've got to 'line *em* úp/ right/   (8 years; II, p. 229)
58 *Int.:* how do you play Mouse Trap?
    P: wèll/ you 'there's this you 'pick up cárds/ and you 'just um
        you 'carry on from 'where *it* ìs/   (12 years; IV, p. 275)

Sometimes, the older children correct themselves in a way which shows that they have realized that their listener cannot be expected to understand, e.g.:

59 *Int.:* what do you think were the best bits in Star Wars?
    L: um 'when he was 'going in to er wèll/ 'Luke Śkywalker/ was
        'going in to 'attack the plànet/   (12 years; IV, p. 281)

Here, Lewis abandons the inexplicit *he*, replacing it with *Luke Skywalker*.

We can now briefly consider children's comprehension of pronominal reference. One thing they have to learn is when a pronoun can refer to a noun in the same sentence and when it cannot, for example:

60 If he wins the race Pluto will be happy.
61 He found out that Mickey won the race.

In (60) *he* can mean *Pluto* but it does not have to – it can also refer to some other unspecified person; in (61) *he* CANNOT refer to Mickey. Carol Chomsky (1969) tested children's understanding of the 'nonidentity requirement' of sentences like (61). Her youngest subjects (aged 5;0 to 5;3) made enough errors for her to say, 'since this construction is one of the simplest and clearest examples of the nonidentity requirement, . . . the evidence strongly suggests that these children have in fact not yet acquired knowledge of this restriction' (p. 107). Almost all of the subjects aged six and over showed full comprehension of the 'nonidentity' test sentences. She emphasized, however, that they needed the support provided by the toy figures of Mickey Mouse and Pluto Pup. A similar experiment, but without supporting toys, was conducted by Berkovits and Wigodsky (1979) with older children. They reported that eleven-year-olds were aware of the nonidentity requirement of sentences like (61) but that nine-year-olds had only a 28 per cent success rate.

Comprehension of pronouns in reading has been studied by Richek (1977) and Barnitz (1980). Richek's eight-year-old subjects read paragraphs which included a compound sentence with either a pronoun or a repeated noun in the second clause, e.g.:

62 . . . Marsha had a box for bracelets and other kinds of things and
    she loved it because it played music . . .
63 . . . Bob had a box for tin soldiers and his other toys and *Bob* liked
    the box because it was big . . .   (p. 152)

After each paragraph, they had to answer a test question, e.g. *Who liked the box?* Surprisingly, there was a ten per cent difference in the results for the two types, with the less common repeated noun structure of (63) gaining an overall score of 86 per cent and the pronominal form of (62) scoring only 76 per cent. Using similar methodology, and subjects aged seven to twelve, Barnitz assessed the effect of a pronoun that precedes its referent rather than following it,[8] e.g.:

64 ... Because *it* was on sale they wanted to buy a large train set ...
(p. 275)

Test questions for such sentences were answered correctly by under half of the children aged 7;10 and by only two-thirds of those aged 11;11. He also tested understanding of pronouns that refer to a whole sentence rather than to an NP, e.g.:

65 ... Mary told Steve that she rides her skateboard in the busy street but Steve did not believe *it* ... (p. 275)

Performance on these structures was rather better, with 67 per cent success for the younger children and 86 per cent for the eleven-year-olds.

Co-ordinated noun phrases. Not surprisingly, co-ordinated noun phrases first appear rather later than the simpler NPs and pronouns, probably between 2;6 and 3;0. The earliest forms of co-ordination to occur are N + N sequences, e.g. *mommy and teddy* (de Villiers *et al.*, 1977). In the pre-school years the construction is not used extensively. O'Donnell *et al.* (1967, p. 70) found a noticeable increase in its use between the ages of five and six and a doubling of frequency between eight and thirteen.

Several studies have shown that the earliest co-ordinated noun phrases occur almost exclusively in object position; subject position is harder. Slobin and Welsh (1973) encouraged two-year-old 'Echo' to imitate sentences she heard; this technique showed that between 2;3 and 2;6 she could produce co-ordinated object phrases, e.g.:

66 here's *a brown brush an' a comb* (p. 492)

but that she divided the adult's co-ordinated subject phrase between two clauses, e.g.:

67 *Adult:* *The red beads and brown beads* are here.
'Echo': *brown beads* here an' *a red beads* here. (p. 490)

Using an experimental procedure where children had to act out with

---

8 Some of the test sentences in this study are very unnatural, so the results must be treated with caution, but they do suggest some possible areas of comprehension difficulty in reading.

toys the sentences that they heard, Ardery (1980) found that virtually all her subjects aged 2;6 to 6;0 were successful with:

68 The giraffe kissed *the tiger and the cat.*

but only three-quarters of them could manage:

69 *The tiger and the turtle* pushed the dog.   (pp. 313–4)

Strickland (1962, p. 42) makes the interesting point that six- to seven-year-olds tend to use a *with* phrase rather than a co-ordinate phrase in subject position, e.g.:

70 I went to school *with my sister* yesterday.

but that eleven-year-olds rarely use this pattern, preferring,

71 *My sister and I* went to school together yesterday.

(When children do use a co-ordinate NP like this in subject position, there is a strong tendency for them to use the object pronoun and say, *My sister and me . . . .*)

The verb phrase

Single-word verbs.   The child has to learn to form and use the past and present tenses of verbs appropriately. Past tense forms, referring to events in the past, usually appear some time after the age of two, as in these examples from Daniel's speech (Fletcher, 1979, p. 272):

72 I *spilt* my juice   (2;0)
73 Mummy *painted* the wall   (2;2)

By the age of three, such past tenses have become very frequent (though with some errors of form that are noted in the section on Word Structure, p. 112). In addition to its role in the expression of past time, the past tense is also used to talk about unreal conditions, that is, happenings which the speaker does not expect to come about, e.g.:

74 If he *went* to France, his French accent would improve.

Predictably, this use of the past tense is acquired considerably later; Fletcher says that it was very rare in Daniel's speech even at the age of four.

    Although simple uses of the past tense occur very early, maintaining the right tense in a sequence of clauses or sentences can cause problems for many years. Fletcher (1979) comments on Daniel's difficulty with this at the age of three, although it seems hardly surprising, seeing that Fawcett and Perkins' (1980) transcripts provide examples of inconsistent tense sequence at least until the age of ten:

75 the 'mice *were* 'going to 'go in the aéroplane/ but the 'aeroplane
   has just flew òff/ and there *was* a 'bird líving/ at the 'top of the
   télegraph pole/ (6 years; I, p. 84)

76 they *were* 'trying to 'find the ghóst/ and 'when they *'find* the ghóst/
   he *was* scàred/ (8 years; II, p. 212)

77 and she and and 'at the énd/ she's um . . . these er 'two mén/ and
   um 'they *were* aǹgels/ *stop* you knów/ and he's 'going to run óut/
   and she *'came* through the doòr/ . . . and 'then they *played* rùgby/
   (10 years; III, pp. 154–5)

(It is true that adults often move from the past tense into the present in
the course of a narrative in order to make it immediate and vivid; the
difference with these immature examples is that they seem to arise from
difficulties in discourse production rather than from skill in storytelling.)

The verb + particle VP.   The earliest two-word verb phrase for most
children is the verb and particle, e.g. (from Braine, 1976):

78 *sit down* (Jonathan, 2;0)
79 Daddy *pick up* (Kendall, 2;0)
80 Kimmy *look at* Kimmy (Kendall, 2;0)

The only difficulty that this construction presents is getting the particle
in the right position when there is an SVO sentence and the object is a
pronoun. With prepositional verbs (see p. 55), e.g. *look at*, the order
remains the same, e.g.:

81 Kimmy looked at her.

But with phrasal verbs, e.g. *pick up*, the particle has to leave its verb and
follow the object pronoun, e.g.:

82 Daddy picked me *up*.

There are examples in Menyuk's (1969, p. 94) data of children's failure to
move the particle, e.g. *you pick up it, he beat up him.*

The catenative VP.   Another early type of two-word verb phrase is the
catenative VP (see p. 53), where two lexical verbs are linked together.
Limber (1973) suggests that the first catenative verb to appear is *want*; in
his data, *want* + v phrases first occur at about age two. Initially, the
linking *to* is unlikely to be present, e.g. *want get, want open door.* Menyuk
(1969, p. 87) notes that even at the age of four the *to* is still occasionally
omitted, e.g. *I like do it, I want draw it.* She also points out that, although
all her subjects (aged three to seven) used the infinitive in this construction, less than half of them used the stem + *ing* form, e.g. *he tried **riding**
my bike.*

The auxiliary VP. The first auxiliaries to be used are *is, can, will* and *could* (Fletcher, 1979; Limber, 1973). Their earliest appearance is usually in negatives and questions, e.g. *Can I fix it?* By about 2;6 they are used in statements too. The progressive forms of the verb, consisting of *be* + stem + *ing*, develop considerably before the perfective aspect, with *have* + past participle. An American study by Eisenberg (1981) gives a mean age of 3;4 for the first use of the present perfective by five children, but other American studies suggest that the form is not always fully mastered by the age of six. Among British children the perfective seems to be established rather earlier, probably by about 3;6. This may be because this form of the verb is used more extensively in British than in American English (Fletcher, 1979).

Although the progressive aspect is an early acquisition, omitting the auxiliary *be* is an error that persists for some years. Fawcett and Perkins' (1980) six-year-olds provide several examples:

83 'I making a sêat for him/ nów/   (I, p. 2)
84 we 'making lôts of things/   (I, p. 245)
85 you 'doing yóurs/   (I, p. 246)
86 my 'sister always 'turning it ôver/   (I, p. 258)

By the age of eight, such omissions seem no longer to occur.

A study of the modal auxiliaries by Major (1974) showed that the commonest modals, *can, could, will, would* and *should*, are well established in the speech of five-year-olds but that *shall, may, might* and *ought to* can still cause difficulties up to the age of eight. When children use an unfamiliar modal, they have a tendency to couple it with one they already know (for safety as it were!), e.g.:

87 Can you may go?
88 He'll might get in jail.

Both Major (1974) and Menyuk (1969) have records of such errors in the speech of children between the ages of six and eight; one of Fawcett and Perkins' eight-year-olds seems to be uncertain about the operator status of *shall* and so uses *do* as well:

89 shall we 'don't make a hotél/   (8 years; II, p. 66)

and a ten-year-old uses *will* and *would* together:

90 it'll would be a 'funny cólour/   (10 years; III, p. 45)

(This could just be a slip of the tongue but there are no pauses marked to suggest that the child is correcting herself.)

The modal *would*, and its perfective form *would have*, enable speakers to make hypotheses, either about what might happen in the future or about what could have happened (but did not) in the past. In this role it occurs with *if* clauses expressing unreal conditions. There has to be a past tense verb in the *if* clause, and *would* or *would have* in the main clause, e.g.:

91 If he *jumped* off that tree he *would* break his leg.
92 If he *had jumped* off that tree he *would have* broken his leg.

Using both naturalistic and experimental techniques, Kuczaj and Daly (1979) found that when children first begin using explicit hypothetical expressions, at about 3;6, they tend to use the wrong modal, e.g.:

93 *Adult:*   Who would fix your breakfast if I slept as late as Daddy?
   HK: Nobody will. I'll just watch TV if you would sleep so late.
                                                               (p. 570)

Here, HK uses *will* instead of *would* in the main clause (and she also gets the verb in the subordinate clause wrong).

Generally, young children have more success with references to a hypothetical future (e.g. (91)) than to a hypothetical past (e.g. (92)). Even so, mistakes in both types persist for quite a long time; Fawcett and Perkins' transcripts suggest that errors occur until the age of ten. Taking the future form (with *would*) first, we can see that some children use a simple form of the verb instead of a verb phrase with *would*:

94 *Int.:*   if you came to school and someone said . . . there is no school today what would you do then?
   J: well 'I just '*go* hóme/   (8 years; II, p. 54)
95 *Int.:*   why would you like to be an air hostess?
   R: 'cos I '*go* all 'over the wórld/ in a pláne/
                                                  (10 years; III, p. 120)

Another kind of error is to use a modal, but in the wrong form. So, instead of *would*, the following sentences have *would have* and *will*:

96 *Int.:*   why would you like to be a teacher?
   G: I 'think it *would've have* 'been 'nice jòb/
                                                (8 years; II, p. 207)
97 *D:*   the ràin'*ll* get in/ if it was a réal house/ wòuldn't it/
                                                (10 years; III, p. 288)

Mistakes in referring to the hypothetical past can be classified in the same way. Thus, some children use a simple verb instead of a verb phrase with *would have*:

98 *Int.:*   what d'you think you'd have done if you'd had more time?
   L: I '*put* . . . 'one of those 'trees by thére/
                                                  (10 years; III, p. 166)
99 *Int.:*   how would you have made a pond?
   S: we '*put* 'these kind of brícks/   (10 years; III, p. 217)

Or, as with the hypothetical future, they may use a modal but get it wrong, saying *would* instead of *would have*, e.g.:

100 *Int.:*   what would you have made if you'd had more time?
    C: 'I *would* make a 'bigger hideout/   (6 years; I, p. 15)
101 *Int.:*   if you'd had more time what else would you have done?
    G: 'I *would* 'do an'other càr/   (6 years; I, p. 172)

However, it is worth emphasizing that, although errors can still be found at the ages of eight and ten, they occur alongside sentences that demonstrate the ability to handle hypothetical reference successfully, e.g.:

102 *Int.:*   if you'd had a lot of time what do you think you'd have done?
    J: I 'think we would've finished it/   (8 years; II, p. 129)

There has been surprisingly little research done on the development of the verb phrase after about 3;6. Comparing the speech of children aged six and ten, Strickland (1962) comments that their verb phrases look very much alike. She gives examples from both age-groups of phrases with two auxiliaries, but has apparently collected no instances of more complicated structures involving both auxiliaries and catenatives. From the limited information available it seems that, unlike noun phrases, children's verb phrases do not develop markedly in length or complexity between the ages of five and ten. Evidence of linguistic maturity is to be found in the varied and error-free use of modal auxiliaries; in the correct handling of sequences of verbs in a discourse, and in the selection of appropriate verb forms for the expression of hypothetical reference.

Word structure

The study of word structure is called **morphology**. Words are made up of one or more **morphemes** – meaningful linguistic units which cannot be further broken down into meaningful components. A morpheme may be a whole word or a part of a word: *garage* is one morpheme because it contains no smaller meaningful components, but *unkind* consists of two morphemes because both *un-* and *kind* have a meaning which contributes to the meaning of the whole. A morpheme may even be a single sound, e.g. the /s/ in *cats*. Here the /s/ has meaning because it makes the difference between the singular and plural of *cat*; this same contrast of sound and meaning occurs in thousands of other words, e.g. *book/books*, *puppet/puppets*, etc. (Obviously /s/ is not always a morpheme. The /s/ at the beginning of *sun* or the end of *bus*, for example, is not a morpheme but simply an individually meaningless part of the whole.) In this section, we shall consider children's acquisition of those grammatical morphemes which are attached to nouns and verbs. In addition to the stem form, nouns have a plural and a possessive form; verbs have a third person singular form (in the present), a progressive, a simple past and a past participle.

Studies by Brown (1973) and de Villiers and de Villiers (1979) indicate that the earliest grammatical morphemes to be acquired are the plural -s and the progressive -ing. They are followed by the possessive -'s and the simple past -ed. By this time, children have usually already learnt individual irregular past tenses such as *went* and *ate*. When they learn to apply the past tense morpheme to regular verbs such as *walk* and *play*, they often overapply it, adding it to the irregular verbs so that they now say *goed* and *eated*. The next acquisition is the third person singular -s, added to the stem of lexical verbs in the present tense. About the same time, children also learn to use the contracted forms of both copula and auxiliary *be*. All of these morphemes are likely to appear between 2;0 and 2;6. According to Fletcher (in Crystal, 1979a, p. 139), the past participle differs in often not being used systematically until sometime after the age of three.

By the time they go to school, children are firmly established in their use of the regular grammatical morphemes. They still make mistakes, though, with nouns and verbs that have irregular morphology. Here are some examples of errors in irregular past tenses and noun plurals from Fawcett and Perkins' (1980) transcripts of six- and eight-year-olds:

Six-year-olds

Verbs: shooted (48), rided (194), runned (199), bringed (199), keeped (213), digged (214), comed (215).

Nouns: rooviz [roofs] (23), mouses (83), roofses (180).

Eight-year-olds

Verbs: keeped (22), catched (213), builded (144), blowed (222).

Nouns: mouses (106)

There are errors in the past participle too, whether it is used to form the perfective aspect, as in (103) to (105), or the passive voice, as in (106) to (108):

103 they've *gét* them/	(6 years; I, p. 37)
104 the 'aeroplane has 'just *flew* òff/	(6 years; I, p. 84)
105 I 'haven't '*make* mìne/ yét/	(6 years; I, p. 126)
106 he'd 'been kìdnapped/ and *took* '*tooken* thère/	(8 years; II, p. 26)
107 it's just '*drawed* on the wàll/	(8 years; II, p. 229)
108 he 'got *blew* ùp/	(8 years; II, p. 231)

So far, I have referred to the plural morpheme as -s and the regular past tense morpheme as -ed but a closer examination will show that the facts

TABLE 10   Noun stems and plural allomorphs

Noun plural allomorph	Type of stem	Example of stem	Phonemic transcription (stem + plural)
1 /ɪz/	-ending in /s, z, ʃ, tʃ, dʒ/	vase hutch	/vɑz/ + /ɪz/ /hʌtʃ/ + /ɪz/
2 /s/	-ending in any other voiceless sound	laugh pit	/laf/ + /s/ /pɪt/ + /s/
3 /z/	-ending in any other voiced sound	rug bee	/rʌg/ + /z/ /bi/ + /z/

are more complex than these simple labels suggest. Consider the plural forms *cats*, *dogs* and *horses*. All of these are written by adding an ⟨-s⟩ to the stem of the word. But the pronunciation of each ⟨-s⟩ is different: respectively, /s/, /z/ and /ɪz/.[9] There are thus three variants, or **allomorphs**, of the plural morpheme. This variation is not arbitrary. The choice of allomorph is governed by the last sound of the stem. The grouping of these sounds can best be explained by introducing the distinction between **voiced** and **voiceless** sounds. Voiced sounds are produced when the vocal cords vibrate during speech. (This vibration can be felt by placing the fingers lightly on the Adam's apple while saying 'aaaah'.) Typical voiced sounds are all the vowels, and the consonants /b, d, g, v, z, m, n/. In contrast, voiceless sounds are produced without any vibration of the vocal cords; examples are, /p, t, k, f, s, tʃ /. Using this distinction, the relationship between different noun stems and the three plural allomorphs is shown in table 10.

Like the plural morpheme, the regular past tense morpheme also has three allomorphs, because the form that is written ⟨-ed⟩ is pronounced either /t/, /d/, or /ɪd/, depending on the last sound of the verb stem. The pairing of verb stems and past tense allomorphs is shown in table 11.

In a study that has become one of the most famous of all language acquisition experiments, Berko (1958) set out to discover the extent to which young children have internalized these morphological regularities in English. Her subjects were aged four to seven. To test their knowledge of plural allomorphs, Berko showed them, for example, a picture of a little bird-like creature and said, 'This is a wug.' She then produced a picture of two of the creatures and said, 'Now there is another one. There are two _____ ' and the child had to supply the plural 'wugs'. (As *wug* has a voiced final sound, like *rug*, this item was testing the child's knowl-

---

9 The slant brackets indicate a **phonemic** transcription; for an explanation of the term **phoneme**, see p. 166. There is a complete list of the phonemic symbols used in this book on p. xv.

TABLE 11   Verb stems and regular past tense allomorphs

Past tense allomorph	Type of stem	Example of stem	Phonemic transcription (stem + past)
1 /ɪd/	-ending in /t, d/	knot nod	/nɒt/ + /ɪd/ /nɒd/ + /ɪd/
2 /t/	-ending in any other voiceless sound	kick pass	/kɪk/ + /t/ /pɑs/ + /t/
3 /d/	-ending in any other voiced sound	wing glue	/wɪŋ/ + /d/ /glu/ + /d/

edge of the /z/ allomorph.) Other nonsense nouns used were *gutch* and *niz* (like *hutch* and *vase* in table 10), and *heaf* (like *laugh*). A similar methodology was used to find out how children formed the past tense of nonsense verbs like *mot*, *rick* and *bing* (compare, in table 11, *knot*, *kick* and *wing*). The results showed, as would be expected, that in most cases, the older children (aged 5;6 and over) did significantly better than the younger ones. Overall, there was a very high rate of success with the /s/ and /z/ plural allomorphs and a very low rate with /ɪz/: only 28 per cent of the children could make *niz* into *nizzes*. Most of the children said firmly, 'There are two niz.' Similarly, the past tense allomorphs /t/ and /d/ were applied correctly by roughly three-quarters of the children, but only a third could use /ɪd/ where it was required. The remainder said, for example, 'Yesterday he mot.'

Commenting on these results, Berko says, 'it is evident that the morphological rules these children have . . . are not the same as those possessed by adults' (p. 163). Indeed, it is clear that even a junior school pupil, faced with a new noun or verb that requires a 'type 1' allomorph, cannot be assumed to have the requisite morphological knowledge. In this connection, it is noteworthy that some of the commonest verbs that end in /t/ or /d/ are irregular and so not followed by the /ɪd/ allomorph in any case, e.g. *bite*, *cut*, *eat*, *fight*, *hit*, *meet*, *put*, *shut*, *write*; *feed*, *find*, *hide*, *read*, *ride*, *stand*. In young children's vocabulary, these may well outnumber the regular verbs, such as, *lift*, *paint*, *plant*, *rest*, *wait*, *want*; *end*, *mend*. If so, it is perhaps not surprising that the /ɪd/ allomorph, at any rate, is a late acquisition.

Negatives

Any contact with small children makes it clear that they learn to express negative reactions very early by means of *no* and *not*, e.g.:

109 not my bed
110 wear mitten no

At first these two negative words are tagged on to the sentence as a whole. Then gradually the child learns to incorporate the negative into the verb phrase. The first step towards this is usually taken around 2;3 with the appearance of the negative modal auxiliaries *can't* and *won't*, e.g.:

111 I can't catch you.

These forms are apparently learnt as unanalysed wholes, rather than as an auxiliary plus a negative morpheme, because they generally occur before the positive *can* and *will* (Fletcher, 1979; Klima & Bellugi, 1966). By about 2;9 (Miller, 1973) the negative transformation is productively established with the various forms of auxiliary *be* being negated and with *do* introduced to negate lexical verbs, e.g.:

112 I don't like porridge.

When a past tense verb is negated, this sometimes leads to the error of double past tense marking, with both the auxiliary and the lexical verb in the past, e.g.:

113 I didn't made it.

(There is an example of this mistake by a six-year-old in Fawcett & Perkins (1980, I, p. 249): *they 'didn't 'caught ús/*.)

According to de Villiers and de Villiers (1979), children between the ages of three and four show mastery of a wide range of auxiliaries in both positive and negative forms. A much later acquisition, however, is the correct use of the forms *any, anyone, anywhere* etc. after a negative, in place of *some, someone, somewhere* etc. Well into the school years we find expressions like: *I haven't got some windows* rather than, *I haven't got any windows*. Even more frequent is: *I haven't got no windows*. It is difficult, however, to make developmental judgements about this last use since it occurs widely in adult speech in some regional dialects. For some children it will be an immature form, discarded when they reach full adult competence; for others it will be normal usage in adulthood.

We can now consider some aspects of the comprehension of negative sentences. Generally, the results of experimental studies suggest that, both for children and adults, negative sentences are harder to process than affirmative ones (Just & Carpenter, 1971; Phinney, 1981). If a two-clause sentence has a negative verb phrase in both clauses then processing becomes very difficult indeed. When Harris (1975) gave children aged four to eleven sentences like this:

114 The teacher did not know that Tim was not absent.

only 60 per cent could correctly answer the question, 'Was Tim absent?' A large-scale Scottish study that involved six thousand fifteen-year-old pupils assessed the effect of various alterations to the wording of 'O' level chemistry questions. One alteration was the rewriting in the affirmative of a multiple-choice question that contained a negative, e.g.:

115a ... Which one of the following could *not* be the atomic weight of the element? ...

115b ... Which one of the following could be the atomic weight of the element? ...

The number of correct answers was 12 per cent higher for the affirmative than for the negative version of the same question. The author, Johnstone (1978, p. 433), comments:

> The negative presentation of a question sometimes has the effect of a 'double think' and if by chance two negatives stray into a question even the strongest candidate quails.

Another source of difficulty is the 'concealed negative', that is an expression that has a negative meaning without an explicit negative marker such as *no, not* or *never*. In an experiment with undergraduate students, Just and Carpenter (1971) found that their subjects needed more time to process sentences that contained a concealed negative word like *scarcely* or *hardly* than sentences that were more obviously negative. The comprehension of concealed negative expressions was also tested in Reid's (1972) investigation into the effect of syntactic structure on seven-year-olds' reading. Her subjects read either the A or B version of a set of sentences and then answered the same binary-choice question after each one, e.g.:

116A Tom's mother was anything but pleased.
116B Tom's mother was not pleased at all.

Question: Was Tom's mother pleased? (yes/no)

Those who read the explicit negative in (116B) scored on average 80.5 per cent but on (116A) the success rate dropped sharply to 43.7 per cent. Another example was:

117A If only David had known, the dog was quite tame.
117B The dog was quite tame but David did not know that.

Question: Did David know that the dog was tame? (yes/no)

Here the results were 81.7 per cent for (117B) but only 57.5 per cent for (117A). The compound co-ordinator *neither ... nor* is an explicit negative marker but the evidence from Reid's study suggests that, for young children at any rate, it functions more like a concealed negative. The test sentences were:

118A Mary's dress was neither new nor pretty.
118B Mary's dress was not new and it was not pretty.

Questions: Was Mary's dress new?   (yes/no)
Was Mary's dress pretty?   (yes/no)

The combined scores for the answers to the two questions were (118A): 37.95 per cent and (118B): 81.1 per cent. So well over half the children who read sentence (118A) thought that the dress was new and pretty.

The last aspect of negation we shall examine is what happens in complex sentences, where the object or complement is expressed by a nominal clause, when the main clause is negated. This is a particularly intricate area of English grammar and the few psycholinguistic studies that have been conducted suggest that full understanding of all the different sentence types is not acquired until rather late – probably some time in the early secondary years. Different verbs, and verb plus adjective combinations (e.g. *be true*), behave in different ways when they are negated. Consider the affirmative and negative versions of sentences (119) to (122):

119a Mary knew that John was angry.
119b Mary didn't know that John was angry.

120a It was true that John was angry.
120b It was not true that John was angry.

121a Mary pretended that John was angry.
121b Mary didn't pretend that John was angry.

122a Mary said that John was angry.
122b Mary didn't say that John was angry.

In all of these examples there is a main clause followed by a subordinate nominal clause; in the negative versions the verb of the main clause is negated. Nevertheless, although the grammatical structure looks identical, the effect on the subordinate clause of the negative in the main clause differs from sentence to sentence. In (119), John is angry in both (a) and (b): the negative in the main clause does not affect the subordinate clause. In (120), John is angry in (a) but not in (b): the negative in the main clause 'carries over' into the subordinate clause. The strange thing about (121) is that the positive subordinate clause has a negative meaning regardless of whether the main clause is positive or negative; that is, in both (a) and (b) John is not angry. In (122) we cannot tell whether John is angry or not; this uncertainty remains the same whether the main clause is positive or negative. A further complexity arises if we compare (122) with (123):

123a Mary thought that John was angry.
123b Mary didn't think that John was angry.

At first sight (122) and (123) look similar in that, in both cases, an outsider does not know for certain whether John is angry or not. But if the negative is moved from the main to the subordinate clause a major difference becomes apparent:

122c Mary said that John wasn't angry.
123c Mary thought that John wasn't angry.

The meaning of (123b) and (123c) seems to be much the same, regardless of where the negative is placed, whereas (122c) clearly does not mean the same as (122b).

Children ranging in age from three and a half to fourteen have been tested for their comprehension of these different sentence types by a variety of experimental methods in studies by Harris (1975), Hopman and Maratsos (1978), Phinney (1981), and Scoville and Gordon (1980). Phinney, who only used sentences like (119) in her test, found that it was not possible to chart any development of understanding in chronological terms because, within each of her age-groups from five to nine, different children made widely varying numbers of errors. She discovered, though, that there was a strong correlation between overall error rate and reading ability: better readers, whatever their age, made fewer errors. Hopman and Maratsos did not find a completely consistent pattern of errors in their subjects, aged 3;6 to 7;11. With sentences like (120b), *It was not true that John was angry*, some of the children failed to realize that the negative in the main clause applied to the subordinate clause – with the result that they believed that John was angry. In complete contrast, other children thought that sentences like (119b), *Mary didn't know that John was angry*, meant that John was NOT angry – they seemed to be inappropriately extending the meaning of the negative from the main to the subordinate clause. This error seemed to be more common among the younger children and had disappeared by the age of seven. However, Scoville and Gordon, who also tested structures like (119b) but with working-class subjects and a different methodology, reported that over-extension of the negative still occurred at fourteen and accounted for a third of all responses in children with a mean age of 11;11. They commented, 'The development of adult-like performance in this task seems to be a rather protracted affair' (p. 390). Harris tested all the sentence types except (120) and (123), and concluded:

A clear finding ... is that comprehension of this type of complex sentence is a difficult and gradual process which, though it may begin in pre-school years, is often not equivalent to adult comprehension until sometime after sixth grade [eleven to twelve years]. (p. 432)

These studies suggest that complex sentences that contain negatives may well cause comprehension difficulties in reading, particularly when the subject matter is unfamiliar, so that the child's knowledge is not secure enough to act as a support to grammatical processing. Indeed, Harris says that his results 'suggest the tremendous importance to children of knowledge about the world in making linguistic judgments' (p. 431).

Questions

Wh- and yes/no questions

The first questions that children ask are not marked grammatically at all. Rather, they consist of a statement structure with a rising intonation, e.g. *daddy come*? Then at about the age of two, embryonic *wh-* questions appear. The earliest are often item-learnt wholes such as, *what dat*? or *whatisdis*? (de Villiers & de Villiers, 1979, p. 62). After that come, probably, *what, where, who* and *why* (psycholinguists differ somewhat over the precise order and time-scale of these). At this stage, children are not using auxiliaries or the copula, *be*, so there is no operator and there can be no subject-operator inversion, e.g.:

> 124 where doggy go?   (Kendall, 2;0. Braine, 1976, p. 19)

Inversion occurs first in *yes/no* questions. Sentences like:

> 125 will you help me?

are first used productively by Miller's (1973) subjects at some time between 2;5 and 3;4. Although present tense *yes/no* questions match adult structures at this age, there are still immaturities in past tense questions because children frequently add a tense marker to both the auxiliary and the lexical verb, e.g.:

> 126 did I saw that in my book?   (Klima & Bellugi, 1966, p. 204)

At the time when children are using subject-operator inversion in *yes/no* questions they may also use the operator in *wh-* questions, but without inversion, e.g.:

> 127 where we can go?

Many *wh-* questions in this period, however, do not have an operator but do have a lexical verb with tense or number markers, e.g.:

> 128 how he opened it?   (Brown, 1968, p. 285)
> 129 what he wants?

Such examples show that the child is putting a *wh-* word at the beginning of a statement structure and is not making a reduction of an adult question form. (An adult would say, for example, *what does he want*? So if the child were to reduce this by omitting the operator he would say *what he want*? rather than *what he wants*?) Generally, negative questions are rare at this age but some children do use *why not* as a unitary question word, e.g.:

> 130 why not you see any?   (Brown *et al.*, 1969, p. 59)

Other *wh-* questions that develop rather slowly are those introduced by *how* and *when*.

About three months after the establishment of subject-operator inversion in *yes/no* questions, the process becomes evident in *wh-* questions, e.g.:

131 where is my teddy?

There can still be double marking of past tense questions, e.g.:

132 why did Rachael left one of her domino cards behind?
(Daniel, 3;5. Fletcher, 1979, p. 272)

Another difficulty is caused by negative questions; even if the child is able to invert subject and operator in affirmatives, he may still say:

133 why he can't go out?   (Slobin, 1973a, p. 334)

Between the ages of three and a half and six, errors in *yes/no* and *wh-* questions gradually disappear. These are some of the mistakes that may still occur during this period:

i) combining question and statement forms so that the auxiliary is repeated, e.g.:

134 how can he can look?   (4;8. Menyuk, 1969, p. 75)

ii) failing to invert subject and operator, e.g.:
135 where she's going?   (6;2. Menyuk, 1969, p. 75)

iii) double marking the past tense, e.g.:

136 'did he made a rácing car/ (6 years. Fawcett & Perkins, I, p. 4)

Tag questions

Yes/no and *wh-* questions are the commonest question forms in English. A less frequent, but socially important, type is the tag question, which can help speakers to establish a conversational rapport. The tag question consists of an operator, which copies the tense of the verb in the main clause, and a pronoun which has to match the person and number of the subject; generally, there is reversal of polarity, with a positive statement being followed by a negative tag and vice versa. This means that there is not an invariant form for tags, since each one is dependent for its structure on the pattern of the preceding statement. A forerunner of these complex tags is the lexical (or 'stereotypical') tag, where a statement is followed by an item such as *OK*, *right*, or *see*, which has the same communicative function as a grammatical tag, but a simple, invariant form, e.g.:

137 I'll hold your teddy bear, *OK*?

Given the complexity of grammatical tags, it is not surprising that children use lexical tags more extensively at first and that errors in the grammatical type persist for a long time.

In a study of 72 children aged 2;10 to 5;7, Berninger and Garvey (1982) noted that the youngest children, aged 2;10 to 3;3, were three times more likely to use lexical tags, like (137), than grammatical ones, like (138):

138 Yes, we do need it, *don't we*?   (p. 156)

The oldest children, aged 4;7 to 5;7, were still using twice as many lexical as grammatical tags. Even when the grammatical forms are well established, the lexical expressions continue to occur, as these examples from Fawcett and Perkins' (1980) transcripts demonstrate:

139 'that one and thàt one is these two/ *sée*/   (6 years; I, p. 129)
140 we'll 'leave the 'gate òpen/ *right*/   (8 years; II, p. 5)
141 we 'need a 'red dóor/ *sée*/   (10 years; III, p. 201)
142 'this one's 'coming along the róad/
  . . . 'coming along the róad/ *right*/   (12 years; IV, p. 65)

There is probably considerable variation in the age at which children begin using grammatical tags. In a personal communication to Crystal (1979a, p. 90), Gordon Wells suggests that data from the Bristol Child Language Project indicate an onset age of about two and a half. However, Mills (1981) and Todd (1982) give 3;6 as the age when tag questions first appeared in the speech of (respectively) Nicky and Adam. Quite apart from individual variation, there are also notable differences in the occurrence of this construction according to the situation – the spontaneous speech samples recorded by Fawcett and Perkins make it very clear that children hardly ever use tags to an adult stranger, though they use them freely in their conversation with each other. This means that data bases derived chiefly from child-adult interactions are unlikely to provide many examples of tag questions; this may be one reason why there is rather little information in the language acquisition literature about their development.

The six-year-olds in Fawcett and Perkins' study show correct use of the auxiliaries *be, have, do, can, will, should,* and *would* in both positive and negative tags with a full range of pronouns, e.g.:

càn you	(I, p. 29)	àre they	(I, p. 227)
wàs there	(I, p. 242)	shòuldn't I	(I, p. 1)
dîdn't we	(I, p. 226)	wôn't it	(I, p. 1)

Nevertheless, alongside correctly formed tags, mistakes can be found for several years. The errors can be classified according to whether they are connected with the operator (i–iii), the subject (iv), or the reversal of polarity (v):

i) failure to copy the main clause operator in the tag, e.g.:
143 they 'both *gotta* 'be the 'same côlour/ – *mûstn't* they/
(6 years; I, p. 28)
144 'somebody *might* thínk/ 'that's a bit of the hòuse/ as wèll/ *wòuldn't* they/ (10 years; III, p. 46)
145 you'*ll* 'have to have 'single ròoms/in thát though/ *dôn't* you/
(12 years; IV, p. 194)

ii) failure to copy the tense of the main clause operator in the tag, e.g.:
146 he '*turns* it aròund/ *dìn*' he/ (8 years; II, p. 254)
147 they'*re* hòrrible/ *wèren't* they/ (10 years; III, p. 73)
148 'that *could* be the gráss/ *càn't* it/ (12 years; IV, p. 169)

iii) failure of concord between the operator and the subject pronoun, e.g.:
149 Jènnifer/ got êverything you can 'áve/ '*àven't* she/
(8 years; II, p. 252)
150 it's 'got to go out hère/ *hàven't* it/ (12 years; IV, p. 129)

iv) failure to copy the subject of the main clause in the tag, e.g.:
151 *there* 'was a 'Lego bòat/ wàsn't *it*/ (6 years; I, p. 3)
152 *there*'s sup'posed to be twò in together like/ ìn *it*/ [i.e. isn't it]
(8 years; II, p. 180)
153 *it* 'could be a bûngalow/ côuldn't *he*/ (12 years; IV, p. 36)

v) failure to use a positive tag after a negative main clause, e.g.:
154 I'*m nót*/ *àren't* I/ (6 years; I, p. 95)
155 you *don't* have 'time at 'see chìldren/ réally/ *dón't* you/
(10 years; III, p. 163)

In an experimental study, Major (1974) found that eight-year-olds could not make tag questions with the auxiliaries *might, may, ought,* and *shall*. It is worth noting, though, that many adults feel uneasy about the forms *mayn't I?* and *oughtn't I?* And in the naturalistic data of Fawcett and Perkins, there is an eight-year-old who uses a tag with *shall*:

156 we'll 'make a 'big 'hotel in the mìddle/ *sháll* we/
(8 years; II, p. 63)

Studies of the comprehension of questions show that *yes/no, what* and *where* questions are the earliest to be understood, with *who* and *why* following fairly soon. Ervin-Tripp (1970) notes that comprehension of each *wh-* word generally precedes its production by several months. The same point is made by Brown (1968), with the comment that *why* is an exception as children often ask strings of *why* questions before they can give 'reason' answers. When children make mistakes in answering *wh*-questions, they do it by giving the answer to a *wh*- word that they have already mastered. So the earliest replies to *who* questions may sound like responses to *where*, e.g.:

> 157 *Adult*:   who put the car in?
>   *Carol*:   in that hole.   (Carol, 2; 6. Ervin-Tripp, 1970, p. 86)

Similarly, *how* questions may receive an answer that would be appropriate to a *why* question. A six-year-old in Fawcett and Perkins' study provides an example of this:

> 158 *Int.*:   how would you do that? [put the fire out]
>   *D*:   be'cause they'll diè/   (6 years; I, p. 236)

A general feature of language acquisition is that the successful use or comprehension of a linguistic form at a particular age does not necessarily mean that full adult control of that item has been achieved; it can happen that a period of apparent mastery is followed by a fresh spate of mistakes as the child changes from one processing strategy to another. There is an example of this apparent regression in Ervin-Tripp's account of children's responses to *who* questions. *Who* can function as the subject or the object in a question; Ervin-Tripp found that, up to the age of three, children could answer correctly questions like *who is he feeding?* where *who* is the object, but that between three and four there was an upsurge of errors because they treated *who* as if it was the subject.

Although the precise ranking of difficulty of *wh*- questions differs from one study to another – partly because of differences in experimental method – it is generally agreed that *when* and *how* questions are the hardest (Cairns & Hsu, 1978; Ervin-Tripp, 1970; Tyack and Ingram, 1977). Indeed, none of Ervin-Tripp's subjects could understand past tense *when* questions by the age of 4; 2 and Cairns and Hsu's five-year-olds scored only 72 per cent in their responses to all *how* questions.

The passive

First of all, we need to distinguish between two different kinds of passive construction. There is the full passive, with an agent phrase, e.g.:

> 159 The toddler was bitten *by a dog*.

and there is the truncated passive, with no expressed agent, e.g.:

> 160 The jug was knocked over.

The truncated passive occurs earlier than the full passive in children's speech and is always much more frequent. (It was noted on p. 52 that in adults' speech, passives without an agent occur four times as often as the full form.) Horgan (1978) used a picture-description task to elicit passive constructions from children aged two to thirteen; her examination of the data convinced her that, for young children at any rate, truncated passives are more closely related to SVC constructions (e.g. *The jug was expensive*) than to full passives; in other words, the past participle is functioning more like an adjective than a verb.

The full passive is one of the latest grammatical structures to appear in children's speech. A few children in the three- to four-year age-range will use it, but it is not universally present for several years after that. Palermo and Molfese (1972, p. 420) say that the five-year-old 'very seldom uses the passive in his own spontaneous speech'. The naturalistic, longitudinal data collected by O'Donnell *et al.* (1967) suggest that, between the ages of five and eleven, there is, on average, only one occurrence of the passive in every two hundred utterances but that this incidence increases among thirteen-year-olds to one in every one hundred and twenty utterances.[10] Horgan found that full passives were used by approximately 15 per cent of her five-year-olds, 20 per cent of the seven- and nine-year-olds and 30 per cent of the eleven-year-olds. Most of the passive expressions that occur in the speech of Fawcett and Perkins' (1980) six-year-olds do not have an agent, e.g.:

161 the 'Princess was caùght/ (6 years; I. p. 48)

But there are a very few instances of the full passive, e.g.:

162 'all the góodies/ were alíve/ ex'cept the 'one who was 'killed by Da Vèda/ (6 years; I, p. 48)
163 my sìster/ 'she got 'cut on her fìnger/ by my scìssors/ (6 years; I, p. 183)

This last example sounds as if the passive is being used to avoid accepting responsibility for the accident! From a grammatical point of view, it illustrates an observation that many people have made (e.g. Menyuk, 1969; Turner and Rommetveit, 1967), namely that young children frequently use *get* rather than *be* to form the passive verb phrase.

Up to the age of five, children may omit the auxiliary in the passive, e.g.:

164 It broken by that.

Under the pressure of an experimental task, they frequently reverse the word order, so they may say:

165 The cat was chased by the girl.

10 More precisely, 'an utterance' is a T-unit; that is, a 'minimal terminable syntactic unit'. A T-unit consists of a main clause and any subordinate clauses that belong to it; so a simple sentence and a complex sentence would each be one T-unit but a compound sentence would be two or more, depending on the number of main clauses it contained. Therefore, 'two hundred utterances' means two hundred main clauses plus any related subordinate clauses.

when they are describing a picture of a cat chasing a girl. Mistakes in the form of the past participle are still being made at eight and nine, e.g.:

166 The fly was catched by the frog.

(9 years; Turner & Rommetveit, 1967, p. 657)

(See also examples (106) to (108) on p. 113 for errors made by Fawcett and Perkins' eight-year-olds.)

From a semantic point of view there are two types of full passive. In one type the two noun phrases can be interchanged, giving two different but perfectly sensible sentences, e.g.:

167 The dog was chased by the cat.
168 The cat was chased by the dog.

Such sentences are called **reversible** passives. It is noticeable that if they are misread as active sentences they still make sense (though the meaning is not what the author intended); so if 'was' and 'by' are ignored in (167) it becomes:

169 The dog chased the cat.

The other type of full passive is **non-reversible**: if the noun phrases are interchanged, a nonsense sentence results, e.g.:

170 Goliath was killed by a stone.
171 !A stone was killed by Goliath.

Unlike the reversible sentence (167), if (170) is misread as an active, it does not make sense. In her study of children's use of passive sentences, Horgan (1978) made the rather surprising discovery that some of her young subjects used reversible passives and others used non-reversible passives but no child under the age of eleven used both types. She also found that the children who used the non-reversible passives showed a marked preference for sentences like (170) above, where the subject is animate and the noun in the *by* phrase is inanimate. Not until the age of nine did they use sentences with an inanimate subject and animate agent, e.g.:

172 The vase was broken by the girl.

There was no evidence of reluctance to use this type of passive among Horgan's adult subjects, who produced roughly equal numbers of sentences like (170) and (172). Commenting on children's use of only a restricted range of passives, she says, 'Although the children's passives were syntactically well formed at a very early age, they appear to be semantically very different from adult passives' (p. 79). It is perhaps worth noting that there seems to be a strong tendency for young children to begin a sentence with an animate noun and to work out the rest of the structure, whether active or passive, from that starting-point.

We can now turn to children's comprehension of passive constructions. In general, passive sentences are harder to understand than active ones. In an archetypal active sentence, an actor performs an action that affects someone or something; this sequentially-expressed relationship is violated in passive sentences, where the affected person or thing occurs first and the actor last (if at all). Passive sentences are very infrequent even in adult speech, so it is not surprising that a rare alteration of the expected actor-action sequence can hamper comprehension. Intuitively, it seems likely that reversible passives will be harder to understand than non-reversible ones because, in reversible sentences, both the correct and the incorrect interpretations are plausible, so comprehension depends entirely on accurate processing of the grammatical relationships with no help from the meaning. On the whole, studies bear out this intuition, though they vary as to the age when the difference between the two types ceases to have an effect. Slobin (1966) measured the time it took children and adults to decide whether a given sentence matched a picture or not and found that even adults needed more time to respond to a reversible passive than to a non-reversible one. A particularly marked difference in response time was found in children aged six to eight. Turner and Rommetveit (1967) and Baldie (1976) used two slightly different picture/sentence matching tasks and measured their subjects' accuracy of response.[11] The earlier study showed that children aged four to eight made more errors on reversible than non-reversible sentences; by nine there was no significant difference. Baldie's youngest subjects also found reversible passives harder to understand, but by the age of six their error rate on the two types was roughly the same. Thus, the two studies diverge in their results for children in the six to eight age-range. These differences may derive from the difference in experimental method or may possibly reflect individual preferences of particular children, similar to those identified by Horgan.

3.3 THE ACQUISITION OF COMPOUND SENTENCES

Co-ordination

The precursor of explicitly-marked co-ordination is the bare juxtaposition of two semantically related simple sentences. Limber (1973) has many examples of this type from children aged 2;0 to 2;6, e.g.:

173 you lookit that book; I lookit this book.   (p. 181)

---

11 Turner and Rommetveit showed one picture and gave two sentences, asking their subjects to select the sentence that matched the picture; Baldie had five pictures and one sentence, so his subjects had to choose the picture that matched the sentence.

Phrasal co-ordination generally precedes clausal co-ordination (de Villiers *et al.*, 1977; Hakuta *et al.*, 1982), but once it is established, then the use of a co-ordinator – usually *and* – to link clauses can begin. There is an early example in Limber:

174 you play with this one *and* I play with this.   (2; 8, p. 181)

The clauses in compound sentences like (174) are reversible without any change of meaning. A slightly later development is the use of conjunction that also reflects temporal sequence, where the clauses are not reversible, e.g.:

175 you snap and he comes.   (Brown, 1973, p. 26)

Clausal co-ordination with *and* is extremely frequent in young children's language (as it is in adults' spontaneous speech). Menyuk reports that it is used by 95 per cent of her subjects in the three to seven age-range. An examination of Fawcett and Perkins' (1980) transcripts reveals that the rate of occurrence of compound sentences is significantly affected by the language situation: when the children talk to the adult interviewer, their language is predominantly narrative and descriptive; in this situation co-ordination abounds. When the children talk to each other, their language consists chiefly of running commentary, argument and banter; in these circumstances, co-ordination is much less frequent.

Substitution

Where there are common elements in two clauses that are joined by co-ordination, it is normal in adult language for this repetition to be avoided, either by substitution of a pro-form, or by ellipsis. Slobin and Welsh (1973) asked 'Echo' to imitate the following compound sentence when she was 2;4:

176 *Adult:*   the pussy eats bread and the pussy runs fast.
     'Echo':   pussy eat bread and *he* run fast.   (p. 493)

Her imitation shows that she was able to substitute a pronoun for the repeated NP, *the pussy*. In spontaneous production, such pronominal substitution probably appears rather later; it has already been suggested (on p. 104) that very young children tend to use a full NP in the second of two co-ordinated clauses where older children and adults are more likely to use a pronoun.

When the common element in the second clause is the predicate, then the substitute is a verbal pro-form. There is slight evidence in a study by Thieman (1975, p. 266) that younger children are more likely to repeat the full predicate but that older children and adults prefer to replace it. In a recall task, cued by pictures that had already been described, one of his subjects produced sentences (177) and (178):

177 The truck hit the wall and the car *did too.*
178 The cat jumped over the fence and the dog *did too.*

(Suzanne, 4; 10)

In contrast, Lloyd, who was only 3; 8, said:

179 The truck hit the wall and the car *hit the wall too.*
180 The cat jumped over the fence and the dog *jumped over* there.

I do not know of any other descriptions of children's use of verbal pro-forms in compound sentences. It is true that repetition of the predicate is less common than repetition of the subject, so verbal substitutions will always be rarer than nominal ones. Nevertheless, there are several examples in Fawcett and Perkins' (1980) transcripts of six-year-olds where a verbal pro-form could have occurred and did not, e.g.:

181 and 'then 'we count and 'then thèy *count/*   (I, p. 102)
182 and then 'we hide and thèy *hide/*   (I, p. 102)
183 I 'done a gárden/ and 'Chris and 'Alex *done a 'garden* as wéll/
(I, p. 107)

These sentences suggest that all the possibilities of co-ordination are not yet being exploited, but in the absence of normative data from older children and adults, it is not possible to be sure that they are truly indications of linguistic immaturity. It would be interesting to know whether, when children do start using verbal pro-forms, they prefer *too* or *so* with the auxiliary: that is, would they say, *we count and they do too*, or would they use the form with subject-auxiliary inversion, *we count and so do they?*

Ellipsis

Compound sentences with an ellipted second subject appear rather later than those with a pronominal second subject. Although 'Echo' could imitate and produce substitutions at 2; 4, she could not manage ellipsis:

184 *Adult:*   The owl eats candy and runs fast.
   'Echo':   Owl eat candy . . . owl eat the candy and . . . he run fast.
(p. 493)

Slobin and Welsh (1973, p. 493) comment:

Her hesitations and false starts indicate she was working hard to produce an imitation matching her image of the model. The introduction of a pronoun for the second noun phrase suggests that her rules do not yet allow for the total deletion of a repeated noun phrase in this sort of structure.

Similarly, Thieman (1975) noted that, while children aged four to five produced sentences with a pronominal or ellipted second subject, three-year-old Lloyd used either the full NP or pronominal substitution in preference to ellipsis. And Menyuk (1971) found that co-ordination with ellipsis was used more frequently towards the upper end of the three to seven age-range. Ardery (1980) asked children aged 2;6 to 6;0 to describe the actions of toys that she manipulated; they often ellipted the second subject but never a verb or object. It seems likely that the use of such ellipsis will be a particularly late linguistic development.

There are several studies which provide information about children's comprehension of ellipsis in co-ordinate clauses. Lahey (1974) had children aged 3;11 to 5;11 act out with toys the sentences that they heard. She used various grammatical structures and a range of modes of presentation but here we need only be concerned with the normal presentation of sentences with an ellipted second subject, e.g.:

185 The cow hit the pig and [   ] chased the deer.

Her four-year-old subjects scored 66 per cent on this task and the five-year-olds achieved 80 per cent. Tavakolian (1978) and Ardery (1980) tested the comprehension of similar sentences using the same task. Their subjects ranged in age from 2;6 to 6;0 and in both studies the average score was about 95 per cent. It is possible that Lahey's results were lower because she presented her subjects with tape-recorded rather than 'live' sentences. In any case, together these experiments suggest that by the time children start school, ellipsis, in speech, of the subject of the second clause should not cause comprehension problems.

The position is remarkably different in reading. Richek's (1977) study (described in part on p. 106 above) included sentences where the subject of the second clause was either a repeated NP, as in (186a), or was ellipted, as in (186b):

186a Bobby was standing by his sister's side in the station and *Bobby* saw her laughing when the train pulled in.
186b Bobby was standing by his sister's side in the station and [   ] saw her laughing when the train pulled in.   (p. 156)

Her eight-year-olds had to read the sentences and write one-word answers to test questions, e.g. *Who saw her laughing when the train pulled in?* The surprising result was that, although they scored 86 per cent when the second subject was a repeated NP – an unusual structure in adult language – they only managed 60.7 per cent when there was ellipsis in the second clause.

It is possible for there to be ellipsis of common elements other than the subject. Ardery (1980) tested comprehension of sentences with an ellipted verb as in (187) and (188), and an ellipted object, as in (189):

187 The horse bumped into the cat and the dog [   ] into the turtle.

188 The giraffe kissed the horse and the frog [   ] the cat.
189 The cat kissed [   ] and the turtle pushed the dog.

Children aged 2;6 to 6;0 acted out these sentences with toys. Their scores on (187) and (188) were 42 per cent and 10 per cent. In (187), where there is a prepositional verb, *bump into*, and only *bump* is ellipted, it seems that the remaining preposition acts as a signal for at least some children, enabling them to recover the verb. In (188), there is no such help. A typical error here was for the children to interpret the second clause as if it was part of the object in the first clause – *The giraffe kissed the horse and the frog and the cat.* The results for (189) were even lower, with only 4 per cent correct answers. This is an exceptionally difficult construction because the object at the end of the second clause (the *dog*) has to be processed before the gap in the first clause can be mentally filled. We need to know the age by which children have mastered these advanced elliptical constructions.

Co-ordinators

As children learn to use compound sentences they are obviously learning to use the co-ordinators that are required; the commonest are *and* and *but*, with *or* and *yet* being used less often. Bloom *et al.* (1980) report that their subjects had *and* well established as a clausal co-ordinator by the age of two and a half. *But* develops rather later, probably between three and four. At 2;4, 'Echo' showed that although she could handle *and* she was not yet ready for *but*:

190 *Adult*:   This one is the giant *but* this one is little.
     'Echo':   dis one little *annat* one big.
                                    (Slobin & Welsh, 1973, p. 490)

Katz and Brent (1968) found that their seven-year-old subjects used *but* occasionally in spontaneous speech but that it was much more frequent in the speech of twelve-year-olds. There are many examples of the correct use of *and*, *but* and *or* – though not the more literary *yet* – as clausal co-ordinators in Fawcett and Perkins' (1980) data from six-year-olds:

191 they 'just put their 'hand in páint/ *and* 'put it on the pàper/
                                    (6 years; I, p. 70)
192 we 'haven't got any bùckets/ *but* we 'have got spădes/
                                    (6 years; I, p. 21)
193 'he's gotta cóunt then/ *or* 'she's gotta còunt/   (6 years; I, p. 37)

Various studies have assessed children's understanding of *and*, *but* and *yet* in their role as clausal co-ordinators. Children aged eight to twelve were tested by Robertson (1968) in a study of fifteen conjunctions and two adverbial sentence connectives. They had to read a clause followed by a conjunction and then choose the best clause out of a set of four to complete the sentence.[12] The average score for all children on the fifteen conjunctions was 67 per cent. The scores for the three co-ordinators tested were: *and*, 60.9 per cent; *yet*, 63.7 per cent; *but*, 66.6 per cent. Here the most surprising result is the apparent difficulty of *and*. It seems possible that, because in the early days children use *and* as an all-purpose connector, it does not have a precise set of meanings for them and they are therefore more liberal than adults in joining clauses by this means; given a choice of four clauses to follow *and*, they find them all acceptable. This interpretation is borne out to some extent by a study by Hutson and Shub (1975), who examined the understanding of *and* and *but* in subjects aged six to fifteen. The test consisted of pairs of clauses with a gap to be filled by either *and* or *but*, e.g.:

194 Mr Green is rich _____ his son is poor.

The results revealed 'an early largely undifferentiated stage during which *and* predominated' (p. 51). The six-year-olds got 75 per cent of the *and* sentences right, but only 42 per cent of those that required *but*. As they used *and* inappropriately in *but* sentences, their score of 75 per cent for *and* does not reflect differentiated understanding but simply their preferred usage at that age. By the age of twelve, scores were 96 per cent for *and* and 84 per cent for *but*.

A different technique was used by Katz and Brent (1968) to test understanding of *but*. The subjects, aged six to seven and eleven to twelve, were asked to choose the better sentence from the following pair, giving reasons for their choice:

195 Jimmie went to school but he felt sick.
196 Jimmie went to school but he felt fine.   (p. 503)

Only 19 per cent of the younger children chose (195), the sentence the authors required, whereas 68 per cent of the older children made the correct choice.

Secondary children were tested for their understanding of nearly two hundred sentence connectives and conjunctions by Gardner (1977). They were given both a sentence completion task (like Robertson's) and a multiple-choice gap-filling task. For the two co-ordinators included in the test, the approximate average scores (combined from the two tasks) were:

	11-year-olds	*15-year-olds*
but	60%	78%
yet	58%	75%

12 A weakness in this study is that one of the 'distractor' clauses in each set was wrong only because it contained a grammatical error, not because it did not follow appropriately from the conjunction. So, by selecting such a clause, children scored nought on the item even though they might have understood the conjunction. Nevertheless, this methodology applied to all the seventeen items tested, so comparisons between items are reasonably valid even though absolute scores are almost certainly too low.

It seems fair to conclude that apparently simple words like *but* and *yet* are not fully mastered in all their uses until some time after the age of eleven.

3.4 THE ACQUISITION OF COMPLEX SENTENCES

Children begin to use embryonic subordinate clauses within main clauses once they are commonly using simple sentences of four or more words (Bowerman, 1979). For many children, this will be sometime between the ages of two and three. We shall consider the development of each of the major subordinate clause types in turn, but first it is worth noting a general point that applies to them all: that is that the extra difficulty of processing a complex sentence can cause children to make errors they no longer make in simple sentences. So Fletcher (1979, p. 264), speaking of command of the tense system, says, 'a child whose usage was error-free when assessed on simple sentences might now omit past tense in the second or third clause of complex structures'. And a study by Wren (1981) of the language of fifteen six-year-old children showed that – bearing in mind that they made very few errors anyway – they made nearly three times as many mistakes in complex sentences as in simple ones.

In order to set the development of different clause types in perspective, table 12 shows their comparative frequencies in the speech of the children in O'Donnell *et al.*'s (1967) study. It highlights the fact that, for all except the kindergarten children, nominal and adverbial clauses are by far the most frequent, with relative clauses much less common. Table 13 shows the actual rate of occurrence of these clauses and reveals a rather uneven increase in overall frequency between the ages of six and thirteen.

Nominal clauses

From about the age of 2;3, children begin to use finite nominal clauses to express the grammatical object of the sentence. These clauses may be introduced by a *wh-* word or by optional *that*, e.g.:

197 <u>I</u> <u>show</u> <u>you</u> *what I got*
    s   v O_i O_d

198 <u>I</u> <u>think</u> *it's the wrong way*
    s   v   o

Gradually, they also begin to appear as complements, but throughout the early years of childhood they are very rare indeed in subject position. Menyuk (1969) found no examples of subject nominal clauses in her data from children aged three to seven; neither did Strickland (1962) in a

TABLE 12   Types and proportions of finite subordinate clauses in children's
speech
(*based on O'Donnell et al., 1967, pp. 59, 61, 68*)

American grade level	Age	Percentage of each clause type		
		Nominal	Adverbial	Relative
Kindergarten (N = 30)	5; 3–6; 4 (mean 5; 10)	34	37	29
1 (N = 30)	6; 3–7; 4 (mean 6; 8)	38	47	15
2 (N = 30)	7; 2–9; 3 (mean 7; 10)	39	44	17
3 (N = 30)	7; 4–10; 2 (mean 8; 9)	40	48	12
5 (N = 30)	10; 2–11; 8 (mean 10; 10)	30	53	17
7 (N = 30)	12; 2–14; 6 (mean 13; 0)	35	50	15

*Type of speech: telling story of silent cartoon film
children had just seen*

sample of 750 utterances from children aged six and eleven. In Loban's
(1963) study, where the children were grouped according to their language ability, there were no examples of subject nominal clauses from
the low-ability children in the five to twelve age-range and only a very
few from the ablest children. The speech samples collected by Fawcett
and Perkins (1980) provide numerous examples of nominal clauses
expressing the object or complement, but only a handful functioning as
subject, e.g.:

199 *who'ever gets the mòst/* *wìns/*   (6 years; I, p. 73)
      s   v

TABLE 13   Rate of occurrence of finite subordinate clauses per 100 T-units in
children's speech
(*based on O'Donnell et al., 1967, pp. 59, 61, 68*)

American grade level	Mean age	Rate of occurrence of each clause type			
		Nominal	Adverbial	Relative	Total
Kindergarten	5; 10	5.57	6.07	4.77	16.41
1	6; 8	7.27	9.17	3.00	19.44
2	7; 10	7.00	7.87	3.15	18.02
3	8; 9	8.42	10.12	2.63	21.17
5	10; 10	5.81	10.05	3.26	19.12
7	13; 0	8.87	12.83	3.90	25.60

200 <u>'what I've gót/</u> <u>is</u> <u>draùghts/</u>   (8 years; II, p. 81)
     S   V   C

It was noted in chapter 2 (pp. 67–8) that subject clauses are infrequent even in adults' spontaneous speech and that, where appropriate, the extraposition construction is used. This fills the subject slot with *it*, allowing the 'heavy' nominal clause to occur after the verb, so that the end-weight principle is satisfied. Children can use this construction too, e.g.:

201 <u>it</u> <u>'doesn't</u> <u>'really</u> <u>'matter</u> *whàt colour we do/*   (8 years, II, p. 9)
   S   V   A   (V)   (extraposed subject)

A mistake that young children can make in a *wh-* clause is to give it the structure of a question (as if the *wh-* word were signalling a question rather than a subordinate clause), e.g.:

202 I 'know *where's his fire bell come from/*   (6 years; I, p. 242)
203 I 'can't re'member *'what was it abòut/*   (6 years; I, p. 13)

Despite these errors, it is worth noticing that the majority of *wh-* nominal clauses in Fawcett and Perkins' data are correctly formed, e.g.:

204 I 'know *what I can 'use for mý man/*   (6 years; I, p. 22)

As well as finite nominal clauses, young children also use non-finite clauses in the predicate, e.g.:

205 'I know *how to màke/ televísions/*   (6 years; I, p. 9)
206 I 'tell you *what to dó/*   (6 years; I, p. 106)

Examples (205) and (206) illustrate the commonest type of non-finite clause, the one with the infinitive; clauses with the stem + *ing* form of the verb occur less often:

207 we 'talked a'bout *'making a brìdge/*   (8 years; II, p. 85)

On the whole, children do not use non-finite clauses in subject position. Occasionally, the extraposition construction is used, with the result that the formality of a nominal clause at the beginning of the sentence is avoided, e.g.:

208 *it* 'cost me about 'ten 'pound *to bùy it/*   (8 years; II, p. 13)

Various aspects of the comprehension of nominal clauses have been studied. Considering finite clauses first, we can compare (209) and (210):

209 David knew *that he was in trouble.*
210 David pretended *that he was in trouble.*

In (209) David really was in trouble whereas in (210) he was not. Harris (1975) has shown that sentences with verbs like *pretend* are significantly harder for children up to the age of eleven to understand than sentences with verbs like *know*, presumably because in (210) the meaning of the italicized nominal clause cannot be correctly interpreted independently of the main clause.

As for non-finite clauses, these have been studied in both subject and object roles. Using the act-out technique, Tavakolian (1976) tested children's understanding of sentences with non-finite subject clauses, e.g.:

211 *To kiss the lion* would make the duck happy.

She found that only a third of her three- to five-year-olds could interpret such sentences correctly. Similar subject clauses were tested in a reading comprehension task by Bormuth *et al.* (1970). The nine-year-old children in this study were asked to read a paragraph which included a test sentence like this:

212 *For us to find him* was difficult.

They then had to write answers to *wh-* questions, e.g., 'What was difficult?' Nearly a third of their responses were wrong.

Non-finite clauses functioning as object have been a particular area of interest for researchers because there are some structures which are exceptions to the general pattern; it is reasonable to predict that exceptions will be acquired later than regularities. The verbs that have been the focus of study, because of the clause structures that follow them, are *promise, tell* and *ask.* Consider these pairs of sentences:

213a Laura told Joanna to feed the doll.
213b Laura asked Joanna to feed the doll.

214a Laura told Joanna to feed the doll.
214b Laura promised Joanna to feed the doll.

215a Laura told Joanna what to feed the doll.
215b Laura asked Joanna what to feed the doll.

In both sentences at (213), it is Joanna who is to feed the doll. This is the regular pattern in English, with the noun phrase (*Joanna*) that immediately precedes the non-finite verb (*to feed*) functioning as the subject of that verb. It contrasts with the exceptional structure at (214b) where it is not Joanna but Laura who will feed the doll. The verb *promise* is unique, being the only one in the language to behave in this way. In the sentence at (215), the non-finite clauses are introduced by the *wh-* word *what*, and this new structure brings about a contrast between *ask* and *tell* that was not present in (213): in (215a) it is Joanna who will feed the doll, whereas in (215b) it is Laura. This means that *ask* is particularly difficult since its use in (215b) is different both from the general pattern and from its own use in (213b).

First, we can examine children's understanding of the *tell/promise* distinction exemplified in (214). In a classic study, C. Chomsky (1969) tested children aged five to ten, using toy figures of Donald Duck and Bozo. Each child heard sentences like:

216 Bozo tells Donald to do a somersault.
217 Bozo promises Donald to do a somersault.

and then had to make the toys perform the appropriate actions. The
results showed a stable developmental sequence, although the children
differed very considerably in the rate at which they progressed through
the various stages. The youngest children treated both sentences as if the
verb was *tell*; this was followed by an inconsistent stage where, realizing
that there was something unusual about *promise*, they made mistakes on
both sentences. The next stage was when *tell* was always right but
promise sentences still contained errors. In the last stage, both types were
correctly understood. The average age of the children who had reached
this final stage was 7;11; however, children up to the age of 9;7 were
still making mistakes.

Chomsky's results have led people to believe that children between the
ages of five and about eight have a tendency to interpret the noun phrase
nearest the non-finite verb as the subject of that verb. A more recent
study, by Tavakolian (1978), suggests that children younger than five
might use a different strategy and therefore make different errors. She
too used toys, asking children aged three to five to act out sentences like:

218 The lion tells the pig to stand on the horse.
219 The pig promises the rabbit to jump over the duck.

Surprisingly, her youngest subjects were successful with the *promise* sentences (e.g. 219) and not with *tell*. Tavakolian suggested that these children were interpreting the sentences as if there were two main clauses
joined by co-ordination, e.g.:

220 The pig promises the rabbit and the pig jumps over the duck.

By chance, such a strategy works for the exceptional *promise* but gives
the wrong interpretation for the more frequent *tell* pattern.

Now we can consider the development of children's understanding of
tell and *ask* when these verbs are followed by a *wh-* clause, as in (215).
Chomsky (1969) studied these structures too and found, as predicted,
that *ask* was harder than both *tell* and *promise*. The majority of her forty
subjects, when instructed to 'Ask Joanna what to feed the doll', said,
'What are *you* going to feed the doll?' rather than, 'What should *I* feed
the doll?' The average age of the fourteen subjects who interpreted the
ask sentences correctly was 8;4 but children up to the age of ten were
still making mistakes. Chomsky concluded, 'this structure is still imper-
fectly learned by some children even at age ten' (p. 120). Using a different
methodology, Kessel (1970) also studied children's comprehension of the
ask / *tell* distinction. Like Chomsky, he found that young children interpret *ask* as if it were *tell*, but, unlike her, he reported complete mastery of
ask by the age of eight. In contrast with Kessel's results, a study by

Kramer *et al.* (1972) concluded that even adults are not consistently successful in interpreting instructions such as:

221 Ask Helen which book to read.

The technique used was the 'act-out' method (which is probably more demanding than the picture-selection task adopted by Kessel). The experimenters found that, by the age of twelve, they could expect 70 per cent success, but that performance did not improve after that, even in nineteen-year-olds. These older subjects frequently expressed doubts about their interpretation of the structure and this led Kramer *et al.* to suggest that:

> it seems possible that syntactic structures . . . that are learned late in life . . . may never be quite as automatic as structures learned earlier (p. 125).

To sum up this section on nominal clauses, we can note that evidence of linguistic maturity will be found in the occurrence of clauses in subject position – particularly if they are non-finite – and also, to a lesser extent, in the use of non-finite clauses that have the stem + *ing* form of the verb. Comprehension of non-finite clauses in subject position is likely to cause problems well into the junior school years; and *wh-* clauses after *ask* may not be confidently understood even by teenagers.

Adverbial clauses

The earliest adverbial clauses to appear, often when the child is only just over two, are those of time, e.g.:

222 *When Jack finish this* Mummy have some.

(Jack, 2; 2. Marsland, 1980)

The first temporal subordinator to be used is *when*, followed later by *while*, *after* and *before* (Clancy *et al.*, 1976). Bloom *et al.* (1980) point out that *when* appears in its role as a subordinator long before it is used as a question word. Other finite adverbial clauses that occur fairly commonly are those of reason, introduced by *because*, of result (*so*), and condition (*if*). Menyuk (1969, p. 92) notes that 82 per cent of her sample of children aged three to seven used *because* clauses, 39 per cent used *so* clauses, and 36 per cent used *if* clauses.

As far as school-age children are concerned, O'Donnell *et al.*'s (1967) data show a significant increase in the number of finite adverbial clauses used between the ages of five and six, and then again between eleven and thirteen (see table 13 on p. 134 above). Adverbial clauses of time, reason and condition are all very common in Fawcett and Perkins' (1980) speech samples. By the age of eight, their children are using a wide range of subordinators to introduce temporal clauses, e.g. *when*, *until*, *by the time that*, *after*, *before*, *whenever*, *every time that*, *while*. Noticeably less frequent than the clauses of time, reason and condition are those of result, introduced by *so*, and purpose, introduced by *so* (*that*):

223 we 'didn't have e'nough colour brícks/ to 'make a 'sort of all réd/
      'so we 'put àny old colour bricks/   (8 years; II, p. 11)
224 you 'must 'move it òver/ *so the bùs can go in/*   (6 years; I, p. 92)

Other adverbial clauses, such as those of place, manner and concession, occur rather rarely in the speech of primary school children. For example, in Strickland's (1962) data there is, on average, only one clause of place for every eight time clauses; and Katz and Brent (1968) found no *although* clauses in their samples of speech from children aged six and eleven. There is just one in Fawcett and Perkins' transcripts of six-year-olds:

225 [it's] 'much bétter/ *though it 'doesn't rhỳme/*   (6 years; I, p. 98)

The only non-finite adverbial clauses to occur at all commonly in children's speech are those of purpose – all the others have a markedly formal or even literary flavour. (For examples, see p. 72). Fawcett and Perkins' six-year-olds provide several instances of purpose clauses introduced by an infinitive, e.g.:

226 the 'man's going 'up and úp/ *to 'mend the aèrial/*
                                                    (6 years; I, p. 79)

The appropriate use of various adverbial clauses in speech does not necessarily mean that the child has full adult comprehension of the relationships they express. It seems likely that young children sometimes connect two clauses appropriately either by chance, or by copying an adult model without complete understanding. Vygotsky (1962, p. 46) comments that the child uses grammatical forms and structures correctly before he understands the meanings they encode: 'The child may operate with subordinate clauses, with words like *because, if, when, . . .* long before he really grasps causal, conditional or temporal relations.' Therefore, we now turn to a consideration of some of the studies that have been made of children's understanding of adverbial clauses of time, reason, condition and concession.

The time clauses that have been studied in greatest detail are those introduced by *before* and *after*. Children in the three to seven age-range have been asked to act out with toys test sentences containing a main and a subordinate clause, related in a time sequence. Several studies, including Clark (1971) and Coker (1978), have established the following order of difficulty, from easiest to hardest:

227 Ellie pushed the boat *before she waved the flag.*
228 *After Ellie pushed the boat* she waved the flag.
229 *Before Ellie waved the flag* she pushed the boat.
230 Ellie waved the flag *after she pushed the boat.*

The two easiest sentences, (227) and (228), preserve the order of events; in fact, the subordinators can be omitted altogether and the correct interpretation still obtained. In contrast, the two harder sentences violate the chronological order, since the first clause in each case describes the second event. Another difference is that in sentences (227) and (229), where *before* is the subordinator, the first event is in the main clause; but in the *after* sentences, (228) and (230), it is the subordinate clause that describes the first event. Where the researchers differ is in their explanation for the agreed order of difficulty. Clark (1971) suggests that *before* is easier than *after* for semantic reasons. But French and Brown (1977) believe that young children process the main clause more readily than the subordinate clause and that, therefore, *before* sentences are easier for the grammatical reason that the main clause always describes the first event: a strategy that interprets the main clause first and then the subordinate clause necessarily gets the order of events right when *before* is the subordinator. Coker's (1978) results support the view that, for young children, the processing of the subordinate clause can cause difficulties, especially when the order of mention conflicts with the chronological sequence. Only 65 per cent of her oldest group, aged 6; 3 to 7; 7, interpreted sentence (230), with *after*, correctly. It seems to combine two different kinds of difficulty: the order of the clauses does not match the sequence of events; and the first event is expressed not by the main but by the subordinate clause. In a study of reading comprehension in children aged nine, Bormuth *et al.* (1970) included these test sentences:

231 *After we entered*, the play began.
232 *Before we arrived*, people had already been seated.

(These sentences have the same clause order as (228) and (229) respectively.) Comprehension scores were 80 per cent for (231) but only 65 per cent for (232). This suggests that, for nine-year-olds at any rate, the violation of the chronological sequence in (232) is more disturbing than the use of a subordinate clause to describe the first event in (231).

Children's understanding of reason clauses introduced by *because* seems to be affected by four factors. First, young children rely heavily on semantic cues, so at an early age they interpret sentences correctly when they express a familiar cause-effect relationship, e.g.:

233 The cup broke *because it fell on the floor*.

Here the child does not really need to understand *because* in order to understand the relationship between the two events and their sequence in time. If the ideas expressed are unfamiliar, however, comprehension is less certain: using a multiple-choice sentence-completion task, Gardner (1977) tested teenage children's understanding of *because* in scientific contexts and reported the rather low scores of 50 per cent for eleven-year-olds and 73 per cent for fifteen-year-olds.

Second, some kinds of causal relationship are easier than others. Corrigan (1975) distinguishes three types: **physical, affective** and **concrete logical**. In the **physical** type, actions and objects in the physical world are related in predictable ways, e.g.:

234 The window broke *because the boy threw a stone.*

When the relationship signalled by *because* is an **affective** one, events or actions are linked to emotional responses, e.g.:

235 *Because Jon laughed at Sue*, she hit him.

In **concrete logical** sentences, ideas or judgements are joined in a relationship of logical necessity, e.g.:

236 Jon had a white block *because there were only white ones.*

The results of Corrigan's study suggest that children find the affective use easiest and the concrete logical use hardest.

The third factor that affects comprehension of *because* is the order of clauses within the sentence. Emerson (1979), Flores d'Arcais (1978) and Pearson (1975) have all shown that, at least until the age of twelve, children have a preference for a linguistic order that matches the sequence of events, with the cause mentioned before the effect. Thus, sentences with the *because* clause first are generally easier than those with the main clause first.

Fourthly, non-reversible sentences are easier to process than reversible ones. A reversible sentence is one where both clauses can equally sensibly express either cause or effect, e.g. (Emerson, 1979, p. 284):

237 He could hear the loud noises and laughing.
    He went outside.

These clauses can be causally joined in two ways, expressing two differ-ent meanings:

238 He could hear the loud noises and laughing because he went outside.
239 He went outside because he could hear the loud noises and laughing.

Emerson found that, when the *because* clause was second in a reversible sentence, only 66 per cent of her ten-year-old subjects could arrange a pair of pictures appropriately to reflect the meaning. Using a more demanding forced-choice question task, Irwin (1980a) found that only 46 per cent of her ten-year-old subjects were successful on reversible *because* sentences (regardless of clause order). On the same test, college students achieved average scores of 93 per cent when the *because* clause was first but their scores dropped to 89 per cent when it was second.

All this means that, although children show comprehension of affective *because* by about five, even teenagers may have difficulty in interpreting logical *because* clauses accurately if they occur in second position in an unfamiliar context in a potentially reversible sentence, e.g.:

> 240 There was diminishing wealth in the state coffers because the number of territorial conquests was declining.

Conditional clauses can be introduced by *if*, *unless* or *provided that*. Emerson (1980) tested children aged 4;10 to 8;7 on the recognition of anomalous *if* sentences by asking them if sentences like (241) were 'sensible' or 'silly':

> 241 He cycled a long way if his legs were tired.

She found that their judgements were more appropriate when the *if* clause was first rather than second: even the oldest group did not perform at an above-chance level when they heard an illogical sentence with the *if* clause second. She concluded that 'full comprehension of *if* in naturalistic sentences appears to be a late-developing ability' (p. 151). In a test of reading comprehension, Bormuth *et al.* (1970) gave nine-year-old children paragraphs that each included a sentence designed to test a particular structure; one contained a sentence with an *if* clause expressing a real condition (242), and another contained an *if* clause expressing a hypothetical condition (243):

> 242 *If we don't hurry*, we'll miss the show.
> 243 *If you had some money*, you would buy some.

The results suggested that the hypothetical condition was the harder one to interpret, as the average scores were 71 per cent for sentence (242) but only 61 per cent for sentence (243). (Though it is worth noticing that, in this particular example, the ellipsis at the end of (243) may have contributed to the difficulty of the sentence.) In fact, it seems to be the case that adult speakers are not entirely agreed about the meaning of hypothetical *if* clauses. The evidence lies in a study by Scholnick and Wing (1982). Using a methodology that did not allow their subjects to capitalize on their real-world knowledge, they presented children and adults with sentences like this:

> 244 If these were number 70 rocks, they would have palium.

The experimenters believed that this meant that the rocks were not 'number 70 rocks', but 57 per cent of their adult subjects did not share this interpretation, believing rather that it was not possible to tell whether the rocks were 'number 70' or not. Given so much uncertainty, it is hard to see by what standard children's comprehension of this structure should be assessed. Another difficult use of *if* is illustrated in (245):

> 245 If the 3rd Symphony is heroic then so too is the 5th.

Here, the meaning is something like, 'If it is true that the 3rd Symphony is heroic (and I have just said that I think it is), then it is also true that the 5th Symphony is heroic.' It seems likely that children may still have problems with this abstract, inferential use of *if*, as with hypothetical conditions, long after they have shown a clear grasp of its meaning in practical situations, e.g.

246 If I give you a sweet, will you play with me?

Unless clauses seem to cause serious comprehension problems. They are concealed negative constructions, with *unless* usually meaning 'if . . . not'. Young children do not recognize the negative meaning but treat *unless* as if it meant *if*. Palermo and Molfese (1972) refer to a study by H. F. Olds which revealed that children do not understand *unless* until they are ten. Other studies suggest that full comprehension may not be established until considerably later than that. For example, in a difficult experimental task involving logical reasoning, Wing and Scholnick (1981) found that only 47 per cent of their ten-year-old subjects could respond appropriately to *unless* clauses. In an experiment conducted by Carrell (1981), children aged four to seven were given a sheet of circles and one red and one blue crayon; they were then told to make a circle a particular colour by an experimenter who used instructions that took a variety of grammatical forms. When they heard:

247 I'll be happy *unless you make the circle blue.*

it is perhaps not surprising that only 42 per cent of the seven-year-olds realized that this meant that they should colour the circle red. Amidon (1976) asked five-, seven- and nine-year-olds to move a car round a game board according to instructions they received, e.g.:

248 You move the car *unless the light comes on.*

Her nine-year-olds had only a 33 per cent success rate on this task. When she added a negative to the *unless* clause, e.g.:

249 You move the car *unless the light does not come on.*

their scores fell to 11 per cent. (This construction is so difficult that it would be interesting to know how much success adults would have.) As they carried out the task, the children's verbalizations showed that they thought *unless* was synonymous with *if*, and *unless not* with *if not*.

The compound subordinator *provided that* has the meaning 'if and only if'. Gardner (1977) tested secondary pupils' understanding of it in both everyday and scientific contexts, using a multiple-choice sentence-completion task. He reported average scores of approximately 55 per cent for eleven-year-olds and 75 per cent for fifteen-year-olds.

Among the hardest of the adverbial clauses is the clause of concession introduced by *although*. Katz and Brent (1968, p. 504) gave the following pair of sentences to two groups of subjects, aged six to seven and eleven to twelve:

250 The meal was good *although the pie was good.*
251 The meal was good *although the pie was bad.*

Asked to say which sentence was 'the best', even at the age of eleven nearly a third of the subjects wrongly selected sentence (250), showing that they did not yet recognize the sense of contrast that is an essential part of the meaning of *although.* Other studies have used a sentence-completion task, where the subject is given a sentence fragment ending in *although* and is either asked to finish the utterance or to select an appropriate conclusion from a multiple-choice set. The results of five studies are given in table 14. They suggest that nine is the earliest age at which a rudimentary understanding of *although* can be expected and that comprehension is not fully established by fifteen.

The last point to consider in this section is whether, even where children have imperfect mastery of a particular subordinator, the explicit marking of the relationship between clauses is preferable to a link that has to be inferred. Katz and Brent (1968, p. 502) found that all their subjects, from six to nineteen, preferred a complex sentence containing *because* to two juxtaposed simple sentences, e.g.:

252a We did not sit down because the benches were wet.
252b We did not sit down. The benches were wet.

TABLE 14   Percentage of correct responses to a comprehension test of *although* in five studies

		Age						
Study	*Task*	6	8	9	10	11	13	15
Watts (1944, p. 83)	sentence completion			43	51	57	69	75
Vygotsky (1962, p. 106)	sentence completion (non-scientific contexts)		16		66			
Robertson (1968, p. 407)	multiple-choice sentence completion			47	59	69		
Gardner (1977, p. 16)	multiple-choice sentence completion (non-scientific contexts)					65		80
Katz & Brent (1968, p. 504)	selection of appropriate sentence from pair	14				68		

A study by Pearson (1975) showed that nine-year-olds recalled causal sentences better when *because* was included, and Irwin (1980a) found that both ten-year-olds and college students gave evidence of better comprehension of reversible causal sentences when the link was explicit. Other studies (e.g. Marshal & Glock, 1978; Irwin, 1980b) have shown enhanced understanding of conditional and temporal relationships when subordinators such as *if* and *after* are included. So, although some subordinators cause comprehension problems well into the secondary years, the solution does not seem to be simply to leave them out.

Relative clauses

Relative clauses function within the noun phrase, post-modifying the head noun. They develop rather later than nominal and adverbial clauses. Bloom *et al.* (1980), who describe the development of both compound and complex sentences in four children aged two to three, say, 'Relativization . . . was the last structure to appear [and] was always infrequent' (p. 250). Limber (1973, p. 180) notes that the earliest examples occur after a non-specific head-word, such as *thing* or *one*, e.g.:

253 I show you the thing *I got.* (2;9)

In young children's speech, relative clauses occur only in noun phrases that follow the verb, not in subject noun phrases. When Slobin and Welsh (1973, p. 494) asked 'Echo' to repeat sentences that had a relative clause following the subject, she altered the structure, either by making two conjoined clauses, e.g.:

254 *Adult:* The owl *who eats candy* runs fast.
    'Echo': Owl eat a candy *and* he run fast. (2;4)

or by converting the relative clause into the main clause (and vice versa), with the result that it was the object, not the subject, that was post-modified:

255 *Adult:* The man *who I saw yesterday* runs fast.
    'Echo': I saw the man *who run fast.* (2;4)

By the age of five, a few children are using relatives in the subject noun phrase (Menyuk, 1969) but Strickland (1962) notes that, even at nine, only 40 per cent of her sample use them in this position. In Fawcett and Perkins' transcripts, the majority of relative clauses occur in the clause elements that follow the verb – the object, complement and adverbial – e.g.:

256 I 'wish I 'had a hòverboat/ *which can 'fly and 'drive and flòat*/
    (6 years; I, p. 87)

However, there are a few that modify the subject head noun, e.g.:

257 the 'ones *who got the mòst*/ win/   (6 years; I, p. 36)

As far as the internal structure of the relative clause is concerned, it is clear that primary school children can use the relative pronoun both as subject and object of the clause, e.g.:

258   it's a gòblin/ '*which is kìng*/   (8 years; II, p. 106)
              s   v   c

259 I 'like the gàmes *that they 'played there*/   (8 years; II, p. 89)
                        o   s   v   a

The relative pronouns that they use most frequently are *which* and *that*; *who* is used less often; *where* occurs only very occasionally, e.g.:

260 'that's a 'sort of lìving room/ *where we 'eat our dìnner*/
                                                         (8 years; II, p. 12)

Generally, primary school children do not use relative clauses introduced by *whom, whose,* or a preposition plus a relative pronoun (e.g. *the bed in which he slept*). Presumably, that is because these structures hardly occur in informal speech, being characteristic of written language, so children are unlikely to meet them until they are themselves fluent readers. This point will be taken up again in chapter 5.

Throughout the primary school years, children use far fewer relative clauses than nominal and adverbial clauses. Surprisingly, several studies have shown that the number of relative clauses is at its highest at about five years of age and then dips until the teens, when it starts to climb again. (See table 13 on p. 134.) This has puzzled researchers. O'Donnell *et al.* (1967, p. 60), say:

> One of the most enigmatic features in the whole array of data collected in this study is the showing that kindergarten children used relative clauses more frequently than did children at any other stage.

A possible explanation might be that young children use relative clauses to compensate for gaps in their vocabulary; that is, they use a general word and post-modify it to make it specific when they do not know a more precise noun. Certainly, in Fawcett and Perkins' transcripts of six-year-olds, many of the relative clauses have vague antecedents such as *the one* and *the thing*. The following example shows a child using a relative clause as part of a circumlocutory description; he is hesitantly describing a game he has got:

261 *S:*   with 'those 'little 'round bàlls/ *that are whìte*/
     Int.: yeah table tennis balls   (6 years; I, p. 165)

The same point about young children's vocabulary is differently made in a poem by D. J. Enright, which begins:[13]

> *'The thing that makes a blue umbrella with its tail –*
> How do you call it?' you ask. Poorly and pale
> Comes my answer. For all I can call it is peacock.

[my italics]

It is very rare to find two or more relative clauses in one sentence in children's speech. Where they do occur, there may be a muddle, e.g. (from Fawcett & Perkins):

262 the 'last one *I sáw/ which was the 'most excíting bit/* 'when 'Starsky and Hútch/ were 'driving the cár/ (8 years; II, p. 105)

Otherwise, the most frequent mistake in relative clauses is the use of the wrong *wh-* word, e.g.:

263 there 'was a 'sports céntre/ *which* you could do 'lots of things/
(6 years; I, pp. 77–8)

Here, either *where* or *in which* is needed. In the next example, *which* has been used to refer to a human antecedent requiring *who* or *that*:

264 there 'were a 'little girl/ *which* a 'naughty làdy/ got from the sèa/
(6 years; I, p. 83)

A fairly frequent non-standard form, even with older children, is the use of *what*, which is not a relative pronoun, to introduce a relative clause, e.g.:

265 you 'got dágger/ or 'something like thát/ *'what* they kílled it with/
(10 years; III, p. 212)
266 'this mán/ *'what*'s 'Kelly's bóyfriend/ (10 years; III, p. 154)

As this is common in many dialects, examples (265) and (266) may be instances of dialect rather than immaturity. Occasionally, when they use the *wh-* word as object of the relative clause, children make the mistake of repeating the object, e.g.:

267 one of them things/ *what* they 'hold *them* like thàt/
(8 years; II, p. 266)

It is generally suggested that non-finite constructions post-modifying nouns are rare in children's speech. This is not true of the six- and eight-year-olds in Fawcett and Perkins' samples, where there are several

13 'Blue Umbrellas' from: D. J. Enright (1956) *Bread rather than blossoms*, Secker & Warburg.

examples of post-modifying clauses with an infinitive or stem + *ing* form of the verb, e.g.:

268 those are 'things *to 'open and shùt/*   (6 years; I, p. 79)
269 [the winner is] the 'first one *to 'find the mùrderer/*
                                                        (8 years; II, p. 20)
270 'I got a 'lady and màn/ *'peeping through the windows/*
                                                        (6 years; I, p. 33)
271 we could 'have a màn/ *re'pairing the hòuse/*   (8 years; II, p. 7)

The stem + *en* form of the verb can also occur in this type of clause (e.g. 'They hit a tree *blown down by the wind*'), but it is more characteristic of written than spoken language and probably does not appear in children's speech until they are reading extensively.

We can now turn to children's comprehension of relative clauses. It is affected by three factors: the position of the relative clause (whether it is modifying the subject or a clause element in the predicate); the grammatical function of the relative pronoun (as subject or object of the relative clause); and the presence or absence of a relative pronoun. We can begin by considering the effect of the position of the relative clause, holding other factors constant.

The contrasting positions that the relative clause can occupy are illustrated in sentences (272) and (273):

272 The cow *that hit the pig* chased the deer.
273 The cow hit the pig *that chased the deer.*

Studies by Lahey (1974) and Tavakolian (1978) have required children aged three to five to act out such sentences with toys; Fluck (1978) used a similar procedure with five- to nine-year-olds. These three researchers all found that sentences like (272), with the relative modifying the subject, were easier than (273). In Fluck's experiment, even nine-year-olds scored only 50 per cent on sentences like (273). This result is strange as, in their spontaneous speech, children use object relative clauses earlier and more frequently than subject ones. Three other studies, by H. Brown (1971), de Villiers *et al.* (1979) and Sheldon (1974), using either picture selection or the act-out task with three- to five-year-olds, have found no significant difference in the difficulty of relative clauses that could be attributed solely to their position in either the subject or the predicate.[14]

The picture with regard to the function of the relative pronoun is rather clearer since the majority of studies that have examined this factor have found that relative clauses that begin with a subject pronoun are

14 For summaries and interpretations of the rather confusing research findings concerning children's comprehension of relative clauses, see Bowerman (1979) and de Villiers *et al.* (1979).

easier than those that begin with an object pronoun; so higher scores have been achieved for (274) than for (275):

274 The turtle hit the pig *that touched the giraffe.*
                                   s   v   o

275 The turtle hit the pig *that the giraffe touched.*
                                 o   s   v

When the interaction between the two factors, clause position and pronoun function, is considered there is a great deal of evidence to suggest that a clause modifying the subject, with its relative pronoun functioning as object, is the hardest type to comprehend, e.g.:

276 The turkey *that the gorilla patted* pushed the pig.

There are two sources of difficulty in this sentence: first, the main clause subject, *the turkey*, is separated from its verb, *pushed*; and, second, the order of the clause elements in the relative clause is OSV, which is a reversal of the normal English clause order, SVO.

When the relative pronoun functions as object of its clause, it can be omitted, e.g.:

277 The turkey *the gorilla patted* pushed the pig.

The effect of this omission of the pronoun has not been so extensively examined as the other two factors in studies of the comprehension of speech (though it has in reading). It is noticeable, however, that when 'Echo' (Slobin & Welsh, 1973, p. 494) was given such a sentence to repeat, it was meaningless to her and she reproduced it as a mere string of words:

278 *Adult:*   The boy the book hit was crying.
     'Echo':   boy the book was crying

Experiments to assess the comprehension of relative clauses in reading have chiefly used adult subjects. As far as the position of the clause is concerned, a study by Edwards (1969) – which required students to paraphrase what they had read – revealed a strong preference for relative clauses that occurred in the predicate rather than in the subject noun phrase. Studies of readers' eye-movements, by Levin and Kaplan (1970) and Wanat (1976), give support to the suggestion that the processing of subject relative clauses is particularly demanding for the reader. So, while the findings with regard to the comprehension of SPOKEN relative clauses are rather confused, with at least some researchers saying that subject relatives are easier, it seems to be the case that, in reading, relative clauses modifying a clause element in the predicate are easier.

Another factor that has been studied for its effect on reading comprehension is the omission of the relative pronoun. Beaumont (1982) tested seven-year-old children's understanding of subject relative clauses in reading and found that their comprehension deteriorated noticeably when the relative pronoun was omitted, e.g.:

279 The lady *the man is touching* is thin.

This effect has also been reported for adult subjects by Fodor and Garrett (1967) and Hakes and Foss (1970).

Adjective + clause

Post-modified adjectives do not occur commonly in young children's speech; there are just a very few examples in Fawcett and Perkins' (1980) transcripts, e.g.:

280 I'm *'good at máking them/*   (6 years; I, p. 3)
281 I'm *'glad I 'didn't 'put my finger in thére/*   (8 years; II, p. 68)

Strickland (1962, p. 40) gives one example from a twelve-year-old subject:

282 . . . real *hard to hit.*

It was noted in chapter 2 (p. 80) that when an infinitive follows an adjective, the subject of the finite verb is most often also the understood subject of the non-finite clause, e.g.:

283 Paul is eager to please his mother.

But a few adjectives, e.g. *easy, hard*, behave differently. With these, the subject of the main clause has a semantic relationship with the infinitive like that of an object, e.g.:

284 Paul is easy to please.

(As this sentence means, 'It is easy to please *Paul*', it is not possible to put an object after please: **Paul is easy to please his mother.*) Children's understanding of 'eager' and 'easy' sentences has been investigated in a number of studies. C. Chomsky (1969) tested children aged 5;0 to 10;0 by showing them a blindfolded doll and asking them if it was easy to see or hard to see. The youngest children thought it was hard to see (presumably because the doll itself could not see) but by the age of seven, most of them realized that it was easy to see. Even so, there were two subjects out of forty who were still making mistakes at the age of eight. Chomsky's methodology was criticized by Kessel (1970), who felt that the prominent and unusual blindfold on the doll could 'trick' the child into a wrong answer. He also pointed out that the procedure did not test children's comprehension of adjectives like 'eager'. He studied both 'easy' and 'eager'-type adjectives using a hide-and-seek game played by 'Peanuts' puppets, e.g.:

285 Lucy was sure to see.
286 Charlie Brown was hard to see.

In each case, the child had to say which puppet was doing the hiding and which the seeking. Kessel found that sentences with adjectives like *eager* (e.g. 285) were always interpreted correctly before those with adjectives like *easy* (e.g. 286). The majority of his subjects could get both types right by the time they were eight. R. F. Cromer (1970) also tested these two constructions; his subjects had to act out instructions using glove puppets. Like Chomsky and Kessel, he found that children varied widely in the age at which they mastered the harder 'easy'-type adjectives, so he clarified his results by presenting them in terms of mental ages as well as chronological ages. He noted that only children with a mental age of 6;8 and above were consistently successful in distinguishing the two constructions; their chronological ages ranged from 6;7 to 7;5. Children with a mental age below 5;7 always interpreted the 'easy'-type adjective as if it were 'eager'; their chronological ages ranged from 5;3 to 7;4.

3.5 THE ACQUISITION OF DISCOURSE CONNECTIONS

So far, this chapter has been chiefly concerned with grammatical structures within the sentence. It is important, however, not to lose sight of the fact that we rarely speak in isolated sentences and that the acquisition of language entails learning to produce longer stretches of speech where the individual utterances are cohesively bound together. Similarly, it entails learning to reply to someone else's speech in such a way that the response is not only logically and semantically appropriate but also grammatically harmonious. This involves, for example, selecting the right verb tense, the right pronominal reference and the right common elements for ellipsis. We have seen already that maintaining a sequence of tenses (p. 108) and handling pronominal reference skilfully (p. 105) are difficult for young schoolchildren.

Researchers such as Givon (1979) and Ochs (1979) suggest that young children string sentences together without explicit linking devices, with the result that the listener has to infer the connections as best he can from the context. Gradually they learn various means of structuring their discourse and signposting the relationships between utterances. This ability to organize discourse develops at different ages for different uses of language. For example, narrative is a form that is acquired early – the typical story structure of an opening followed by one or more events is apparent in the language of many five-year-olds. Umiker-Sebeok (1979) recorded the simple narratives that children incorporate in their spontaneous conversations and found that 57 per cent of the narratives produced by her three- to five-year-old subjects had both an introduction and at least one event. In contrast, explicitly-organized descriptive or explanatory discourses do not occur until much later. (Even in adults they are more likely to appear in planned than unplanned speech.)

We can now briefly consider some of the grammatical devices which bind sentences together in a discourse. The characteristic of these devices is that they can be interpreted only by referring to another sentence elsewhere in the discourse.

Reference and substitution[15]

Garber (1979) found that her six-year-old subjects could use both these categories of discourse connection, though it was noticeable that reference was twenty times as frequent as substitution in their speech. The spontaneous speech of children aged seven to fifteen was studied by Scinto (1977), who noted that the younger children's pronouns were not always clear in their reference; he concluded, 'there would appear to be evidence to support a gradual developmental picture of control of pronominal use in discourse' (p. 32). There is abundant evidence of pronominal reference in Fawcett and Perkins' (1980) transcripts – we have seen already (p. 106) that the pronouns are not always easy for the listener to interpret: this is especially true of the speech of the six- and eight-year-olds. Less frequent, but also well established, are nominal and verbal substitution, e.g.:

> 287 *K:*   'anybody 'got another dòor/ . . . I 'need anòther *one*/
> (6 years; I, p. 29)
> 288 *K:*   I 'need a gáte/ for my gârden/
> *T:*   'so do Ì/   (6 years; I, p. 29)

The studies of children's comprehension of these discourse connections present a confused picture. When Lesgold (1974) replicated in part an experiment by Bormuth *et al.* (1970), he obtained significantly different results. He suggested that semantic factors had not been properly controlled in the earlier study. Moberly (1978) reported on both studies and added her own results; as they were different again she concluded that understanding of discourse connections was a very difficult aspect of language competence to assess experimentally. All three studies are summarized in table 15.

Moberly showed that performance improved between the ages of nine and twelve. Unlike the other researchers, she also investigated the effect of the distance between a lexical item and its pro-form replacement. She found that scores deteriorated when substitution items were separated by

15 As explained in chapter 2, section 6, I am using the analysis and terminology put forward by Halliday and Hasan (1976) (rather than Quirk *et al.'s* description) because it is their framework that has been used by most of the researchers who have studied the development of cohesive features in children's language.

TABLE 15   Comprehension of reference and substitution in discourse[16]

| Study | Task | Age of subjects | Results | |
			Reference	Substitution
Bormuth *et al.* (1970, p. 354)	Read paragraph and give written answer to multiple-choice *wh-* question	9–10	74%	82%
Lesgold (1974, p. 336)	Read paragraph and give oral answer to *wh-* question	8–11	84%	60%
Moberly (1978, p. 99) (immediate location only)	Write in the item that has been substituted	9–12	73%	75%

a sentence or more from the lexical expressions they were replacing, but that this distance effect did not apply to reference items.

Ellipsis

In order to produce or understand elliptical constructions, the speaker has to be able to hold the full utterance in his mind, recognize which elements have already been produced, and provide the appropriate remainder, e.g.:

289   What are you doing tomorrow?
[I am] visiting a friend in Wales [tomorrow].

The words in square brackets are those that are recoverable from the question – *I am* having undergone the necessary changes from *are you*. Although it is grammatically possible (but socially odd) to produce a full response, it is not possible for the speaker to introduce individual variation into the ellipted part of the utterance, and reply, for example, **am visiting a friend in Wales*. So ellipsis involves both recognition of common elements (even when their form is transmuted) and knowledge of the rules governing their omission. It is not surprising, therefore, that many studies (e.g. Bloom *et al.* (1975), Katz & Brent (1968)) have sug-

16 The results have been reanalysed in terms of Halliday and Hasan's (1976) classification of reference and substitution.

gested that elliptical utterances occur after the comparable full structure has been mastered.

Miller (1973, p. 387) gives examples of Christy's spontaneous speech at 2;10 showing errors in ellipsis, e.g.:

> 290 *Int.:*   Are you gonna make coffee for Liz?
> *C:*   Yeah I do.

At 3;1 there are signs that she is acquiring mastery, in responses like this:

> 291 *Int.:*   It's not blue.
> *C:*   Yes it is.

It is worth noting, though, that this example is easier than her earlier attempt, since it does not involve any change in the form of subject or verb.

An examination of Fawcett and Perkins' (1980) transcripts reveals that, although their six-year-olds can certainly use discourse-level ellipsis, they have a tendency to give full responses where an elliptical one would be possible, e.g.:

> 292 *Int.:*   what was it about?
> *C:*   I 'can't re'member 'what was it abŏut/   (6 years; I, p. 13)
> 293 *Int.:*   do you make things like that?
> *F:*   'sometimes I 'make things like thát/   (6 years; I, p. 17)
> 294 *Int.:*   do you play the mother or the father?
> *M:*   I 'play the mòther/   (6 years; I, p. 81)

The eight- and ten-year-old children seem to make greater use of elliptical responses.

Comprehension of ellipsis in discourse has not been extensively studied. (One reason for this is that it is difficult to find an appropriate methodology.) Bormuth *et al.* (1970) asked their nine-year-old subjects to read paragraphs containing sequences like this:

> 295 There are ripe and green apples. The green [   ] are mine.

79 per cent of the children could successfully answer a *wh-* question after reading this. Similarly, Moberly (1978) reported scores of 78 per cent obtained by children aged nine to twelve responding to ellipsis that referred to the immediately preceding sentence. She noted that comprehension deteriorated significantly if the antecedent was more than one sentence away: in that case, scores fell to 58 per cent.

Sentence connectives

Conjunctions and adverbs can be used to link sentences in a discourse; the connected sentences may both be spoken by one speaker or they may form part of a conversation between two speakers. By means of connectives, the second speaker is able to 'tie' his response to what has gone before. Garber (1979) collected speech samples from six-year-olds and found that they used connectives to link their sentences into a cohesive discourse. The most frequent words used were *and* and *then*. Fawcett and Perkins' (1980) six-year-olds provide examples of all the four types of connective classified by Halliday and Hasan. They use **additive** connectives, such as *and* and *as well*, e.g.:

296 *T*: 'I've been in 'one of thém/ a yéllow one/ . . .
    S: I've been in a 'red one *as wèll*/   (6 years; I, p. 31)

Their **adversative** connectives include *though* and *anyway*, e.g.:

297 *F*: we'll 'have to 'bash them back ŭp again/
    C: but we can 'make them at hòme *though*/ cân't we/
                                     (6 years; I, p. 2)

The **temporal** connective *then* is used very often; the children also use sequencing words such as *in the end* and *first of all*, e.g.:

298 *K*: they shòoted/ and they had 'Star Wars 'swords as wéll/ . . .
      and '*in the énd*/ Da 'Veda 'wasn't kílled/   (6 years; I, p. 48)

Understandably, these connectives are used most often when they are telling a story. **Causal** connectives, such as *else* (meaning 'if not') and *so*, also occur, e.g.:

299 *K*: I 'haven't 'really 'gotta 'man Trícia/ . . . *so* it 'isn't fàir/ ìs it/
    Sháron/   (6 years; I, p. 32)

All these connectives are quite general in their meaning and are very common in speech.

    Naturally enough, young children do not use in their spontaneous speech those connectives with a rather more specific meaning that are characteristic of written discourse and of fairly formal planned speech – for example, *nevertheless, thus, accordingly*. Henderson (1979) selected sixteen sentence connectives and asked college students to write sentences incorporating them. They were least successful with *likewise, besides, moreover, consequently, instead*, and *hence*. This is an example of the type of error they made:

300 He would like to go on a vacation. *Consequently*, he cannot
    afford it.   (p. 72)

In her results, there was a very noticeable difference in the performance of able and poor readers: able readers used the connectives appropriately 86 per cent of the time whereas weaker readers scored only 55 per cent on average.

    Studies of the comprehension of sentence connectives suggest that some of them are acquired very late. Robertson (1968) tested children aged nine to eleven on *however* and *thus* and reported average scores of 61 per cent for *however* and 45 per cent for *thus*. Gardner (1977) tested eleven- and fifteen-year-old children on a large number of connectives: the following were understood by fewer than 50 per cent of the older children: *similarly, further, that is*; scores for *moreover* were below 30 per cent. In Henderson's (1979) study with college students, even the able readers scored below 30 per cent on *instead, also* and *moreover*.

3.6 CONCLUSION

During the Seventies, it was commonplace for books on language acquisition to suggest that, apart from vocabulary, children had virtually completed the learning of their mother tongue by the age of five; for example, Slobin (1971, p. 40) wrote:

> a little child ... masters the exceedingly complex structure of his native language in the course of a short three or four years.

I hope that this chapter has shown that, although children have acquired a remarkable amount of language by the time they start school, the developmental process continues, albeit at a slower rate, until they are in their teens.

There are many grammatical constructions that are more likely to occur after five than before – some, indeed, that are not at all frequent until adolescence. They include: complex NPs, particularly in subject position; some modal auxiliaries, e.g. *shall, may, ought to*; nominal clauses as subjects; adverbial clauses of place, manner, concession and hypothetical condition; non-finite adverbial clauses (apart from those of purpose); relative clauses introduced by *whom, whose*, or a relative pronoun plus a preposition; clausal substitution; some types of ellipsis, and all but the commonest sentence connectives.

Another process that continues for many years after the age of five is the gradual increase of fluency, with a reduction in the number of mazes and hesitations. In addition, errors of immaturity are slowly eliminated. These include: lack of concord between subject and verb; use of the wrong determiner; inappropriate pronominal and determiner reference; omission of auxiliary *be*; failure of tense sequence; mistakes in the morphology of irregular nouns and verbs; errors in tag questions and hypothetical expressions; and the selection of the wrong relative pronoun.

As far as comprehension is concerned, it is clear that when the child starts school there are still many grammatical constructions that are not fully understood. These include the $SVO_i \, O_d$ clause pattern, *how* questions, reversible passives, the *ask/tell* distinction, and ellipsis of the verb or object in compound sentences. Furthermore, it is generally several years before the following constructions are interpreted in an adult way: concealed negatives; sentences where both the main and the subordinate clause are negated; sentences where the clause sequence conflicts with the chronological sequence; adverbial clauses introduced by *although, unless* and *provided that,* as well as hypothetical and inferential 'if' clauses; many sentence connectives; and discourse-level ellipsis that is remote from its antecedent.

It is worth considering briefly why there should have been such an emphasis on early language acquisition with less attention paid to later developments. First, some psycholinguists believe that there is, innate in human beings, a specifically linguistic ability (as distinct from general cognitive abilities); they have emphasized the speed with which children learn language, seeing it as evidence that the human brain is specially adapted for formulating hypotheses about linguistic structures from the rather small amount of data provided by older language-users. Second, many educationists stress how much language children have already learnt by the time they start school, lest teachers should think of their pupils as empty vessels, waiting to be filled. Third, linguists concentrate very heavily on descriptions of the spoken language, and it is certainly true that a very large proportion of the linguistic forms that occur frequently in informal speech are acquired by children while they are still very young. However, a full description of the language also has to include structures such as complex grammatical subjects, non-finite and verbless clauses and certain types of ellipsis – all of which occur much more frequently in writing and formal, planned speech than they do in spontaneous speech. Naturally enough, children do not acquire these constructions until they are reading fluently, and then they are more likely to use them in writing than in speech. (This notion will be elaborated in chapter 5.) Finally, the linguistic abilities of a school-age child can easily be over-estimated, because the immaturities are not very obvious – unlike those of a three-year-old. They consist, on the whole, of comprehension difficulties that may only come to light in experimental settings, and of a failure to exploit all the resources of the language. Because it is not very easy to notice that a child is not using clausal substitution, for example, it is all too easy to think that the process of language learning is more nearly complete than it really is.

As well as showing that language acquisition is by no means complete by the age of five, the studies that have been outlined in this chapter have also provided evidence that development does not follow a smooth, unbroken, forward progression. For example, although very young children correctly produce irregular past tenses such as *went* and *came,* a little later they start making errors and saying *goed* and *comed.* Likewise, Palermo and Molfese (1972, p. 422), describing various studies of pronominalization, say, 'the child seems to grasp pronominal constructions at one age only to lose them and reacquire them again, with final errorless performance coming relatively late in language acquisition'. Also, table

13, p. 134, shows that between the ages of five and six there is a notice-able increase in the number of subordinate clauses used, but that the level then stays fairly constant for several years until about eleven, when there is another marked jump. This is one piece of evidence for the observation made in several studies (e.g. Loban, 1963; O'Donnell *et al.*, 1967) that there appear to be periods of particularly active language development in the early school years and then again around eleven. Palermo and Molfese (1972, p. 422) comment that these periods are 'marked by instability . . . and are followed by growth to new levels and subsequent stable linguistic performance . . . It is during these two periods that large increases in new grammatical constructions and high error rates on some kinds of constructions are reported'.

It is not only the development of language production that is charac-terized by instability; comprehension, too, may appear to regress. For instance, we have seen (p. 124) that, at three, children can understand *who* when it is functioning as an object, but that, at four, they tend to interpret it as the subject. Similarly, the exceptional structure with *promise* seems to be understood by three-year-olds but not by five-year-olds (p. 137). Slobin (1973a, p. 465) suggests that such 'regressions' may occur as the child learns to use new, more powerful language-processing strategies and, at first, applies them inappropriately, with the result that 'comprehension does not uniformly improve with age'. It is obviously helpful for teachers to be aware that children's language acquisition – both production and comprehension – does not proceed in a series of steady, incremental steps.

The findings reported in this chapter have implications for the teach-ing of reading and writing. When children learn to write, there are still immaturities of many kinds in their speech. Therefore, given the difficulty of the task, it is not surprising that these immaturities occur more notice-ably in their writing. In chapter 5 we shall see how, gradually, children's grammatical control in writing comes to match their oral ability and then, eventually, to overtake it. A very important factor in this develop-ment of linguistic skill in writing is the input that comes from reading. The next chapter will show that, for a variety of reasons, the competent writer has to use constructions that rarely occur in unplanned speech. These can be acquired only through reading – and reading a wide range of different kinds of language. Yet it is clearly unreasonable for young children – who are still struggling to master the mechanics of reading – to be faced with grammatical constructions that are remote from the language they speak. So a delicate balance has to be maintained, whereby pupils learn the basics of reading by using books that have language which is close to their everyday speech, but progress, with help and support, to more literary material that will serve to enrich the lan-guage of their own writing and, ultimately, their spoken language too.

CHAPTER 4

Some differences between speech and writing

Not enough account is taken of the fundamental differences that exist between speech and writing.

(DES, 1975, p. 143)

4.1 INTRODUCTION

In the last chapter we saw that normally-developing children acquire the most frequently occurring grammatical structures of the spoken language in a period of two to three years, from the age of about eighteen months. If no speech emerges during the first five years (and if the child is amongst people who talk normally) this is, in itself, a sign of some abnormality, such as deafness, autism, or some kind of brain damage. For this reason, doctors include a simple check on language development in their routine clinic examinations of children between the ages of two and five. When something is found to be wrong, it is important for remedial help to be given as soon as possible because the brain seems to be especially suited to the learning of a first language in the years before puberty; later, it is probably impossible for anything like normal competence in the mother tongue to be achieved. A tragic example of excessive delay in language learning is a girl called Genie who has been studied by Curtiss (1977). Because her psychotic father kept her locked up alone, away from all human contact, Genie had acquired no language at all by the time she was thirteen, when she was discovered and taken into care. She was given intensive individual instruction but, despite this, over the next five years she was able to learn only the most rudimentary vocabulary and sentence patterns. Her difficulty was probably caused, at least in part, by the fact that she was past the stage when the first language is most easily acquired. In normal circumstances, of course, when children learn to speak before they are five, they do not need any formal teaching at all.

All these characteristics of learning to speak contrast markedly with learning to read and write. It is very rare for children to acquire these skills unaided or before they go to school; indeed, teachers spend a great deal of time and effort on teaching reading and writing – and, even so, many pupils fail to become fully literate. However, for those who are not successful there is, fortunately, no maturational barrier (such as puberty) after which there is little chance of learning: the Adult Literacy Project has shown that people in their seventies can learn to read and write.

Human beings have been speaking for roughly a million years but have been writing for only about five and a half thousand (Stubbs, 1980), so, in terms of the whole span of human history, writing is a very recent development. Moreover, for most of those five and a half thousand years only the smallest minority of the earth's population has been able to read and write. Until the development of printing in the fifteenth century, written texts were available only to monasteries and the very wealthy. In Britain, it was not until the advent of compulsory education, about a century ago, that there was any expectation that the whole population should be literate. Even today, according to Stubbs (1980), more than 40 per cent of the world's adult population cannot read or write at all and a further 25 per cent do not have sufficient mastery of a writing system for it to be of significant practical use. Many languages have been written down for the first time during this century and there are still hundreds of communities who have no written form of the language they speak. So spoken language preceded writing in the history of the human race and of individual tribes or nations. It is clear, I think, that writing is not 'natural' in the way that speech is. Speaking is as fundamental a part of being human as walking upright, but writing is an optional extra – exclusive to human beings, certainly, but not a defining characteristic of the species.

Some of the difficulties that children experience in composing effective written language and in understanding books and workcards derive from the differences between spoken and written language. As educated adults, we are, almost by definition, people who feel at home with written language, so it is not always easy for us to see the learning task from the child's viewpoint. An explicit awareness of the differences between speech and writing – and of the characteristic strengths and weaknesses of each mode – may provide ideas for leading pupils from the known forms and functions of speech to the unknown forms and functions of writing.

Physical differences

Speech consists of sounds that are produced in a sequence in TIME; writing consists of marks, made on a surface such as paper, in an arrangement in SPACE. The spatial arrangement is two-dimensional: some writing systems progress across the page, others from top to bottom, but all involve both horizontal and vertical movements. The time sequence, on the other hand, is necessarily uni-dimensional. Speech is perceived by the ear, writing by the eye. Confining ourselves now to English, we can say that normally skilful adult readers read at roughly twice the rate that they speak; rates vary, of course, according to mood, situation, purpose and so on, but as a guide we can take 300 words per minute as an average reading speed and 150 words per minute as an average speaking speed.[1] The listener's rate is necessarily fixed by the speed of the speaker. The writer, on the other hand, is very much slower than either the reader or the speaker: Horowitz and Newman (1964, p. 642) suggest that six minutes' writing time is needed to produce the equivalent of one minute's speech.

A piece of writing is relatively durable; it can be read and reread; it can be carried about and it can be accurately reproduced. Once written, it no longer needs an author, since it then has an independent existence. Therefore, by means of writing, the same words can be faithfully transmitted through the centuries and across continents to an infinite number of people, without the identity of the writer necessarily being known. In contrast, speech is typically impermanent, local and personal. Until the invention of the tape-recorder, speech was ephemeral; it could not be stored, 're-heard' or transported, and it had no existence independent of the speaker. Before the telephone and the radio, the speaker's words could travel no further than his voice could carry them. Even today, most spoken language is not recorded, broadcast or transmitted by telephone. When spoken messages are passed on, they are notoriously subject to distortion. This is best illustrated by the (apocryphal) story of the military order, 'Send reinforcements, we're going to advance', which, by the end of a chain of messengers, had become, 'Send three and fourpence, we're going to a dance.'

The reader is a free agent. He can read at his own speed, slowing down if the language is difficult, or particularly enjoyable and worth savouring; skipping sections that are of no interest; running his eye over the pages to locate a piece of information, such as a name or a date, and moving backwards and forwards in the text to reread, check, compare, cross-reference, and so on. The listener, on the other hand, is tied quite closely to the speaker. For example, if he is listening to a formal talk and misses a few words, he cannot 're-hear' them; and if he fails to understand a point, he cannot reflect on it without losing what comes next; nor can he look ahead to find out how the argument will develop. The contrast between the two types of language-processing is highlighted by some of the techniques that are used by radio news presenters. Knowing that the audience may be giving the programme only the most fleeting attention,

---

1 As Foulke and Sticht (1969, p. 52) say, there is 'considerable variability in published estimates of word rate' in speech. They give 125 wpm for conversational speaking rate, and 174 wpm for oral reading rate; a mid-point between these two figures is 150 wpm.

they attempt to simulate the scanning technique that, as readers, we typically use with newspapers – glancing at one headline after another until we find a topic that interests us. Thus, the newsreader frequently tells us what we are going to hear 'in the next fifty minutes' and also reminds us of what we have just been told. According to Self (1980) such attention-getting techniques are known in radio circles as 'the Mabel Factor':

> The Mabel Factor is that element in any radio news sequence programme, such as *Today*, *A.M.*, or *P.M.*, which makes a listener shout to his wife, 'Here Mabel, listen to this'.

The reader, especially of non-fiction, has the benefit of a whole range of visual clues on the page – running headlines at the top, chapter headings and side headings, sometimes abstracts or summaries set off from the main text by a different style of print. An interesting example of the difference between spoken and written forms of presentation is the use of the footnote. In footnotes the writer can give references, further examples, additional information and opposing viewpoints without distorting the balance or disguising the main thread of the argument. The reader is then able to choose the level at which he will read: if he is new to the topic, he can ignore the footnotes, confident that all the basic material will be included in the body of the text; if he is an expert, however, he can choose to follow up any or all of the footnotes. Unlike the reader, a person listening to a lecture is completely dependent on the selection of material made by the speaker. And whereas the listener rarely knows how long a talk will last until the speaker stops, the reader can judge at a glance the extent of a work and the proportion devoted to each topic. In *Northanger Abbey*, Jane Austen acknowledges that her readers must be aware that the story is reaching its close, since they can see 'in the tell-tale compression of the pages before them that we are all hastening together to perfect felicity'.

Situational differences

The most frequent type of spoken language is face-to-face conversation. This kind of language is a co-operative product: a question is followed by an answer, a request by a response, a statement by agreement or contradiction or additional information, and so on. There is no time for careful planning – if a speaker pauses too long to collect his thoughts or think of a word, he will almost certainly be interrupted. Despite this pressure on production, serious misunderstanding is rare because the speaker can generally sense if he has not made himself clear and can repeat or rephrase what he was saying. In this type of situation, language is only one aspect of the total act of communication. People communicate non-verbally by means of noises such as sighs, laughter, snorts and intakes of breath and by body posture, gestures and facial expressions. (A person who says, 'I'm terrified' while lolling in a chair and smiling broadly clearly means something different from the person who uses the same words but whose body is tense and whose face is taut with anxiety.) When the participants in a conversation know each other well, they can take for granted shared knowledge, ideas and attitudes. Being in the same physical situation, they do not need to make fully explicit any references to their surroundings.

In stark contrast with this, writing is a lonely and isolated endeavour. Most typically the writer does not write in the presence of the reader, so he receives no prompting about what to write, no encouragement to continue and no indication of any ambiguity or lack of clarity in his message. However, being alone, the writer can take his time, can search for the exact expression of his meaning without fear of interruption. Unlike the speaker, he can look back over what he has written so that each sentence flows smoothly from the last. (Speakers who lose track of what they are saying sometimes have to ask their listeners what they have just said.) The more demanding the topic, the more necessary such rereading is. Britton (1975, p. 115) describes how the Writing Research team at London University tried experimentally to perform various writing tasks without being able to reread what they had just written:

> We sensed no difficulty in writing a letter . . ., some handicap in trying to write a story, and considerable frustration in writing a research report. Our recorded writings when we read them lent support to our feelings.

The writer can correct, alter and polish his work, presenting finally a fair copy that shows no trace of earlier, rejected versions. Such effort is often necessary because, in writing, the language has to bear the whole burden of communication – there are no gestures or other non-verbal signals to support or interpret the words. This means that much greater linguistic explicitness has to be achieved. In addition, in many kinds of writing the readers will be unknown to the writer, so he cannot make assumptions about their knowledge and attitudes. All this tends to make writing more impersonal than speech.

A study by Walker (1976) compared sixteen-year-olds' comprehension of spoken and written language. Videotape recordings were made of discussions between two students on clearly defined themes; these were transcribed, and the information they conveyed expressed in normal written style. One group of subjects watched the videotapes and the other group read the written versions of the material. Both groups then had to write down what they could recall of the ideas that had been presented. Regardless of their reading ability, students who read the written versions recalled more ideas and expressed them more accurately than those who had watched the videotapes. One reason for this result is probably that writing is a more unified kind of communication than speech. All the information is in the language; ideas are, literally, disembodied. They stand by themselves, in clear isolation on the page, whereas in speech, ideas are perceived as being part of a person, whose appearance, voice quality, emotions and attitudes all contribute to a much more diffuse act of communication. Listeners learn more than readers about the author of the idea, but less about the ideas themselves. Walker concludes, 'Reading comprehension appears to possess at least one unique characteristic that sets it off from listening comprehension of spontaneous speech; it . . . permits relatively greater precision of communication' (p. 164).

Functional differences

Speech can often be satisfactorily written down and a great deal of writing can be intelligibly read aloud, so there is obviously a relationship between these two forms of language, but this should not disguise the fact that, on the whole, they have different functions. After all, if speech could perform all the linguistic functions that society requires, there would be no need for the slow and laborious process of writing at all. In the beginning, writing was almost certainly devised because there was a need to keep records – of property, of commercial transactions, of legal judgements and so on. Most of the early writing that has been found consists of lists of one kind or another. It is this capacity to store accurately the details found in documents like statutes, contracts, wills, census records, and registers of births, marriages and deaths which gives writing its place at the heart of a complexly organized, centrally administered society. No human memory can hold all that information. It follows that writing enables the knowledge of centuries to accumulate; each new generation can build on the ideas, discoveries and inventions of the one before. Academic subjects such as history, geography and all the sciences owe their very existence to writing.

Although the permanence of writing is fundamental to its storage function, it is not that alone which makes it an essential tool of academic study. (After all, in modern times oral language also can be stored, by means of tapes or cassettes.) Almost as important is the physical layout of the material. Foss and Hakes (1978, p. 327) point out that, 'The eye differs from the ear in that the former accepts information in parallel while the latter is a serial device.' This, and the fact that the eye can skim rapidly back and forth through the text, means that the reader can make comparisons, note contrasts and detect inconsistencies in a way that is impossible for the listener.

Another function of writing not served by speech is labelling. We can think of street names, signposts, nameplates on shops, offices and public buildings, as well as the brand labels of thousands of products. Together with these we can include the instructions for use, and danger warnings found on many packages and containers. It is true that in earlier times this naming role was often fulfilled by symbols, such as the striped pole outside the barber's shop and three brass balls outside the pawnbroker's. There ARE pictorial labels in use today, especially in international settings like airports, because it is easy to designate facilities like telephones and restaurants in this way or to draw attention to dangers such as inflammable or explosive substances, but most of the name labels that surround us daily defy such simple replacement. I cannot think, for example, of symbols that would unambiguously express 'Education Office' or 'Department of Health and Social Security'.

The most basic uses of writing, then, are concerned with the recording of facts, ideas and information. Although speech too has an informative function, at least as important is its role in establishing and maintaining human relationships. A great deal of everyday speech with friends, acquaintances and chance contacts has more to do with being sociable than with any kind of intellectual enquiry.

An advantage that writing has over speech is that it enables ideas to be explored at leisure and in private, without fear of interruption or disagreement. It can therefore become a means of extending one's own thinking and of clarifying one's ideas. When a controversial topic is raised in conversation, there is a tendency for opinions to polarize; if someone tries to express more than one point of view, he will be pressed to say 'what he really thinks' – and he may well find himself defending a position he does not really hold. In such circumstances it is very difficult to follow through all the ideas clearly; many people have had the experience of thinking of the telling point, the clinching argument, hours later. In writing, however, it is perfectly possible to take an 'on the one hand, on the other hand' stance (as some newspaper editorials, notably in *The Guardian*, demonstrate). Because there is time to develop a line of thought, to look back over the accumulating evidence, to weigh opposing arguments, to notice errors in reasoning, it can happen that, in the process of writing, the writer makes a new synthesis of ideas, sees a new connection, or even espouses a new viewpoint. So writing is a vital intellectual tool not just because it allows information to be stored but also because it enables a different kind of thinking to take place. (Anthropologists such as Goody (1977) and Greenfield (1972) suggest that there is evidence of differences in cognitive style between oral and written cultures.)

A specialized function of writing is found in literature. Societies with a strong oral culture have an oral literature but it has to be restricted to rather a few types: ballads and epic poetry; drama based on traditional stories; and folk stories, myths and so on, where the basic narrative is well known and the teller embroiders the tale as he goes along. Mnemonic devices, such as alliteration, rhyme, refrains and set phrases, are a necessary characteristic of oral poetry. With writing, it is possible to have a wide range of types of poetry, as well as plays with original plots, and novels too – a form not found in oral cultures at all. Not only are there far more examples of a much wider range of literary genres, but also they are available to anyone who can read them. Readers are not dependent on a travelling poet or storyteller.

Normally, a choice does not arise over whether to use speech or writing for a particular purpose: school registers have to be written, instructions in a PE lesson have to be spoken. Sometimes there is the possibility of either a letter or a phone call, of either a written memo or a personal conversation. Even here the choice is not always as open as it may seem: if the message is important and a record of it will be needed, then the written form will be preferred; if the message is urgent, and the recipient far away, then the telephone will be more appropriate.

Some rather general differences between speech and writing have been outlined; we can now turn to more specifically linguistic differences in form, structure and discourse organization.

4.2 DIFFERENCES IN FORM

Speech sounds: phonemes

The most obvious difference in form between speech and writing is that speech consists of sounds and writing of letters. It is easy to think that the letters represent the sounds. In order to see how far this is true, we must introduce some technical description of speech. If we take the word *rip* we can analyse it into three minimal units of sound: *r-i-p*. However, the term 'sound' is not very helpful because it is too vague. If we think of the different ways in which a Scotsman and an Englishman pronounce the word *rip* it becomes clear that there are (at least) two different 'r' sounds. The important point is that these different pronunciations of 'r' are not **contrastive**. That is, although they make the word SOUND different they do not give it a different meaning. Sounds are said to be **in contrast** when the substitution of one for another brings about a change of meaning. Thus the sound 'l' is in contrast with 'r' because the substitution of 'l' gives the new word *lip*. It is the lack of contrast between the various 'r' sounds that enables us to think of them in some way as 'the same sound', although they are physically different. All the possible pronunciations of 'r' are manifestations of the **phoneme** /r/. The phonemes of a language are those minimal sound units which contrast with each other. (They are always written between slant brackets.) Thus /r/ and /l/ are phonemes because they are in contrast. The different pronunciations of /r/, however, are not phonemes because they are not in contrast; they are called **allophones** of the phoneme.[2] Therefore, there are many differ-

2 Compare the pair of terms, **morpheme** and **allomorph**, on p. 114.

ent 'r' sounds but only one /r/ phoneme in English. Now we can consider the allophones of the phoneme /l/. If you say *lip* and then *pill*, you will notice that the two 'l' sounds are very different: the first is made at the front of the mouth (and is sometimes called 'clear l'), the second is made at the back of the mouth (and called 'dark l'). It is quite possible to say *lip* with a dark *l*; it sounds odd but it does not produce a word with a different meaning. So clear and dark *l* are not in contrast but rather are allophones of the phoneme /l/.[3] Now, instead of saying as we did at the beginning of this paragraph that *rip* consists of three sounds we can say more accurately that it consists of three phonemes.

There are approximately forty-four phonemes in English. (The precise number depends upon the particular accent of English that is being described and the system of analysis that is being followed.) These phonemes are referred to as **segmental** features of the sound system because they are discrete units, they occur in sequence and they can (more or less) be produced and identified in isolation from each other.[4]

Speech sounds: non-segmental features

As well as the segmental phonemes, there are also two non-segmental aspects of the sounds of speech: these are **paralinguistic** features and **prosodic** features. Both aspects relate to the production not of individual phonemes but of whole words, phrases and clauses.

Paralinguistic features

Paralinguistic features include the pitch and timbre differences which usually enable us to distinguish male from female voices; general voice quality, such as breathiness or nasality; and the overall manner of speech production – whether an utterance is shouted, spoken, or whispered, for example.[5] These features do not generally affect the meaning of an utterance. They may reveal something of the speaker's attitude to what he is saying or of the physical conditions in which he is speaking, but the meaning of 'Bob isn't going to China' remains the same whether it is shouted or whispered and whether it is said by a man or a woman.

3 For a more detailed account of the phoneme, see Wells & Colson (1971, pp. 81–6).
4 This does not mean, however, that phonemes are unaffected by their phonemic environment. On the contrary, surrounding phonemes have an important influence. For example, a vowel is affected by the consonant that follows it – the /i/ is longer in *bead* than it is in *beat*, for instance; and some consonants are **aspirated** (i.e. produced with audible breath) in some environments but not others, e.g. /p, t, k/ are aspirated at the beginning of a stressed syllable but not when they occur after /s/, so the /p/ in *pin* and *spin* is pronounced differently.
5 By restricting the term 'paralinguistic' to non-linguistic uses of the voice, I am using it more narrowly than some writers who also include all non-verbal communication, such as gesture, eye contact, body posture, and so on.

Prosodic features

Prosodic features include intonation, stress and rhythm. Together, these features make up the characteristic 'tune' of the language (or, more accurately, of the various dialects of the language, since prosodic aspects are noticeably different from region to region: for example, the varieties of English spoken in Wales and Northern Ireland differ prosodically from each other and from the English spoken in southeast England). The easiest way to think of this cluster or prosodic features is to contrast normal spoken English, of any region, with the speech of Daleks, or other fictional robots. Characteristically, robots are made to talk in a monotone (losing the pitch variation of intonation), and to give even stress to each syllable, forfeiting the contrast between light and heavy stresses which is an important feature of English rhythm.

We need to note three formal aspects of prosodic features:

i) **the nuclear syllable.** This is the most prominent syllable in a sequence because it receives the intonation **nucleus**; that is, it is the place where the pitch movement of the **nuclear tone** begins. This movement may be a simple fall or rise, in which case the nuclear syllable is marked ` or ´; or it may be bi-directional, with a fall-rise marked ˘ and a rise-fall marked ˆ. (These symbols were used in the extracts from Fawcett & Perkins (1980) in chapter 3.) Because the nuclear syllable is intonationally prominent, it is always perceived as being stressed. An example of a nuclear syllable with a falling nuclear tone is given in (1):
1 he fell òver/

ii) **the tone unit.** This is a group of words that are bound together by one intonation **contour** (or **tune**). The tone unit has a nuclear syllable and a number of other syllables which may be stressed or unstressed. Following Fawcett and Perkins' practice, the boundaries between tone units are marked / in this book; non-nuclear stressed syllables are marked ', e.g.:
2 the pol'iceman fell o'ver/

There is generally a high degree of grammatical cohesion between the words within a tone unit. In other words, there are likely to be closer grammatical relationships between words within one tone unit than between those that are separated by a tone-unit boundary. It is not surprising, therefore, that a tone-unit boundary often coincides with a clause boundary: Crystal (1980, p. 160) reports that in a sample of casual conversation among adults, '54 per cent of clauses are exactly one tone unit in length'. In example (3), there are two tone units, each one clause long:
3 he fell óver/ when he 'ran across the ròad/

However, when speech is particularly emphatic, tone units may

correspond with smaller grammatical units, such as phrases, e.g.:
4 the políceman/ fell óver/ when he 'ran across the ròad/

Whether a clause has more than one tone unit partly depends on length; as a very rough guideline, Quirk *et al.* (1972, p. 938) suggest that a tone unit is generally not more than about ten words long.

iii) **the intonation contour.** We have seen that a nuclear syllable is prominent because it begins the pitch movement called the nuclear tone. Pitch patterns before the nuclear tone are very variable but a common pattern has a high-level pitch beginning on the first stressed syllable in the tone unit and continuing up to the nucleus. The combination of the pre-nuclear pitch pattern and the nuclear tone forms the overall contour or tune of the tone unit. There are very many contours that can be used in English, but a rather small number occur with great frequency – O'Connor and Arnold (1961, 1973, pp. 40–90), for instance, describe ten.

Functions of prosodic features.   There are four major functions of prosodic features:

i) Intonation can enable the communicative role of an utterance to differ from its grammatical form. For example, sentence (5a) has the grammatical structure of a statement:
5a He's lost it.

Typically, this would be said with a falling nucleus on *lost*, i.e.:
5b he's lòst it/

If a speaker says this with a rising nucleus, then it will have the communicative effect of a question:
5c he's lóst it/

ii) The speaker uses prosodic features to group words into information units, since each tone unit represents one unit of information. This grouping – which is often but not necessarily delimited by a pause – enables the listener to divide the flow of words into grammatically related clusters, so that, for example, all the items in a long NP are perceived and processed as one constituent. We are not normally aware of this grouping function of intonation, but it becomes immediately obvious when someone who is reading aloud gets it wrong. This sometimes happens when a television newsreader is reading the news from the autocue in front of him. He may say:
6a the 'new version of the práyer book/ was intro'duced by the Archbìshop/

He then sees the next line of the autocue, with the words *of Canterbury* and he adds the correction:

6b . . . by the Arch'bishop of Cànterbury/

Because the falling nuclear tone on *-bishop* in (6a) has indicated a completed information unit, it is not possible simply to add *of Canterbury*; rather, the whole phrase has to be repeated so that the nucleus can be moved to *Canterbury*.

iii) Prosodic features enable the speaker to place emphasis on any word in the tone unit. The normal placement of the nuclear tone is on the stressed syllable of the last lexical word in the unit – as in examples (1) to (6). However, for special purposes, the nucleus can occur earlier in the tone unit, e.g.:

7   Bŏb didn't fall 'over/

Here, the meaning is contrastive: that it wasn't Bob who fell over but someone else. This function of prosodic features is very important in revealing the **focus of information**; that is, the part of the communication which the speaker wants to highlight, usually because it is new to the listener. (We saw on p. 31 that new information characteristically occurs at the end of a clause. As the end of a clause often coincides with the end of a tone unit, this shows why there is a strong tendency for the nuclear syllable to occur at the end of a tone unit. This characteristic of English is referred to as **end-focus**.)

iv) The fourth function of prosodic features is to convey the speaker's attitude. The literal meaning of an utterance may be insignificant in comparison with the overtones imparted to it by stress, rhythm and intonation contour. It is well known, for example, that rudeness may lie more in the way words are said than in the words themselves. Similarly, it is a common experience that *no* can be pronounced with a falling nuclear tone to sound dogmatic and final, or with a fall-rise to mean 'no, but . . .' or even, 'perhaps yes'. It is not only the choice of nuclear tone, though, that reveals attitude; the whole contour is important. For example, *yes/no* questions usually begin with a fairly high stressed syllable and end with a low rising nuclear tone, e.g.:

8   'are you staying to lúnch/

Said like this, the question sounds warm and enthusiastic. If the sentence begins on a low pitch, however, but still ends with a rise, the speaker then sounds uncommitted, sceptical or even disapproving.[6]

We can now consider how far the English writing system is able to represent the sounds of speech – that is, the segmental phonemes and the non-segmental paralinguistic and prosodic features.

6 A fuller account of formal and functional aspects of prosodic features will be found in Quirk *et al.* (1972, pp. 937–43 and 1034–52) and in O'Connor & Arnold (1961, 1973).

Written representation of speech sounds: segmental units

The phonemes of speech are represented in writing by letters, or **graphemes** (by analogy with the term 'phoneme'). A grapheme is not a particular letter form but rather an abstract unit that subsumes all the different shapes that are functionally equivalent, e.g. A, a, *a*, ɑ, etc. It is well known that, in English, the relationship between the set of phonemes and the set of graphemes is peculiarly complex. It becomes clear that it must be, when we realize that there are forty-four phonemes and only twenty-six graphemes.[7] Nevertheless, despite this complexity, phonemes CAN be represented in writing.

Even so, there are two ways in which this representation falls short of being a transcription of the actual segmental units of speech. First, the phoneme is an abstract unit; the physical manifestations are its various allophones. Graphemes represent phonemes, not allophones, so the written form ⟨*rip*⟩ does not distinguish between the pronunciation used by the Scot and the one used by the Englishman, although the two pronunciations are clearly distinguishable in speech. It is worth noting that this apparent limitation of the writing system is, in fact, one of its great strengths, since spelling is neutral with respect to accent. If writers all used a spelling that reflected their own pronunciation, so that books written by Scots were spelt differently from books written by Cockneys, the reading task would be extraordinarily complex and many people would be able to read only those written varieties which bore a close relationship to their own pronunciation. The freeing of the writing system from particular types of pronunciation gives it a currency throughout the English-speaking world and makes it comprehensible across centuries, despite the substantial sound changes that have occurred.

The second reason why graphemes do not represent exactly the segmental units of speech is that written forms are generally invariant whereas speakers are very flexible, changing their style of speech according to whether they are chatting informally with friends, addressing a formal meeting or conducting a telephone conversation against a great deal of background noise. When a word is pronounced in isolation by a careful speaker, all its constituent phonemes can be heard. This is known as the **citation** form. In normal conversational speech, not all words occur in their citation forms because various phonetic alterations take place. We can consider three here.

The first is the change to a **weak form**. This is characteristic of function words, which are usually unstressed in connected speech. Weak forms

---

7 Further reasons for the complexity of the relationship are given in Perera (1979, pp. 136–42). A clear account of the principles underlying the English spelling system is to be found in Stubbs (1980, pp. 43–68).

are shorter than citation forms; they often have elision of some phonemes; and they usually have one of the following vowels: /ə, ɪ, ʊ/. Table 16 gives the citation and weak forms of some common function words.

TABLE 16   Citation forms and weak forms of some common function words

Written form	Citation form	Weak form(s)
and	/ænd/	/ənd, nd, ən, n/
do	/du/	/dʊ, də, d/
him	/hɪm/	/ɪm/
must	/mʌst/	/məst/, məs/
of	/ɒv/	/əv, v, ə/
them	/ðem/	/ðəm, əm, m/

Several function words have the weak form /ə/. This is illustrated in (9b), which is a transcription of a fairly rapid, casual pronunciation of (9a):

9a Two or three girls are having a cup of tea.
9b /tu ə θri gɜlz ə hævɪŋ ə kʌp ə ti/

The second type of alteration is **assimilation**. This is a process whereby two adjacent different sounds become more alike, or even identical; typically, it occurs across word boundaries. For instance, phrases like *cut price* and *ten men* will often be pronounced /kʌp praɪs/ and /tem men/. In each of these examples, the last consonant of the first word has been changed so that it is the same as the first consonant of the second word.

The third type is **elision**. Here, the last consonant of a final consonant cluster may be omitted when the next word begins with a consonant; so *next day* is pronounced /neks deɪ/ and *just right* becomes /dʒʌs raɪt/. All these alterations are a perfectly normal feature of spoken language. They occur in the speech of educated people who are not considered to be careless or sloppy speakers. A pronunciation that uses the citation form of every word sounds either foreign or absurdly stilted.

On the whole, the phonetic alterations of speech are not reflected in writing. There are a few written forms which represent the weak forms of some function words, e.g. *I'll, you're, he's, we've, they'd, can't,* but these are not generally acceptable in formal writing. In teenage magazines other spelling reductions occur, presumably with the aim of capturing the flavour of colloquial speech, e.g. *'cos, boys 'n' girls, f'rinstance, y'know, I spose.* On the whole, though, the abbreviations that are acceptable in formal writing are those that do NOT reflect a particular style of pronunciation, e.g. *Mr, St* (street or saint), *no.* (number), *p.,* etc., *mm., cwt, lb.* For example, the writer's choice of either *doctor* or *Dr* does not reflect the difference between a casual and a formal style; rather, it depends on whether or not the next word is a proper noun; thus, (10) is possible, (11) is not:

10 I saw Dr Smith.
11 *I saw the Dr.

Written representation of speech sounds: non-segmental features

Having considered the extent to which segmental features are represented in writing, we can turn to paralinguistic and prosodic features. Generally, paralinguistic features have no written counterpart. Occasionally in a novel the author will use capital letters for a character's speech to show that he is shouting, and comic strips sometimes use print of increasing size to indicate a crescendo, but such effects are both rare and limited – there is, for example, no written way of representing a whisper. For this reason, a very wide range of words is used in writing to describe the manner of speech. A few examples are: *whine, wheedle, cajole, rant, roar, bellow, murmur, mumble, mutter, wheeze, croak, snuffle, bluster, hector* and *retort*.

As for prosodic features, four functions have already been outlined. These functions differ in the extent to which they can be fulfilled by aspects of the writing system. The first function is changing the communicative role of an utterance. This can be done in writing by means of punctuation, so a sentence used to make a statement will end with a full stop and one used to ask a question will end with a question mark, regardless of grammatical form, e.g.:

12 He's lost it.
13 He's lost it?

Similarly, an exclamation mark and a question mark serve to differentiate two contrasting uses of the same form of words, e.g.:

14 Doesn't she look well?
15 Doesn't she look well!

Secondly, prosodic features are used to group words into grammatically related units. Punctuation does this job only patchily. Sentences are demarcated by an initial capital letter and a final full stop, question mark or exclamation mark. Clauses within compound and complex sentences may be separated by commas, semi-colons or colons. It is sometimes suggested in traditional grammar books that co-ordinate clauses joined by *and* do not need a comma between them; however, in some cases, the use of such a comma can prevent the reader co-ordinating units at the wrong level, e.g.:

16 The headmaster taught the girls, and the boys who had forgotten their games kit had to sit in the cloakroom.

Here, if there were no comma, the reader might co-ordinate the two NPs – *the girls* and *the boys who had forgotten their games kit* – rather than the two clauses. An initial adverbial can be separated from the rest of the sentence by a comma, e.g.:

17 While they were eating, great platefuls of steaming hot food were placed on the table next to them.

Again, if there is no comma, the reader may group the words wrongly, treating the subject of the main clause – *great platefuls of steaming hot food* – as the object of *eating* in the subordinate clause.

In the description of relative clauses (pp. 77–8), it was pointed out that non-restrictive relatives differ from restrictive relatives in being spoken as a separate tone unit and in being enclosed, in writing, between a pair of commas. Similarly, phrases or clauses that in some way interrupt the basic grammatical structure of the sentence, and that are given separate tone units in speech, are set apart in writing by paired punctuation marks: either commas, dashes or brackets, e.g.:

18 They had, *although they were hungry*, refused all food.
19 Because he constantly comes into contact with the larger society – *indeed, is forced to do so* – he comes up against the power of social evaluation.
20 The most common type (*there is probably one of this kind hanging on the wall in your classroom*) consists of a small glass bulb filled with mercury.

Punctuation can also distinguish between an adverbial that modifies a verb and one that modifies a whole sentence, e.g.:

21 He wasn't speaking honestly.
22 He wasn't speaking, honestly.

In (21) *honestly* is spoken in the same tone unit as the verb phrase *wasn't speaking* to give the meaning that he was speaking dishonestly. In (22) there is a separate tone unit for *honestly* and now the sentence means that he was silent.

Next we can consider examples where separate tone units in speech cannot be delimited in writing by punctuation. The most obvious case is the long subject NP. In speech, such an NP always has its own tone unit but there is a strict convention in writing that subject and verb are not separated by punctuation (except when the head noun is followed by an appositional phrase or by a non-restrictive relative clause). This leads to sentences like (23) which are rather awkward to read but present no trouble to the listener:

23 Everyone who knows John knows he will be successful.

The clear prosodic break between *John* and *knows* is not reflected in the writing system. In the following example, the enforced absence of a comma at the end of the subject NP gives the reader a momentary doubt about the role of the adverbial *frequently*:

24 My entirely unscientific opinion poll of over 400 Europeans who visit the USA frequently produced an overwhelming number of votes for San Francisco as the country's most pleasant city.

The adverbial could either modify the verb *produced* in the main clause or the verb *visit* in the relative clause. (In this sentence the writer could have avoided the ambiguity by placing *frequently* before *visit*, i.e. 'Europeans who frequently visit the USA'.)

Here are some further examples where our punctuation conventions are not powerful enough to represent all the word-grouping distinctions that are made by intonation in speech:

25 The struggles of the common people have not yet succeeded, but they have wrested from the rich and powerful institutions which – here and there – defend the poor against the rich.

It looks to the eye of the reader as if there is an NP *the rich and powerful institutions* but to the ear of the listener it would be clear that the NP is *the rich and powerful* and that *institutions* is the object of *wrested*.

26 At a three-hour meeting at Downing Street last night with Mr Callaghan, Mr Len Murray, TUC general secretary, and Mr Moss Evans, TGWU general secretary, seem to have persuaded the Prime Minister that the Government should grant a stay of execution.

The comma is used both to link items in a list and to separate an initial adverbial from the rest of the sentence. In (26), the comma after *Mr Callaghan* is being used to mark off the adverbial, but because two names follow, it is very easy to read *Mr Callaghan, Mr Len Murray . . . and Mr Moss Evans* as a list. (If the author had worded the adverbial, 'At a three-hour meeting *with Mr Callaghan* at Downing Street last night', the problem would have been avoided.) Listing also causes difficulties in (27):

27 He denounced the Corrie Bill on abortion, jury vetting, multi-nationals and the mixed economy.

Here it is not, at first sight, clear whether the denunciation was of the Corrie Bill (which covered a range of topics from abortion to the mixed economy) or of four quite separate subjects, including the Corrie Bill on abortion. Common sense suggests that the second interpretation is the right one because, although a wide range of disparate things may be denounced, they would not normally be yoked together in one parliamentary bill. It is noticeable, however, that general knowledge has been needed to support a linguistic interpretation. (The writer of (27) could have prevented the possible ambiguity by placing *the Corrie Bill on abortion* at the end rather than at the beginning of the list.)

Punctuation, then, has only a limited role in signalling which words belong together in information units. While examples (16) to (22) have shown that some groupings can be demarcated, examples (23) to (27) have revealed two shortcomings of the punctuation system: first, it is not always possible to use a punctuation mark where a tone unit boundary would occur in speech, e.g. after *John* in (23), *frequently* in (24) and *powerful* in (25). Secondly, even where a punctuation mark does correspond to a tone-unit boundary – e.g. the commas after *Callaghan* in (26) and *abortion* in (27) – it may not reveal the grammatical structure, because it cannot convey other relevant features such as pause length and intonation contour.

The third function of prosodic features is to distribute emphasis appropriately throughout the utterance. We have seen that the placing of the intonation nucleus establishes the focus of information in the clause. This is particularly noticeable in questions, where the nuclear tone pinpoints the part of the sentence that is being queried. In the question at (28), the nucleus – and thus the focus of interrogation – can fall on a range of words; the appropriate answer to the question differs according to the placement of the nucleus:

28a 'did John fly to 'Edinburgh on Sáturday/
      No, Sunday.
28b 'did John fly to Édinburgh on 'Saturday/
      No, he went to Aberdeen.
28c 'did John flý to 'Edinburgh on 'Saturday/
      Yes, he went from Heathrow.

In fact, although the question is long, the speaker is treating most of it as given information and querying only one aspect of it. So (28c) could be paraphrased like this:

29 I know John went to Edinburgh on Saturday. Did he fly?

In writing, it is difficult for the writer to show that he wants the emphasis placed other than on the last lexical word in the clause; he may use underlining, or italics, or (as in this book) small capitals. But heavy use of these devices is disapproved of in formal styles so, as the author cannot easily move the emphasis to the word of his choice, he has to move the word to the end of the clause. Leech (1966, p. 89) expresses it like this: 'One of the skills of writing formal English consists in arranging one's ideas so as to make the end of each sense group . . . as far as possible the appropriate place for emphasis.' There are several rather literary grammatical constructions which enable the writer to do just this and they will be described in section 4.3. Nevertheless, there are numerous examples in print of failure to get the emphasis in the right place.

Halliday (n.d., p. 9) illustrates this point with the following sentences taken from a book written for young children:

30 This was the first railway engine. Steam made it go.

He comments that the emphasis in the second sentence falls naturally on *go*, when clearly the focus of information is *steam*. The author could have achieved the desired effect by writing, for example, 'It was driven by steam.' Such a simple solution is not always available. A recent newspaper article about Sir Ralph Richardson contained this statement:

31 The desk has a drawer full of pipes and another of photographs, both of Sir Ralph and by him.

Here, emphasis is required on the normally unstressed function words, *of* and *by*, but there is no easy way for the author to indicate this.

It is not only nucleus placement which is significant in speech but also the choice of nuclear tone. Quirk *et al.* (1972, p. 1044) state that, 'a tone unit has a falling nucleus unless there is some specific reason why it should not.' One reason for the use of a rising tone is to show that a statement is functioning as a question; it has already been pointed out that this is readily indicated in writing by a question mark. Another reason is to signal that the utterance is incomplete; this is sometimes marked in writing by trailing off into dots . . . But, in addition, there are some contrasts of meaning that are conveyed in speech entirely by the choice of nuclear tone which are impossible to convey directly in writing. For example, a falling tone can have a neutral meaning where a fall-rise is contrastive:

32a Tom 'likes 'Jean's sìster/
32b Tom 'likes 'Jean's sǐster/

(32b) suggests that although Tom likes Jean's sister, there is someone else that he does not like – her brother, perhaps. In (33), the two different tones on *any* also produce two distinct meanings:

33a you 'won't find 'fossils ànywhere/
33b you 'won't find 'fossils ǎnywhere/

(33a) is a straightforward negative, whereas (33b) means that you will find fossils in some places, but not everywhere. It is obvious from the use of special notation for prosodic features and from the need for rather elaborate glosses that the contrasted meanings expressed in the spoken versions of (32) and (33) cannot be captured by the conventional writing system.

The fourth function of prosodic features is to convey the speaker's attitude. This is achieved partly by the choice of nuclear tone (a rising nucleus may sound tentative or guarded, for example) but also by the overall contour of the tone unit, and by speed, rhythm and stress. O'Connor and Arnold (1961, 1973, p. 5) comment:

To describe exactly the attitude which a given pitch pattern expresses is not always easy, for the very good reason that such attitudes are more often conveyed in tunes than in words, so that the words are not readily available. *It is this difficulty that writers are constantly facing,* and one measure of a writer's success is his ability to solve the problem of suggesting the exact meaning he has in mind even though he has no direct method of conveying intonation. (My italics)

A dramatic way of discovering how much attitudinal information is conveyed by prosodic features is to compare a transcript of spontaneous speech with the original tape-recording. A journalist who listened to one of the Watergate tapes wrote this about Nixon:

Once you hear the tapes, and the tone in which he uttered the comments which previously have only been available in a neutral transcript, any last shred of doubt about his guilt must disappear.

I have attempted to delineate the extent to which the writing system represents the sounds of speech. To summarize: graphemes represent the phonemes of the citation forms of words; punctuation signals the grammatical function of a sentence and marks some, though by no means all, tone unit boundaries. However, the writer has no conventionalized means of expressing regional accent, voice quality, volume, speed, rhythm and intonation patterns. He has to exercise skill and to employ rather literary grammatical structures in order to convey his intended emphasis. All of this means that the signalling of the focus of information can be difficult in writing and that the expression of emotional attitudes is very hard indeed.

Written forms with no oral counterparts

Having considered those aspects of speech which cannot be successfully written down, we can now look at aspects of writing which cannot be easily expressed in speech.

First, there are features that arise from the physical format of the text. Most obviously, written language clearly identifies words (by a white space on either side), sentences (by an initial capital letter and a final punctuation mark), and paragraphs (by indentation). None of these units is unambiguously and consistently demarcated in speech. In the following examples, there is just one phonetic transcription for the two phrases in each pair because they are physically identical in speech, despite the fact that word boundaries fall in different places; in writing, the two members of each pair are evidently different:

a tax on buildings	attacks on buildings	/ə'tæks ɒn 'bɪldɪŋz/
a nice cream	an ice cream	/ə'naɪs krim/

In addition, various written genres are distinguishable by their layout on the page. The reader can usually tell at a glance whether he is looking at a newspaper, a diary or a letter; a work of fiction or non-fiction; a play, a poem or a novel. A similarly brief snatch of speech heard on the radio is not always so readily identified. In print (as opposed to hand-written text or typescript) there is a variety of type fonts that can be used for different purposes. This is probably most clearly illustrated in news-papers, where a wide range of styles is used for headlines, subheadings, picture captions and sometimes for the key sentence in a paragraph. Such diversity allows a subtle grading of the news, according to the editor's view of its importance. On radio news bulletins, prominence has to be achieved solely by the ordering and length of the news items, not by the manner of their presentation. Dramatists are able to differentiate their stage directions and the names of the characters from the text of the play by the printer's use of italics and small capitals. Even in novels, which generally have a rather uniform style of printing, distinctions can be made that are not possible in speech or handwriting. Italics, for example, are used for the names of books, newspapers and ships. This is exploited in the following sentence about a ship and its eponymous owner – some of the meaning would be lost if it were read aloud:

34 *Maurice* was deserted, Maurice having been invited, as he quite often was, to go down for the day to Brighton.

Secondly, there are features of the spelling system that do not have an equivalent in speech. For example, proper names are distinguished from common nouns by a capital letter in writing, so *Cook, cook*; *Baker, baker* and *Teachers, teachers* cannot be confused. Then, many pairs of words that sound the same are spelt differently: there are more than one thou-sand homophones in English but only about 160 homographs (Whitford, 1966).[8] Thus, some misunderstandings which occur in speech would be avoided in writing. A journalist reported the following exchange between a television interviewer and Nancy Reagan:

35 The TV interrogator burbled, 'And now Mrs Reagan, tell us about your famous Gaze.' Nancy's tight little smile tightened into invisi-bility. 'Gays?' she said coldly.

A mistake which reveals the usefulness of both capital letters and spelling differentiation occurred in a local authority where the colour of a new fleet of buses was to be decided. An official asked the transport manager what colour they were to be painted. 'See Green,' he replied, and the authority got sea-green buses. Although, generally, written forms are more finely differentiated than spoken forms, there are occasional

8 These figures are based on American English and would be slightly different for British English. For example, the following pairs – given as homophones by Whitford – are not homophonous for British speakers: *awful/offal*; *balm/bomb*; *marry/merry*; *hostel/hostile*.

instances of one spelling having two pronunciations, e.g. *read, row* and *tear*. This allows the creation of visual puns that have no oral counterpart. The following example is a cumulative piece of graffiti (a specifically WRITTEN form of humour) provided by two anonymous authors:

36 In Communist China the workers take the lead.

In Capitalist Britain the thieving sods take the brass, the copper and the fillings from your teeth as well.

Thirdly, some aspects of punctuation have no direct equivalent in speech. The apostrophe which marks the possessive form of the noun enables the reader, unlike the listener, to distinguish between singular and plural possessors and between the possessive and plural forms of nouns. These contrasts are shown in the (a) and (b) versions of sentences (37) and (38):

37a He was surprised by the Union's decision.
37b He was surprised by the Unions' decision.
38a We saw the ships sail.
38b We saw the ship's sail.

Quotation marks serve a very useful function in writing. It is not uncommon to hear someone giving a lecture say, 'And I quote' and, 'end of quotation', because he has no simpler means of delimiting the borrowed words.

Then brackets have a number of uses. Square brackets are most often used when a writer is quoting from someone else and wants to add a gloss or insertion of his own. By using square brackets, he is able to include a comment at the appropriate moment, while making it visually clear that the words are his and not part of the quotation. If such a text is read aloud, the reader has to insert an explanatory sentence to give the parenthetic material its correct status. Even curved brackets can be used to enclose items which could not be read aloud unchanged. This happens especially in non-fiction, such as history and geography textbooks, where there are accepted conventions for this type of highly elliptical reference, e.g.:

39 Benvenuto Cellini (1500–1571) of Florence was the most famous Renaissance goldsmith.

(It is worth noticing that when dates are given after the name of a king they sometimes span his life and sometimes his reign.)

40 They are found in Bohemia (Czechoslovakia), South Africa and the United States.

If (40) were read aloud, it would sound as if Bohemia and Czechoslovakia were two places on the list whereas, in fact, Czechoslovakia is an (inaccurate) gloss on Bohemia. Brackets are frequently used in children's books to enclose a simpler version of a technical term, e.g.:

41 Ancient Egyptian jewellers used *motifs* (patterns) such as *scarabs* (sacred beetles), lotus blossoms or falcons.

Sometimes a whole clause would be needed to express the bracketed information in speech, e.g.:

42 On the plain (Jan. 4°C) snow falls on perhaps only twenty days each year.

An oral version of (42) would have to be something like, 'On the plain, *where the mean January temperature is 4 degrees centigrade . . .*' Brackets can also be used to offer the reader two alternatives at once from which he can make a choice, e.g.:

43 It would be a brave government which would bring in such changes in a (the?) principal medium of modern world communication.

The compression of meaning in (43) has no counterpart in speech. To be read aloud the sentence would have to be expanded, e.g. '. . . such changes in a principal medium of modern world communication – indeed, some might consider it THE principal medium.'

Lastly, there is the use of inverted commas, which have a variety of functions apart from marking direct speech. They can be used to draw attention to a technical term, e.g.:

44 The oil is 'cracked', to form some of the products from which petrol is made.

Or they can show that a word is being used metaphorically:

45 Some torpedoes can 'listen' for the noise of a ship's engine.

In formal writing, authors use inverted commas to apologize for the presence of nicknames and colloquialisms, e.g.:

46 One of the sets of instruments on a submarine in the US Navy is called the 'Christmas Tree'.
47 This was called the *dividend*, or 'divi'.

Inverted commas can be used to show that something is not genuine, e.g.:

48 In 1680 a way of making imitation pearls was invented and strings of these 'pearls' became very popular.

More subtly, they express two points of view at once:

49 The Romans could dash out to fight off any northern 'barbarians' trying to cross to the south.

Here the author is saying, in effect, 'The Romans considered the Scots to be barbarians but we know that they were not really.' In rather similar vein, writers use inverted commas to mean, 'I am using this term as a convenient piece of shorthand although we all know that it is not strictly accurate,' e.g.:

> 50 Bereiter and Engelmann's programme consists of intensive drills in the use of 'correct' English.

It is hardly surprising that not all these various meanings can be directly expressed in speech; speakers often use the term 'so-called' before saying the word that would be highlighted in writing by inverted commas.

Amongst educated people, the conventions of the writing system are so firmly established that they are frequently fed back into the spoken language. So a speaker will spell out a word to distinguish it from its homophone, or make inverted commas in the air with his fingers. He will even say, 'As a footnote, let me add . . .,' or 'In parenthesis, may I say . . .,' or 'I must underline this point' – all, in effect, metaphorical expressions derived from writing.

4.3 DIFFERENCES IN GRAMMATICAL STRUCTURE

The physical, situational, functional and formal differences between speech and writing lead to significant differences in the grammatical structure of spoken and written language. In other words, it is not simply the case that writing cannot provide an exact transliteration of speech sounds but rather that the two modes each have their own distinctive patterns of organization. We can consider the grammatical structures that are particularly characteristic of either speech or writing under the headings of the four types of difference that have already been outlined.

Differences related to physical production

High redundancy in speech

Speech is typically produced spontaneously. This means that there is little time for planning, so spoken language is characterized by false starts, incomplete utterances, hesitations, repetitions, rephrasings, fillers such as *well* and *you know*, and voiced pauses (usually written *er* and *umm*). We can start by looking at two transcripts of spontaneous speech that illustrate some of these rather general features. The first is an extract from a televised interview with Bill Beaumont, the former English Rugby Union captain (dashes in the transcription indicate pauses):

> 51 *Int.:* What was the atmosphere like in the morning?
>   *B.B.:* 'well – the side's mor'ale was grèat/ that er – – I 'opened my bedroom window/ on the 'morning of the gáme/ I 'thought

mm 'typical 'Lancashire wèather/ [laughs] this er – just just our cup of tèa this/ that er these er – 'guys off the er – – the high vèldt/ aren't going to be 'too keen on this weather/ must be – conditions very wèt/

This extract has hesitations, voiced pauses, the filler *well*, a false start (*must be – conditions very wet*), repetitions (e.g. *just just*), and an incomplete utterance (*the side's morale was great that er – –*). Although the visual appearance of the transcription suggests that the language was hesitant and disjointed, the auditory impression of the interview was that it was fluent and coherent. In this connection we can note a comment by Goldman-Eisler (1964, pp. 119–20):

An average of 40 to 50 per cent of utterance time is occupied by pauses. Evidently pausing is as much part of the act of speaking as the vocal utterance of words itself, which suggests that it is essential to the generation of spontaneous speech.

False starts, rephrasings and so on arise because there is usually insufficient time for the speaker to plan a whole utterance before starting to talk and he may change his mind in mid-course. The fillers and voiced pauses tell the listener that the speaker has not finished yet but is searching for a word. (An unfilled pause is often taken by the listener as a signal that he can start speaking.)

Another notable feature of (51) is that, despite the fact that it falls into clear information units, delineated by tone unit boundaries, it is not easy to punctuate it using the conventions of the writing system. This leads some grammarians to distinguish between the SENTENCES of written language and the UTTERANCES of spoken language, on the grounds that sentences are clearly delimited constructions, consisting of one or more clauses with obvious structural relationships, whereas utterances are looser collections of information units that cannot always be analysed unhesitatingly and exhaustively in terms of sentence structure. Writing of informal conversational speech, Crystal (1980, p. 159) says:

This variety of English . . . does not seem to be readily analysable in terms of sentences. Rather the CLAUSE is the unit in terms of which the material is most conveniently organized.

It is generally the case that the information units of speech are most often linked by devices of co-ordination, while clauses in writing are frequently joined by the hierarchical processes of subordination, which gives a more tightly integrated texture to the language.

The second transcript, (52), provides a clear example of a high level of repetition in spontaneous speech. It comes from Quirk (1972, p. 108) and, apart from pauses, prosodic features are not marked:

52 All the time he tries to maintain a balance he talks about naturalism in education and and – he's started on pragmatism – I haven't

had time to follow up this in in my reading at all but – all the time – he tries – – er to maintain a balance I mean he he he criticizes points of the naturalistic approach of the – approach of of of er the er er um originating from Rousseau – and then he criticizes um points in the pragmatic approach – test of experience all the time he criticizes that he says it doesn't allow enough weight – for – the value er of tradition – all the time he tries to maintain this balance.

Even ignoring 'stammer-type' strings of words (e.g. *he he he*), there is still a great deal of repetition in this extract: *all the time* occurs four times and *he tries to maintain a balance*, *criticizes* and *approach* three times each.

The use of co-ordination, repetition and rephrasing causes spoken language to have a low level of **lexical density** and a high level of **redundancy**. This means that lexical words are spaced out, separated by grammatical words, and that a high number of words is used to convey a given amount of information. Obviously, these features aid not only the speaker's production of language but also the listener's reception. Such assistance is necessary, since the listener does not have the reader's opportunity to backtrack in order to retrieve a forgotten word. (This is sometimes forgotten by people writing scripts for radio and television; Edward Blishen commented in a review of television programmes: 'I could not, alas, watch the recent *The Shock of the New* because Robert Hughes spoke too densely for me – I had not time to decide whether I understood what he was saying or not.')

In addition to the fairly general features of co-ordination, repetition and rephrasing, there are also some grammatical constructions which occur more commonly in speech than in writing and which have the effect of decreasing lexical density and increasing redundancy. Most of the illustrations which follow are taken from Fawcett and Perkins' (1980) transcripts; there is no suggestion, however, that these structures are immature – they are widespread in adult speech too.

Extraposition of clausal object.   Here the clausal object is delayed until the end of the sentence, its structural position being filled by the pro-form *it*, e.g.:

53a I 'worked *it* out where the trèe [should] be/   (8 years; II, p. 34)

In writing, the unextraposed version at (53b) would be more likely:

53b I worked out where the tree should be.

Extraposition of subject participial clause.   Even in writing it is common for a finite subject clause to be delayed by means of the extraposition transformation (e.g. 'It is certain *that he will come*' rather than '*That he will come* is certain'). But the use of extraposition with non-finite participial subject clauses is more common in speech than writing, e.g.:

54a It's a waste of time *doing that.*

Again, the structural position of the delayed element (*doing that*) is filled by the pro-form *it*. The sentence is derived from the SVC sentence at (54b):

54b <u>Doing that</u> <u>is</u> <u>a waste of time.</u>
      S   V   C

Tag statement. In this construction, the subject and verb of a statement are repeated in the form of a pronoun and an operator tagged on at the end. It is very common in the Fawcett and Perkins transcripts, particularly when the children are talking to each other rather than to an unknown adult, e.g.:

55 I'm en'joying this/ *Í am/* (12 years; IV, p. 5)

Amplificatory noun phrase tag. In this case, a pronoun is used to fill the appropriate grammatical position in the sentence and the reference of the pronoun is clarified by the addition of a noun phrase at the end of the sentence, outside the basic clause pattern, e.g.:

56a it was 'really prècious *that cat/* (10 years; III, p. 134)

The written version would be briefer:

56b That cat was really precious.

Recapitulatory pronoun. This construction was described and exemplified in chapter 3 (p. 96). Here is a further example:

57 the 'women 'teachers – *they* 'do 'stop them from shŏuting/
(12 years; IV, p. 126)

Quirk (1972, p. 104) comments that the colloquial recapitulatory pronoun 'involves disjuncture, with the effect of *foregrounding* a lexical cluster of special importance in the communication'. He carried out an experiment to discover the effects of this foregrounding on listeners' comprehension of spoken language. Two passages were constructed, each containing the same information. In passage A the key noun phrase (italicized below) was introduced early and recapitulated by a pronoun later:

A He's doing research on *the mineral resources of various parts of the Commonwealth* – the procedures for assessing, the methods of surveying and the techniques for exploiting them.

In contrast, in passage B, this noun phrase occupied the position it would have in written English:

B He's doing research on the procedures for assessing, the methods of surveying and the techniques for exploiting *the mineral resources of various parts of the Commonwealth.*

Each passage was read to a different group of thirty-five undergraduates studying English, who were then asked to give a written recall of what they had heard. The students who heard passage A remembered, on average, 60 per cent of the information while those who heard passage B recalled only 45 per cent. This result suggests that there are sound psycholinguistic reasons for the more redundant constructions that occur in speech.

It is worth pointing out that a great deal of the apparently spontaneous speech that we hear on radio and television is, in fact, written language either read or learnt by heart. Dramatists do not often write scripts that contain all the repetitions and rephrasings of genuine speech – if they did, their audiences would get very bored – and actors rarely use the hesitations and voiced pauses of the ordinary speaker, since such naturalism makes it sound as if they have forgotten their lines. When reporters talk fluently and articulately to the camera they are usually reading from an autocue. Abercrombie (1965, pp. 1–9) calls such language 'spoken prose', to distinguish it from spontaneous speech. The widespread occurrence of spoken prose, which is really written language read aloud, can easily blind us to the fundamental differences between speech and writing.

Low redundancy in writing

Written language is typically produced slowly, with the author planning, drafting and rewriting in order to remove errors and false starts – though occasionally professional writers deliberately retain their inaccurate first thoughts in an attempt to achieve a personal, casual style, e.g.:

58 There are just two – no, three – points to remember about making a soufflé.

The laborious style of production (together with the reader's ability to proceed at his own pace, rereading when necessary) allows writing to be less redundant than speech and to have higher lexical density. Britton (1975, p. 113) comments on the growing tendency of writers to dictate their material rather than drafting it on paper, and says:

There are people . . . who do very little to the draft produced by a typist from their dictation and in my experience this seems to result (for reasons I do not fully understand) in writing that I can only call tedious.

I believe that two reasons for the tediousness Britton notes are, first, that language produced in such a way – basically, oral language – tends to lack variety of vocabulary and sentence structure and, second, that it is more prolix than writing need be. In speech, lexical repetition is both less avoidable and more tolerable than it is in writing. The writer can avoid it because, unlike the speaker, he has time to search his memory for the precise word he wants without losing track of his train of thought. The reader finds repetition more irritating than the listener partly because he is processing the language twice as quickly and, therefore, repeated words follow on each other's heels more rapidly and more noticeably. In addition, the reader has only the disembodied text in front of him, while the listener can hear and, usually, see the speaker; the more attention he pays to the speaker's tone of voice, physical appearance and so on, the less he has to spare for the language itself.

Lack of variety in sentence patterns is not necessarily evident in oral language because the speaker is able to vary the rhythm, speed and volume of delivery and to place the intonation nucleus anywhere in the clause. In writing, however, these paralinguistic and prosodic features are absent, so any monotony of grammatical structure is thrown into prominence.

The natural prolixity of speech derives both from repetitions and re-phrasings and from the use of constructions, like those illustrated on p. 185, that increase redundancy. Writing, on the other hand, favours compression, so grammatical structures which decrease redundancy and increase lexical density are typical of the written mode. Here are some examples:

Non-finite subordinate clauses

59 *Paraded through the streets*, he is said to have shown such defiant courage that the Emperor spared his life.

In speech, it is more likely that the subordinate clause would be finite, which would entail the addition of a subordinator, subject and auxiliary verb, i.e. *when he was paraded through the streets*.

Verbless subordinate clauses

60 *When very hot indeed*, the atoms of the other chemicals fit into the hydrocarbon chain.

The finite subordinate clause that would again be more usual in oral language would need a subject and operator: *When they are very hot indeed*.

Ellipsis. We have seen (p. 61) that ellipsis involves the omission of common elements either within or between sentences. This is a very obvious way of reducing redundancy. In the following examples the ellipted words are enclosed in square brackets:

61 Either a magnet is made to spin near a coil of wire or a coil of wire [is made] to spin near a magnet.
62 Other kinds [of larvae] get into some crack or corner above ground.

Nominalizations.   It is sometimes possible for a whole clause to become a long subject noun phrase in the transformed sentence. Example (63a) shows the nominalized version that is typical of writing, whereas (63b) illustrates the less dense style that is more normal in speech:

63a *The extension of fishing limits by Iceland and other countries* has meant that Fleetwood's traditional Distant Water fishing grounds have been closed to its trawlers.

63b <u>Iceland and other countries</u> <u>have extended</u> <u>their fishing limits</u>
       s   v   o

and this has meant that Fleetwood's traditional Distant Water fishing grounds have been closed to its trawlers.

Attributive adjectives.   Lexically-dense subject noun phrases also result if the writer includes several adjectives. Saukkonen (1977, p. 212) gives as an example from written language, *poor lands, unsuitable for intensive cultivation*, and suggests that, in speech, it is more common for the adjectives to occur after a copula verb, in predicative position, e.g. *the lands are poor and they are unsuitable for intensive cultivation*. In the sentences at (64), the attributive adjectives of the written (a) version are expressed in the more colloquial (b) version by a variety of constructions: *better* and *increasing* are replaced by the verbs *improve* and *increase*; *more mechanized* occupies the predicative rather than the attributive position; and *Scottish, mainland* and *employment and population* each become the head of a post-modifying prepositional phrase.

64a *Better, more mechanized farming on Orkney and the increasing efficiency of the Scottish mainland fishing industry* have aggravated employment and population problems.
64b Farming on Orkney has improved and become more mechanized and the efficiency of the fishing industry on the mainland of Scotland has increased; these factors have aggravated problems of employment and population.

These two examples show clearly the contrasts between high and low levels of redundancy and lexical density. (64b) takes thirty-two words to express the same information that is conveyed by (64a) in only twenty-two, so the spoken style of (b) is considerably more redundant than the written style of (a). In (a), the ratio of lexical to grammatical words is

14:8 (or 1.75:1), whereas in (b) it is 16:16 (or 1:1); therefore the written passage is markedly higher in lexical density than the oral one.

The most extreme examples of low redundancy in writing occur in newspaper headlines, telegrams and lecture notes where, for reasons of space, economy or speed, grammatical words are omitted, e.g.:

65a Police seek two men after gasworks explosion.

In speech, thirteen words could well be used to express this seven-word headline, e.g.:

65b The police are looking for two men after an explosion at a gasworks.

There is no oral equivalent of the telegraphic compression illustrated in (65a). It is true that the ITN *News at Ten* programme begins with a sequence of headlines, but I find that they sound very odd. Apart from this and the shipping forecast, abbreviated constructions are not generally read aloud and they are certainly not produced by adults in spontaneous speech.

Differences related to situational factors

Context-dependence in speech

Having considered some of the ways in which physical factors of production and reception influence the grammatical structure of speech and writing, we can turn to the effect of situational factors. Speech is typically produced face-to-face, so speaker and listener share the non-linguistic setting. This means that people and objects that are visible can be referred to by pronouns rather than noun phrases (even though they have not been mentioned before); and a whole range of adverbials, such as *next to me*, *in the corner* and *bolt upright* can be expressed by *here*, *there* and *like this*. The Fawcett and Perkins (1980) transcripts of play sessions with Lego provide abundant examples of this context-dependent reference, e.g.:

66 will '*that one* fit in by *thére*/   (12 years; IV, p. 1)

Speakers also make use of context-dependent ellipsis, where the omitted words can be understood from the situation, rather than from elsewhere in the discourse. To distinguish this type of contextual omission from true language-dependent ellipsis, Quirk *et al.* (1972, pp. 544–5) use the term **sub-audibility**; it is as if the speaker starts the sentence under his breath. In the following examples, the likely 'sub-audible' words are enclosed in square brackets:

67 [it] 'won't fit/ down thère/ nów/   (12 years; IV, p. 2)
68 [I] don't 'need little ones any more/   (12 years; IV, p. 38)

In a conversation, the speaker is typically interacting with the listener, so he does not use statements alone, but also *yes/no* questions and tags to elicit a response, and *wh-* questions which serve to pass the conversational ball to the listener. He may also use exclamations and commands, though it is more normal for the latter to have the grammatical form of questions in a conversation between equals, e.g. *Would you mind shutting the door?* rather than *Shut the door*. Understandably, commands, exclamations and questions do not occur frequently in the more impersonal mode of writing, apart from dialogue and certain specialized styles such as instructions (*Pierce with a pin*), advertisements (*What an amazing offer this is!*) and rhetorical journalism (*Can the industry survive a prolonged strike?*).

Autonomy in writing

Written language has to be more explicit than speech because it stands alone. Therefore, it uses fewer pronouns and pro-forms, more noun phrases and open-class adverbs. Long subject noun phrases, very rare in speech, are frequent in academic writing. Olson (1977, p. 261) makes the point that there is a continuum of explicitness in language: at one end, there is the highly context-dependent oral language of the young child who uses an utterance like *Mommy sock* to mean a variety of things, including *Here is Mommy's sock* and *Mommy is putting my sock on*, according to the situation; at the other end, there is formal written language, capable of standing alone as an autonomous representation of meaning.

It is also the case that the writer makes less overt contact than the speaker with his audience; this is particularly true of factual prose, where the author tends to use an anonymous style and not to acknowledge the existence of the reader. Even in fiction, it is now fairly unusual for the author to address the reader directly – rather rare in modern writing is the Victorian novelist's relationship with the reader, typified by Charlotte Bronte in this sentence in *Jane Eyre*: 'Reader, I married him.'

Differences related to functional contrasts

Informality in speech

The structures used in speech and writing are also affected by the different functions of the two modes. Speech is as much concerned with establishing and maintaining personal relationships as with conveying information, so it makes use of what Quirk (1972, p. 105) calls 'intimacy signals' – expressions like *you know, you see, well*. Spontaneous speech generally fulfils functions that are less formal than those performed by either spoken prose or written language. The informality is evident in the use of contracted auxiliaries and the negative *n't*, e.g. *you've, he'll, can't,* which are not widely acceptable in writing. In addition, the following constructions are notably colloquial and therefore do not occur in styles typical of written language:

'This' and 'these' for indefinite reference. This structure was described in chapter 3 (p. 103); here is a further example (from Fawcett & Perkins):

> 69 well 'there's *this* bòy/ and he 'stays with *these* 'two 'horrible aùnts/ and um 'in his gárden/ – you knów/ there's *this* 'giant pèach/
> (10 years; III, p. 54)

Clause completers. In casual speech, a clause may be completed by a vague expression like *and that, and all* or *and everything*, e.g.:

> 70 it was 'time for 'everybody to 'cut the córn *and everything*/
> (12 years; IV, p. 110)
> 71 I 'like doing êxercises *and that*/ (12 years; IV, p. 117)

Formality in writing

There are a number of constructions that are markedly formal which, for that reason, occur far more frequently in writing than speech. Their informal counterparts are felt by many to be inappropriate in a written text. In a study of such attitudes, Mittins *et al.* (1970) gave a questionnaire to five hundred respondents, who were students, teachers, examiners, lecturers and other professional people, with ages ranging roughly from twenty to sixty-five. They were asked whether or not they would find particular sentences acceptable in four different contexts: formal and informal speech, and formal and informal writing. The average acceptability rating for fifty debatable usages was 41 per cent; in the spoken settings alone, the score rose to 46 per cent whereas in written uses it dropped to 35 per cent. With some items, the contrast between the two scores was more pronounced. All the following examples of formal style are taken from written English; where a comparison can be made with an item in Mittins *et al.*'s study, I shall give the scores they obtained.

Fronting of preposition in relative clause

> 72 Climate to a great extent controls the activities *in which* it is possible for us to engage.

Less formally, the relative clause would be: *which it is possible for us to engage in.*

Whom. This is the objective case of a pronoun that can introduce either a question or a relative clause. The form *whom* may occur when the pronoun is the object of the clause (as in (73)); it HAS to occur when the pronoun follows a preposition (as in (74)):

73 *Whom* did he meet?

74 The people *to whom* she spoke seemed satisfied with the situation.

These are very formal constructions; the only occasion when *whom* is grammatically essential is when it follows a preposition. (Example (72) shows that preposition fronting is, in itself, generally formal.) With a FINAL preposition the relative clause in (74) can easily be expressed, (*who/that*) *she spoke to* but **to who she spoke* is impossible.

Masculine pronoun after unspecified singular noun or pronoun. On p. 38 it was pointed out that there is no sex-neutral pronoun to refer to nouns like *teacher* or to pronouns like *anyone*. In formal writing, the masculine pronoun is frequently used, e.g.:

75 Everyone had completed *his* application and claim forms before the manager returned.

Mittins *et al.* included in their study an item with *their* rather than *his* (*Everyone has their off days*); although 72 per cent of the respondents found this permissible in informal speech, only 19 per cent would accept it in formal writing.

Singular verb after indefinite pronoun

76 None of the farmers in the highland areas *is* confident of a secure future.

Where the indefinite pronoun refers to a plural idea, as in (76), it is often followed in speech by a plural verb.

Indefinite one

77 The kind of thermometer that is used to take *one's* temperature when *one* is ill works in the same way.

In informal settings it is more normal for the pronouns *your* and *you* to be used. This particular example is taken from a school textbook; the use of *one* means that the writer avoids addressing his readers directly and so maintains an impersonal style.

Impersonal use of the passive. The passive has a number of different stylistic functions: one is to minimize references to people. Where there is more than one noun phrase in a clause and only one is animate, English has a stylistic preference for putting the animate noun in subject position. It is not grammatically possible to omit the subject of a clause so, if the writer wants to avoid using an animate noun phrase, he can employ the passive transformation since, by this means, the subject becomes the agent phrase which is then omissible (see p. 52). Obviously this helps to make the style more impersonal, e.g.:

78a Holidays *were spent* in resorts.

The active version would have to have a subject noun phrase like *people*:

78b People spent their holidays in resorts.

Negated negative adjective

79 Out of the total number of burials in London in 1739, *not an untypical year*, over half were of children under eleven years of age.

This cautious style – the author is not prepared to go so far as to say that the year was actually typical – is particularly common in academic writing.

Subjective case pronoun after 'than'

80 Latin-American peoples have a lower incidence of heart disease and cancers than *we*.

In informal settings, the objective case *us* would be more normal. Mittins *et al.* recorded an average acceptability of 42 per cent for the object pronoun, with a marked divergence of scores according to situation: 78 per cent of the subjects considered it appropriate in informal speech but only 16 per cent in formal writing.

Possessive pronoun or noun before a present participle

81 The possibility of *their* being defeated made the Prime Minister pause.

Even more formally, a writer may use a noun rather than a pronoun in the possessive, e.g.:

82 There was no sign of that *amendment's* being adopted.

Speakers are much more likely to use the object pronoun (*them* in (81)) or the stem form of the noun. Mittins *et al.* assessed responses to the object pronoun; they do not give figures for their results but comment that over half accepted it in informal speech, far fewer in formal writing.

Differences related to absence of prosodic features in writing

End-focus

The last factor responsible for structural differences between the two modes is the absence in writing of the prosodic features of speech. We have seen (p. 176) that the writer, being on the whole unable to alter the placement of information focus, has to employ grammatical constructions that enable the word which is to be emphasized to occur at the end of the clause. The examples that follow are of syntactic patterns which are more frequent in written than in oral language because they serve stylistic purposes fulfilled in speech by intonational means. Many of them illustrate the fact that the principle of end-focus often works in harmony with the principle of end-weight; that is that 'the predicate of a clause should where possible be longer than the subject' (Quirk *et al.*, 1972, p. 968).

There is no problem in obtaining end-focus when the word that should be prominent is expressing one of the elements that occur clause-finally anyway, i.e. adverbials, objects and complements. Special effort is required, however, to achieve final position for the subject or verb. Here are some constructions which have that effect:

Passive. One result of the passive transformation is that the subject of the active sentence becomes the agent phrase and follows the verb, e.g.:

83 He was welcomed by the Chancellor of the Exchequer.
    S   V   Agent Phrase

[Active Subject]

It is noticeable in this example that the passive usefully allows 'new' information to appear in its favoured position, at the end of the clause. The passive can enable the verb, too, to be the focus. This comes about if an SVO sentence is passivized and the agent phrase omitted, e.g.:

84a Someone ransacked the house.
     S   V   O

84b The house was ransacked.
     S   V

Fronting of place adverbial. Place adverbials usually occur after the verb; in literary style, however, they may begin a clause, in which case the subject and verb are inverted. By this means, the subject can be placed at the end of a sentence which has the underlying form SVA, e.g.:

85 Beside the entrance way,
         A

    looking at her with dark, unblinking eyes, stood
               A   V

    the biggest rat she had ever seen.
           S

The change of word order provides a dramatic climax to the sentence, in contrast to the more mundane version: 'The biggest rat she had ever seen stood beside the entrance way, looking at her with dark unblinking eyes.' If the subject is a pronoun, rather than a noun or NP, subject-verb inversion does not result from adverbial fronting. Thus the pattern becomes ASV, achieving prominence for the verb, e.g.:

86 <u>Up the steep cliff face</u> <u>they</u> <u>struggled.</u>
   A   S   V

Cleft sentences. This construction was described on p. 82. It allows contrastive focus to be placed on the subject, object or adverbial, but not on the complement or verb, of the underlying clause. Because two clauses are made from one, there are two positions for end-focus. Consequently, the transformation is particularly useful when the original simple sentence is of a length which would, in speech, attract two intonation nuclei, since it specifies where the non-final nucleus should fall. In example (87a), the italicized cleft highlights the subject of the simple sentence:

87a Thus *it is the lowland areas of Scotland* which have the least rainfall and the most sunshine.

The untransformed version would read:

87b Thus the lowland areas of Scotland have the least rainfall and the most sunshine.

This is fourteen words long and in speech would probably be divided into two tone units with two nuclei. The advantage of the cleft construction, for the reader, is that it splits the clause into the appropriate information units for him.

Existential 'there'. The description of this transformation on p. 30 suggests that it can be applied in speech if the simple sentence contains part of the verb *to be*. In literary style, an SV sentence can sometimes undergo the transformation even if it does not include the verb *to be*, e.g.:

88a <u>A complex series of secret negotiations</u> <u>followed.</u>
   S   V

88b There followed a complex series of secret negotiations.

Clearly, the effect of the transformed version, (88b), is to achieve both end-weight (by placing the longest element after the verb), and end-focus on the subject.

Fronting of object. Placing the object at the beginning allows the verb in an SVO sentence to occupy final position, e.g.:

89 <u>That</u> <u>he</u> <u>would not endure.</u>
   O   S   V

Emphasis

The last five constructions illustrated have given prominence to either subject or verb by placing them in clause-final position. Another way of highlighting a particular word in a sentence is to follow it by an 'interrupting construction', that is, one that delays the completion of the basic clause pattern. Interruptions form separate information units and so have a tone unit of their own; this means that the preceding lexical word has nuclear stress, regardless of its position in the clause. In the following examples, the interrupting constructions are italicized:

90 The students' results, *to their surprise and delight,*
       S   A

   were outstanding.
    V   C

When this sentence is spoken, there have to be three intonation nuclei: one on *outstànding*, because it is at the end of the clause; one on *delíght*, since it concludes the interrupting construction; and one on *resúlts*, as it is the last lexical word before the interruption. In this example, it is the subject that is given special prominence; in (91), the verb in the main clause is emphasized by the interrupting adverbial:

91 The economists expected, *in short,*
      S   V   A

   that they would be proved wrong.
               O

The emphatic effect of an interruption is illustrated particularly clearly when the author inserts it in the wrong place, as in this unfortunate example from a newspaper report:

92 Seven young people, mostly in their teens and in clothes (except for a dearth of neckties) acceptable among the City of London congregation, had positioned themselves on either side of the altar.

If the bracketed phrase had followed 'acceptable', the sentence would not have sounded as if the journalist had expected the young people to go to church naked.

So far, I have concentrated on showing how a writer can give prominence to a clause element that otherwise would be unmarked. Now we can consider what happens if he wants to obtain special emphasis not at clause but at phrase level. That is, the appropriate clause element may be in the right position as far as focus is concerned but it may be expressed by a long phrase. Normally the focus falls on the last word of the phrase (which may or may not be the head), e.g. *a large flamboyant straw* HAT, *the mainland fishing industry in* SCOTland. If the writer wants to highlight another word, e.g. *a large flam*BOY*ant straw hat*, there are various constructions that he can use. Unusual word order naturally draws attention to itself, e.g.:

93 She bought a straw hat, *large and flamboyant.*
94 Henry VIII was married six times and of his children *only three* survived him.

This is more arresting than the prosaic *only three of his children.* As at clause level, interrupting constructions serve to accentuate the preceding word, e.g.:

95 Prince Charles has developed a religious – *literally so* – sense of duty.

In the noun phrase the writer can often choose whether to use a word as an attributive adjective or in a post-modifying prepositional phrase or relative clause. The choice leads to a difference of emphasis in each member of the following pairs:

96a The mainland fishing industry in Scotland . . .
96b The fishing industry on the Scottish mainland . . .

97a The following examples . . .
97b The examples which follow . . .

Thematic prominence

As well as manipulating the focus of information, the writer can exploit the stylistic effects of **theme.** This is the initial element of the clause; Quirk *et al.* (1972, p. 945) say:

Apart from the last stressed element of clause structure (that which most naturally bears information focus) the theme is the most important part of the clause.

Subjects and most adverbials occur naturally in initial position; other elements may be fronted to give them thematic prominence. This change of word-order usually interacts with the achievement of end-focus for the important part of the communication. The lexical verb of a passive VP can be fronted (the remaining auxiliary has to precede the subject), e.g.:

98 *Situated* on the east coast is the steel industry.

Complements and objects can also occur as themes:

99 *Small and strange* was the writing.

100 *This problem* he chose to ignore.

Example (85) on p. 194 showed that place adverbials can be fronted; particularly with adverbials of direction, this thematic prominence gives a very literary style, e.g.:

101 *Onward, toward the tiny light,* the weary refugees dragged

                 A   S   V

their precious burden.

             O

I have been illustrating the kinds of construction that the writer can use to compensate for the fact that he lacks the prosodic resources of the speaker. Apart from the cleft sentence, they all function within a single clause. It is necessary, therefore, to point out that the overall arrangement of clauses within a complex sentence also has a stylistic effect. Leech and Svartvik (1975, p. 174) comment:

> In writing you cannot point to important information by using intonation, so you have to rely on ordering and subordination of clauses instead. The general rule is that the most important information is saved up to the end, so that the sentence finishes with a sort of climax.

I do not want to give the impression that writers regularly make conscious decisions to employ the various literary constructions that I have described. It would be absurd to suggest that an author says to himself, 'I shall use a cleft sentence' or, 'I shall front this adverbial'. Nevertheless, the ability to write effectively, unambiguously and elegantly does depend to some extent on the mastery of these linguistic resources and on a sensitivity to the effects they achieve. Similarly, one aspect of advanced reading skill is the (tacit) recognition and comprehension of the grammatical patterns that occur rather rarely in speech.

4.4   DIFFERENCES IN DISCOURSE ORGANIZATION

In conversation, people normally give small amounts of information at a time and add more if the listener seems to want it. This is partly to avoid density of content but also because it is not socially acceptable to assume total ignorance on the part of the listener, or to treat him as if he were a member of a lecture audience. Therefore, (102) is a more likely conversational exchange than (103):

102   *A:*   Where's the director?
       B: He's visiting Senegal.
       A: Where's that?
       B: Africa.
       A: Southern Africa?
       B: No, it's on the west coast, I think.

103 *A:* Where's the director?

    B: He's visiting Senegal, on the west coast of Africa.

In writing, (103) would be perfectly normal. The difference between the two styles of presenting information is nicely (though unintentionally) illustrated in the following extract from a leaflet issued by the Rioja Wine Information Centre:

104 Just the mention of the name [Rioja] enlivens the conversations of wine aficionados all over Europe. *'Yes'*, they say, *'that fertile valley in Spain only two hundred miles south of Bordeaux that is justly famous for extraordinary wines.'*

It is hard to imagine any conversation that would be enlivened by the italicized sentence in (104).

Example (102) shows that spontaneous speech is generally a co-operative product, with different people contributing in turn. This, together with the lack of opportunity for planning and the impossibility of revision, means that, in conversation at any rate (as opposed to debate, for example), speakers characteristically wander freely over a wide range of topics that are not necessarily related in any way. Crystal and Davy (1969, p. 103) comment that, 'at any place in a conversation one may, if desired, "change the subject" without this being felt to be linguistically inappropriate.' However, in most writing, an overall theme is necessary. The material has to be carefully organized so that it forms a coherent, unified whole – with changes of topic justified and made explicit.

An interesting difference between the two forms of language is that exaggeration is much more acceptable in speech than in writing. This is conventionalized in certain expressions that occur only in informal settings, e.g. *He waited* **ages**, *She was carrying* **hundreds** *of parcels, I've got* **tons** *of work to do*. But it is more widespread than that. It is possible in speech for sentences and even whole discourses to be, in a literal sense, untrue without the speaker being a liar. Such episodes occur frequently in the narration of jokes and anecdotes. So long as they are accompanied by the appropriate paralinguistic and non-verbal features, such as laughter, raised pitch and volume, animated facial expression and extravagant gestures, there is little risk of misunderstanding. So a person who is recounting how he was stopped by the police for speeding and who says, in self-justification, 'The road was ten lanes wide at that point' does not expect his listener to reply, 'There aren't any roads as wide as that in Britain.' In writing, when the words have to stand alone, the language is much more likely to be taken literally. This means that fantasizing, teasing and joking are all very much harder on paper. It is not unusual for those who attempt satire or humour in their letters to newspapers to have their efforts misinterpreted. One correspondent wrote to *The Guardian* suggesting that the date of a child's conception should be celebrated, rather than its birthday, since the one was pleasurable for the mother and the other painful. After several earnest responses from readers extolling the joys of natural childbirth, she had to reply, 'My letter was meant to be a light-hearted joke!'

A similar problem is that a great deal of writing skill is needed to express the liveliness and commitment that are non-linguistically evident in spoken language. Therefore, it is not surprising that children's writing often seems either inappropriately exaggerated or flat and dull. A group of pupils who spoke to the Schools Council (1976, p. 17) Writing Across the Curriculum team had a strong feeling that their orally expressed enthusiasm should not be written down. A twelve-year-old boy called Gerald said:

> If you're telling it to friends . . . you say, cor blimey we had a smash-ing time . . . . You can say it to your friends but you can't really write it down, can you? . . . It just wouldn't seem right, you know, you're writing, 'we climbed over the pipes to look at them and it really was great, you know. It was rather fun, you know.'

He concluded that in writing he would have to say, 'We had a very nice time.'

4.5 TYPES OF SPOKEN AND WRITTEN LANGUAGE

This chapter has focused on the differences between spoken and written language. It is important, though, not to think in terms of a simple dichotomy because, although there are sharp contrasts between arche-typal speech and archetypal writing, each mode encompasses a whole range of varieties and some types of speech display some of the charac-teristics of written language (and vice versa).

It is in conversation that archetypal spoken language is to be found. Abercrombie (1965, p. 3) suggests that it:

> contains the most natural, the most frequent and the most widespread occurrences of spoken language. . . . The other uses of spoken lan-guage are adaptations, or specializations, of this basic category.

Conversation is typically spontaneous, informal, ephemeral and inter-active; most often it takes place among people who know each other. The language is supported both by non-verbal communication and by the situational context. Any of these characteristic features can be altered to produce another kind of spoken language. So speeches and lectures are, typically, planned monologues, not necessarily addressed to a known audience; telephone conversations and radio talks lack the visual dimen-sion of a face-to-face encounter; tape-recordings, whether of personal memos or public broadcasts, are durable – and so on. Then there is the spoken language which is writing read aloud or recited – it may be a news broadcast, a church service, or the dialogue in a play.

I do not think that there is a single archetypal variety of written language to compare with conversation. The most distinctive characteristics of writing are that it is planned, organized and durable; it is not bound to any physical setting and is frequently read by people unknown to the author. Two very substantial categories of written language fulfil all these criteria: literature and serious informative prose. Both types tend to be printed rather than hand-written, to be widely disseminated and to be stored for future reference. A difference between them is the relationship of the author to the work. Non-fiction writing is frequently anonymous and, in the case of government reports, legal documents, college prospectuses and so on, may indeed be drafted by a committee. Academic articles and books are frequently written by two or more authors. It is rather unusual for people to comment on the style as opposed to the content of such writing (except perhaps to note that it is particularly obscure or pellucid). Literary writing, on the other hand, is nearly always by a named author whose personal style is an essential part of the work. We do not, therefore, find novels written by a committee or poems by a partnership. Publishers' editors confronted with a non-fiction manuscript may alter idiosyncratic grammar, correct spelling and standardize punctuation; they will not, without consultation, alter so much as a comma in a work of literature, since they know that the language has been shaped and polished with deliberation.

Considered from the point of view of production, it does not seem sensible to suggest that one of these varieties is more typical of the written mode than the other. From the standpoint of the recipient, however, it is worth noticing that whereas literature can generally be read aloud and enjoyed by the listener, there are some kinds of non-fiction that are very hard to comprehend aurally. This is because the complexity and density of the language goes beyond what we can process by ear; in passages like the following (from Cutts & Maher, 1980, p. 6) we need to be able to move backwards and forwards through the text at our own pace:

105 'Mixed hereditament' means a hereditament which is not a dwelling house but in the case of which the proportion of the rateable value of the hereditament attributable to the part of the hereditament used for the purposes of a private dwelling is greater than the proportion thereof attributable to the part used for other purposes.

Faced with such an example, it is easy to understand Whitehall's (1951, p. 1) assertion that 'serious written English may be regarded as a rather artificial dialect of our language'.

There are some types of writing which differ from both of the two most highly developed varieties; examples include personal letters, diaries, lecture notes, memos and shopping lists. These are characteristically hand-written and addressed to a known audience (often the writer himself). They are not generally extensively planned, nor do they regularly undergo drafting, revision and rewriting. The more casual instances are also less likely to be kept for posterity. Obviously these more spontaneous varieties share some of the characteristics of both spoken and written language. In these circumstances, writing is chosen in preference to speech in order to achieve a special purpose: it may be to bridge a physical distance between the sender and receiver of the message, to aid the writer's memory, or to enable him to give verbal expression to his thoughts while keeping them private.

4.6 CONCLUSION

Is writing obsolescent?

It is sometimes suggested that now that letters can be replaced by telephone calls, written memos by dictaphone messages, newspapers by radio and television programmes and printed books by pre-recorded cassettes, there is no longer any real need for writing. I hope that the cumulative effect of this chapter has been to demonstrate that the functions and structures of the two modes are, in most cases, so distinct that the one cannot simply replace the other. Nevertheless, as so much time, money and effort is spent on teaching reading and writing, it seems worthwhile to refute the obsolescence argument explicitly.

There are obvious criticisms that can be made on practical grounds: tape-recorders, radios, televisions and telephones are not so cheap or portable as pens, paper, newspapers and books. More important, it is not possible to skim through the contents of an audiotape, nor is it easy to provide an index or find a particular place, so pinpointing information is much harder than it is in a book. Students sometimes think that tape-recording lectures is a good substitute for lecture notes. Experience rapidly reveals the flaw in this idea. Note-taking necessitates summarizing – we can only write about one-sixth of the words we hear spoken at a normal rate (see p. 161). So, notes of a one-hour lecture, reread at the speaker's original speed, will occupy about ten minutes; but because we read at roughly twice the speed of speech, the gist of the lecture can, in fact, be reviewed in five minutes or so. A tape, on the other hand, faithfully recording every hesitation, voiced pause and repetition, consumes as much time as the original and makes no distillation of the essence of the lecture.

When the news is broadcast on television, or a novel presented on radio or tape, the speaker is, of course, reading from a written text. Therefore, even with all our technology, some of the population have to be able to read and write. To choose to have only a small élite who could do so, and who could control the dissemination of information, would, to most people, be politically unacceptable.

Above all, writing allows the planning, shaping, organization and revision of ideas so that the style of thinking it fosters is qualitatively different. (When authors compose by dictation into a tape-recorder, they make their alterations and corrections to a transcribed typescript; it is not possible to achieve the same effects by editing the tape itself.) The Schools Council (1976, p. 7) team emphasize that 'there are meanings which can't be expressed in talk because you can't hold enough in your head to get a coherent organization'. Similarly, the skilled reader can process greater complexity of language and ideas by eye than the listener can by ear. (A study by Durrell (1969), for example, suggests that by the time children are thirteen years old their reading comprehension is 12 per cent superior to their listening comprehension.) Therefore, the teacher of reading and writing is not only enabling pupils to have independent access to everything that is written but is also providing them with the key to new kinds of thought processes.

Implications for the classroom

Finally, we should consider how an awareness of the fundamental differences between speech and writing might affect classroom practice. At the level of physical differences in production we have seen that writing is characteristically planned and, unlike speech, has the advantage of allowing revision and polishing. This suggests that, at least when the writing requires original thought and when it is to be kept, pupils should have the opportunity of making a rough draft before they produce a finished copy. (I have heard students tell children to write a composition in their best handwriting without any crossing out. We need to see crossing out as evidence of thought, not carelessness – though that does not mean that it should remain in the final version.) When young children first start to write they do not reread what they have just written. As their handwriting is slow and laborious they naturally lose their train of thought, so the text becomes muddled and incoherent. They are experiencing the physical difficulties of writing without benefiting from the fact that it provides a permanent record. Explicit encouragement to reread as they go along will not only improve the structure of their work but will also draw attention to one of the advantages that writing has over speech.

A major situational difference is that speech involves interaction between people, whereas the writer works alone. This leads to an intrinsic difficulty in any written work that involves answering questions. The question and answer format derives from speech where the answer is typically elliptical, omitting any elements that can be understood from the question. Being very familiar with oral elliptical responses, children understandably give elliptical written answers as well. So, if in a textbook there is the question, 'Which animal provides our daily pint of milk?', children will probably write in their exercise books, 'The cow'. The result is that, in writing – unlike speech – the answer is divorced from the question. Since such responses do not make sense on their own, teachers often instruct children to answer questions 'in complete sentences'. Linguistically, this is an unnatural thing to do. Therefore, it is probably sensible to allow short answers if they are not going to be referred to again. However, if they are to be reread at some later date, it is obviously essential for the answers to be fully meaningful; an explanation to pupils in these terms should help them to see the necessity of an expanded response.

Learning to read and write is hard work. If young children are to see any purpose in their labour, it is important that they should be aware of the things that writing can do that speech cannot. There are many occasions in the infant classroom when the functions of writing can be illustrated even before the children begin to learn to read. I remember watching a student with a nursery class making gingerbread men. As they all weighed and measured and mixed and stirred the oral language work was excellent. But the student missed a splendid opportunity by keeping the recipe tucked in her bag and glancing at it surreptitiously when she needed information. She felt that, as the teacher, she should appear omniscient. The children would have learnt something of great value, however, if she had explained that, as no one can remember all the recipes there are, they are written down so that they can be referred to whenever they are needed.

Junior children can experiment with passing both oral and written messages round the class so that they discover for themselves the greater reliability of writing. (This could lead on to a consideration of the differences between written literature and orally transmitted plays, stories and poems.)

A study of the range of uses that writing has in society can begin in the classroom, where there may well be labels of various kinds, a register, a weather chart, guides to radio and TV programmes, lists of teams, and instructions for the use of equipment – quite apart from books both for information and enjoyment. With older pupils such an approach can develop into an exploration of the kinds of thinking that are actually facilitated by writing. This is important because, although some children write willingly enough, others, lacking a sense of purpose, consider it a waste of time and effort. A thirteen-year-old boy called David, who was intelligent and had a keen desire to learn, showed he had not yet perceived any distinctive value in writing when he said:

I think that talking brings out more things in you than just writing it down on a piece of paper. I mean you write it down to show the teacher that you've done it but it doesn't bring out any more knowledge in you, I don't think. (Schools Council, 1976, p. 3)

As far as formal differences are concerned, an important aspect is the absence of prosodic features in writing. Children are well aware that the same words can have different meanings depending on how they are spoken; they often enjoy demonstrating that a written dialogue can be presented orally in a variety of ways. Similarly, they will work with imagination when asked to try to capture a particular tone of voice in writing. In reading, it is worth drawing attention to some of the helpful features of print, such as headings, layout and different styles and sizes of typeface.

We have seen that the structures of writing are, to a considerable extent, different from those of speech. This means that, although oral work is undeniably of great value in pupils' learning, it does not specifically help them to acquire the kinds of grammatical patterns that they need in their writing. Those have to be learnt from good written language. But children who find reading difficult are largely denied this valuable stimulus to their linguistic development. Therefore, there is much to be gained from reading aloud to pupils across a wide age-range – and not just from fiction but from good non-fiction too – because, in this pleasurable way, they gain experience of sentence structures and patterns of discourse organization which they would have difficulty in processing in their private reading. Hearing good prose well read should be beneficial for both their reading and their writing.

It is widely agreed that unusual sentence patterns create difficulties for the young or unskilled reader. This suggests that, at least in the early stages of reading, children's texts should not contain a significant proportion of structures that are rare in speech. This view is sometimes overstated, however. For example, the Bullock Report (DES, 1975, p. 92) comments that 'a printed text is easier to read the more closely its structures are related to those used by the reader in normal speech'. Taken to its logical conclusion, this would mean that a transcript of speech should provide the easiest reading material of all. The following sample of spontaneous speech by an eight-year-old boy, taken from Fawcett and Perkins' (1980) transcripts, reveals the fallacy of such a conclusion:

106   um there was 'this um witch doctor/ and 'Scooby Dóo/ was 'he was 'he was he 'was 'standing by the witch doctor/ and the 'witch doctor 'went in and he and he 'went he 'went chásing him/ he 'went Scooby Doo 'went in the cúpboard/ with Shággy/ and 'got

um some clóthes on/ and the àcting clothes/ and 'they were 'they
were 'they were 'they were àcting on/ and then and the 'witch
doctor 'pressed the 'button and they 'turned òn again then/ and
'then they were 'act and then 'Scooby was ácting/ then and then
they just 'take him and he 'switched he 'keeped on switching it/
un'til they 'all came róund/ and the 'all clòthes fell off him/

(8 years; II, p. 22)

I believe that pupils can be helped in both their reading and their
writing if some of the differences between the spoken and written modes
are referred to explicitly, when appropriate, in the course of classroom
activities: physical, situational, functional, formal and organizational differences, for example. However, personally I do not think it is a good
idea to deal with structural differences in the same way; I would not
want, for example, to try to teach children to identify and label the
various literary constructions I have illustrated in this chapter. The
teacher needs to be aware of them and to be alert for the problems that
they may cause, but children can absorb and master them gradually and
naturally by reading, listening and writing – just as they acquired the
structures of oral language by listening and talking.

I have briefly outlined some rather general implications for the classroom that arise from the ideas in this chapter; more detailed points will
emerge in chapters 5 and 6.

CHAPTER 5

Children's writing

*The teacher should take deliberate measures to improve his pupils'
ability to handle [written] language.*

(DES, 1975, p. 169)

5.1 INTRODUCTION

Learning to write, as the last chapter has shown, entails mastering not
only the physical forms of letters, spellings and punctuation, but also the
structural and organizational patterns that characterize written language. For adults, the structural differences between speech and writing
are blurred to some extent because we both hear and produce a great
deal of spoken language that is parasitic on the written mode; that is,
language that we are able to use only because we are already competent
readers and writers. For children, whose experience of language before
they go to school will have been largely of the archetypally spoken kind
– that is, unplanned, face-to-face, interactive conversation – the differences are more stark.

When children begin to learn to write, they have not fully mastered the
spoken language. Indeed, just as their writing grows out of the oral
language patterns they bring to school, so, in turn, what they learn
through writing and reading feeds into the development of their speech.

Bearing in mind these interrelationships between speech and writing,
Kroll (1981) has proposed four phases in the acquisition of writing
ability. He calls these **preparation**, **consolidation**, **differentiation** and **integration**. The preparation phase is the time when the basic mechanisms of
handwriting and spelling are learnt. During the consolidation phase,
children express in writing what they can already say; in other words,
their writing 'catches up' with their spoken language. Naturally enough,
such writing will have many of the personal, colloquial, context-bound
qualities of speech. When composing has become automatic, when the
physical task of writing no longer absorbs all the child's attention, then

the movement into the differentiation phase can begin. Now writing begins to diverge from speech, to take on its own distinctive functions, syntactic structures and patterns of organization. Not surprisingly, during this stage there is often awkwardness as children try out new constructions, adopt forms they have met in their reading, and swerve erratically from over-formality to colloquialism and back again. In the fourth phase, integration, the language user has such assured control of both oral and written language that he is able to make appropriate linguistic choices in any circumstances and, indeed, has the confidence to allow his own personal voice to influence his writing style. Kroll (1981, p. 53) comments, 'the expressive qualities most typical of speech (voice, tone, naturalness) are important to advanced writers.' Not all writers reach this stage: Kantor and Rubin (1981, p. 62) say, 'many writers . . . perhaps the majority of high school graduates, remain at a middle level of development, suspended awkwardly between speech and writing.' This chapter will not cover the preparation for writing but will focus chiefly on the consolidation and differentiation phases.

It is not easy to assign chronological ages to the onset of these phases, partly because children vary so much but also because the phases themselves are not discrete periods, arranged end-to-end with clear-cut boundaries between them, but rather indications of progression along a complex developmental continuum. However, accepting that the figures are the roughest of guidelines, it is possible to suggest that the consolidation stage begins at about six or seven and the differentiation stage at around nine or ten. The justification for the first age-range is found in large-scale surveys of children's writing (e.g. Harpin, 1976; A. Wilkinson et al., 1979), where the researchers have certainly been able to collect samples of independent writing from many seven-year-olds. Then, for the second age-range, there are many studies, which will be referred to in 5.3, which suggest that grammatical structures rarely found in speech begin to appear in children's writing during the third and fourth years of the junior school, thus providing evidence of differentiation between the two language modes.

Since this chapter is about children's developing ability to handle the structures of written language, it is worth emphasizing that this is only one aspect of learning to be a writer and, therefore, it is only part of the teaching of writing. Good writing depends, first and foremost, on having something to write about; it requires from the writer such non-linguistic qualities as truthfulness, vigour, imagination, and so on. It is quite possible for a piece of writing to contain varied vocabulary, mature sentence structures and well-planned paragraphs, and still to be unsatisfactory, because the writer was not committed to it. The Bullock Report (DES, 1975, p. 164) emphasizes that:

> a writer's intention is prior to his need for techniques. The teacher
> who aims to extend the pupil's power as a writer must therefore work

first upon his intentions and *then* upon the techniques appropriate to them.

I am sure that that priority is right. Therefore the information provided in this chapter about the growth of technique in writing is intended as a means whereby teachers can help their pupils to express their meanings more clearly and satisfyingly; it is not seen as an end in itself.

Before turning to structural development in children's writing, it is worth outlining briefly some of the findings from research on how pupils and students behave during the process of writing. This is a burgeoning research area, popular in the United States. Subjects are closely observed, and videotaped, while they write. Sometimes they are also asked to compose aloud, to read what they have written or to provide a commentary on their videotaped behaviour. Using these methods in a long-term project, Graves (1979) found that his youngest subjects, who were just learning to write, did not reread or alter what they had written. Then, gradually they learnt to make small revisions, such as correcting a faulty letter-shape or changing a spelling. These alterations were usually made with a rubber. At the age of eight, many children reached a plateau where their writing was fluent but not subject to revision. But, when they learnt to cross out rather than depend on a rubber, their work changed dramatically:

> Once crossing out enters the picture ... the units of revision expand. . . . The draft now takes on an important, temporary quality. Words can be written in; others excluded. The section may be written from three to four times before the words are true to the meaning of personal experience. (Graves, 1979, p. 315)

Calkins (1980) noted that, by the age of nine, some of her abler subjects were aware of the needs of an external audience. One girl alternated between being a writer and a reader of her work – when she took on the role of reader, she deliberately adopted a different posture. A study of nine- and twelve-year-olds by Birnbaum (1981) suggested that the older and abler children were more aware of the possibility of revising a written text; their less proficient counterparts were more concerned about producing a neat, error-free end-product. This differentiated attitude was borne out in research that Atwell (1981) conducted with adult subjects. She found that, while competent students were ready to make changes to their work, remedial students were reluctant to abandon anything they had managed to get down on paper. Finally, a study of remedial adult writers by Perl (1979) drew attention to the difficulty these students experienced in correcting their work, because they could not read it accurately enough. When Perl asked them to read aloud what they had written, on the whole they read what they had intended to write, not what they had actually written; so omissions, repetitions and transpositions were generally ignored. All the researchers who have studied the processes of writing make it clear that many of the patterns of behaviour they have observed are not the product of maturation alone but also of teaching. This indicates the importance of fostering approaches to the writing task that will be beneficial in the long term and, particularly, it highlights the danger of an over-emphasis on neatness and the avoidance of errors.

Research on the process of writing provides a valuable reminder that different types of behaviour are involved. A finished product may have undergone several stages of drafting, revision, editing and proof-reading. These stages overlap to some extent but, broadly, drafting involves getting ideas on to paper, regardless of form, order and expression; revision entails shaping and structuring the raw material as the writer's intentions begin to emerge. Editing can be seen as a final process of revision which specifically takes the reader into account; the writer tries to reread with the eye of an outsider, looking for ambiguity, vagueness, lack of coherence, irrelevance and so on. This is very demanding, because the writer has to imagine himself into the position of a naive reader. Equally demanding is proof-reading. At this stage, the writer checks to see if he actually wrote what he intended, since haste or distraction can lead to the omission or repetition of words, particularly function words. Finding such errors requires slow and deliberate reading, quite different from our normal reading for meaning.

Not all these processes are involved in every piece of writing – I doubt whether many people proof-read their shopping lists – but, generally, the more difficult or unfamiliar the subject matter and the more distant the intended readership, the harder it is to achieve a final form of words at the first attempt. Yet, often, this is required of children in school. The Bullock Report (DES, 1975, p. 167) criticizes this approach:

> In much of the writing that takes place in school, the pupil's first attempt is expected to be the finished article; there is not enough encouragement of the idea of a first draft to be followed by a second, more refined production.[1]

If teachers are to intervene constructively during the process of writing in order to assist with revising, editing and proof-reading, then they need to know what problems of composition confront children at different developmental levels and what linguistic difficulties are associated with different types of writing. Accordingly, section 5.3 of this chapter looks at the structure of writing from a developmental perspective, while 5.2 and 5.4 include a consideration of the demands made by various kinds of writing task.

As far as possible, the examples used in this chapter come from

---

1 For detailed examples of drafting in practice, see Harris & Kay (1981), chapter 9; Schwartz (1977); and Thornton (1980), chapter 5. For a theoretical framework for editing, see Collins & Gentner (1980).

published collections of children's writing, in order that readers who are interested to restore an extract to its original context can do so. Many of the examples come from Burgess *et al.* (1973), Harpin (1976) and Rosen & Rosen (1973). (Quotations from these sources are followed by author and page number alone; extracts from other sources have a full reference.) In addition, I have been fortunate to be able to study ninety pieces of writing produced by eighteen nine-year-old children who form a sub-sample of the Bristol Longitudinal Language Development Programme.[2] This corpus is not published, but information about it and many examples of the children's work appear in Kroll *et al.* (1980) and in Kroll & Wells (1983). In all the examples presented in this chapter I have corrected the spelling mistakes so that attention can be focused on the structure of the language and not on its sometimes bizarre surface appearance. Occasionally, to make reading easier, I have made slight alterations to the punctuation; these have been kept to a minimum and have never involved more than the insertion of a full stop. No other changes have been made to the children's writing.

5.2 LANGUAGE VARIETIES

In describing a language there is always a danger of making it sound uniform, as if there were one kind of language for all users and all occasions. The aim of this section is to counteract any such impression by indicating some of the ways in which language varies. So far in this book distinctions have been made between spoken and written language and between informal spontaneous speech and formal planned speech. It is clear that there are grammatical structures (as well as vocabulary) which are entirely appropriate in conversation between friends but which will not work in a formal written text. In addition, there are other differences that have only been mentioned in passing – those of accent and dialect, which, broadly, are varieties associated with different geographical regions.

Accent and dialect

Everyone is aware that someone born in Newcastle pronounces words differently from a Londoner or a Liverpudlian. Nowadays, it seems to be generally agreed that it is not the place of the school to attempt to alter a child's accent. The Bullock Report (DES, 1975, p. 143) is unequivocal:

We believe that a child's accent should be accepted and that to attempt to suppress it is irrational and neither humane nor necessary.

2 I am most grateful to Barry Kroll and Gordon Wells for generously providing me with copies of their data and allowing me to quote from it.

We have seen already that accentual variation is not reflected in English spelling; however, as children learn to spell, some of their errors may well arise from the characteristic pronunciation of their region. For example, young Cockney children sometimes write ⟨fanks⟩ for 'thanks' and ⟨breve⟩ for 'breathe' (Nuttall, 1982).

The term 'dialect' is generally used to refer to features of vocabulary and grammar that are characteristic of a particular region and do not have nationwide currency. (Regional dialects are always spoken with a regional accent.) For example, northern English speakers may use the word *maiden* for the standard English term *clothes horse*, or *mardy* to describe a bad-tempered child. Then, to give an example of a grammatical difference, people in East Anglia may use the stem form of the verb in the third person singular present tense, e.g. *he go*, where standard English has the stem+*s* form, *he goes*. Such dialectal variation can occur in writing as well as in speech.

It is necessary to make the point that, linguistically, regional dialects are not inferior to standard English. (Historically, standard English has itself developed from a regional dialect which, because it came to be associated with influential people and institutions, gained social prestige and, hence, widespread currency.) All varieties of the language have their own grammatical rules; therefore, all are fully grammatical – but the grammar of each variety is slightly different. This means that suggestions that standard English is 'better' or 'more correct' or 'more acceptable' than regional varieties reflect social rather than linguistic judgements. In other words, when people criticize the grammar of a sentence like *I ain't done nothing*, they are really saying that it does not conform to the grammar of standard English, which is the variety generally spoken by people who have status in our society. If children who would normally use such a sentence adopt the standard form instead, they are, by doing so, separating themselves, to some extent, from their own community and aligning themselves with a different social group. This raises psychological, social and even political issues that are too complex to explore here.[3] In schools, opinions range from those who feel that all non-standard uses of language should be eliminated to those who think it is an impertinence to reject the language of the child and his family. Perhaps a middle way is to seek to extend children's linguistic resources by teaching standard English for formal contexts while accepting dialect expressions in more casual situations. By this means, when pupils are old enough to make a choice, they can decide whether to use standard English or dialect in any particular set of circumstances. If standard English is never taught they do not have that choice.

3 These issues are discussed in J. R. Edwards (1979) and in Trudgill (1975). Both authors . argue the case for the appreciation of dialectal variety within schools and for the adoption, where appropriate, of a bi-dialectal approach. There is a full exploration of the complexity of the issues in Milroy & Milroy (forthcoming).

The issue becomes particularly salient in written language. Because a written text is relatively autonomous, having an existence of its own independent of its author, it can, potentially at least, reach a much wider audience than most everyday speech. The audience may be distant in either time or place. Thus, from a practical point of view, it is sensible for the writer to use a form of language that is widely understood and accepted. This explains why the convention has arisen that, generally, standard English rather than regional dialect is used in writing. It follows that dialect expressions call more attention to themselves on the page than they do in speech. So, one aspect of learning to write involves learning to use standard English.

Teachers need to consider at what stage of the learning sequence this will be appropriate. J. R. Edwards (1979, p. 120) thinks standard English should be encouraged in writing 'from the earliest school years'. On the other hand, Richmond (1979, p. 53) feels that it should not be expected until about the age of fourteen. My own view is that it is probably too difficult to learn to write and to learn to handle a new variety of the language at the same time, so I would favour some delay in the introduction of standard English features – but perhaps more than halfway through the secondary school is rather late. A study by Cheshire (1982, p. 56) provides some evidence that children aged eleven to fourteen are already aware of contexts where their dialect forms are inappropriate. Her eight subjects came from Reading, where local dialect speakers may use the stem + s form of the verb throughout the present tense, e.g. *I wants, you wants* etc. Although her pupils used the non-standard stem + s form 60 per cent of the time in small group discussions in school, they did not use it at all in their writing. Accordingly, it seems to me that, once the consolidation stage is complete and children are becoming increasingly aware of the differences between speech and writing (on average, about the age of nine or ten), that is an appropriate time to talk about the nature and role of standard English and to illustrate the major ways in which it differs from the local dialect. It is worth noting that, although all children have to alter their language significantly as they move from casual speech to formal writing, those whose oral language differs markedly from standard English will have a particularly demanding adjustment to make.

If teachers are to provide examples of contrasts between different language varieties, then it follows that they themselves need to know the distinctive characteristics of the dialect of their region. Such knowledge also enables them to respond more sensitively to their pupils' writing, as they will be able to distinguish between dialect expressions, and errors – like the omission of words – that are probably caused by haste. This distinction has important consequences for marking written work: there is obviously no point, for example, in instructing a pupil to reread his work to 'find the mistake' if the item in question is something he uses habitually in speech. In addition, awareness of dialect features can help the teacher to make sense of otherwise inexplicable mistakes. For example, if a pupil in East Anglia writes *they goes* this might, at first sight, seem very odd because it is neither a standard English form nor an East Anglian one. What has probably happened is that the child – who would normally say both *they go* and *he go* – is conscious that he needs to add an *-s* to some of his verb forms in writing and, being anxious to get it right, has simply overdone it. (When speakers of standard English try to write in a regional dialect they experience similar difficulty.)

There are three grammatical areas where dialect differences are particularly noticeable: these are verbs, pronouns and negatives.[4] We have seen already that East Anglian speakers may use the stem form of the verb throughout the present tense and that people in Reading (and indeed in a wide area of central southern and southwest England) may use the stem + *s* form throughout. Further, in many parts of the country, a few common irregular verbs tend to have their past forms regularized to some extent, as illustrated in table 17. In addition, it is common for

TABLE 17 Dialect forms of common irregular verbs

Verb	Simple past	Past participle
do	*done	done
see	*seen	seen
come	*come	come
go	went	*went
eat	ate	*ate
write	wrote/*writ	*wrote/*writ
give	*give	*give

asterisked forms are non-standard.

the two past forms of the verb *to be* to be reduced to one, giving either *I was, you was* etc. or *I were, you were*. As the verb *to be* is used not only as a lexical verb but also as an auxiliary in verb phrases, to make the progressive aspect and the passive voice, it is clear that this one difference from standard English will appear particularly prominent. Here are examples from children's writing which probably illustrate the influence of dialect on verb forms:

1 They *done* this to find out which is the longest day of the year.
June, 12 years (Burgess *et al.*, p. 134)
2 We *was* so cold we went to the village again.
Darin, 9 years (Harpin, p. 66)

4 For a fuller account of these differences, with reference to specific regions, see Hughes & Trudgill (1979).

The second area is pronouns. The personal pronouns *them* and *us* may appear as determiners (in place of *those* and *our*), e.g. *I want **them** books*; *we'll have **us** tea*. The reflexive pronouns *himself* and *themselves* may be replaced by *hisself* and *theirselves*; and the subordinator *what* may function as a relative pronoun, e.g.:

3 His dog came with him to get the birds *what* the man killed.

Allan, 9 years (Kroll et al.)

The third area is negatives. First, the form *ain't* may be used as the negative of all present forms of auxiliary and lexical *be*, e.g. *I **ain't** going*, *he **ain't** there*, and also of auxiliary have, e.g. *we **ain't** done it*. Second, multiple negatives occur commonly, e.g.:

4 The hunter . . . give the bones to his dog to eat because he did *not* kill *no* birds and *no* elephant.   Allan, 9 years (Kroll *et al.*)
5 When you get a white you *don't* go *nowhere*.

Judy, 9 years (Kroll et al.)

Third, the word *never* often refers to a single occasion (like standard *didn't*), e.g. *I **never** broke that jug*, where standard English has, *I didn't break that jug*.

Although it is true that, in general, standard English is used in writing, there are occasions when dialect forms are perfectly appropriate. An obvious example is in the written representation of speech. In a story called *Town Boy*, Clive tells how a London boy named Steve has to move to the country to live with his aunt. Clive skilfully uses dialect to emphasize Steve's alienation from his new surroundings:

6 . . . He was used to the dirt and smoke of the back streets of London. But he suffered from a chest complaint and could not carry on living there.
   'You're to start the village school tomorrow Steve.'
   'School I ain't going t no school.' Next day he was taken to the school. He sat at the back of the classroom doing nothing and then at break he went outside where all the other children started to push him around. He punched one boy in the eye. *He weren't scared he Steve Parker leader of the gas work gang weren't scared of no country bumpkins* . . .   Clive, 12 years (Burgess *et al.* p. 171)

Types of writing

Accent and dialect variation differentiate the language of one person (or group of people) from another. A further kind of variation is that which arises from the situation and purpose of the communication. Confining our attention to written language, it is clear that there are different types of writing which derive from the varying intentions of the author. For example, we can generally distinguish fiction from non-fiction, a novel from a poem, a scientific report from a letter, and so on. Through the centuries, there have been very many classifications of types of writing. A frequently-occurring one has four divisions (the labels used may vary slightly): narration, description, exposition and argument.[5] These labels can often be confidently applied to the mature products of adult writers but they are not necessarily revealing of the developmental processes in children's writing.

In order to try to overcome this problem, Britton *et al.* (1975, pp. 88–91) devised a three-way system of language functions to classify their large corpus of writing by secondary pupils. Their basic category is **expressive** writing. This they describe as 'language close to the self' and 'thinking aloud on paper'. Out of this fundamental type develop two more advanced categories: **transactional** and **poetic** writing. Transactional writing is used to get things done in the real world, to inform, advise, persuade or instruct. Poetic writing, on the other hand, is an artifact, something 'that exists *for its own sake* and not as a means of achieving something else'.

Although in broad terms these categories make intuitive sense, in practice they raise certain difficulties. First, there are no linguistic features which serve as identifiers of one type or another, so classification is inevitably a subjective process.

Next, there is no psycholinguistic evidence of a developmental sequence in writing from the expressive to the poetic. Indeed, elsewhere Britton (1970, p. 164) has himself suggested that children's earliest writing is poetic in function:

> I am inclined to believe that young children rely upon speech for all that they want to communicate and that when they write before going to school their writing takes the form of a 'construct' or performance. I have seen many examples of stories written, illustrated and decorated, the pages stitched or clipped together to make little books. They exist as objects in the world: miniature or even make-believe objects. . . . A good deal of early writing in the primary school is not aimed at telling anybody anything but at producing 'written objects' . . . something that deserves to be embellished, illustrated and to go along as part of the possessions of the group.

There is also some doubt about the developmental place of transactional writing. A. Wilkinson *et al.* (1979, p. 75) say:

> It is sometimes suggested that young children cannot handle 'transactional writing'. Judging by the response of some seven-year-olds to our transactional task, this may be because they are not asked.

5 For a history and criticism of these categories, see Britton *et al.* (1975, pp. 3–6).

A third weakness of Britton *et al*'s classification is that their three categories do not reveal anything about the organizational demands that different types of writing make on the writer.

To try to meet these objections, I shall suggest a framework which might be used to consider such demands. It has been devised with school writing specifically in mind, and is certainly too simple to account for all the many types of writing that skilled adult writers employ. The first dimension of this framework concerns the organization of subject matter in the text. Here, there is a broad division between texts that are organized chronologically and those that are not. (This division is made, for example, by Longacre and Levinsohn (1978) and by Winter (1977).) In a chronologically ordered text (which can loosely be called a **narrative**) the sequence of events in time structures the material; in a non-chronologically ordered text, the relationships between the parts are not temporal but logical, e.g. comparison, contrast, similarity, whole–part, cause–effect, and so on. Linguistically, a chronological text can be identified by its high use of verbs that describe actions or events and by the fact that sentences which contain such verbs can generally be joined by connectives like *then, next, after that*.

There is widespread agreement that, when children start to produce coherent pieces of written work (rather than primitive collections of random ideas), they find chronological texts the easier of the two types. For example, Burgess *et al.* (1973, pp. 91–2), describing a piece of factual writing about HMS Victory by nine-year-old Kerry, decide that she can handle the facts because she can marshal them along a time continuum:

> The narrative principle . . . becomes the central principle of organiz-
> ation. When, however, a principle of organization other than narrative
> is required, Kerry flounders about. She either throws the facts
> together in almost any order, or, when she can, shifts as quickly as
> possible back into a time sequence.

Bereiter (1980), commenting on data he collected, reported that narrative writing was established by eight or nine but that expository writing developed 'much later'. A. Wilkinson *et al.* (1979), who gave four written tasks to children aged seven, ten and thirteen, found that the seven- and ten-year-olds predominantly used chronological organization but that the thirteen-year-olds could also manage other patterns. Kantor and Rubin (1981, p. 74), however, noted that even thirteen-year-olds would 'lapse into the narrative mode' if faced with a task that required them to theorize. Similarly, J. B. N. Harris (1980, p. 198) found that pupils aged twelve to fifteen experienced more problems with non-chronological than with narrative writing; he commented particularly on the difficulty of any assignment that involved sustaining a comparison or contrast throughout the text.

The second dimension of the framework is less clear-cut; it concerns the relationship of the writer to his subject matter and to his reader.

Here, there is not a straightforward division between types but rather a continuum ranging from 'close' personal writing at one end to 'distant' impersonal writing at the other. (This dimension is similar to Moffett's (1968, p. 35) scale of abstraction.) The linguistic feature which serves to identify rough divisions along this continuum is the number and kind of personal pronouns in the text.

First of all, let us consider the writer's relationship to his subject matter. At the personal end of the continuum, pupils write about themselves and about people they know – friends, relatives, teachers and so forth. (We can probably include pets in this personal group.) In addition, in their stories they invent characters who belong to the creator's own private world rather than to the public world of the teacher. Writing at the personal end of the continuum is characterized by an extensive use of personal pronouns, particularly *I*, *we*, *he*, *she* and *they*, as illustrated in this extract:

> 7 *I* don't remember much about the next few days. *We* – the children – that is, my brother cousins and *I* alternated between fits of hysterical laughter silence and irritability. *I* remember *we* read through all the letters of consolation and awarded each a certain amount of points – points being taken off for clichés like wherever *he* is *he* is happy now. These made *me* furiously angry for to *me he* was nowhere.   Judith, 20 years (Burgess *et al.*, p. 44)

In this 70-word passage there are ten personal pronouns (and one instance of the related determiner, *my*).

At the opposite, impersonal end of the continuum, the subject matter is not people but objects, processes, phenomena, ideas, explanations and theories. The personal pronouns that occur in this kind of writing are restricted to *it* and impersonal *they* but, generally, the language is characterized by a heavy use of NPs rather than pronouns, e.g.:

> 8 In order for acetic acid to be formed, an H atom must detach itself from the other branch so that the number of hydrogens is right prior to oxidation. The substance left is maloric acid, which agrees with the question. If the same reaction is considered with structure f), acetic acid might be formed but the remaining hydrogens are in the wrong positions for maloric acid to be formed.
>
>   Jane, 17 years (Burgess *et al.*, p. 40)

This 69-word passage contains no personal pronouns and just one reflexive pronoun, *itself*. (Judith and Jane are both mature writers, so the comparison between the two pieces is a fair one.)

It is easy to identify writing at the two ends of the continuum. Between these two extremes there is a large, rather indeterminate area where we find writing that is personal in the sense that it is about people, but people who are not personally known to the writer. Such writing occurs frequently in history and religious education. Predominant pronouns are *he, she* and *they*. The following 77-word extract is from an essay about the young Elizabeth I:

9 Unlike most adolescents her flirtings ended not in scoldings but in death and violence. Seymour her artful step-father and would-be husband was smashed under her nose and Elizabeth was forced to play cool to keep her life. *She* thus learnt early to show no hint of her emotions. During Edward's reign, *she* watched her brother being used by his councillors, during Mary's *she* felt again the thinness of the thread on which her life hung.

Jessica, 17 years (Burgess *et al.*, p. 107)

In addition to the three personal pronouns, there are seven occurrences of the related determiner *her* and one of *his*. (In this intermediate category, the proportion of personal pronouns varies widely depending on the nature and complexity of the subject matter.)

Now we can turn to the writer's relationship with the reader. At the personal end of the scale, he writes for himself or for a known reader. Examples are notes, memos, diaries, letters and stories written for himself, the teacher, or his parents. Such writing frequently includes the pronouns *I* and *you*. At the impersonal end of the scale, the writing is for a distant, unknown and possibly large audience. The writer does not appear in any way in his text, nor does he acknowledge the presence of the reader. *I* and *you* never occur in this kind of writing. At the intermediate stage, the writer may use *I* or *you* or, occasionally, both. In this case, *you* is addressed to a generalized audience rather than to a specific person, e.g.:

10 Slave trading is cruel. Can *you* imagine being in a cage, with tied arms, having people staring at *you*.

Rosemary, 10 years (Rosen & Rosen, p. 126)

We can include in the intermediate category writing which is about impersonal subject matter yet which recognizes the existence of the author or the reader, or both, e.g.:

11 The aim of my project is to weigh objects on a spring. *I* found by experimenting that the spring stretches five and a half inches.

Andrew, 11 years (Rosen & Rosen, p. 138)

12 Have *you* ever visited a pond, well really visited a pond. *You* will honestly be surprised at the number of different insects and creatures *you* see. Elaine, 10 years (Rosen & Rosen, p. 130)

Summing up the personal-impersonal dimension we can say that 'close' personal writing uses the full range of personal pronouns and uses them extensively. 'Distant' impersonal writing uses very few personal pronouns and then only *it* and *they*. The intermediate category uses predominantly *he, she, it* and *they*; *I, we* and *you* are used rather rarely – all the pronouns (except *I* and *we*) refer to people unknown to the writer.

Personal writing is closer to everyday speech than impersonal writing and, naturally enough, it is the kind of writing that children produce first. Fully impersonal writing is not normally found until about the third year of the secondary school. It is worth considering what the movement towards impersonality entails for the writer. It requires the avoidance of constructions that occur in speech but not in formal writing (e.g. dialect expressions, recapitulatory pronouns, amplificatory noun phrase tags); it requires the creation of a self-sufficient text in which the writer treats the audience as strangers who cannot be expected to share his knowledge and experience; and it requires the use of constructions more common in writing than in speech (such as the passive), which allow the personal pronouns to be avoided altogether. The demands that all these features make on young writers will be illustrated in section 5.4.

The two dimensions (organizational and personal-impersonal) are combined to show the structure of the framework in figure 2. An example of a typical kind of writing in each category is given in each of the six boxes.

	Writer's relationship to the subject matter and to the reader		
	Close personal (known to writer)	Intermediate personal (unknown to writer)	Distant impersonal
Organization of the subject matter	he, she, they I, we, you	he, she, they (I, we, you)	it, they
Chronological	e.g. autobiographical account story	e.g. biographical account	e.g. account of a process
Non-chronological	e.g. description of a friend	e.g. description of a type of person (e.g. pirates, Eskimos)	e.g. description of a structure evaluation of an idea

FIGURE 2   A schematization of kinds of writing showing typical pronoun use

It is not possible to rank in strict order of difficulty all the six broad categories that are represented in the framework; there is no evidence to suggest, for example, whether chronological 'distant' writing is harder or easier than non-chronological 'intermediate' writing. (In any case, it seems likely that the pupil's interest in and knowledge of the particular subject matter will have an effect on any such ordering.) What can be said with some confidence, though, is that categories towards the left of the framework are easier than those to their right and that those on the top row are easier than the ones directly below them. (This schematization suggests a reason why Britton *et al.*'s (1975) expressive–poetic–transactional model is not revealing about the relative difficulty of various kinds of writing: all three of their types may be organized either chronologically or non-chronologically and, although transactional writing is usually fairly impersonal, it is possible for all three types to be placed at the personal end of the continuum. In other words, in terms of the kind of language and organization that is required, there may be more important differences between two pieces of writing that both fall in the same category than between pieces that belong to two different categories.)

·Teachers do not normally have any need to classify their pupils' writing, and the presentation of figure 2 is certainly not intended to suggest that they should do so. Rather, I feel that the information it displays has relevance to the TEACHING of writing; for example, it relates to the choice of topics, the preparation for writing, the guidance given during the writing process, and the response to the finished product.

To start with the teacher's response: it is always necessary to judge a piece of writing in terms of the kind of writing it was intended to be – there is no such thing as 'good writing' in a vacuum. The point can be illustrated by the following extracts from two letters, both on the topic of loft insulation:

A Would you kindly inform me from whom I might obtain the booklet about loft insulation referred to in paragraph three of your letter?
B In your last letter you mentioned a booklet about loft insulation. Can you let me know sometime where I can get one from?

It is not possible to say that one of these pieces is better than the other. Instead, we notice that they differ in respect of the writer's relationship to the reader, since letter B is more personal than A. (On figure 2, B would belong in the Personal (known) category and A in the Personal (unknown) category.) If the writer knows the *you* of B and does not know the *you* of A, then each letter is appropriate to its purpose; if, however, letter A is intended for someone the writer knows well, then we would be justified in criticizing it on the grounds that it is inappropriately impersonal.

It follows from this that children need to know what type of writing is required of them whenever they write. That they do not always have this knowledge is clear from the following example from Harpin (1976, p. 46):

After a history lesson on the Stone Age an eleven-year-old was set to 'write about life' in the period. His writing took the form of a narrative, a tale of hunter and hunted, which carried, in fictional form, much of the information from the lesson. The comment was 'a good story – but not much history'.

Presumably, the teacher expected a piece of writing in the non-chronological, 'intermediate' category but her instruction was too vague and the pupil interpreted it as a request for a personal narrative. (Another important point that is raised by this example is whether children should always have to use the conventional academic forms to write about subjects like history.) It is worthwhile not only for individual teachers to think about their expectations of their pupils' writing, but also for teachers in different departments within a school, and in associated primary and secondary schools, to consider the various types of writing that they each expect in their different subjects.

An awareness of the different types of writing can help teachers to ensure that their pupils are gradually extending their repertoire. One aspect of the development of writing skill is the ability to handle appropriately a range of kinds of writing. The Bullock Report (DES, 1975, p. 166) says:

> We believe that progress in writing throughout the school years should be marked by an increasing differentiation in the kinds of writing a pupil can successfully tackle.

Quite apart from the usefulness of controlling a range of flexible responses to the task of writing, it will become clear in section 5.3 that different types of writing are characterized to some extent by different grammatical constructions. Therefore, syntactic as well as sociolinguistic resources are extended by the provision of a variety of writing assignments.

Finally, the framework presented in figure 2, schematic though it is, may enable teachers to think of the work they set in terms of the demands it makes on the writer. It is true that we lack clear indications as to the precise ordering (and related normative chronological ages) of the six broad categories outlined; as the Bullock Report (p. 164) suggests:

> There has not been enough thought given to the different varieties of English and to the stages of language development at which children can begin to cope with them.

However, this means that there is a good opportunity for teachers to conduct their own classroom-based investigations to see what kinds of writing their pupils can handle confidently and where they experience particular difficulties. If pupils are struggling with written language, they can be helped by having the topic formulated in such a way that it falls within one of the easier categories. Similarly, if the subject matter is conceptually demanding, the teacher can choose a familiar form in which it can be expressed. Thus, if a chronological plan of organization is not possible, then perhaps the writing can be in a personal style; conversely, if a personal style is inappropriate, then maybe the facts can be presented in the form of a narrative. When a type of writing is set that is known to present difficulties, then it is opportune for the teacher to provide more help at the planning stage than would be necessary if the pupils were writing, say, a story or a biographical account.

5.3 GRAMMATICAL DEVELOPMENT IN CHILDREN'S WRITING

Several large-scale studies, both in Britain and the US, have examined the grammatical structures that children use in writing, covering between them the age-range seven to eighteen (e.g. Harpin, 1976; Hunt, 1965, 1970; O'Donnell et al., 1967; Yerrill, 1977).

Clause structure

As far as clause structure is concerned, apart from the fact that clause length increases as writers mature, there are only a few trends that can be associated with development. Yerrill (1977) reports that older children show more flexibility in the positioning of adverbials and will sometimes insert one between subject and verb, e.g.:

13 We *unfortunately* had no luck.   12 years (Yerrill, p. 187)

Also, according to O'Donnell et al. (1967, p. 73) the use of the passive increases threefold between the ages of eight and twelve. In their study, subjects watched a cartoon film of a fable, without the soundtrack, and then wrote the story of the film. Since the language task was the same for all the children, the more frequent use of the passive cannot be attributed to the increase in impersonal writing that usually takes place during the middle years of schooling. The following example shows a thirteen-year-old confidently handling the passive in personal writing:

14 When I was quite small I felt quite sure I *should be expected* to play something myself, so that when a half-size cello *was discovered* almost by accident, it seemed to everybody the obvious solution.   Philip, 13 years (Burgess et al., p. 62)

A change in clause structure that reveals a growing recognition of the grammatical differences between speech and writing is the rapid decline after the age of nine in the use of the recapitulatory pronoun, e.g.:

15 My second to best friend Jeffrey *he* is a very new person to me.
9 years (Yerrill, 1977, p. 173)

In Yerrill's data this construction still appears occasionally in twelve-year-olds' speech (as it does in adults') but never in their writing. However, it is worth noticing that examples do occur in the writing that Shaughnessy (1977) collected from American adults attending a 'basic writing' course (which would probably be called a 'remedial writing' course in Britain), e.g.:

16 The boy's father *he* has a job and a family to take care of.
Adult (p. 67)

This suggests that the avoidance of the construction in writing depends more on one's maturity as a writer than on simple chronological age.

In speech, school-age children do not make many errors in clause structure, the only one that occurs with any frequency being a failure of concord between subject and verb. We can add to this the fact that the false starts and hesitations characteristic of all unplanned speech are more numerous in the speech of six-year-olds than of ten-year-olds. In writing, errors of concord occur spasmodically until about the age of nine; however, with the exception of the verbs *have, be* and *do*, the only marking of concord is the final -*s*. This is so easy for a young, inexperienced writer to omit that it would be unwise to regard the odd error as a sign of immaturity. The following examples, taken from Kroll *et al.*'s (1980) data, all involve more than the omission of -*s*:

17 He *do* not bark.   Janet, 9 years
18 Eight of them have a got a home and one of them *have* not.
Mary, 9 years
19 The player *have* to get the same colour.   Derek, 9 years

When Christine, a skilled ten-year-old writer, makes an error of concord it appears to be because the prepositional phrase modifying the head noun contains a singular noun, *weed*, which misleads her:

20 The purple stems of chick weed *is* sleek and is covered with tiny hairs which are like a baby's hair when it is first born.
Christine, 10 years (Rosen & Rosen, p. 102)

The hesitations of speech, naturally enough, have no counterparts in writing. But if we think of false starts as a consequence of the way in which speech is produced, then it is possible to find a parallel in young children's writing. Some of them have a marked tendency to forget what they have written and, apparently, not to reread more than the last word when they add to their writing. Sentences like these (from Kroll *et al.*) result:

21 So the man got out his gun out.   Andrew, 9 years

22 In the morning he likes to come in about nine o'clock in the
   morning.   Paul, 9 years
23 There were some jungle animals were there.   Andrew, 9 years

Another production problem is that the writer's thoughts race ahead
of his pen; this makes it very easy to omit words. In the following
examples, the word that has, presumably, been left out is given in square
brackets at the end of the sentence:

24 But it must not be that drives away every night. [one]
                                   Michael, 7 years (Burgess *et al.*, p. 85)
25 The giraffe said they would it back to its tree house. [take]
                                         Sandra, 9 years (Kroll *et al.*)
26 My nearly gave way when I stepped out. [legs]
                                          David, 9 years (Kroll *et al.*)

Such omissions are very frequent in David's writing, making it particularly demanding to read: in one piece of 116 words there are at least
seven omissions. As writers mature, they do not necessarily make fewer
of these errors but they become more skilful at correcting them at the
proof-reading stage.

Phrase structure

In chapter 3 it was noted that phrase structure gives clearer indications
than clause structure of children's linguistic development in speech; the
same is true of writing.

The noun phrase

Far more research has been done on the development of the noun phrase
than of the verb phrase. It shows that the following types of NP are used
with increasing frequency from seven to seventeen: d adj n; NP
prep NP; noun phrases in apposition. From the age of nine or ten, these
patterns are used in writing more often than they are in speech. Here are
some examples from children's writing of fairly complex NPs:

27 We saw *the church at Threekingham with the jaw bone of*
             NP   prep   NP
        NP   prep   NP   NP   prep

a whale.
                                        Wendy, 9 years (Harpin, p. 34)
   NP

28 There are *three parts to arithmetic, problems, mechanical*
             NP   NP in

and mental.
   apposition   9 years (Yerrill, 1977, p. 170)

29 *The recently televised 'Six Wives of Henry VIII' and*
   d   adj   n   c

'Elizabeth R' are my idea of a dream.
    n

Annabel, 13 years (Burgess et al., p. 67)

We have seen (p. 100) that children rarely use complex NPs in subject position in their speech; neither do adults in talk that is unplanned and informal. Similarly, while they are novice writers, young children employ only simple noun phrases as subjects – that is, pronouns, proper nouns and dn phrases. By the age of ten, though, they use expanded NPs as subjects more often in their writing than in their speech. The gradual increase in the complexity of subjects is a continuing trend, which can be illustrated by data from a study by Hunt (1970). He asked all his writers, from nine-year-olds to adults, to rewrite 'in a better way' a passage that consisted of thirty-two very short, simple sentences. It is true that this task is not the same as free writing but, because it is identical for everybody, it does make possible a valid comparison of the types of subject NP produced at various ages:

30 *The chemical* is powdery.   (9 years; p. 64)
31 *The other substances* form a mass.   (13 years; p. 65)
32 *A light, lustrous metal* is formed.   (17 years; p. 66)
33 *Aluminium, an abundant metal of many uses,* is obtained from bauxite.   (skilled adult; p. 66)

All writers use simple subject NPs a great deal; only writers with some linguistic maturity are able to write subject phrases that tap some of the other very varied structural possibilities of the noun phrase.

Harpin (1976) made an interesting discovery about children's use of pronouns in his study of the junior age-range. He found that, when they were composing stories, the youngest writers preferred a third person narration but, with increasing maturity, they gradually changed to the first person; for most children the crossover in preference occurred roughly at the age of nine. On the other hand, when they were engaged in factual writing, the youngest pupils found it easier to use *I*, changing to *he, she* and *it* only at nine or ten. These tendencies were true for the group as a whole but, in a small number of children, a particular aspect of personality appeared to have an effect that ran counter to the general result. Those who were very silent – who were slightly more syntactically mature than the most talkative pupils – used *I* earlier in their story writing than their peers; in factual writing they had made only a modest movement towards the third person by the top of the junior school. Harpin (p. 154) speculated that quiet, isolated children saw themselves as both writer and reader of their work while the talkative, gregarious children were more oriented towards an external audience.

In chapter 3, two late-occurring errors in the spoken noun phrase were noted: the use of the objective case pronoun *me* in co-ordinated subject phrases, and a violation of the co-occurrence restrictions between determiner and head noun. In speech, 'me and someone' as subject is only marginally an error. In other words, educated adults will produce it in unplanned casual conversation and only in rather formal contexts is it markedly inappropriate. Because written language can be planned and because it is intrinsically more formal than most speech, we are more conscious of inappropriateness when *me* is used as a subject in writing. It is a form that occurs quite extensively during the junior school years, e.g.:

34 *Me and Andrew* went swimming.   Robert, 7 years (Harpin, p. 146)
35 *Me and my family* looked out of the window.
                                        Susan, 9 years (Kroll *et al.*)
36 *Jill and me* got a bowl.   11 years (Burgess *et al.*, p. 74)

In the ninety pieces of writing by nine-year-olds which constitute Kroll *et al.*'s sample, there are just seven uses of the first person singular pronoun in a co-ordinated subject; six of these have the form 'me and someone' (or 'someone and me'). There is only one 'someone and I'.

Characteristic determiner errors in speech are listed in table 9 on p. 102 above. The only one that occurs with any frequency in children's writing is the use of *a* rather than *an* before a noun or adjective that begins with a vowel, e.g.:

six- and seven-year-olds:

a elephant (Harpin, p. 89); a ant (Rosen & Rosen, p. 92); a underwater cave (Burgess *et al.*, p. 88)

nine-year-olds:

a aeroplane (Harpin, p. 89); a hour (Kroll *et al.*); a elderly lady (Burgess, p. 89); a American game (Kroll *et al.*)

eleven-year-olds:

a 1882 hearse (Harpin, p. 88)

This determiner error is the one that seems to persist longest in children's speech, also. In the transcripts of Fawcett and Perkins' (1980) twelve-year-olds, there is a tendency for the error to be associated with the use of relatively unfamiliar nouns, e.g. *arcade*, *accountant*. In writing, it might come about because the writer pauses after the determiner, having not yet chosen the next word, and then continues the phrase without rereading.

The verb phrase

As far as the verb phrase is concerned, Hunt (1970, p. 7) reports that older students use 'significantly more perfect tenses, progressive forms, more passives, more modals'. Characteristically, young children use simple, active verbs, e.g.:

> 37 One day two boys *went* fishing and they *had* some jam-jars and they *caught* some sticklebacks and they *saw* a mill and they *explored* it.   Mark, 7 years (Harpin, p. 57)

They can also use auxiliary verb phrases – the following examples are from seven- and eight-year-olds in Harpin's study:

> 38 The shadow *was coming*.   (p. 65)
> 39 They wondered what *had happened*.   (p. 62)
> 40 I *don't like* snow.   (p. 148)
> 41 I *could hear* the wind.   (p. 65)

In addition, there are examples of catenative verb phrases and verb plus particle phrases, e.g.:

> 42 The house *seemed to creak*.   (p. 65)
> 43 My spell *has worn out*.   (p. 65)

These two- and three-word phrases seem to be the most complex VP structures that occur at all commonly at this age. Older children use modal auxiliaries more frequently and also constructions that combine both auxiliary and catenative phrases: the examples are from twelve-and thirteen-year-olds' writing, collected by Burgess *et al.*:

> 44 We *must have looked* like a row of rheumatic Can Can girls. (p. 47)
> 45 This *would have been* an encouragement.   (p. 62)
> 46 I *have decided to put together* all the general facts.   (p. 40)
> 47 He *had been longing to go*.   (p. 60)
> 48 I *should be expected to play* something.   (p. 62)

In speech, children are not always able to maintain agreement between tenses in successive verb phrases. This difficulty also arises in their writing: when there is a complex sentence with two or more clauses, young writers sometimes change tense within the sentence, e.g.:

> 49 There *was* a swimming pool which you *can go* in.
>   Mary, 9 years (Kroll *et al.*)
> 50 The Africans *are getting* tired of continually thatching their houses, every time a drip *came* through the roof.
>   Rosemary, 10 years (Rosen & Rosen, p. 125)
> 51 It *was* hopeless to escape because the window *is* about $4\frac{1}{2}$ yards off the ground.   Steven, 10 years (Harpin, p. 48)

However, the greatest difficulty that children experience with the verb phrase in speech is the selection of the right modal and tense forms in hypothetical reference (see p. 111). There is evidence of a similar struggle in writing, e.g.:

52 If you *would try and step* on it your feet would go straight through
   it.   Mary, 9 years (Kroll *et al.*)
53 We have a nice headmaster who hardly ever grumbles at us. I
   don't blame him if he did.   Andrew, 10 years (Harpin, p. 28)
54 I dared not pick them up in case they *would fall* to pieces.
                                    Annabel, 13 years (Burgess *et al.*, p. 59)
55 Even if China became a member there is no saying if she *will agree*
   on most political opinions.   John, 14 years (Burgess *et al.*, p. 77)

The teenagers, Annabel and John, are very competent writers, who have
produced mature, carefully crafted pieces. Yet they both still have difficulty with this type of verb phrase. Completely assured mastery of this
form must be a very late development.

Word structure

We have seen that, in their oral language, children make errors in the
past tense forms of irregular verbs at least until the age of eight. Such
errors occur in writing too; some examples are presented in table 18. It is

TABLE 18   Errors in irregular verbs in children's writing

| | Verb form required | | | |
| | Simple past | | Past participle | |
Age	Erroneous form	Study	Erroneous form	Study
7 years	swum	Harpin (p. 146)	fell	Harpin (p. 62)
	sunk	Harpin (p. 46)		
9 and 10 years	drived	Harpin (p. 89)	saw	Kroll *et al.*
	eated	Harpin (p. 89)	trod	Rosen & Rosen (p. 120)
	catched	Kroll *et al.*		
	shined	Rosen & Rosen (p. 186)		
11–13 years	rised	Burgess *et al.* (p. 134)	rose	Harris (1980) (p. 161)
	setted	Burgess *et al.* (p. 134)		
	sunk	Burgess *et al.* (p. 74)		

not always possible to tell whether the error is in the form of the verb or
in the selection of the right tense. Sometimes, spelling problems confuse
the issue further. For example, when nine-year-old James writes:

56 The lions ran away and *hide*.   James, 9 years (Kroll *et al.*)

we cannot tell whether he has moved from the past to the present tense; or whether he thinks the past tense of the irregular verb *hide* is the same as the present (as it is in the verb *spread*, for example); or whether he knows the form *hid* and simply cannot spell it properly.

Compound sentences

The position with regard to main clause co-ordination is straightforward: young children use it a great deal. O'Donnell *et al.*'s (1967) study shows that it is very pervasive in their speech; and, as Harpin (1976, p. 68) points out, 'by the time they come to write, it is a powerful habit, which gives way only slowly and reluctantly to the very large number of different joining methods provided for in English.' This kind of writing is very familiar to primary school teachers:

> 57 One day, Mel and me took the dog for a walk and the dog ran away and David ran after it and caught it and we went home and had our tea. David, 7 years (Harpin, p. 89)

'And' can signal several different relationships. It can indicate chronological sequence (*then* or *next*), e.g.:

> 58 I started the engine and I put it in gear.

Here, the order of the clauses cannot be reversed without a change of meaning. The same applies when 'and' expresses causality (*so*):

> 59 It was raining and I got soaked.

King and Rentel (1981, p. 65) suggest that seven-year-olds may also use 'and' in an adversative sense, where adults would use *but* or *yet*. Again, the order of clauses cannot be changed:

> 60 They tried to destroy this bridge and they had airplanes and bombers *and* they could not reach it.

In contrast, the conjoined clauses are reversible when 'and' expresses either simultaneity (*while*):

> 61 Alan read the newspaper and Margaret wrote a letter.

or an additive relation (*in addition*):

> 62 James broke his glasses and Sarah lost her passport.

The wide range of meanings that 'and' can express makes it a temptingly easy choice for the writer but a source of some difficulty for the reader, who would be helped by a more precise expression of inter-clause relationships.

Young writers use 'and' not only to signal the relationships outlined above but also, sometimes, simply to keep the discourse moving forward, with no temporal or logical link implied at all. This can lead to some unfortunate co-ordinations, e.g.:

> 63 [The Vikings] killed and slaughtered the mums and children. They poked them with spears *and* they were also very good craftsmen, for they carved their own boats and ships.
>
> June, 12 years (Burgess *et al.*, p. 135)

As they mature linguistically, developing a range of ways of connecting their ideas, so their dependence on clausal co-ordination decreases. Hunt (1965, p. 52) notes that, compared with nine-year-olds, seventeen-year-olds use less than a quarter of the number of clauses joined by *and*.

Complex sentences

The decline in the use of compound sentences is matched by an increase in the number of complex ones. With increasing age, children use not only more subordinate clauses but also a wider variety of clause types. At the age of eight, there is rather more subordination in samples of children's speech than there is in comparable samples of writing; by ten, the relationship is reversed, with about a third more subordinate clauses in written language; by seventeen, the difference between the two modes is even greater. Table 19 gives the figures for subordination in speech and writing in O'Donnell *et al.*'s (1967) study; their subjects were aged 7;4 to 14;6, but only one type of language – narrative – was sampled.

In general, it is very noticeable that young writers 'lose their way' more often in a complex sentence than in a simple one. For example, if they begin a complex sentence with an adverbial phrase or clause, they sometimes appear to have forgotten the structure they have embarked on, and to be re-interpreting a noun phrase in the adverbial as the subject of the main clause:

> 64 When *we* had got level with Karim Khan Zand flyover when we saw a paylcar [sic] burning with tyres around it.
>
> Jenny, 9 years (J. Wilkinson, 1981, p. 90)
> 65 In *this particular rockpool that I looked in* was so crammed with all kinds of marine life . . .
>
> Russell, 11 years (Rosen & Rosen, p. 134)

Other errors will be mentioned in the following sections on the three major clause types. The proportions of these types in children's writing are shown in table 20, which presents data from studies by Harpin (1976), Hunt (1965) and O'Donnell *et al.* (1967). The figures in the three studies differ somewhat, almost certainly because they are derived from different types of writing. (Table 21 shows what a dramatic effect the task has on the use of subordinate clauses.) Nevertheless, the broad picture is clear: nominal and adverbial clauses occur extensively throughout the

TABLE 19 Comparison of rate of occurrence of finite subordinate clauses per 100 T-units in children's speech and writing
(based on O'Donnell et al., 1967, pp. 59, 60, 61, 62, 68)

| American grade level | Age | Rate of occurrence of each clause type | | | | | | | |
| | | Speech | | | | Writing | | | |
		Nom.	Adv.	Rel.	Total	Nom.	Adv.	Rel.	Total
3 (N = 30)	7;4–10;2 (mean 8;9)	8.42	10.12	2.63	21.17	7.75	8.93	0.99	17.67
5 (N = 30)	10;2–11;8 (mean 10;10)	5.81	10.05	3.26	19.12	7.50	15.65	3.37	26.52
7 (N = 30)	12;2–14;6 (mean 13;0)	8.87	12.83	3.90	25.60	7.47	17.60	4.46	29.53

Type of language: story of silent cartoon film children had just seen

TABLE 20 Proportions of subordinate clause types used in children's writing in three studies

| | | Hunt (1965, p. 89) | | | Harpin (1976, p. 71) | | | O'Donnell et al. (1967, pp. 60, 62, 68) | | |
| | | Varied | | | Varied | | | Narrative | | |
American grade level	Age (approx.)	Nom.	Adv.	Rel.[7]	Nom.	Adv.	Rel.[7]	Nom.	Adv.	Rel.
					Percentages of each clause type[6]					
	7				46	43	11			
3	8				38	46	16	44	50	6
4	9	48	36	16	36	45	19			
5	10				34	44	22	28	59	13
7	13							25	60	15
8	14	39	39	22						
12	17	44	31	25						

6 The least common types, e.g. adj + *that* clause, are not included.
7 Hunt and Harpin use the term 'adjective clause' for the constructions that are labelled 'relative clause' in this book.

seven to seventeen age-range; relative clauses are initially infrequent but their occurrence increases significantly during the school years.

Nominal clauses

Children readily use nominal clauses as objects in their writing (as they do in speech). They are particularly frequent in dialogue and in personal narratives, where verbs like *say, think* and *know* occur naturally. In descriptive writing they appear much less often, as Hunt (1970) found when he asked three hundred subjects, from nine-year-olds to adults, to describe the process of aluminium smelting; although the descriptions contained hundreds of subordinate clauses there were no nominal ones at all. It would clearly be a crass misinterpretation of this data to suggest that the subjects had not yet mastered such clauses. On the whole, then, variation in the use of nominal clauses is related to type of writing rather than to developmental level. However, there are two trends that are indicative of linguistic maturity. First, nominal clauses functioning as clause elements other than the object are never frequent; indeed, subject clauses are especially rare and are more likely to occur in the writing of older and abler children, e.g.:

> 66 Very little is known about how and what the infant perceives and *what is known* is inconclusive.
>
> Danny, 17 years (Burgess *et al.*, p. 28)

In Hunt's (1965) data, out of 247 nominal clauses produced by thirteen-year-olds, only nine (3.6 per cent) were functioning as subjects. Secondly, Harpin (1976) found that, whereas seven-year-olds use object clauses more often to express direct speech than indirect speech, eleven-year-olds show the opposite preference. During the years in between, it is not unusual for them to make the mistake of blending the two constructions, e.g.:

> 67 A jungle boy stopped him and said, 'That the elephant is already dead.'
>
> Philip, 9 years (Kroll *et al.*)

It is not just Philip's punctuation that is wrong: to be successful with the indirect speech form (which he has signalled by *that*) he would have to use the past tense – 'the elephant *was* already dead'. The next example illustrates a pronominal problem the writer experiences in attempting indirect speech:

> 68 Then someone advised some of us to stay with us in the Ferdowni compound.
>
> Jenny, 9 years (J. Wilkinson, 1981, p. 84)

Here, 'stay with *us*' repeats the speaker's actual words when the indirect form, 'stay with *them*', is required.

Adverbial clauses

Adverbial clauses of time occur early and often in children's writing. Naturally enough, they are particularly common in any piece that has a chronological pattern of organization. Harpin (1976, p. 69) suggests that other adverbial clauses appear in children's writing in the following order of frequency; reason, condition, place, result, purpose, manner, concession. Eleven-year-olds use twice as many clauses of concession as eight-year-olds but, even so, they write only one concession clause for every sixty time clauses. The nine-year-olds' writing that Kroll *et al.* collected provides numerous instances of clauses of time, reason and condition; there are also several examples of purpose and result clauses, e.g.:

69 Then you throw the counter *to see who starts.*   David, 9 years
70 You would not sink right into the mud *so that you could not be saw.*   Mary, 9 years

Place and manner clauses, however, occur only rarely, e.g.:

71 If it is on white then you stay *where you are.*   David, 9 years
72 The lion started running *like no man ever could.*   David, 9 years

In all the ninety pieces of writing in Kroll *et al.*'s sample, there is only one possible attempt at a clause of concession. In this sentence, John is trying to describe his joy at finally owning a puppy he had longed to have:

73 When you get sudden fear something *though you like that but with happiness.*   John, 9 years

Evidently, the language structure collapses as John tries to use complex subordination to express demanding ideas.

It is noticeable that, out of the eighteen children in Kroll *et al.*'s sample, it is only a small, able group who use the more unusual types of adverbial clause. It seems, then, that the production of a variety of clause types, including such rare kinds as place, manner and concession clauses, is a sign of linguistic maturity.

Another indication of maturity is the use of non-finite adverbial clauses (other than those of purpose, which occur early). There are very occasional examples from nine-year-olds, e.g.:

74 She will walk away *as if knowing you don't want her.*

9 years, David (Kroll *et al.*)

Yerrill (1977, p. 183), who notes that more such clauses occur in the writing of older and abler pupils, provides the following examples from twelve-year-olds:

75 *Having done that,* I was soon able to iron out my faults.

76 He, *realizing my enthusiasm with regards to football*, gave me my first season ticket for my eleventh birthday.

77 The sounds, *although totally disconnected*, seemed to form a weird symphony which was going somewhere.

Such language is literary, clearly differentiated from the language of spontaneous speech.

Relative clauses

Table 20 (p. 233) shows that the occurrence of relative clauses in writing doubles between the ages of seven and ten and that the increase, in relation to the other subordinate clauses, continues throughout the secondary years. Linguistic maturity is signalled, though, not only by the number of relative clauses but also by the type, since some are noticeably late developments. As in speech, relative clauses in writing occur in subject noun phrases later than in predicate noun phrases, and non-finite forms appear after finite ones. Clauses introduced by *whom*, *whose* and a preposition plus a relative pronoun (e.g. *in which*) are the production of mature writers: Hunt's (1965) thirteen-year-olds produced 136 relative pronouns without a single occurrence of these forms; the seventeen-year-olds used 205 relative pronouns, which included one example of *whom*, two of *whose* and five of a preposition plus a relative pronoun. Similarly advanced are series of relative clauses within one sentence. A study of children's writing and of the available research evidence suggests a possible developmental sequence, so I have tentatively grouped the various relative clause types into four stages. The hypothesis is that a writer who used a pattern from one of the later groups would also be able to use all the constructions in the previous groups. (There is no suggestion of ordering WITHIN each group.) It is possible, of course, that some very able children will acquire the constructions in several groups almost simultaneously, but it is probably more normal for there to be a progression through the stages, with the structures in stages I and II appearing during the primary years and those in III and IV not normally occurring until children reach the secondary school.

Stage I. This group contains the earliest-occurring relative clauses, which are finite clauses, in the predicate, introduced by *that, who, which* and zero, e.g.:

78 He shot a few rabbits *that the witch might like.*
Susan, 7 years (Burgess et al., p. 55)

79 I have a sister *who's always doing things wrong.*
Michael, 7 years (Burgess et al., p. 84)

80 It was the first time *I had played on that green.*
Jimmy, 8 years (Rosen & Rosen, p. 146)

An error that occurs in clauses of this type is the use of the wrong relative pronoun, e.g.:

81 [all the children] stayed up except the two youngest **which** *went with Saramy the eldest.*   11 years (Burgess *et al.*, p. 123)

Stage II.   Slightly more advanced are:

a) finite clauses modifying the subject,
b) non-finite clauses in the predicate,

e.g.:

82 The chair *I am waiting in* is comfortable.
Christopher, 10 years (Rosen & Rosen, p. 116)
83 You flick the counter *marked with blue and yellow.*
Philip, 9 years (Kroll *et al.*)
84 We went in and found a witch *sitting on a chair.*
Ruth, 9 years (Harpin, p. 86)

Occasionally, children make the error of omitting the subject relative pronoun when the clause modifies the subject, e.g.:

85 The girl or boy *get up the circles* wins the game. [*i.e.* The girl or boy *who gets up to the circles* wins the game.]
Allan, 9 years (Kroll *et al.*)

Stage III.   Rather later, clauses appear that are introduced by *whom, whose* or a preposition plus a relative pronoun, e.g.:

86 When I first entered this school, the Headmaster was Mr. H. *whom I liked and respected even though I was terrified of him.*
12 years (Yerrill, 1977, p. 179)
87 One of the girls, *who's* [*whose*] *name was Josephine but they called her Jo for short*, first saw Laurie looking out of a window.
12 years (Yerrill, 1977, p. 180)
88 He is just a ghost *to whom I pay no attention at all.*
Stephen, 13 years (Burgess *et al.*, p. 56)

Young writers obviously recognize the formality of these constructions and sometimes try to introduce them into their work – presumably because they are striving to achieve a formal style – only to get into a muddle, e.g.:

89 Place your specimen (*the most suitable of which being a small rodent*) onto a piece of paper.   10 years (Burgess *et al.*, p. 134)

Here, the writer does not need *of which* at all. In the next example, an adult remedial writer makes the mistake of including a preposition that is not required:

90 You know what you want and you can just about demand the price *in which you think you should receive.*
Adult (Shaughnessy, 1977, p. 64)

Another error is the repetition of the preposition, e.g.:

91 This year it is Pirates of Penzance *in which I'm in.*
12 years (Yerrill, 1977, p. 179)
92 The college bound student would like to find out *in which field he or she would be most interested in.*
Adult (Shaughnessy, 1977, p. 65)

The relative pronoun *whose* seems to be particularly difficult, e.g.:

93 It was great to learn Staniflovsky's method *which I know I just spelled his name wrong.*   Adult (Shaughnessy, 1977, p. 63)

This writer seems to have been aiming for: *whose name, I know, I just spelled wrong.*

Stage IV.   The most mature relative clause constructions are:

  a) non-finite clauses modifying the subject (excluding the almost formulaic use of *called* and *named,* e.g. 'a man called John'),
  b) series of relatives within one sentence,

e.g.:

94 One colt, *lying down on the hay,* was trembling.
(Hunt, 1966, p. 735)
95 I turned away from the door as Nanny, *helped by Philip,* swayed drunkenly out of the lounge into the dim lit hall.
15 years (Yerrill, 1977, p. 246)

Yerrill comments that, out of approximately 650 pieces of writing by pupils aged nine to fifteen, this was the only example of a non-finite relative with a past participle, modifying a subject. It is also in his data that the following, competently handled series of relative clauses occurs:

96 You couldn't blame them really, because not many people would like to be seen with a person *whose appearance was appalling, whose teeth hadn't been brushed for days or maybe weeks, who hadn't had a bath for weeks and whose hair was dirty and untidy.*
15 years (Yerrill, 1977, p. 244)

Even skilful sixteen-year-old writers can make mistakes in the production of such a series, e.g.:

97 The agents of erosion that act on a temperate desert are – Wind, *which picks up sand and hurls it at objects in its path and wearing it down where it is weaker.*   16 years (Yerrill, 1977, p. 270)

Whereas the clauses in stages I and II occur as readily in speech as in writing, the examples in stage IV are undoubtedly more typical of written language.

To conclude this section on complex sentences it is important to emphasize that the occurrence of different types of subordinate clause is heavily dependent on the nature of the writing. A clear illustration of this is provided by the samples in the Kroll *et al.* (1980) corpus. Their eighteen subjects wrote five different pieces, over a period of five weeks. These included a story, which the children made up to accompany a cartoon picture of a hunter being confronted by some wild animals, and a set of instructions for a board game. All the children had been taught how to play the specially devised game (without verbal instructions) and they were told to 'write instructions so that another child your age could read your explanation and then know how to play perfectly.' As the same children produced writing of different types, it is valid to compare the kinds of subordination engendered by the two situations.

Both pieces of writing can be organized chronologically, though the instructions also require superordinate statements of principles and exceptions. The story is personal writing, with the pronouns *he* and *they* occurring frequently in subject position. In contrast, the instructions are further along the continuum towards impersonal writing, as the subjects of clauses are most often **generalized** people, e.g. *the player, the other person, two people, the winner.* The commonest subject is generalized *you*, e.g. *You can't move until you get the right colour* (where *you* could be replaced by *one*). An interesting point about the instructions is that they entail describing actions that are simple to perform but difficult to express in words. For example, the rule that explains which of the two players makes the first move on the board needs to be formulated something like this:

> One player flips a counter that is yellow on one side and blue on the other. The player with the bird which matches the colour that lands uppermost is the one to begin.

That procedure is easy to demonstrate yet hard to write about. It seems reasonable, therefore, to predict that Kroll *et al.*'s subjects would find the story the easier of the two writing tasks. There is some evidence to that effect. A majority of the children wrote more for the story than for the instructions (on average, the stories were 18 per cent longer). Furthermore, when all the pieces were evaluated by independent markers, the average score for the story was 8 out of 18 (44 per cent); it was lower for the instructions at 11.5 out of 30 (28 per cent) (Kroll & Wells, 1983). However, that does not mean that the story stimulated the writers' most mature language. The occurrence of subordination in the two pieces is dramatically different, as table 21 shows. Not only are there

TABLE 21   Types of subordinate clause in two pieces of writing by seventeen nine-year-old children

	Story	Instructions
Total number of words in 17 pieces:	*2230*	*1886*
Subordinate clause types		
Nominal object ⎫ *very*	14	6
Adverbial time ⎭ *common clauses*[8]	14	10
Adverbial condition	0	40
reason	3	2
result *less*	3	1
place *common*	0	2
manner *clauses*[8]	1	0
other	0	6
Nominal after prep	0	3
Relative modifying 0	6	13
Relative modifying S	1	11
Adj + 'that' clause	2	0
Total number of sub. clauses	44	94
Number of sub. clauses per 100 words	2	5
Proportion of less common clauses	36%	83%

more than twice as many subordinate clauses in the instructions, there is also a much higher proportion of the less common clause types. Perhaps it is the very complexity of the instruction-writing task that forces the writers to exploit all the linguistic resources they have at their command.

The overall comparison is striking but the figures for individual children are even more telling. Every one of the seventeen pupils who completed both pieces used more subordinate clauses per hundred words in the instructions than in the story. Four children, Paul, Janet, Elizabeth and Ann, produced no subordinate clauses at all in their stories but from three to seven in the instructions. This shows clearly that it would be very misleading to make a judgement about a pupil's linguistic ability on the basis of only one type of writing. It also suggests that children need the opportunity, from a fairly early age, to write in a number of different styles. They may get in a muddle sometimes, as Wendy does here:

> 98 Then you toss the counter in the air. If it lands on yellow then that person starts who ever has the yellow bird.
>
> Wendy, 9 years (Kroll *et al.*)

But this can be seen as a sign of growth, as she stretches her linguistic ability to the limits in the struggle to express a complex idea. If such

8 The division into very common and less common subordinate clauses follows Harpin (1976, p. 60).

demands are never made, it is hard to see how the young writer can develop to the full. One way of ensuring that the task does not become unproductively overwhelming is to prepare the subject matter before-hand (as in the bird game) so that children do not have to work out WHAT to write as well as HOW to write it.

Discourse connections

For a passage to form a satisfactory discourse, it is necessary for there to be agreement of tenses. We have seen already that young writers some-times change tense within a complex sentence. Not surprisingly, they do the same between sentences, e.g.:

> 99 In a field the bulls *are crunching* the fresh green grass or basking in the sun. Suddenly a lot of children *creep* up near the bulls, trying not to look suspicious. They *knelt* down to sketch the bulls. The bulls *start* to surround them.
>
> Ian, 10 years (Rosen & Rosen, p. 113).

Sentences in a discourse can be linked together by the grammatical processes of reference, substitution and ellipsis, and by connective words such as *then* and *however*. Crystal (1979b) reports that teachers of primary school children are particularly concerned about their pupils' inability to handle these connectivity features skilfully. He notes that there are two broad problems – the overuse of some resources and the underuse of others.

Reference

Pronominal reference is used early and extensively in children's writing. Indeed, the repetition of the same pronoun as subject of several consecu-tive sentences is characteristic of immature work, e.g.:

> 100 I have got a nice puppy. *He* do not chase cats and *he* is a good puppy and *he* do not bark. *He* is furry and very very good. *He* is clever.   Janet, 9 years (Kroll *et al.*)

Much rarer than pronouns are pro-forms such as *there*, e.g.:

> 101 They had to climb the mountain. But when they got *there* there were some jungle animals . . .   Andrew, 9 years (Kroll *et al.*)

The following sentence shows the kind of nominal repetition that arises when a writer does not make use of a pro-form:

> 102 When he went to his pocket there was not anything *in his pocket*.
>
> Andrew, 9 years (Kroll *et al.*)

Apart from the overuse of pronouns and the underuse of pro-forms, there are two major difficulties that children experience with reference items. The first is maintaining pronominal agreement and the second is avoiding ambiguity. Pronouns have to agree with their antecedent noun in number and gender. Failure to do so is exemplified in the following sentences:

> 103 *Privateers* were paid by the government to be a pirate and *he* couldn't be hanged if he was caught.
>
> Kerry, 9 years (Burgess *et al.*, p. 92)
>
> 104 Two *people* can play it. *One* of them puts two metal birds behind *its* back.   Sandra, 9 years (Kroll *et al.*)

Kerry seems to have been led astray by her singular use of *pirate* after the plural *privateers*. Sandra's error may have been caused by the absence in English of a sex-neutral third person singular pronoun; the options available to her are *his, her, his or her*, and *their*. All of these have their drawbacks, which may have led, unconsciously, to her choice of *its*.

Once the writer has selected a pronoun to refer to a noun, he must be consistent in its use. Children seem to have particular difficulty when they want to refer to nouns that are animate but non-human. In writing that I have read about dogs, snails, spiders, flies and ants, the pronouns swing between *it, he*, and occasionally *she*, e.g.:

> 105 I saw a harvestman spider. *It* was shy and began to run away on its eight long flimsy legs. *It* had a minute body and great long legs like stabilizers. *He* was very light and hairy like. *He* soon ran back under the log. *It* crawled right under and came out the other side.   Christopher, 10 years (Rosen & Rosen, p. 113)

Evidence of the pervasiveness of this error comes from Kroll *et al.*'s sample of nine-year-olds, who all had to write a letter persuading someone to buy a dog. Eleven of the seventeen children who used pronominal reference in their letters were inconsistent in the forms they used; most fluctuated between *he* and *it* but three included *she* as well.

A rather different problem of pronominal sequence occurs in narratives where the narrator switches from observing the action to being a part of it, e.g.:

> 106 When *you* take him out for walkies he run away from *me*.
>
> Judy, 9 years (Kroll *et al.*)
>
> 107 Suddenly a *lot of children* creep up near the bulls . . . *They* knelt down to sketch the bulls. The bulls start to surround *them* but *we* discover their plan so *they* slowly walk away to leave them crunching the grass in the field.
>
> Ian, 10 years (Rosen & Rosen, p. 113)

The second difficulty with pronouns is ambiguity of reference. This problem is not confined to the youngest writers. J. B. N. Harris (1980) studied the writing done in history, geography and biology by able children aged twelve to fifteen and he was struck by the fact that when they had to weave together two or more strands of action or description, pronominal confusion often resulted. In other words, if there is one central character in a narrative, who typically occupies the subject slot in successive sentences, pronominal reference presents no serious problems. But when, for example, the actions of two opposing armies have to be described, then the pronoun *they* has to be very skilfully employed, as it may have two possible antecedents, e.g.:

108 When the French reached the English *they* pushed *them* back when the English began steadily fighting.

12/13 years (Harris, 1980, p. 106)

Substitution and ellipsis

Substitution and ellipsis are used very much less than reference by young writers. (In adult writing, too, reference is the most frequent of the three processes.) King and Rentel (1981) found hardly any examples in six- to eight-year-olds' writing and, even with data from fifteen-year-olds, J. B. N. Harris (1980) noted that both of these discourse processes were very rare. The nine-year-olds in Kroll *et al.*'s sample provide a handful of instances of nominal substitution, e.g.:

109 He saw a lot of animals. Do you know which *one* he saw?

Mary, 9 years (Kroll *et al.*)

There is just one example of clausal substitution:

110 I wondered if you would like it. If *so*, please write to this address.

Judy, 9 years (Kroll *et al.*)

There is no verbal substitution at all in this corpus. Ellipsis occurs occasionally at both clause and phrase level. In the following examples, it is indicated by empty square brackets:

111 Would you like to have a puppy? Because my aunt May said that you would [ ]. Ann, 9 years (Kroll *et al.*)
112 First you hold the two birds behind your back and let your opponent choose one hand. He has that bird. You have the other [ ]. David, 9 years (Kroll *et al.*)

The overriding impression that is gained from a study of writing by children aged between about seven and twelve is that they do not use reference, substitution and ellipsis in the same way as adult writers. Frequently, the result is a repetitive text, e.g.:

113 There is a lovely black and white dog waiting to be sold. If you would like the dog come to Pennard Farm West Bradley Somer-

set. The dog has a fluffy warm tail. The dog has bright black eyes. The dog has been trained about a year ago. The dog does not bite you and does not bite anything else.

Derek, 9 years (Kroll et al.)

Here, Derek uses ellipsis only once (in the last sentence) and no pronominal reference at all. In the next example, Mary misses an opportunity to use ellipsis:

> 114 I was wondering if you might want it. I will be glad if you do *want it.*　　　　　　　　　　　　　　　Mary, 9 years (Kroll *et al.*)

Lastly, Judy repeats a noun phrase rather than using the indefinite pronoun *one*:

> 115 I was wondering if you would like a Jack Russell. Her name is Elcid. My grandfather told me that you would like *a Jack Russell.*　　　　　　　　　　　　　Judy, 9 years (Kroll *et al.*)

Not only are these examples unlike adult writing, but they also seem more repetitive than the speech of children of the same age. What they resemble most closely is the kind of writing that is found in early reading books, e.g.:

> 116 Here is a ball in a shop. Jane likes the ball.
> Jane has the dog and Jane has the ball.
> The dog has the ball. The dog likes the ball.

This makes one wonder whether some young children are unconsciously modelling their writing style on texts of this type.

Such an explanation is unlikely to apply to older pupils, and yet J. B. N. Harris (1980) found that a few of the teenagers he studied also produced repetitive texts by failing to use pronominal reference in the expected way. He suggested that they were composing in discrete 'event units'; that is, each new action, signalled by a time adverbial, is perceived as an autonomous whole. Therefore, the processes of reference and ellipsis work WITHIN event units but not BETWEEN them. For simplicity, I have chosen an example that has one event unit per sentence, but very often a unit spans two or more sentences. Each new event unit begins on a new line:

> 117 Henry V claimed the throne to France.
> In August 1415 *Henry* sailed to Harfleur and captured it.
> On October 9th *Henry* set off for Calais, leaving half of his army at Harfleur and taking the other half with him.

12/13 years (Harris, 1980, p. 81)

In this passage, we would expect the italicized nouns to be replaced by pronouns.

Sentence connectives

Sentence connectives are not used very extensively by young children in their writing. King and Rentel (1981) found that, although their use of connectives increased fourfold between the ages of six and eight, eight-year-olds still produced fewer connectives in their writing than they did in stories that they dictated for an adult to transcribe. In the primary school years, the connectives that do appear are generally the ones that are frequent in speech, such as *and, but, so, then, first, next, later, after that*. Apart from the ubiquitous *and*, it is the temporal connectives that are used most often. The commonest may be overused, e.g.:

118 In the morning I had some cornflakes. *Then* I had a practice kicking the judo bag. *Then* I had to do some judo exercises. *Then* I got changed and my dad took me to my friend. *Then* later on he took me home.   Paul, 9 years (Kroll *et al.*)

In fact, a discourse with a chronological pattern of organization does not strictly require connectives at all, since, in the absence of indications to the contrary, readers assume that the order of sentences reflects the order of events. Therefore a young writer does not actually need to employ a wide range of temporal connectives. However, a discourse that is not organized in a chronological sequence is heavily dependent on logical connectives to signal the relationships between the sentences. Young writers experience particular difficulty with the causal and adversative connectives. Thus there is the paradoxical situation that children cope with the connectives they do not strictly need and yet struggle with those they do. Fiction generally has a chronological pattern of organization, so children are unlikely to learn those logical connectives that are more formal and precise than *but* and *so* by reading stories. Unless they read well-constructed non-fictional descriptions, explanations and so on before they have to write their own in subjects like geography and science, they are unlikely to have at their command the connectives they need.

In his study of writing in the 'subject areas', J. B. N. Harris (1980) discovered that it was very common for pupils to be instructed to take notes from the teacher's exposition during the lesson and then to write an essay based on the notes. He felt that this technique led to the writing of strings of unconnected sentences because, in order to take economical notes, the pupils wrote down only the facts, leaving out the connections between them. At the essay-writing stage they seemed unable to recover the missing links.

Three general points will conclude this section on grammatical development. First, linguistic maturity in writing has been seen in terms of the writer's increasing ability to handle complex constructions successfully.

This notion needs to be treated with caution. There is no virtue in complexity for its own sake – indeed, a great deal of adult writing would be better if it were grammatically simpler. Moreover, short, simple sentences can sometimes be used to great stylistic effect. In the following extract, Wendy is recalling the time when, at the age of two and a half, she was sent away to her grandmother's:

> 119 I went there for a week. On Sunday I came back home. We rang on my doorbell. Daddy came. Come in. We went upstairs. I said hello mummy. But on the floor was a little baby girl. She is your little sister. Her name is Chloe.   Wendy, 9 years (Kroll *et al.*)

All the sentences in this extract are between two and six words long, except, *But on the floor was a little baby girl,* which is nine words long and clearly the heart of the whole piece. Wendy gives this sentence special prominence both by surrounding it with much shorter sentences and by reversing the normal word order so that the subject *a little baby girl* appears, climactically, at the end. In addition, it does not seem far-fetched to suggest that she is trying to create the impression of a two-year-old's world-view by using childlike language. (In the whole piece, the average sentence length is 5.76 words, whereas in another piece of her personal writing it is 8.83 words, which proves that she is not using very short sentences just because she is incapable of anything else.) This extract shows how important it is to evaluate linguistic features in relation to the writer's purposes rather than in a vacuum. The teacher's aim, therefore, in seeking to foster more complex constructions, should be to ensure that pupils have a wide range of linguistic resources and can select from them appropriately as the occasion demands. Simple sentences are fine if they reflect a writer's intentions but not if, being his only available option, they become a straitjacket for his thoughts.

The second point concerns the relationship between maturity in speech and in writing. Up to the age of nine, or thereabouts, most children reveal a lower level of grammatical maturity in their writing than in their speech. From then on, writing becomes increasingly differentiated from spoken language, employing a higher proportion of complex constructions, and some structures that rarely occur at all in spontaneous speech, such as long subject NPs, 'Stage IV' relatives, and non-finite adverbial clauses. This strongly suggests that, by this stage, linguistic development is being influenced at least as much by reading as by oral language. Some of the literary constructions which appear first in children's writing may later appear in their formal speech. Undoubtedly, as children become literate they gain access to a powerful new stimulus to their language development.

The third point relates to the use that teachers can make of knowledge about normal grammatical development in writing. For example, it should enable them to anticipate grammatical problem spots in particular writing assignments and to prepare pupils to cope with them. Thus, in setting a piece of work about an animal, a teacher could draw attention to the need to choose between *he, she* and *it* and to be consistent in pronoun use thereafter. Likewise, such knowledge should enable teachers to provide specific guidance about things to check at the editing stage of writing, such as confusions between direct and indirect speech, or instances of *and* that could be replaced by a more precise connective. It should also make it possible for teachers to distinguish between errors caused by a failure to reread (either during or after writing) and those that indicate growth-points – new constructions attempted but not yet fully mastered. Obviously the response to these two kinds of error needs to be different – there is no point in exhorting a pupil to reread his work if he will not recognize the mistake when he meets it.

5.4 THE EMERGENCE OF A DIFFERENTIATED WRITTEN STYLE

In some ways the separation between this section and the last is an artificial one, since both deal chiefly with grammatical features. However, here the emphasis will be on characteristic differences between spoken and written language rather than on children's developing ability to handle complex linguistic constructions. There are three reasons for making the separation. First, in the previous section it was possible to follow the pattern of organization that was established in chapters 2 and 3, moving from clause to phrase to word levels and from simple to compound to complex sentences. But in this section, in order to focus on some of the typical features of written language, it is necessary to cut across that pattern. For example, one such feature is thematic variation, which, in grammatical terms, may be achieved by the use of the passive, by the fronting of a clause element (such as the object or a place adverbial), by clefting, by substitution and so on.

Secondly, unlike 5.3, this section cannot be supported by findings from large-scale, statistically-oriented studies, because very little research has been done in this area. Presumably this is because, although it is easy enough to identify constructions that are characteristic of written language, it is much harder to be precise about their effects. For instance, a researcher can count the number of occurrences of the passive but is unlikely to be able to say unequivocally whether the writer selected that particular form to achieve an impersonal style, to maintain thematic continuity, to bring about thematic variation or to create end-focus or end-weight – frequently, several of these effects will combine. A further deterrent to large-scale research is that the structures that are generally confined to the written mode occur rather rarely in children's writing and so cannot be fruitfully subjected to statistical analysis. Nevertheless, I am convinced that, when we are considering a particular piece of work by an individual pupil (rather than referring to some notional 'average' child), a single occurrence of a construction may be very important as far as the quality of writing is concerned, regardless of the fact that it would not reach a level of statistical significance in a counting study. This can be illustrated by referring again to the extract from Wendy's writing, on p. 246. Here, in a pivotal position in her account, she uses the sentence *But on the floor was a little baby girl*, where the fronting of the adverbial – and consequent inversion of subject and verb – allows the information focus to fall, dramatically, on the subject, *a little baby girl*. Simply counting the number of instances of adverbial fronting would tell us nothing about the use and effectiveness of this sentence.

The third reason for separating the two sections is that, on the whole, it is not possible to provide a developmental perspective for this one, in contrast to the previous section. This, of course, derives from the fact that, generally, age-related studies of children's writing have been concerned with measurable trends rather than with the stylistic function of particular constructions.

Broadly, section 5.3 followed the orientation and organization of chapter 3, on children's acquisition of oral language, whereas this section takes up points raised in chapter 4, on the differences between spoken and written language.

A word of warning is needed about the term 'style', as it has many meanings (Crystal and Davy (1969, pp. 9–10), for example, distinguish four). In using the phrase 'written style', I am referring to a use of language that is felt to be appropriate to the topic, to the author's purpose and to the intended readership, as well as to the mode of communication. Thus the style is an integral part of the expression, not a decorative afterthought like icing on a cake. This means that it is not possible to consider stylistic features in a vacuum without reference to the larger context.

First I shall present some examples that reveal children successfully differentiating the written from the spoken mode. Then we can turn to some of the difficulties they experience.

The use of features characteristic of written language

Conventions of the writing system

In chapter 4 there were examples of features of the writing system that have no counterpart in speech, such as square brackets and the use of italics for the titles of books. The information these features convey is largely or wholly lost if the written text is read aloud. Any examination of writing produced by pupils aged between about seven and fourteen reveals that many are not confident in their handling of the basic conventional symbols – the full stop, question mark (with following capital letter) and comma – so it is not surprising that there are very few examples of more adventurous exploitation of the wider resources of the system. One of the rare ones comes from a piece of history homework: the class of twelve-year-olds, who were studying the Roman occupation of Britain, had been asked to pretend that they were soldiers stationed on Hadrian's wall and to write a letter home to their families in Rome. After an opening complaint about the British weather, one boy wrote:

> 120 This morning I killed VIII Scots.

This is a visual joke that has no aural counterpart. Another example comes from an eerie piece about a boy who sees his double:

> 121 'I'm Peter Warton'. . .
> 'That's funny, m-m-my name's Peter, too.'
> 'Peter what?'
> 'Would you like to come inside?'
> Peter W. wondered why Peter ? hadn't answered his last question.
> Chris, 13 years (Burgess et al., p. 175)

The question mark in *Peter ?* is a skilful, succinct way of focusing on the unrevealed surname. There is some evidence that the ability to take advantage of the purely visual features afforded by the writing system increases between the ages of nine and eleven. In a study related to the one described in the last section, Kroll (1981) asked children aged eight, nine and eleven to write instructions for the board game that he had devised. He found that, on the whole, it was the older children who were likely to use numbering, side-headings and other forms that do not generally occur in speech, e.g. *he/she* and *his/her*.

Thematic continuity

Now we can consider sentence **theme** in writing. In chapter 4 (p. 197), the theme was described as the first element in a clause. (It is worth noting that this is a narrowly technical definition of the term, different from the more general meaning, 'subject matter' or 'overall idea'.) Normally, the theme expresses 'given' information – that is, something that has already been mentioned – so that new information appears in the latter half of the sentence. This means that the skilful choice of theme is very important for the creation of a smoothly flowing text. If new information keeps occurring at the beginnings of sentences, then an awkward, disjointed text results in which it is hard for the reader to follow the writer's train of thought. (One aid for the reader in a well constructed passage is the division of the text into paragraphs, which signal visually the onset of new themes.) The theme occupies a prominent position in the clause or sentence, second only to the last lexical item, which is normally the information **focus** (see p. 170). Accordingly, a well chosen theme has to fulfil two criteria: it must take up an idea that has already been introduced, and it must have enough importance in the developing text to deserve its favoured position.

The clause elements which normally occur as themes are the subject and most adverbials (excluding those of place, which generally follow the verb). If these elements do not meet the two criteria then the writer can change the usual word order by fronting another element, e.g.:

> 122a They [the starlings] got stronger and their eyes had opened. One was getting very intelligent, like plucking at moving things. *This one* we called Charlie.
>
> Annabel, 13 years (Burgess *et al.*, p. 60)

Here, Annabel links the last two sentences by fronting the object *this one* to make it the theme. The unusual word order heightens the theme's characteristic prominence. If she had followed the normal word order and written:

> 122b We called this one Charlie.

she would have had as a theme the word *we*, which has not occurred in the immediately preceding sentences and which is not important in the present one.

In the next example a place adverbial is fronted:

> 123 From there I went up a flimsy ladder. There was a hole in the wall and a cold draught was coming through it. *At the top of the ladder* was a very big wheel attached to the bell.
>
> Christopher, 10 years (Rosen & Rosen, p. 112)

By making the adverbial the theme, Christopher links the sentence smoothly to the preceding text and also allows the phrase *a very big wheel attached to the bell*, which is the information focus, to occur where it is generally preferred, at the end.

Another grammatical device the writer can employ in order to get an appropriate theme is to use the passive. In the following extract Wendy is describing a school trip to a safari park:

> 124a I breathed a sigh of relief when we at last arrived back at the stop for it had taken up most of our time. *We were then allowed to have lunch.* Wendy, 9 years (Harpin, p. 34)

If she had not used the passive, she would have had to say something like:

> 124b Our teachers then allowed us to have lunch.

Here, the new information, *our teachers*, is the theme. This would be all right if the idea was to be taken up in the rest of the story but, in fact, the teachers are not important to Wendy so it would distort her purposes to give them the prominence that new material necessarily has when it is made the theme. Hence, her ability to use the passive helps her both to create a cohesive text and to concentrate on those aspects of her account that matter to her.

Thematic variety

In chapter 4, it was noted that extensive repetition of vocabulary and grammatical structure is less acceptable in writing than in speech. Therefore, mature writers try, often consciously, to introduce thematic variety. At first sight, this might seem to conflict with the idea of the theme maintaining continuity with the preceding text but, in fact, the two notions are compatible, as the following, constructed, example illustrates:

125a Ian saw Helen. She was wearing a new dress. It was dark green. The colour suited her.

Here, the object or complement of each sentence becomes the subject – and so the theme – of the next. This gives four different themes, *Ian she, it, the colour*, with each taking up an idea already introduced in the text. We can contrast this with a similar passage:

125b Ian saw Helen. He noticed her new dress. He liked dark green. He thought it suited her.

Now all four themes are the same – either *Ian* or the pronominal replacement *he*.

Young writers often use the same pronoun repeatedly in subject position, as the extract from Janet's writing on p. 241 demonstrated. Variety can be introduced by means of grammatical processes such as passivization and fronting. For instance, after a succession of clauses beginning with either *we* or *I*, Wendy changes the pattern by using a passive:

126 *The journey home was spent singing* until we reached the Church at Threekingham . . .   Wendy, 9 years (Harpin, p. 34)

Less adventurously, she could have continued with thematic *we* – 'We sang during the journey home until . . .' Sometimes a passive may sound rather stilted, as in this extract:

127 She ran to him. 'Happy Birthday' Sam he said and she gave him a big kiss. *A present was given to her*.
                Kim, 9 years (Crystal, 1979b, p. 24)

As most of the subjects of sentences in Kim's story are pronouns, it is possible that she has used the passive here because she is aware of the need for thematic variation; if this is so, then even though the result is rather clumsy, it is, as Crystal (p. 26) says, 'a quite exciting move in the right direction'.

End-focus

A major difference between spoken and written language is the absence of prosodic features in writing. A speaker is able to select any word as the information focus by assigning it the intonation nucleus. In contrast, the writer, as we have seen, generally has to ensure that the focus occurs at the end of the clause. This may involve changes in word order. Failure to give the appropriate word end-focus can result in a distortion of the writer's intended meaning, e.g.:

> 128a Sir Almroth Wright . . . had a vaccine to prevent typhoid and was in search of a vaccine to cure diseases.
>
> 14/15 years (Harris, 1980, p. 112)

Here there are two clauses, with the information focus falling on the last word in each, *typhoid* and *diseases*. This serves to contrast the two terms and makes it sound as if typhoid is not a disease. In fact, the intended contrast is between the verbs *prevent* and *cure*. It is very difficult to put a transitive verb in clause-final position because, in SVO structures, it naturally occurs in the middle. It could be done, rather awkwardly, by passivization, e.g.:

> 128b Sir Almroth Wright already had a vaccine which enabled typhoid to be prevented and now he was in search of a vaccine which would allow diseases to be cured.

In this case, it would probably be better for the whole sentence to be recast, with the contrast made explicit, e.g.:

> 128c Although Sir Almroth Wright already had a vaccine which prevented typhoid, he was not satisfied simply with disease prevention; he was looking for a vaccine that would provide a cure.

End-focus can be provided not only by the passive but also by fronting and clefting. In the next two examples, children use adverbial fronting, with subject–verb inversion, so that emphasis falls on the subject:

> 129 The snail gently uncoils his body from his spiral shell.
>
> From his flat face come two pairs of antlers.
>   A   V   S
>
> Mandy, 8 years (Rosen & Rosen, p. 129)

> 130 I ran back to where the dead bird lay. There in front of me
>   A
> was a murder.
> V   S
>
> Mary Jane, 10 years (Rosen & Rosen, p. 118)

When an SVA clause contains a progressive verb phrase, with part of the verb *to be* and a present participle, the verb phrase is split if the adverbial is fronted, with the result that the lexical verb moves with the adverbial, e.g.:

131 While walking through the hot jungles of South America we found ourselves in a lot of trouble because standing before us was an Indian brave.

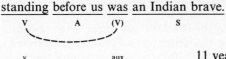

11 years (Burgess *et al.*, p. 125)

132 They all looked in the direction of my pointing arm. Coming up the lane was a figure.

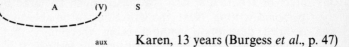

Karen, 13 years (Burgess *et al.*, p. 47)

This is a very effective way of providing a dramatic climax in writing.

Clefting is a useful device in the control of focus, because it makes two clauses out of one and so creates an extra position for information focus. In the following extract, Judith is describing a painful visit to the crematorium after the death of her nine-year-old cousin. She needs to emphasize the close relationship she had had with him:

133 I went with them – the only one from my family. *It was me* who had read him stories.　　Judith, 20 years (Burgess *et al.*, p. 44)

Without clefting, the sentence would have read, 'I had read him stories.' If Judith had written that, no doubt she would have heard in her head a stress on the word 'I'; her use of clefting suggests that she realizes that any other reader needs the emphasis to be made more explicit.

Impersonal style

A great deal of writing is intended for a wide or unspecified audience – it is only things like letters, memos and shopping lists that are addressed exclusively to one particular known reader. A general audience is a remote and impersonal one, so it is not surprising that, on the whole, written language is more formal and impersonal than speech. The impersonality is most noticeable in academic writing, particularly in geography and the sciences, where it has come to be accepted that the writer should distance himself from his topic and his readers. Such language has no counterpart in spontaneous speech. This becomes clear if we consider the reply we might give if we were asked how we had made a particular cake. We certainly would NOT say, '125 gm. butter and 125 gm. sugar were measured into a 3 litre glass bowl. Two hens' eggs were broken into the mixture, which was thoroughly beaten.' Yet this is the kind of description that would be required in a written account of a scientific process.

It is worth considering briefly how an impersonal scientific style is achieved. Most obviously, the writer has to avoid the pronouns *I*, *we* and *you*. But in addition, he has to refrain from mentioning any human agent who has conducted the procedure which is being described. So, rather than 'The teacher set up the apparatus', he has to write, 'The apparatus was set up.' Clearly, this style is heavily dependent on the use of the passive. Since he cannot refer to human agents, neither can he include any direct or reported speech – a device much favoured by children in their personal writing. Next, the writer has to be able to give a precise and detailed description without using vocabulary that reveals his involvement by betraying his own attitudes or feelings. It is obvious that such restraint contrasts sharply with the committed personal response which is more often required from young pupils. In the following extract, Victor, who has not yet reached the stage of the detached, remote author, includes his own evaluation of the equipment:

134 We got some apparatus which was most useful for this experiment.   Victor, 11 years (Rosen & Rosen, p. 140)

Furthermore, the writer of a scientific account has to be able to handle the appropriate technical terminology properly. And if quantities and measurements are given, they have to be precise – to the reader as well as the writer. Humphrey, describing a timer he has made, uses an appealing but non-scientific measure of time:

135 *When I was having my dinner* it dripped $3\frac{1}{2}$ inches. In one hour it dropped $4\frac{1}{2}$ inches.   Humphrey, 7 years (Rosen & Rosen, p. 137)

Moreover, the writer has to leave out any events that were irrelevant to the final outcome, despite the fact that they did occur in the course of the experiment. In the next extract, Anna, unlike an adult scientist, records a mistake that was made in a series of experiments that she and a friend carried out:

136 The copper one was a bit of copper in a test tube that had to be heated. (Amanda left the tube in the flame too long so the tube began to melt.) The copper went black.

                                        Anna, 12 years (Sutton, 1981, p. 18)

Her use of brackets suggests that she recognizes the unofficial status of the comment. Finally, a scientific account has to fit a conventionalized discourse structure, which normally begins with a specification of the equipment and continues with the procedure, results and conclusion.

Naturally enough, when children first start writing about their scientific activities they do not use the kind of language described above, but rather language that is closely related to their everyday speech, e.g.:

137 Jill and me got a bowl with a $\frac{1}{2}$ litre of water and put an egg in it and it sunk to the bottom. Then we got another bowl of water and put six spoons of salt in it and when we put the egg in it floated. Then we put three spoons of salt in the first bowl but the egg wouldn't float. So the egg only floats in the water with the most salt in it. I think it must be like the Dead Sea. Mrs. Norris gave me and Jill an egg each for our tea.

11 years (Burgess *et al.*, p. 74)

However, there are examples which suggest that some young teenagers can handle the impersonal, scientific style, e.g.:

138 The flask shown was connected to a vacuum pump, the clip was opened and the air pumped out. The clip was closed, the rubber tube disconnected from the pump and the flask was weighed. The clip was now opened and the flask was weighed with air. The increase in weight gave the weight of air in the flask.

Chris, 14/15 years (Burgess *et al.*, pp. 105–6)

Important questions are whether school pupils should be expected to follow the conventions of adult scientific writing and, if so, at what age they should begin.[9] If it is decided that they should, the following points could be borne in mind. Since such language has no oral counterpart, pupils cannot be expected to know intuitively how to produce it, so they will need extensive experience of reading good examples of the kind of writing that will be required of them. In addition, they will probably be helped by a precise description of the characteristic features of the style and by an explanation of the purposes it serves. In order to provide a gradual introduction to this particularly demanding type of writing, teachers could ensure that, initially at least, pupils do not have to use it to write about topics that are conceptually very taxing. Grappling with difficult ideas and new forms of language at the same time is bound to cause problems. It is also worth noting that some assignments lend themselves to impersonal writing more naturally than others. For example, it is easier for a writer to be objective about an observed mechanical process, such as the working of a lever, than about an experiment that he himself has conducted. Kroll (1981) has noted a developmental movement towards the impersonal in children's writing. When he asked eight-, nine- and eleven-year-olds to give instructions for his board

9 For alternative approaches see, for example, Burgess *et al.* (1973) pp. 69–82, 159–64, and Watkins (1981).

game, he identified three different relationships that the writer could have with the reader. He called these **subjective**, **objective** and **hypothetical** approaches. In the most personal of these, the subjective, the child writes as if he and the reader are playing the game, e.g.:

139 I move the bird to the blue stripe. Now you roll the die.

In the objective approach, the reader or a generalized 'you' plays with another player, e.g.:

140 You move the bird to the blue stripe and then the other person rolls the die.

The least personal approach, the hypothetical, refers to third persons only and is 'further removed from the context of an actual game in progress' (Kroll, p. 35), e.g.:

141 One player moves to the blue stripe, and then the other player rolls the die.

Kroll's subjects tape-recorded their instructions as well as writing them. The eight- and nine-year-olds predominantly used the objective approach in both speech and writing, whereas the eleven-year-olds, who also chiefly used the objective approach in speech, showed some differentiation between the modes by using the hypothetical approach significantly more often in writing.

A general comment can be made relating to all the constructions described here that are characteristic of written language. It is likely that children will make mistakes when they begin to experiment with structures that are new to them. A technique that teachers often use to help children spot errors is to ask them to read the relevant passage aloud to see if it sounds right. With many errors this technique works well. It is less likely to be successful in this case, however, for the simple reason that most children have insufficient experience of how such constructions should sound. In these circumstances, therefore, teachers may find it helpful to show an individual pupil how the construction he has attempted relates to a familiar oral pattern, though I imagine that most would choose to do so by practical demonstration rather than by grammatical description.[10]

Inappropriate use of features of spoken language

As children begin to develop a differentiated written style a very understandable error they make is occasionally to use a linguistic feature that

10 For an illustration of how this can be done, see Keen (1978, pp. 47–50).

is more typical of speech. It has already been emphasized that stylistic features can only be assessed in relation to the writer's intentions. This is particularly true of colloquial expressions. There are times when they are wholly appropriate – for instance, in a letter, where the sender wants to break down the formality that is inextricably associated with writing by using a personal 'voice' to his correspondent; and, most obviously, in dialogue in a story. For this, Clive's use of dialect (p. 215) and Chris's representation of a frightened stammer – 'm-m-my name's Peter too' (p. 249) – can stand as examples.

Nevertheless, in many kinds of writing, features of spoken language will be stylistically discordant. On p. 224 we saw that, with increasing maturity, young writers seem to recognize the recapitulatory pronoun as inappropriate to written contexts. A rather similar construction is the amplificatory NP tag where the speaker or writer first uses a pronoun and then, as if realizing that the referent might not be clear, adds a noun phrase at the end. Normally this structure is confined to speech but a few examples occur in children's writing, e.g.:

142 In the morning they both went out *the two eldest.*
11 years (Burgess *et al.*, p. 124)

Here the noun phrase seems like an afterthought. A similar impression is given when an NP that is intended as part of the subject is tacked on at the end of a sentence, e.g.:

143 Suddenly he fell down *and his dog.*
Kathleen, 9 years (Kroll *et al.*)
144 All the children started to cry *and the dogs.*
Elaine, 10 years (Rosen & Rosen, p. 186)

We could call this **delayed co-ordination** since, more formally, the two NPs that constitute the subject would be side by side, e.g. *all the children and the dogs.* It is noticeable that both the amplificatory NP tag and the delayed co-ordination construction allow a writer to avoid using a complex NP in subject position, a usage that children find rather difficult. These two constructions can be thought of as expressing additive afterthoughts; that is, ideas that clarify or expand what has gone before. They are characteristic of writers who have not yet learned to edit their work; mature writers also have afterthoughts but, at the editing stage, they move them to the appropriate place in the text.

Another kind of afterthought is the correction, e.g.:

145 A racing yacht has a huge sail. *Well two huge sails.*
Kerry, 9 years (Burgess *et al.*, p. 92)

Kerry realizes that she has made a mistake but instead of crossing out *a* and replacing it with *two*, she lets the error stand and appends the correction – as she would have to in speech, of course. A great advantage that writing has over speech is that it allows the complete erasure of rejected phrases and thus enables the writer to present his considered opinions uncluttered by the groping first thoughts that led to them. It seems very likely that a desire for neatness prevents some children from capitalizing on this advantage.

It is common in speech for a speaker to begin a clause with the idea that is uppermost in his mind and then to develop the rest of the clause from that starting-point. Very often this produces one of the standard clause patterns, but if the ideas are complex or awkward to express for some reason then a looser structure may result. If a skilled writer finds himself in this position he can abandon the sentence and begin again from a different starting-point. In contrast, young writers, like speakers, sometimes persevere with a structure they have embarked on, despite the difficulties it causes. This may again reflect children's reluctance to cross out but it may also suggest that they are not yet consciously aware of the range of grammatical options they command. Extracts from instructions for the bird game illustrate the point:

146 You drop the dice. Whatever colour it lands on the person goes first if the person got the colour.   Ann, 9 years (Kroll *et al.*)

147 Throw the dice and the colour it lands on you move to the colour.   Peter, 9 years (Kroll *et al.*)

148 The player who had the birds behind the back flicks the counter on the table. The colour it lands on that player starts the game.
        Derek, 9 years (Kroll *et al.*)

It is clear that, after the tossing of the dice or counter, it is the colour that is displayed which is the salient idea for these children. For Derek to complete successfully the sentence beginning, 'The colour . . .', he would need to continue with a rather unusual verb, such as 'determine' or 'designate', e.g. 'The colour it lands on determines the player who is to start the game.' Therefore, it would be easier for him to abandon 'the colour' as his theme and begin again with 'the player': 'The player who has the colour it lands on starts the game.'

Another characteristic of speakers is to support their language with non-verbal signals such as shrugs, nods, grimaces, and so forth. Consequently, the links in a train of thought do not always need to be fully expressed in words. As gestural support is absent from writing, writers have to depend wholly on language for the expression of meaning. If they do not realize this, they may not make explicit the necessary connections between ideas, e.g.:

149 My parents never took holidays or vacations, lack of time or money.   Adult (Shaughnessy, 1977, p. 23)

Here there is an effect-cause relationship which, in speech, would probably be conveyed by a pause after *vacations* and an expressive shrug; in writing, it needs to be overtly signalled by *because of* or *on account of* – the comma alone is not enough.

Although the examples in this section have shown that it is possible to find instances of inappropriately colloquial constructions in children's writing, it is the case that, even by nine, their written language is, on the whole, noticeably different from their speech. Chapter 4 gave examples from Fawcett and Perkins' (1980) ten- and twelve-year-olds of constructions that are more typical of speech than writing. They included intimacy signals (*well, you know*); tag statements (*I'm enjoying this, I am*); clause completers (*Use some red ones and all*); *this* used for indefinite reference (*I heard this noise*); subaudibility – where the first words of the sentence are omitted; recapitulatory pronouns (*Kelly, she fell over*); and amplificatory noun phrase tags (*It's difficult, this game*). All except the last two occur with great frequency in children's speech, and not only in the running commentary that accompanies their play with their peers. Several of these colloquial constructions are illustrated in the following extract, which is an oral narrative addressed to an adult stranger:

150 oh well 'there's this bòy/ and he 'stays with these 'two horrible aùnts/ and 'in his gárden/ you knów/ there's this 'giant peàch/ and you knów/ there's a 'little dòor/ and he 'goes ìn it/ you knów/ and he finds 'all these éarwigs/ and áll/

10 years (Fawcett & Perkins, 1980, III, p. 54)

In content, this is much like the stories that children write and yet, although the account is fluent and coherent, it could never be mistaken for written language. The extent to which nine-year-olds have already differentiated their written language from their speech is revealed by the fact that, in the ninety pieces of writing by Kroll *et al.*'s subjects, there are only three instances of the colloquial constructions outlined above:

151 *Well* have a guess. Mary, 9 years (Kroll *et al.*)
152 But then he saw *this* elephant. Philip, 9 years (Kroll *et al.*)
153 *These* men were cannibals. Philip, 9 years (Kroll *et al.*)

Constructing a self-sufficient text

A major way in which a piece of writing differs from most speech is by having its own autonomous existence, separate both from the person who produced it and from the physical situation in which it was created. This means that, to a considerable extent, the language used in writing has to be self-sufficient, capable of standing alone, unlike the language of speech, which characteristically interacts with features of the situation, forming a meaning that derives from the combination of verbal and non-verbal elements. In linguistic terms, to create a self-sufficient text a writer must use the reference system appropriately; that is, pronouns and pro-forms must have explicitly stated antecedents, and definite noun phrases must be specific to the reader as well as the writer (see p. 101–4).

Even in speech it is possible for reference to be insufficiently explicit, but at least the listener usually has the opportunity to seek clarification of any vagueness or ambiguity. We saw in chapter 3 that children up to the age of about nine sometimes assume too much knowledge on the part of their listeners. As writing needs to be more explicit than speech it is not surprising that young writers do not always get it right. In the following examples, the italicized pronoun, pro-form and definite NPs are used inappropriately, since, in each case, the place or thing referred to has not been previously mentioned in the text:

154 . . . I'm in the first team and my friend is the goalie. Chris S —— passed *it* to Alphonso.   Peter, 9 years (Kroll *et al.*)

155 I was happy when I won *the judo match.* I was given a yellow belt and some pips. . . . I slept *there* in the night.
         Paul, 9 years (Kroll *et al.*)

156 My happiest moment is Christmas when I stayed up my Aunty Kathleen's and on Christmas Day I went and saw *the bull* with my dad.   Judy, 9 years (Kroll *et al.*)

In these pieces of personal writing, the children are describing private experiences; that is, experiences they have not shared with the teacher they are writing for. After reading many pieces of children's work, I have formed the impression that inappropriate use of the reference system does not occur often in this type of writing after the age of nine or so.

The picture is very different in other types of writing, however. The following extracts all come from writing related to science lessons; in each case, the italicized NP is the first mention of that noun in the text:

157 The aim of my project is to weigh objects on a spring. I found by experimenting that the spring stretches five and a half inches when you put a pound in *the bucket.*
         Andrew, 11 years (Rosen & Rosen, p. 138)

158 When *the cube* was one inch long the volume was one cubic inch.
         Melville, 11 years (Rosen & Rosen, p. 139)

159 We had a lot of funny results like *the magnesium.*
         Anna, 12 years (Sutton, 1981, p. 18)

Now the children are not writing about private experiences but rather about activities they have shared in some way with the teacher. It is often stated that the difficulty with reference that pupils reveal in their written work derives from their failure to have a clear sense of the audience they are writing for. The examples above suggest that the problem is more complicated than that. After all, these children have been asked to write for the teacher, who is probably the only person who will read their accounts. They know that the teacher knows what materials and equipment were used – indeed she may have set the experiment up – and so they assume that knowledge in their descriptions. As adults, we know that what is required of them is to write for an artificial audience – a teacher who pretends she does not know what she knows better than her pupils. The point has been illustrated with writing in science (where the shared experience of an experiment in the laboratory seems to make the problem particularly acute) but it applies equally to history and geography.

An added complication arises when the writing is accompanied by a labelled diagram. In this case it seems to be acceptable for an NP to be definite the first time it occurs in the text because it is specified by the illustration, e.g.:

> 160 As the iron vibrator is pulled across, *the striker* catches on to *the gong*. *The springy metal strip* also moves across, leaving a gap between the springy metal strip and *the contact screw*.
>
> 13/14 years (Sutton, 1981, p. 44)

These are the first appearances in this extract of the italicized NPs and yet, as their referents are represented in an accompanying diagram, the use of the definite determiner seems appropriate. Science textbooks make extensive use of illustrations so it is likely that pupils will frequently meet in their reading NPs that have definite status by virtue of their pictorial, non-verbal specification. If a textbook serves as a model for the pupils' own scientific writing, then they will be led astray if they adopt the definite NPs without the requisite diagrams.

In his study of teenagers' writing in science, geography and history, J. B. N. Harris (1980) noted that, where they wrote essays based on notes taken from a textbook or from a teacher's instruction, they tended to take over definite NPs which had been used appropriately in the source material and to use them inappropriately by omitting the first, indefinite mention of the noun. He could discern no decrease in this faulty use of definite reference between the ages of twelve and fifteen.

Global discourse coherence

Writing differs from most spontaneous speech in requiring the production of an extended discourse without the support or prompting of a conversational partner. We have already considered the ways in which individual sentences are linked together by means of adverbial connectives and the grammatical processes of reference, substitution and ellipsis. But these features alone do not necessarily create a cohesive text. The fundamental characteristic of a discourse is that it develops an idea or theme (in the general sense) which provides the point and purpose of the text. Typically, discourses can be summarized – the statement of the gist of a passage reflects the discourse theme. A constructed example may clarify the notion of discourse theme:

> 161 On Wednesday Jane went to a political meeting. At first, she found herself admiring the chairman, a good-looking man

wearing an elegant suit. It had been made by a tailor with a small shop in Muswell Hill. The lease would shortly expire so he was planning to move to Wembley. There the football crowds always made life exciting. The game has changed radically since the war. In those days there were few professional players.

Here, although each sentence is impeccably linked to its predecessor, there is no sense of a coherent communicative purpose in the writer's mind. It is impossible to write a summary or identify the gist of a pseudo-discourse of this type. It could be called 'Consequences' writing because it resembles the passages that are produced in the game of Consequences, where each player has to add a word or phrase to a developing story without being able to read what has gone before.

To be truly cohesive, a text must have both an overall discourse theme and connections between adjacent sentences. These two features have been labelled **global coherence** and **local coherence** by Atwell (1981), who studied the writing of twenty undergraduates to see how cohesive their essays were. Ten of her subjects were competent writers and ten were remedial students. She found that both groups produced texts that had connections between adjacent sentences and so were locally coherent. However, the two groups differed dramatically in the extent to which they were able to relate the various parts of their text to an overall discourse theme: on average, the competent writers had a global coherence score that was more than double that of the remedial students. When they talked about their work afterwards, the able students focused on the main idea they were trying to convey whereas the weaker ones appeared not to have a sense of overall structure or organization. Atwell (p. 84) commented that the texts produced by the remedial students often 'failed to state a gist or overriding concept, had erratic or unclear episodes, and few macroconnectors linking episodes to a gist'.

It is clearly not enough to show pupils how to link their sentences together if their work reveals the more fundamental problem of a failure in global discourse coherence. Fortunately, at least in personal narratives, it does not seem to be the case that young writers normally produce work that is completely lacking in a discourse theme. This accords with the findings of a study by Applebee (1978) of children's oral narratives; he found that, by the age of five, the majority of his subjects could tell stories which had some degree of both local and global coherence (which he called **chaining** and **centring**). Even at such an early age, only 16 per cent of the children produced pseudo-discourses without a theme. Nevertheless, although a total breakdown of organization is unlikely, there are still some weaknesses of discourse structure that are quite common in children's writing. These can now be briefly described.

Sometimes children move from a type of writing they find difficult to one that is easier, with the result that there is an uneasy switch of purpose and style in mid-discourse. In the following passage, Kerry is describing the kinds of boats that used the Thames in Tudor and Stuart times:

162 Gilded barges were for the King and Queen, they carried the Queen and King. Merchant ships carried cargo. Light skiffs carry one passenger. Wherries are used for taking passengers across and round the river . . . [6 sentences] . . . More nearer the sea the larger ships were seen, sovereign of the sea, great barges and so on. A ship would be used as a taxi. The buildings towering up, our small little wherry straining, pushing her way to safety. The engine rumbling away, the waves lapping gently against my boat, the boat floating swiftly across the water, night is here, lights vanishing, one by one.   Kerry, 9 years (Burgess *et al.*, p. 93)

The piece starts as a non-chronological, impersonal, factual description of the Thames and its craft during a broad but undefined span of time in the past; the writer is appropriately distanced from her topic. About three-quarters of the way through, Kerry appears to become tired of the impersonal style and she moves into the foreground by taking a place in one of the boats. At this point, the description turns into an imaginative, personal story, set on one particular night. Separately, both types of writing are valid, of course, but together they do not blend to form a satisfactory discourse.

Different types of writing are characterized by different structural components. For example, Hoey (1979) has shown that a great deal of writing has a problem-solution structure, consisting normally of the following elements: situation, problem, solution, result, evaluation. The personal narratives which constitute such an important part of primary school writing typically consist of a setting, followed by a sequence of events and a conclusion.[11] The setting introduces the central participants and announces the time of the action and the place where it occurs. If it is an autobiographical account the time will generally be fairly precise, e.g. 'when I was $2\frac{1}{2}$ years old', 'on April 15th 1978', 'last year'; if it is an imagined story about invented characters then the time will be in the misty past, e.g. 'Once upon a time', 'one day', 'a long time ago'.

A weakness of some young writers is that they do not always include all the necessary components of the discourse type they have embarked on. In Kroll *et al.*'s (1980) data, sixteen of the children wrote imaginative stories based on the cartoon depicting a hunter and a group of wild animals. (The remaining two children produced a series of fairly random sentences about the picture.) All sixteen children introduced the participants and set their story in the misty past; they all also described events in a chronological sequence. Thirteen of the children specified the place of the action but only nine provided a conclusion – the rest simply

11 For a detailed specification of the structural components in seven different types of scientific writing, see Davies *et al.* (1980).

stopped writing. (In the oral narratives studied by Applebee (1978) fewer than half of the five-year-old subjects gave their story a formal conclusion while nearly 90 per cent handled the other story components successfully.) True conclusions are distinguishable from an event which just happens to be the last one the child describes. Derek, for example, ends his story inconclusively, like this:

> 163 The man was lying on the floor. Then the animals started to cry.
>
> Derek, 9 years (Kroll *et al.*)

It would clearly be possible for this story to continue. In contrast, Susan's is very firmly ended:

> 164 That was the end of him and all the animals lived happily ever after.
>
> Susan, 9 years (Kroll *et al.*)

When young writers do provide a conclusion they sometimes introduce it prematurely, presumably because they have tired of their story. Favourite devices are to kill off all the participants or to make the hero wake up, declaring the preceding incomplete event sequence to have been a dream. Another weakness relates to the placing of events: even if the location is specified at the beginning of the piece, the writer may neglect to make explicit a change of scene; J. B. N. Harris (1980) noted this as a common failing in the writing of twelve- to fifteen-year-olds.

A further problem arises when a writer abandons participants he has introduced and continues the story with new characters. Sandra does this, in her story about the hunter. She starts with a giraffe and an elephant:

> 165a Once upon a time on the edge of a jungle there lived a giraffe and an elephant who were best friends.
>
> Sandra, 9 years (Kroll *et al.*)

Then she introduces a hunter, and these three characters are the principal (and opposing) participants throughout the next fifteen sentences. After that, the story ends like this:

> 165b He screamed so loudly that the lion and the rhinoceros came to see what was happening. When they saw the hunter the lion and the rhinoceros pushed him to the edge of the cliff and he fell down. Luckily the cliff wasn't very steep and it wasn't a tall one. So it was all right. But the hunter never went to that jungle again.

To be fully satisfying, this story needs to have the giraffe and the elephant involved in some way in the conclusion.

The structural components that constitute the basic building blocks of different kinds of writing can be of varying lengths; so, the setting may occupy a single sentence or a whole paragraph. Apart from the essential components, there are also (in personal writing at least) optional expansions that can be included, such as descriptions of participants, evaluations of actions, reflections on consequences, and so on. Young writers reveal growing maturity in their control of discourse structure not only by including all the necessary components but also by judging when it is appropriate to use elaborations and expansions. For example, a relatively immature writer may follow the first event in a narrative with a lengthy description which blurs the story line without serving any structural purpose; in contrast, a more mature writer may deliberately place a descriptive passage just before the climax of the action, aware that it will heighten the suspense. In order to achieve the right balance between different discourse components, the writer has to have an overall view of the point that he is trying to make in his writing – structurally harmonious discourse cannot be achieved by a purely additive type of composing where each sentence grows out of its predecessor. This point is made by both Kroll *et al.* (1980) and J. Wilkinson (1980), who use detailed analyses of story structure to illustrate varying levels of maturity in children's global organization of discourse.

Two final weaknesses in the construction of a discourse arise from a failure to revise or edit the text after a first draft. They are repetition of material and faulty sequencing of sentences. Kathleen, writing about a puppy, says:

> 166 . . . He is very nice. I wish I had him. But my nan told me that you want one. He is very nice.   Kathleen, 9 years (Kroll *et al.*)

It seems unlikely that she has used this repetition for emphasis; it is more probable that she is writing so slowly and laboriously that after only two sentences she has forgotten what she has already written.

Muddled sentence order occurs most often in non-chronological texts. This is predictable since narratives require the writer to perform the relatively straightforward task of arranging events in a time sequence, whereas non-chronological discourses follow more abstract principles of organization. Asked to write a description of somebody, a young writer may string sentences together in a fairly haphazard way, as in this example:

> 167 My mummy's name is Joy and she has blond curly short hair. And she has green eyes. And my mummy works at the college on a corridor of her own. My mummy's birthday is on the 30th October. And she watches the moment of truth. And my mummy makes lovely cakes. And other things. My mummy does not wear glasses and she used to type before she was married. When she was a teenager, she delivered papers. She does not go to work on Saturdays and Sundays.   8 years (Burgess *et al.*, p. 119)

Even in chronologically organized texts, writers sometimes place a sentence out of sequence, perhaps because the idea was an afterthought, e.g.:

168 The French began to lose their man-to-man fights and the others fell over their dead comrades. Some French fell and suffocated in the mud.   12/13 years (Harris, 1980, p. 132)

Harris comments that the last sentence should really follow 'man-to-man fights'. On the subject of sentence-sequencing in his corpus of writing by pupils aged twelve to fifteen, he says:

> While in texts by mature writers it is often impossible to reorder sentences without creating incoherence, in the corpus there is at times not only the possibility of reordering with an enhanced sense of coherence but also, occasionally, the desirability of so doing. (p. 102)

In a chronological discourse, the normal – or **unmarked** – order of sentences is the one that matches the order of events in real time. Hoey (1979) gives an example of four sentences in a chronological sequence: out of the twenty-four possible arrangements of these sentences just one is the unmarked order. Most of the other arrangements give sequences that are incoherent. A very few produce discourses with an organization that is possible but **marked**. In order to be able to manage a marked discourse order successfully, the writer has to command fairly advanced linguistic devices. Hoey shows that it can be done by bracketing; another possibility, in some circumstances, is to use the past perfective aspect of the verb. This has the effect of overriding the surface ordering of the text, as the following extract illustrates:

169 We were going as usual until we got south of the Shahanshah expressway. *When we had been in the British embassy compound Mrs. Abbott had said keep your headlights on all the time to show you don't want to fight.* So we had our headlights on.
                                        Jenny, 9 years (J. Wilkinson, 1981, p. 85)

A general conclusion that emerges from this section is that children can only develop a differentiated written style if they read a great deal. Whether we think in terms of the grammatical constructions that are required for thematic variety, end-focus, an impersonal style and so forth, or of the structural components that characterize different types of discourse, it is clear that these forms cannot be acquired by listening to spontaneous oral language, because they do not normally occur in speech. Thus, if children are to learn to write well they need to read well-written material. Stories are very valuable because they provide a pleasurable way for the reader to absorb the characteristic patterns of written language. Nevertheless, there is a need for a more varied diet of reading, since stories alone cannot exemplify all the structures that are found in the impersonal, non-narrative types of writing which cause the young writer so much difficulty. It is particularly important for pupils to read extended passages of good non-fiction so that they acquire a feeling for the overall organization of such discourses and not just for sentence-level details of vocabulary and grammar. Pertinent here is research by Dolan *et al.* (1979, p. 125) for the Effective Use of Reading Project. They found that pupils in secondary schools tended to refer to non-fiction books to winkle out a single item of information rather than to engage in continuous reading. In science and social studies lessons, more than 85 per cent of fifteen-year-olds' reading consisted of short bursts lasting only one to thirty seconds. This is obviously not the way to become familiar with the various kinds of text structure.

As children are necessarily restricted to reading material that is within their competence, it follows that poor readers will be confined to a limited range of simply-written texts. Since such pupils are very likely to be poor writers also, we can see that the children who most need help and support from good models of writing are the ones least able to get it. This highlights the value of the teacher reading aloud to the class, even in the secondary school.

5.5 ASSESSING CHILDREN'S WRITING

Knowledge about grammatical and stylistic development in children's writing can provide a mental framework for teachers as they assess the structural aspects of their pupils' written work.[12] It is important that writing can be assessed in terms of its strengths as well as its weaknesses. For example, linguistic strengths may include: good discourse structure, appropriate style for the topic, thematic variety, skilful handling of emphasis, competent sentence construction, varied phrase structure, and so on. Even children whose work is short, untidily written and poorly spelt can have such strengths lying hidden beneath the unpromising surface. For instance, the following extract, given in its original spelling, ends a short letter asking a farmer to buy a puppy:

> 170 . . . he is very playfull with people I just got read of five I can not keep it so I folt of you becauese I no you are got with animals
> Peter, 9 years (Kroll *et al.*)

Although they are not marked by punctuation, the three sentences in this extract are all well-formed and there is no difficulty in deciding where the full-stops should go. Then the last sentence, with its three competently-managed subordinate clauses, provides a strong ending to the letter. Recognition of such success enables the teacher to provide praise that is both honest and specific, rather than the kindly, but sometimes uncon-

12 For a range of types of linguistic assessment of individual pieces of writing see Crystal (1979b); Gannon & Czerniewska (1980), chapter 4; Keen (1978), chapter 6; J. Wilkinson (1981).

vincing, 'A good effort'. It may also help to prevent teachers from forming unjustly low expectations of their pupils' linguistic abilities.

Weaknesses in writing include the failure to use structures that would have improved the work, as well as the commission of errors. Since mistakes are always easier to detect than non-occurrences, it is worth noting that children tend to underuse relative clauses, sentence connectives, ellipsis and substitution.

The signalling of errors in written work, by underlining, crossing out, exclamation marks and so on, is a very familiar task for teachers. However, not all mistakes have the same cause and will respond to the same treatment. This chapter has already indicated some of the ways in which errors can be differentiated: they are summarized here. Broadly, it is worth distinguishing between problems at sentence level (and below) and those at discourse level.

At sentence level, first there are errors that arise because ideas flow faster than the pen can record them, and those that stem from a failure to reread during the composing process. Typical examples are the omission of words, repetitions, and the conflation of two different sentence patterns. Teaching the techniques of proof-reading and encouraging pupils to check each other's work are the best ways to approach such errors.

Second, there are mistakes that result from the pupil experimenting with new constructions that have not yet been fully mastered. Among children aged roughly nine to thirteen, these will include hypothetical reference, the advanced types of relative clause, and adverbial clauses of concession. Proof-reading will not help with errors of this kind; rather, pupils will need an explicit demonstration of how the attempted construction should be formed and how it relates to more familiar expressions.

Third, there are dialect expressions which may be judged as inappropriate in some types of writing. Again, proof-reading is no answer here. Pupils will need to be taught not only the differences between their dialect and standard English but also the reasons why the standard form is felt to be preferable in those particular circumstances.

Fourth, children may use constructions which are normal in speech but less acceptable in writing. In this case, they will probably benefit from an awareness of the different requirements of writing – especially the need for language that is relatively self-sufficient and independent of context. As they learn the skill of editing, they can be encouraged to view their own work with the eyes of an outsider.

At discourse level, difficulties frequently arise with pronouns and with tense sequence. If pupils are specifically reminded to check these features, they should be able to correct their own errors at the editing stage. As well as looking for agreement of pronouns and of tenses, they can, in pairs, be urged to make sure that the reference of each pronoun is unambiguous.

A more major problem at discourse level is when an essential structural component – often the location or the conclusion – is omitted. After setting a piece of work, a teacher might provide a brief checklist of questions that pupils can use at the revision stage to make sure they have included all the necessary information – e.g. 'Where did it happen?', 'If there was a change of scene, how did it come about?', 'How did it end?' etc. (If the teacher has time, more specific questions can be written on the first draft of an individual pupil's work to provide guidance at the revision stage.)

Another structural difficulty is muddled sentence order, which is especially likely to occur in writing that does not have a chronological pattern of organization. It is not easy for young pupils to correct this by themselves; they will need suggestions as to how they might present their ideas more coherently. To take as an example the description of 'My mummy' on p. 265, the writer could be encouraged to group together sentences about her mother's appearance, about her youth, and about the things she does now.

Lastly, the pupil might produce a piece of writing which the teacher judges to be, overall, an inappropriate response to the task set. For example, the science teacher who asked his pupils to describe the wormery they had made was dissatisfied with this answer:

171 I fetched a bucket of soil and a cup. A jar of sand and some chalk. I fetched a wormery glass which you can see through. I made layers of soil then sand and powdered chalk. I continued like that. Then I put some water in it. I have marked in biro where the water ran. Then I placed four worms into the wormery. They did not stir when they were on the top of the soil but later they will. I put the wormery into a dark cupboard which is closed. 13 years (Burgess, 1971, p. 43)

The teacher's comment was, 'Not very good, but might be all right in English, creative writing, or something'. In this case, it would be better for the teacher to make clear the linguistic requirements of the assignment before the pupils start writing – and to ensure that they know how to fulfil them – than to criticize the finished product and make disparaging remarks about English and creative writing into the bargain!

A differentiated approach to errors in writing enables both teachers and pupils to recognize that some mistakes are less serious than others; indeed, that some are positive signs of growth. Furthermore, it means that children are not instructed to 'correct' a construction that they cannot be expected to recognize as wrong. It also allows a teacher to select, in a principled way, the errors that she chooses to mark on any occasion. For instance, after explaining this to the class, she might concentrate on the way they link their ideas together, or the variety of their sentence openings, or the effectiveness of their conclusion. In addition, it pinpoints the recurring problems that typify some children's writing. If we select just three children from Kroll *et al.*'s sample of eighteen, David, Paul and Derek, we can see that all three have their own characteristic weaknesses. David frequently omits words, producing sentences like this:

172 I don't think you will find it to to train her to round up a flock of sheep.

If he learnt to proof-read effectively he could bring about a significant improvement in his work. Paul uses definite reference inappropriately at the beginning of pieces of writing, e.g.:

173 The animals come from the jungle. The man is singing and his foot is falling off the cliff.

Here Paul is describing a picture he is looking at as if the reader, too, can see it. He needs some help with the self-sufficient, context-free language that is required in writing. Finally, Derek writes very repetitively because he rarely uses pronouns, e.g.:

174 The man started to walk home. The animals started to follow the man. Then the man fell down a cliff.

It would be necessary, first of all, to see how Derek uses pronouns in his speech. If he uses them normally, as is most likely, then he could be shown how to introduce them into his writing. It would also be worth checking his reading book to ensure that his repetitive tendency is not being reinforced by the language of an old-fashioned reading scheme.

5.6 CONCLUSION

To conclude this chapter, I shall draw together briefly some of the key points that have emerged from it. First, it is clear that ability in writing grows initially out of a sound foundation of oral language and that, as children mature, the structures they use in their writing may, in turn, influence the development of their speech. Second, there is a close and vital relationship between writing and reading: to be good writers, children need to be able to read well, for three reasons. By reading, they learn the characteristic structures of written language; as readers, they evaluate and edit their own writing to make it clear for their intended audience; and through proof-reading, they correct many of their superficial mistakes.

Next, different kinds of writing make varying demands on the writer and produce characteristically different linguistic structures. This highlights the need to provide a range of writing tasks for children, related to their developmental level. It also emphasizes the importance of making available a variety of types of reading material, so that they have a wealth of good examples to learn from.

Children need to learn to think of drafting, revising, editing and proof-reading as integral parts of the writing process (essential not just for novices but for skilled professional writers too). Chapter 4 drew attention to the role of writing as a key to a kind of thinking that is not easy to achieve through oral language alone. The writer has time to reflect, to shape his thoughts and, thereby, to reach a new synthesis – in fact, to discover what he thinks. But learning by writing is only possible if there is an acceptance that the first draft is a tentative formulation. The requirement that the first attempt should be a neat finished product is inimical to the full exploitation of the cognitive and expressive resources of the written language. It is important, therefore, that pupils should not think of revising as a process of correcting mistakes but rather as a way of searching for the best expression of their developing meaning. From a practical point of view, revision becomes less of a chore if coloured pens are used to indicate re-ordering, and so on, and if scrap paper is used so that just one side can be written on, enabling it to be cut up and stuck together in new ways without too much tedious copying.

This chapter has shown that an impersonal style is demanding for all pupils and that the movement away from the personal is particularly difficult for those whose dialect is significantly different from standard English. Therefore, within a department or, if possible, a school, teachers need to come to an agreement about the degree of formality they expect in their pupils' writing at each level.

Finally, the aim of this chapter has been to help teachers to have a developmental perspective when they set written work, to offer their pupils explicit guidance related to the difficulties posed by a particular task, and to respond in a constructive way to their finished products.

This chapter was completed before the publication of Gunther Kress's *Learning to Write*, which contains valuable insights into children's cognitive and linguistic development as revealed in their writing.

CHAPTER 6

Understanding written language

... a particularly important teaching skill is that of assessing the level of difficulty of books. ... The teacher who can do this is in a better position to match children to reading materials that answer their needs.

(DES, 1975, p. 113)

6.1 INTRODUCTION

The last chapter suggested that children's written language matures as they become more confident readers, since, through reading, they gain access to a new and powerful source of language enrichment. In this chapter, the structures of language written for children to read will be examined in some detail, with particular emphasis on features that may cause the young reader difficulty.

Many children find learning to read extremely difficult, despite the great deal of time and effort that is expended by their teachers. It is also true that there are a considerable number of adults who are unable to read with ease and confidence. For example, the Bullock Report (DES, 1975, pp. 11–12) notes that there are probably anything between one and two million adults in Britain with a reading age of below 9;0, who are unable to read everyday materials such as recipes, simple newspapers and the Highway Code; in the United States, the figure is around eighteen million.

It is worth considering why it is that reading requires laborious teaching, which may after all be unsuccessful, when oral language is normally acquired without formal instruction and with apparent ease. If learning to read meant simply learning to recognize letters and words – that is, 'decoding' from print to sound – and then applying to the decoded words the normal processes of comprehension that we all use all the time when we listen to speech, then we would not expect so many people to fail. In that case, the only failures should be those who are unable to carry out the initial stage of decoding. However, there are many children and adults who, having mastered that first stage, make little further progress and never become fluent, confident readers. This must be because reading differs from listening in ways which, in the beginning at least, make it a much harder type of language-processing activity.

First, as written texts have to be self-sufficient and largely independent of any physical context, readers – unlike listeners – do not receive any non-linguistic information from the author of the message or from the situation, so there is nothing to support their interpretation of the language. For instance, suppose a primary teacher says, 'The noise of that pneumatic drill is quite intolerable.' Her class may never have heard the words 'pneumatic drill' and 'intolerable' before but the presence of the noise-making drill outside the window identifies the noun phrase, and the teacher's frown and irritated tone of voice show that 'intolerable' has a pejorative meaning. In contrast, if a child were to come across the same sentence in a book, he would be alone with the unfamiliar words, with no situational clues to help him.

Second, written language uses some grammatical constructions and discourse structures that are rare in everyday speech, so the novice reader cannot rely solely on his knowledge of oral language as he processes the grammar of a written text.

Third – and, in my view, most important – written language lacks the prosodic features of intonation, stress, rhythm and pause which, in speech, indicate how words are grouped together in grammatical constituents. To a considerable extent, listeners have the first stage of grammatical processing done for them by the speaker, whereas readers have to work out for themselves which words belong together in phrases. (We saw in chapter 4 that punctuation is limited in the extent to which it can signal the information units of speech. However, in books for the very youngest readers, publishers try to overcome this deficiency in the writing system by using layout and line divisions that reflect the grammatical structure of the text.) Prosodic features also highlight the focus of information in the clause. This means that, as an oral discourse progresses, listeners can tell at any point what the speaker considers to be new and important information because it will be made salient by pitch, stress and, possibly, loudness. Therefore, listeners do not necessarily have to pay close and detailed attention to each successive sentence in a discourse in order to recognize new information. Readers, on the other hand, have to hold the developing text rather carefully in memory so that they can identify the information focus even when it does not occur in its most usual position at the end of a clause.

A study by Oakan et al. (1971) suggests that the ability to organize written words into grammatical constituents is a crucial component of reading skill. Fifty-four children, aged 9; 10 to 11; 3, with a mean of 10; 6, were divided into two groups according to whether they were good or poor readers. The groups were matched for age and intelligence. All the children heard stories read aloud and were given multiple-choice questions to answer. On this oral test there was no difference in score between the two groups. They also read stories and were tested on their reading. As would be expected, the poor readers did significantly worse than the good readers, scoring 44 per cent as against 73 per cent. The interesting feature of the study, though, is that, before they read the passages, the poor readers were taught all the words in the texts so that they could identify them successfully, to ensure that they would have no difficulty at the level of decoding. In spite of this, they still did badly on the comprehension tests. Thus, although recognizing words accurately is an essential component of reading ability, it is not all that is required for understanding written texts. Oakan *et al.* (p. 76) conclude, 'the findings of the study lend support to the argument that an appreciable amount of the poor reader's comprehension difficulties may be attributable to the manner in which he organizes his input.'

Having noted some of the factors that, for several years, make reading harder than listening, we can now turn to the various types of difficulty that readers may encounter in written texts. Most obviously, writing may be hard to read for physical reasons: illegible handwriting, print that is blurred or uncomfortably small, or lack of contrast between the words and the background. Even skilled adult readers can have a struggle to sort out the details about holiday surcharges when they are presented in small print over a deep blue Mediterranean sea. Publishers of books for schools usually go to considerable trouble to make the presentation of the text as clear and attractive as possible. (In passing, it is worth noticing that this can mislead the teacher who is trying to make a rapid assessment of the reading level of a number of books: not all of those with large, clear bold print and full-page, full-colour illustrations will be easy enough to be read by the young children they appear to be designed for.) However, good presentation is not always a characteristic of teacher-produced worksheets. Poor copies, particularly those produced by a spirit rather than an ink duplicator, make the initial process of decoding slow and effortful. This is a much more serious obstacle for the beginner than for the skilled reader. As teachers are all good readers, they often find it difficult to see a worksheet through the eyes of their struggling pupils. In order to gain a rough impression of the decoding problems experienced by weak readers, it is useful to hold a poor-quality copy up to a mirror and to try to read the reflection.

Another source of reading difficulty is when the subject matter is outside the reader's knowledge and experience. In this case, it is possible for all the words of the text to be understood but for the whole not to make sense. The following sentences come from a passage about India in January 1947:

1 What is known about the Ravana gang? That it posed as a fanatical ,anti-Muslim movement, which in those days before the Partition riots, in those days when pigs' heads could be left with impunity in the courtyards of Friday mosques, was nothing unusual.

Here, a knowledge of all the word meanings and grammatical constructions is not enough. It is necessary to know also that the Partition (which took place later in 1947) separated the largely Muslim north of India (which became Pakistan) from the largely Hindu remainder; that mosques are the sacred buildings of Muslims; that Friday is the Muslims' holy day and that, to them, pigs are unclean.

A third kind of difficulty is presented by unfamiliar vocabulary. The following sentence, from a book written for junior school pupils, contains several words which are unlikely to be known by young children:

2 Some plastics articles are made by heating and shaping a piece of thermoplastic sheet which has previously been made by extrusion, or by calendering, or which has been polymerized as a sheet.

Fourth, there may be grammatical difficulties in the text and, fifth, the overall pattern of discourse organization may be unclear or unfamiliar. These last two sources of reading difficulty will be considered in some detail in this chapter.

I have listed five possible sources of reading difficulty; the more they occur together in any one text, the harder the reading task will be. It is easy enough to avoid illegible and badly laid out texts. Very often, though, in instructional writing in academic subjects, it will not be possible to circumvent all conceptual and lexical difficulties. After all, in the early stages, a major part of learning a subject like physics or economics is learning the basic concepts and essential technical vocabulary. In such circumstances it is all the more necessary for the structure of clauses and paragraphs to be as helpful as possible for the reader. In chapter 3, it was shown that children can often only interpret advanced grammatical constructions (like *unless* clauses) when their knowledge of the world gives them a common-sense account of the meaning. This suggests that if unfamiliar subject matter expressed in technical vocabulary combines with intrinsically demanding sentence structure, then the chances of full comprehension are much reduced.

Therefore, the aim of this chapter is to focus on some possible sources of structural difficulty at the levels of the sentence and the discourse. Awareness of potential problems of this kind can have three advantages: first, it means that when the reading ease and comprehensibility of books are being considered, linguistic aspects can be taken into account more sensitively than is allowed for by readability formulae, which depend solely on the two measures of word difficulty and sentence length.[1] Next, it makes possible the planning of activities which will provide young readers with specific help in coping with some regularly occurring difficult constructions. This is very important, since the teacher's response to grammatical complexity in texts should not always be one of avoidance, otherwise her pupils will lose opportunities for linguistic development. Nevertheless, if average and weak readers are to succeed in reading unfamiliar literary constructions, they will need support – unaided, they will experience frustration and failure, which may lead them to reject academic reading altogether. The need to continue with some structured teaching of reading after the initial decoding stage is highlighted in this extract from the Bullock Report (DES, 1975, p. 92):

> The teaching of reading virtually ceases once the child can read aloud with reasonable accuracy at a reasonable speed. Yet to discontinue instruction at this point is rather like halting the training of a pianist once he can play the scales and a few elementary tunes.

Finally, awareness of structural difficulties can be useful for teachers who want to write their own materials or to revise others that are obviously too demanding for their pupils. It seems that a great deal of time is spent on such work, since the Effective Use of Reading Project found, for example, that most of the written materials used by first year secondary pupils in science lessons were produced by their own teachers. Sadly, they also found that they were at least as difficult as published materials and that both books and worksheets were, in general, markedly too hard for these pupils to read. If time and energy are going to be spent on the production of worksheets and so on, then it is important that the effort is not wasted.

In this connection, it is worth noting that there are dangers in the naïve simplification of written texts, since sometimes apparent simplification may make comprehension harder. To illustrate this point we can consider three guidelines that are often given for writing simple prose; although they can be applied successfully in some circumstances, they also have their limitations. The first is the suggestion that the vocabulary used should be as familiar as possible to the intended readership. To this end, writers consult published lists of the most frequently used words. The disadvantage of a slavish following of such lists is that it produces a bland text with words so general that they lack the power to evoke a specific scenario. For instance, if a text begins:

3 A boat was approaching the island.

---

1 For a balanced account of some of the formulae available and their uses, see Harrison (1980). For an outline of some of their limitations, from a linguistic point of view, see Perera (1980).

there is no indication of what kind of boat and, therefore, rather few expectations are established as to how the passage might develop. If, on the other hand, the first sentence is either:

    4 A canoe was approaching the island.

or:

    5 A submarine was approaching the island.

then, in each case, the kind of information that is likely to follow is much more tightly constrained. So, although *boat* might be thought to make reading easier because it – unlike *canoe* and *submarine* – occurs among the first thousand words on lists of English children's vocabulary (e.g. Burroughs, 1957; Edwards & Gibbon, 1964), the less familiar words have the advantage that they enable readers to predict more of the following content and vocabulary. This should make the reading of the rest of the text easier and, indeed, there is some evidence (e.g. Sanford & Garrod, 1981, pp. 118–27) that specific vocabulary early in a passage facilitates the reading of subsequent sentences. Obviously such a notion needs a commonsense application – it would be absurd to suggest that the highly specific *barquentine* and *trireme* would enhance children's comprehension – but it does highlight the limitations of the apparently straightforward advice to 'use familiar vocabulary'.

Another piece of advice frequently given to writers is to keep sentences short. A danger here is that clarifying connections may be omitted in the interests of brevity. Pearson (1975) asked nine-year-old subjects to read sentences like these:

    6a John slept all day. He was lazy.
    6b Because John was lazy he slept all day.

He found that they showed a preference for the longer, more explicit sentences like (6b) and he concluded, 'The data lend no support to the recommendation that the difficulty of written discourse can be reduced by . . . reducing sentence length' (p. 189). Similarly, an obvious way to shorten sentences is by means of ellipsis, but we saw in chapter 3 (p. 130 above) that this can make comprehension harder. The following sentence contains twenty words:

    7 Bradford is the chief town for the marketing of the cloth and Leeds
      for the manufacture of ready-made clothing.

The inclusion of the ellipted words, *is the chief town*, after *Leeds* would increase the sentence length by four words but it would almost certainly make it easier for younger and slower readers to comprehend. An additional problem posed by short sentences is that, if several of them occur in sequence so that there is little variety in sentence length, the result is a style that is jerky and unnatural.

The third guideline we can consider is the suggestion that subordination should be kept to a minimum. In the following pair of sentences, the first is, in grammatical terms, simple because it contains no subordinate clauses, while the second is complex, having three subordinate clauses in addition to the main clause:

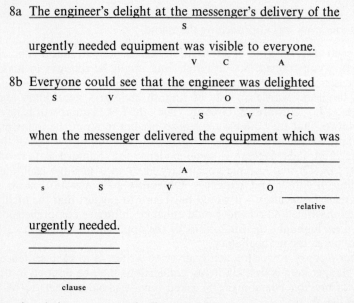

Despite being grammatically complex (and longer than the first sentence), the second sentence seems much easier to read. This illustrates the point that Williams (1979) has made – that the labels **simple** and **complex**, which refer to the clause structure of sentences, are misleading if they are taken to apply to the reader's ease of processing.

It seems clear, then, that producing texts that are easy to read and understand cannot be achieved merely by faithful obedience to a few guidelines. This chapter will therefore attempt to suggest what might be some of the linguistic causes of reading difficulty, so that teachers writing their own materials will have principled reasons for choosing to use, on occasion, a long sentence rather than a shorter one, or a subordinate clause rather than a noun phrase.

In the last chapter, I outlined Kroll's (1981) model of four broad phases in writing development. I feel it is possible, in a limited way, to apply this model to reading development too. We can, I believe, distinguish three phases in reading: preparation, consolidation and differentiation. During the preparation phase, readers learn to recognize letters and words. Then, in the consolidation phase, their reading ability gradually catches up with their oral language ability; that is, they come to be able to read the kind of everyday language that they themselves hear, and use in speech. A great many readers do not progress beyond that phase. It is followed by the differentiation phase, when reading comprehension outstrips auditory comprehension. We know that, as skilled readers, we can often understand a written passage that is so dense in meaning that, if it were read aloud to us, we could not make sense of it. Yet, in contrast, young and weak readers may be unable to read with comprehension a passage that they could understand perfectly well if it were read to them. So there must be a point in reading development when the processing of difficult language and ideas actually becomes easier for the reader than for the listener; it seems reasonable to take this as the distinguishing characteristic of the differentiation phase in reading.

In the study by Oakan et al. (1971, referred to on p. 273 above), with subjects aged 9;10 to 11;3, the good readers scored 53 per cent on comprehension questions given after they had listened to a story but a significantly higher 73 per cent on questions that they answered after they had read a story themselves. A large-scale study by Durrell (1969) of readers of a wide range of ability found that listening and reading comprehension were roughly the same at the age of eleven but that reading had a significant advantage by the age of thirteen. So, while good readers may be moving into the differentiation stage at about the age of ten, average readers probably do not reach that level until nearer thirteen. It is during the consolidation stage, when reading ability has not yet caught up with oral language ability, that difficult and unfamiliar grammatical constructions are most likely to present problems.

For the skilled reader, then, reading has the advantage over listening as far as comprehension is concerned. There are two reasons for this. First, the reader is in active control of his language processing because he can scan backwards and forwards across the text, repeatedly if necessary, as he tries to construct a meaning. The listener, on the other hand, is shackled to the speaker. He can neither move ahead nor go back over what has been said; and he cannot alter the speed of language processing to suit the difficulty of the material. Second, the skilled reader can read very much faster than the normal rate of speech. This means that more words can be processed together as a 'chunk'. Hence, it is easier to perceive the grammatical relationships between words by reading than by listening when sentence constituents are long and complex.

As reading rate is so important, it is worth considering speed in relation to age, bearing in mind that, for most readers, reading speed varies according to the difficulty of the material and the purpose for which it is being read. Studies of eye-movements in reading by Taylor, Franckenpohl and Pette (quoted in Massaro, 1975, p. 294) give average reading rates for reading with comprehension as shown in table 22. If, very roughly, we take the average speech rate as something like 150 words per minute (see p. 161 above), we can see that children generally do not read

TABLE 22 Reading speed according to age
(*from Massaro, 1975, p. 294*)

Grade	1	3	5	7	9	11	College
Approx. age	6–7	8–9	10–11	12–13	14–15	16–17	Adult
Words read per minute	80	138	173	195	214	237	280

faster than this until the age of ten. Even at thirteen they still have a long way to go to reach skilled adult reading speeds. A word of caution is needed here. The importance of speed in mature reading should not lead teachers to urge children to read faster. Slow reading is, after all, a symptom, not a cause, of reading difficulty and it is useless to attack the symptom without dealing with the underlying cause.

To illustrate different kinds of structural difficulty I have taken examples from a wide range of materials; these are identified in the text simply as 'Junior', 'Secondary' and 'Adult'. The junior and secondary examples come from textbooks or novels that are predominantly in use in the relevant schools. All of the textbooks have been published since 1970. The adult examples come from novels, newspapers and academic books; their purpose is to show that, even for skilled readers, particular constructions can cause reading difficulty. Such an awareness is valuable because sometimes it is hard for us to see what causes children difficulty in a text which we find straightforward. To put ourselves in something like their position would mean blocking out a great deal of our knowledge of the subject they are reading about, drastically reducing our vocabulary, and virtually halving our reading speed. Therefore, there are advantages sometimes in looking at reading difficulty at our own level.

6.2 READING DIFFICULTY AT SENTENCE LEVEL

Sentence processing

In order to make principled hypotheses about grammatical sources of difficulty in reading, it is necessary to consider what is known about the way in which language is processed. Some of the experimental evidence concerns the interpretation of spoken rather than written language, but it seems reasonable to assume that the processing of the two modes will have some features in common – making due allowance, of course, for the fact that the reader, unlike the speaker, can take in several words at once and can reread what has gone before. I shall say nothing about the first stage of the reading process, which involves decoding words from their physical shape to their meaning. There is fierce controversy about whether words are perceived as whole units or as strings of letters; about whether letters are processed serially or in parallel; and about whether written words have to be decoded to sound before they can be understood or whether it is possible to go direct from print to meaning without the intervention of sound at all. The answers that are given to these questions have important consequences for the teaching of reading to beginners, but it is possible to consider how meaning is derived from phrases, clauses and sentences without being committed to any one view of the decoding of individual words.

There is widespread agreement that, as readers, we actively construct a meaning as we progress through a text; in other words, we do not passively await the perceptual information that is conveyed via our eyes but rather use our knowledge of sentence structure and word meanings, as well as our knowledge of the world, to predict what is likely to come next. As the text unfolds and an interpretation is built up, it adds to our knowledge, thus allowing further predictions to be made. This active processing goes on all the time, so words are not first read as isolated items in a list and then at some later point assigned a cumulative meaning but are grouped as early as possible into units that are both meaningful and grammatically structured. Such grouping of strings of words is called **chunking** or **segmenting**.

In order to work out the syntactic relationships in a segment of text, it is necessary to remember the words verbatim. This memory for exact words in correct sequence is a highly vulnerable kind of storage, capable of retaining just a few items for only a few seconds. It is referred to variously as short-term memory, working memory, primary memory and immediate memory. Each segment of text is held in short-term memory while it is being processed and then, when processing is complete, it is shunted off to a less vulnerable storage mechanism where it is no longer remembered verbatim but as a more abstract, gist-type meaning. The eyes of a skilled reader are always several words ahead of the segment that is currently being processed, so once it has been cleared from short-term memory, another segment can immediately take its place and processing can begin again. Difficulties arise in language processing if a segment being processed is so long or complex that it exceeds the capacity of short-term memory. In that case, comprehension may simply break down or the reader may look back at the segment again so that verbatim memory is revived.

A crucial question concerns the nature of the segments of text that form the units of processing. There is evidence that the clause is a very important unit and that readers strive to hold a whole clause in short-term memory when they can. Where a clause is too long or too complex to be processed as a unit, then the segments can be composed of the major clause elements, such as subject, verb and object.

Some of the evidence for this view of sentence processing can now be briefly presented. The fact that readers are active in predicting what is likely to come next is made clear in studies of reading errors. Clay (1969) and Weber (1970) made extensive records of children's oral reading and found an overwhelming tendency for their errors to make sense and to be grammatically appropriate to the preceding context. So, if a sentence reads:

9 Peter sat on the stool.

children might say, 'Peter sat on the chair' (where *chair* is visually dis-similar but semantically and syntactically appropriate) but they are most unlikely to say, 'Peter sat on the stood', despite the close physical simi-larity of *stood* to the target word *stool*. If readers were totally dependent on the perceptual information provided by the text and did not bring to it their own knowledge, then the second error would be more likely than the first. Skilled adults do not normally make many errors in reading aloud so, to ensure that he would get enough errors to analyse, Kolers (1970) asked his college-student subjects to read passages that were geo-metrically transformed, by rotation, reversal, and so on (as, for example, in a mirror-image text). Even in these very demanding reading condi-tions, he still found that the many errors that were produced nearly always preserved the syntactic structure of the sentence.

The importance of grammatical cues for the reader was demonstrated in a study that Siler (1974) conducted with children aged seven and nine. They were given sentences to read that were (a) normal, (b) syntactically violated, (c) semantically violated and (d) both syntactically and semanti-cally violated, e.g.:

10a I like cold milk with my cake.
10b I like cold with milk my cake.
10c I like cold silk with my cake.
10d I like cold with silk my cake.   (Siler, p. 592)

Both groups of children found the syntactically violated versions, (10b) and (10d), harder to read than the other sentences, taking longer over them and making more errors. Semantic violations, as in (10c), were not so disruptive.

The idea that readers make a start on grammatical processing as soon as there is enough material available for the structure of the clause to be perceived gains support from a study by Isakson (1979). He devised pairs of thirteen-word sentences like these:

11a The weary guard clubbed the hoodlums who attacked him in
          s   v   o

the dark alley.

11b <u>The weary guard clubbed by hoodlums who attacked him</u>

s

<u>fell</u> <u>down the stairs.</u>

v   A

(Isakson, p. 161)

The first sentence has an SVO structure, the second an SVA structure. In (11a), the structure is predictable at the fifth word, *the*: the determiner signals the beginning of a noun phrase, which, following the transitive verb *clubbed*, must be a direct object. In contrast, at the fifth word in (11b), *by*, the subject is still not complete and the SVA structure does not become apparent until the eleventh word, *down*. Isakson presented his test sentences, on film, one word at a time, to adult subjects. At some point in each sentence, the subjects heard a click through headphones and had to press a button in response. The time they took to respond was measured – the idea being that the more attention they were giving to grammatical processing, the more slowly they would respond to the click. When clicks accompanied the fourth word in each sentence in a pair (e.g. *clubbed* in (11a) and (11b)), there was no difference in the subjects' response time. However, when clicks occurred during the fifth word (e.g. *the* and *by*), subjects were significantly slower on sentences like (11a) than those like (11b). Isakson suggested that this was because, with the clause structure already apparent by the fifth word in the (11a) type sentences, the subjects were carrying out grammatical processing (which was absorbing a lot of their attention), whereas in the (11b) type sentences all they could do was hold the words in memory and wait until the grammatical structure became apparent. (Bever (1970, p. 292) reported a similar result with a different sentence structure.) It is important to note that the longer response time for (11a) does not mean that it is harder than (11b); rather it means that in sentences where the structure is predictable at an early stage, processing can begin early, which should lighten the load on short-term memory.

    The burden imposed on short-term memory by an unprocessed string of words was revealed in an unpublished study by Gough and Mastenbrook (described in Foss & Hakes, 1978, p. 112). Their adult subjects heard ten-word strings and were immediately asked to recall them, e.g.:

12a radio arm chief test window melting snows cause sudden floods
12b melting snows cause sudden floods radio arm chief test window

Strings like (12b) were recalled much more accurately than those like (12a). The experimenters suggested that this was because when the first five words could be assigned a grammatical structure (as in (12b)), they no longer took up storage space in short-term memory so the five unrelated words at the end of the string could be held. (Miller, 1956, p. 92, suggests that the adult memory span for unrelated monosyllabic English words is about five.) On the other hand, in (12a) the first five unrelated words either had to remain in short-term memory, leaving no spare capacity for the next five, or they were forgotten while the last five were processed.

Isakson's study suggested that readers begin grammatical processing early in the sentence when they can; Kimball (1973) believes that it is a principle of language processing that a string of words will have the first plausible grammatical analysis assigned to it. If subsequent words show that the clause has been wrongly segmented, then the initial chunk will have to be re-processed. For example, if a reader meets the string:

13a The trains run . . .

it is likely that this will be analysed as SV. . . , perhaps with the expectation of a following adverbial, e.g. *on time* or *to London*. If, however, the next words to be read are:

13b . . . by railway clubs . . .

then the first string has to be reanalysed so that, with (13b), it forms the subject of the clause, with the verb still to come.

If a segment that has been analysed has to be recalled and reprocessed then this is likely to cause difficulty, as there is evidence that once chunks have been processed they are cleared from short-term memory. Caplan (1972, p. 75) tape-recorded pairs of sentences like these:

14a Although we still have not had any snow, storms are expected.
14b Because the weather is cold and damp, snow storms are expected.

In these sentences, the last four words are the same but in (14a) *snow* is the last word in the first clause, while in (14b) it is the first word in the second clause. The tapes were spliced so that the pronunciation and intonation of the last four words was identical in the two sentences. This was to ensure that subjects did not receive any help with grammatical processing from prosodic features.[2] Adult subjects listened to each sentence and then had to press a lever to signal whether or not it had contained a test word they were given. When the test word was *snow*, response times were significantly faster when it was in the last clause, as in (14b). The slower response to (14a) suggests that the first clause, including *snow*, had been processed and cleared from short-term memory

2 As the subjects were responsive to the difference in grammatical structure between the two sentences, without the aid of prosodic features, this would seem to conflict with the point emphatically made on p. 273 above that it is the absence of these features in written language that is a major source of difficulty for the young reader. I feel that the point stands, however, for two reasons. First, children need support from a range of sources – the situation, the linguistic context, prosody – in their interpretation of the more advanced grammatical structures, whereas adults can, if necessary, process complex sentences that are completely decontextualized. Second, processing individual test sentences that have had prosodic cues removed is very different from continuous language processing; I believe that even adults would have difficulty if lengthy oral passages had to be comprehended without the benefit of intonation to signal the structural divisions within sentences.

·so that it was no longer quite so readily accessible as the clause that was still under active processing.

Language that has been processed and removed from short-term memory is less accessible to verbatim recall because, fairly quickly, its exact form is lost, although a representation of the meaning remains. This memory for gist has been demonstrated in studies by Sachs (1967, 1974). In her second study, she asked her adult subjects to read short passages which each contained an unmarked test sentence, e.g.:

15a The founding fathers considered owning slaves to be immoral.

After a given interval, they then had to read another sentence and say whether it had been in the passage. The sentences for comparison either altered the meaning, e.g.:

15b The founding fathers didn't consider owning slaves to be immoral.

or they retained the meaning but altered the form, e.g.:

15c The founding fathers thought owning slaves to be immoral.

The subjects had to make the comparison either immediately after they had read the test sentence or after another twenty, forty or eighty syllables. The results showed that memory for meaning was good, so that even after eighty syllables, sentence (15b) was recognized as a mismatch, but that forgetting of the exact words was substantial within twenty syllables and essentially complete within forty. Sachs (1974, p. 99) concluded:

> The combined outcomes of quick memory loss of the exact words of a sentence together with good retention of the meaning of those words is consistent with the view that the material in a sentence is encoded in an abstract representation, and the exact words are rapidly forgotten.

We can now consider what is known about the segments of language that form the basis of sentence processing. One piece of evidence comes from 'click' studies. In these studies, subjects hear a sentence through one headphone and a brief click through the other. They are instructed to write down the sentence they have heard, marking the point where the click occurred. The idea behind this methodology is that word strings that are perceived as units will resist interruption and, therefore, the subjects' placement of the clicks might indicate natural breaks in the structure of the sentence. In a study by Garrett, Bever and Fodor (1966, p. 31), students heard sentences like these:

16a In order to catch his train George drove furiously
　　　　　　　A　　　　　　　S　　　V　　　A

　　to the station.
　　A

16b The reporters assigned to George drove furiously
               S   V   A

to the station.
    A

Both these sentences contain a non-finite subordinate clause; in (16a) it is an adverbial of purpose and in (16b) it post-modifies the noun *reporters*. From *George* onwards the two sentences are physically identical but, because of their different structures, in (16b) *George* belongs to the subordinate clause while in (16a) it is the subject of the main clause. The tapes were spliced so that intonation was held constant and could not be used as a cue in processing. In both sentences, the click was superimposed on the word *George*. Some subjects reported this placement accurately; of those who did not, most who heard (16a) located the click BEFORE *George* and those who heard (16b) put it AFTER *George*. So, the click tended to 'move' to the boundary between the subordinate and the main clause. This suggests that the boundaries that separate clauses in these examples also mark off the strings of words that are perceived as unified segments in sentence processing. In other words, the grammatical division into clauses has psychological reality for the language user. This result receives support from the study by Caplan (1972), described above, and from a similar one by Jarvella (1971).

Evidence more directly related to reading comes from studies of the eye-voice span; this is the distance, in words, that the eyes are ahead of the voice in oral reading. Subjects are asked to read aloud sentences projected on a screen. In mid-sentence, the experimenter turns off the projector, telling the subjects to continue reporting what they have read. Levin (1979) suggests that the average eye-voice span for adult readers is four to five words. The most revealing fact, though, is that the span is flexible, not fixed. It is responsive to the grammatical structure and complexity of a text. Rode (1974) studied the eye-voice span of children aged nine to eleven as they read aloud eleven-word compound sentences, consisting of two main clauses joined by *and*, e.g.:

17 Big hamburgers were slowly fried and thin hot dogs were grilled.
                                                 (Rode, p. 130)

She found that the eye-voice spans of the nine-year-olds tended to terminate at phrase boundaries, e.g. . . . . *dogs*, suggesting that these younger children were treating as separate segments the two clause elements, subject and verb. In contrast, the older children had a strong tendency to read to clause boundaries. Their eye-voice spans expanded and contracted according to the structure of the sentence at the interruption point; if they were near the end of the first clause when the projector was switched off, they generally did not report words beyond the end of the clause, but if they were near the beginning of the clause, they tried to complete it. Noting that, in the older subjects, there was a particularly marked effort to process the subject and verb together, Rode (p. 137) offered this explanation:

> The information . . . gained from an initial noun phrase is minimal and it is only upon reading the verb phrase that the reader knows what sentential meaning the author intended.

Studies of the eye-voice span, then, suggest that even young readers are sensitive to constituent boundaries since, in reporting words they have seen, they rarely stop in the middle of a clause element. (Though as the longest clause element in Rode's study was only three words long we cannot tell how they would behave when confronted with longer constituents.) The studies also reveal that older and abler readers have a strong tendency to process at least the subject and verb together.

From this view of sentence processing, it is possible to hypothesize three potential sources of grammatical difficulty in reading. First, reading is likely to be harder when the grammatical structure of a sentence is not easy to predict. This follows from the evidence that readers bring active expectations to the task of sentence processing rather than merely being passive receivers of information.

Second, reading is likely to be harder when a sentence does not divide readily into optimal segments for processing. We have seen that even young readers prefer segments to correspond to major clause elements and that in older readers there is a leaning towards chunks that consist of whole clauses where possible. This raises the question of how these grammatical divisions are recognized. Bever (1970, p. 288) comments:

> There is no known automatic procedure that ensures the proper segmentation of actual sequences . . . pronunciation often provides many cues that indicate where the segmentation . . . should occur.

But, of course, it is just these pronunciation cues that written language lacks, and, as was shown in chapter 4, punctuation is an inadequate substitute. I shall suggest in a later section that some types of written sentence enhance the likelihood of profitable segmentation while others diminish it.

Third, reading is likely to be harder when a heavy burden is imposed on short-term memory. It has been said that the words undergoing active processing have to be held together in short-term memory; if it is not possible to work out grammatical relationships without exceeding the memory's limits, then comprehension will be impeded and reading will become more effortful. The capacity of short-term memory is not easy to state precisely, because it is affected by a variety of factors. For example, it is reduced when a processing task requires a great deal of attention. So children's normal memory capacity is likely to be decreased if they are struggling with complex subject matter or unfamiliar vocabulary.

Another difference is caused by age, as memory span is thought to increase throughout childhood. Gamlin (1971), for instance, reports a study with two groups of children, the younger group aged fourteen, the older aged sixteen to eighteen. The younger children had an average memory span for random numbers of 5.8 digits, while the older group had an average span of 6.8. However, there are also differences between one individual and another of the same age. Gamlin's subjects were further grouped according to whether they had a high or a low short-term memory span; the averages for his two groups of fourteen-year-olds were 6.3 and 5.3 digits. It is also well known that the memory span for meaningful material is longer than for random words.

Bearing these various differences in mind, we can note that Sachs (1974, p. 99) found that adult readers could remember something like twenty syllables (or roughly eleven words in her test sentences); Jarvella (1971, p. 412) reported that adults doing a listening task had a verbatim memory for about ten words within one sentence; this is similar to the results obtained by Gamlin (1971) with pupils aged fourteen to eighteen. In all these studies, the subjects knew they would be asked to recall what they had heard or read. Wanner (1974) believed that this might produce longer memory spans than would occur in normal processing, so he devised an experiment where, either with or without warning, subjects were required to recall the instructions they had just been given. His belief was confirmed, since his subjects remembered significantly more in the warned condition; in the unwarned condition they did not remember more than sixteen syllables (roughly nine words). Together, these results suggest that, for young and slow readers, reading will be more demanding when the grammatical relationships within a string do not become apparent within the space of ten or eleven words. We know that in reading, unlike speech, comprehension does not collapse entirely if short-term memory is overloaded, because the text is always available for rereading. Nevertheless, a frequent need to reread is bound to cause frustration and to reduce understanding.

Each of these three possible sources of reading difficulty will now be examined in turn.

Structures that are difficult to predict

Late-acquired structures

Sentence structures that are frequently-used and familiar are likely to be processed more rapidly and accurately than those that are unfamiliar, because they are easier to predict. Therefore, constructions that develop rather late in children's speech, and particularly those that are more often found in written than in spoken language, can be expected to cause difficulties for readers still at the consolidation phase. Studies by Peltz (1974), Ruddell (1965) and Tatham (1970) all provide evidence, in varying ways, that children do indeed experience more reading difficulty with unfamiliar sentence patterns. Now, by taking up material from chapter 3 on grammatical structures that are acquired during the school years, and from chapter 4 on those that are more typical of written than spoken language, it is possible to list and exemplify potentially difficult constructions at clause and phrase level, in simple, compound and complex sentences.

Clause level. Two clause patterns that are acquired fairly late are SVO$_i$ O$_d$ and SVOC. A problem with both these constructions is that they are compressed, with the relationships between the two complementation elements not overtly expressed, e.g.:

18a <u>They</u> <u>found</u> <u>their inhabitants, the Aborigines of Australia</u>
    s   v   o

<u>and the Maoris of New Zealand,</u> <u>definitely hostile.</u>   (Junior)
                                      c

Here, the structure would be more obvious if a subordinate clause was used, e.g.:

18b They found that their inhabitants . . . were definitely hostile.

Some negative constructions are acquired fairly late. Among these are the concealed negatives (where the negative word is not an obvious one like *not, no* or *never*) and the literary constructions with fronting of the negative followed by subject-verb inversion. Concealed negatives occur commonly in books for young children, e.g.:

19 The gibbon is *rarely* seen on the ground.   (Junior)
20 Soon there may be *few* left.   (Junior)
21 These seers *seldom* tried to make the people live better lives.
                                  (Secondary)

There are also occasional examples of literary negatives, e.g.:

22 Nowhere are these forces more clearly shown than in the letters of early immigrants.   (Secondary)
23 Not for many years did Ged set foot on that land.   (Secondary)

A particularly common feature of written language is fronting: we saw in chapters 4 and 5 that this device can be used to maintain thematic continuity, to introduce thematic variety, or to ensure that the information focus falls on the appropriate clause element. When an adverbial is fronted, it is usually easy to recognize because it is introduced by a preposition, e.g.:

24 *In this way* were formed the oilfields from which we get our oil
   today.   (Junior)
25 Consequently, *from carbon atoms* come two things so different to
   look at.   (Junior)

But sometimes an adverbial consists of a noun phrase without a preposition; when such a structure occurs at the beginning of a sentence it is
easy to mistake it for the subject, e.g.:

26a *Every winter* passes are blocked by snow.   (Secondary)

It would be easy to predict a different structure for this sentence, e.g.:

26b Every winter passes more slowly.

Fronting of the object always means that, contrary to expectations, the
initial noun phrase is not the subject. It seems likely that this will cause
more confusion than most adverbial fronting, e.g.:

27 *The thread and screwdriver* we hid.   (Junior)

When a complement noun phrase is fronted there is the same possibility
that it will be misinterpreted as the subject, e.g.:

28 *A platform* it most certainly is, but it is so much more.

                                                        (Secondary)

Complements that consist of adjective phrases, though, cannot lead to
that kind of error:

29 *Very glad* he was to learn this lore.   (Secondary)

To draw the different types of fronting together, it is true to say that they
are all less familiar and less predictable than the canonical order of SV +
complementation; and that those which cause a non-subject noun phrase
to occupy initial position in the clause are probably particularly confusing.

   Another fairly frequent device in written language is the interrupting
construction; that is, at clause level, something that intervenes between
subject and verb or between the verb and its complementation. Slobin
(1973b) has formulated a number of principles which, he believes, reflect
basic cognitive abilities and which may, therefore, apply universally to
language processing. One of these principles is, 'Avoid interruption or
re-arrangement of linguistic units' (p. 199). Bever (1970, p. 299) has also
suggested that interrupted clauses are harder to process. He reports a
study where subjects were asked for immediate recall of sentences like
the following:

30a Quickly the waiter sent the order back.
    A   S   V   O   A

30b The waiter quickly sent back the order.
    S   A   V   A   O

Of the errors in word order, 87 per cent were made by subjects who altered (30b), with its interrupting adverbials, to (30a).

It does not seem likely that single-word adverbials like these normally cause readers much difficulty. However, interrupting constructions can be very much longer than that, e.g.:

31 It then became possible to make polymethylmethacrylate in commercial quantities, and its toughness and transparency – *in sheet form it is as clear as glass* – made it suitable for applications such as aircraft canopies.   (Junior)

32 Meanwhile, the Normans, *who, early in the Confessor's reign, had narrowly failed to gain a commanding position in the kingdom,* were now preparing a landing somewhere along the south coast. (Junior)

33 Because plastics need heat to soften them, the barrel (*that is the part of an extruder between the hopper and the hole at the end, which is called a die*) must be made so that it can be heated and controlled at a steady temperature.   (Junior)

These three interruptions illustrate the different types of punctuation that can be used to signal them – paired dashes, paired commas, and brackets. The number of words in the interrruptions is nine, seventeen and twenty-one respectively. In (32) the interruption is itself interrupted by the adverbial, *early in the Confessor's reign.* All three interruptions occur between subject and verb, which is probably where they have the most disruptive effect on sentence processing since, as we have already seen, it is very important to be able to process both subject and verb as early as possible. This is partly because of a desire to complete the concord relationship which binds subject and verb together; it is also because the clause pattern often becomes clear once the verb is reached. The reason for this is that the sub-class to which the verb belongs, transitive, copular or intransitive, largely determines the structure of the rest of the clause. Coleman (1962, p. 133) refers to the need to link subject and verb:

To understand a sentence, we must connect subject and verb correctly. This connecting becomes easier as fewer words separate subject and verb.

In a study of American children aged eight to eleven, Richek (1976) was able to demonstrate that their reading performance was hampered when sentential relationships were interrupted. She gave matched groups paired paragraphs to read, one containing an uninterrupted sequence, like (34a), the other featuring an interruption, as in (34b):

34a John visited Bill in order to give the gift. Bill was in the house.(. . .)

34b John visited Bill, *who was in the house,* in order to give the gift.(. . .)

At the end of the paragraph there was a question to be answered, e.g. *Who gave the gift?* Although they were all allowed to look back at the paragraph while they answered the question, significantly more of the children who read the uninterrupted version got the answer right. Richek felt that the effects of an interruption were particularly severe when the basic sentence structure was itself difficult for some reason. She concluded, 'authors and editors of children's books should be aware of the rapidly increasing difficulty encountered when several difficult structures are combined in a single sentence' (p. 806).

Phrase level.   We have already seen that in all speech and in children's writing long subject noun phrases are rare. In adult writing they are more common. Like interrupting constructions, they delay the completion of the link between subject and verb. In books written for children, particularly in non-fiction, there are very many examples of subject noun phrases that are more than ten words long, e.g.:

35 *Differences in water temperature, the abundance of food supplies and the availability of the right places to breed or spawn* are the main reasons for the migration of aquatic animals.   (Junior)
36 *The conversion of the products obtained from the crackers of the oil refineries into the basic raw materials of the plastics industry* occupies a large section of the world's chemical industry.   (Junior)

The subjects of these two sentences are 20 and 22 words long. A problem the reader faces is relating the head noun of the subject NP to the verb. In (36), the head noun is *conversion* but five other, potentially distracting, nouns occur before the verb is reached: *products, crackers, refineries, materials, industry.* It sometimes happens that even mature adult writers make an error of concord when another noun intervenes between the head noun and the verb, e.g.:

37 *Active productive control of these structures* are late to develop in children's language.   (Adult)

Here the head noun is *control* but the verb form the author uses shows that he has been distracted by the later plural noun *structures.* Examples like this suggest that NPs that contain several nouns may cause difficulties for both writers and readers.

Phrases, like clauses, can be interrupted. When a phrase is in subject position, an interruption within the phrase may increase the distance between the head noun and the verb, e.g.:

38 Housewives and, *in big houses,* sewing women made all the clothes by hand.   (Junior)
39 Seventy draft ewes (*five-year old sheep come to the end of their life on the hill*) and 130 ewe hoggs (*one-year olds*) are wintered on low ground.   (Secondary)

In (39), what could be a straightforward co-ordinated NP grows to 24 words because of the two definitions given in brackets. This example helps to explain why these cumbersome constructions appear more often in non-fiction than in fiction: they allow a writer to gloss, expand or qualify the information which is being given, so they occur particularly frequently when an author is fulfilling an instructional role.

The head noun of an NP can be modified by an appositional phrase. This is a late grammatical acquisition which is generally more common in writing than in speech. In subject position, it is another construction that has the effect of distancing the head noun from the verb, e.g.:

40 When Elizabeth died in 1603, her cousin, *King James VI of Scotland* (*son of Mary, Queen of Scots*), came from Scotland to be King James I. (Junior)

An additional problem is that, in writing, it can sometimes be difficult to distinguish appositional phrases from a co-ordinated list of NPs. (In speech, intonation differentiates the two structures.) For example,

41 Among them were the secretary of state, Mr Alexander Haig, the Chairman of the Federal Reserve Board, Mr Paul Volcker, and a senior member of the National Security Council. (Adult)

The question is whether three or five people are referred to in this sentence. The answer does not lie in the grammatical structure (which is ambiguous between the two interpretations) but in the reader's knowledge of the world. That alone makes it clear that the structure is not NP, NP, NP, NP, *and* NP but NP(=NP), NP(=NP), *and* NP.

Another kind of noun phrase that is more typical of written than spoken language is the **nominalization**. In this case, a clause is made into a noun phrase, with the verb of the clause being **nominalized** and becoming the head noun of the phrase, e.g.:

42a *The exploration and charting of the coastlines of these new lands* was the work of an English seaman. (Junior)

Here, the clause that underlies the italicized nominalization is, *The coastlines of these new lands were explored and charted*; the verbs *explore* and *chart* have been made into the co-ordinated head nouns of the NP – *exploration* and *charting*. If (42a) is rewritten to get rid of the nominalization, a possible result is:

42b An English seaman explored and charted the coastlines of these new lands.

This alteration has had four desirable effects: it has replaced an abstract subject by a concrete, human one; it has replaced a long subject NP by a short one and, in so doing, it has produced a sentence with end-weight (unlike (42a)); and it has provided a dynamic and memorable VP in place of the static and colourless *was*. A disadvantage of the alteration is that the information focus no longer falls where the author wanted it, on *an English seaman*. This can easily be remedied, without sacrificing the advantages of (42b), by clefting:

> 42c It was an English seaman who explored and charted the coast-lines of these new lands.

Another disadvantage could be that thematic continuity has been lost. This could be restored, without resorting to nominalization, by using the passive, e.g.:

> 42d The coastlines of these new lands were explored and charted by an English seaman.

Examples (42b–d) show that there are various ways of avoiding nominalizations. That this might be worth doing has been suggested in many studies (e.g. Williams, 1979; Harrison, 1980). Williams makes the point that, in the most common English clauses, the grammatical pattern subject-verb reflects the semantic structure agent-action. In a nominalized construction, this parallel is lost, since the subject now expresses not the agent but the action and the verb is reduced to a mere linking word; if the agent appears at all it comes after the verb. Of the breakdown of grammatical and semantic parallelism, Williams (p. 602) says:

> When the subject does not express the agent and the verb does not express what that agent does, then the syntactic and semantic structures of a sentence become to that degree even more complex.

He goes on to describe a study in which seventy typists typed passages where the subject-verb structure either did or did not reflect the agent-action relationship; the typists were both faster and more accurate on the passages in which the semantic structure was reinforced by the grammar.

Compound sentences. Generally speaking, compound sentences should be easy. They occur very early in children's speech and do not present many problems. It is worth remembering, though, that the compound co-ordinator *not only . . . but also* may be misunderstood. For instance, the first clause in the following sentence may be interpreted as a negative ('The earth does not travel . . .'):

> 43 The earth not only travels on its orbit round the sun, it also rotates on its axis, taking 24 hours to make one complete revolution. (Secondary)

Another possible source of difficulty is ellipsis, which occurs frequently in compound sentences. The study by Richek (1977) described on p. 130 above suggested that when there is ellipsis of a repeated subject in the second clause of a compound sentence, the result is a marked fall-off in comprehension among eight-year-old readers, even though this particular type of ellipsis is very common. Other types are less frequent and probably more demanding, e.g.:

44 A camel is well equipped to survive in the desert, and a polar bear
   in the Arctic. (Junior)

Here, reading the second clause entails the mental insertion of 'is well equipped to survive' after 'polar bear'.

Occasionally, if the writer is careless, it may not be clear to the reader which two clauses are being co-ordinated; this makes it difficult to identify the referent of an ellipted subject, e.g.:

45 I still get a tiny shiver of embarrassment when I remember how he
   came to dinner with us when we were very young and couldn't eat
   kidneys. (Adult)

This looks as if 'and couldn't eat kidneys' is joined to 'when we were very young'. If this were the case, the ellipted subject would be *we*. In fact, the rest of the passage reveals that it was *he* who couldn't eat kidneys, so the last clause is actually co-ordinated to 'how he came to dinner with us'. The author could have avoided the ambiguity either by including the subject *he* in the last clause or by placing the adverbial 'when we were very young' immediately after *how*.

Finally, we can note that if the first of two co-ordinated clauses contains a negative, the writer has to take particular care or it may not be clear whether the negation extends into the second clause or not, e.g.:

46 Police are confident that if bank managers do not panic and
   contact them they can contain the problem. (Adult)

In this sentence, bank managers are being advised to contact the police but it is easy to think it means the opposite, because the negative 'do not panic' exerts its influence on the following co-ordinated clause. A similar effect occurs in (47):

47 Don't overcrowd the fridge and keep food covered. (Adult)

Complex sentences. The finite subordinate clauses will be considered first and the non-finite ones will be illustrated at the end of this section. Of the nominal subordinate clauses, the least common and the latest to develop in children's language are subject clauses, introduced by a *wh*-word or (*the fact*) *that*. Like long noun phrases in subject position, they can entail some complex processing before the main verb of the sentence is reached, e.g.:

48 *The fact that the monomers, and similar chemicals that are the
   starting materials for the manufacture of plastics, can now be made
   fairly cheaply and in large quantities* is a result of all the research
   and development that has been carried out in recent years. (Junior)

The italicized subject nominal clause is 28 words long and itself contains a subject NP that is 15 words long ('the monomers ... plastics'). However, it is not only long subject clauses that may be difficult; the following short sentence is not easy at first reading:

49 What people think is important is important. (Adult)

Now we can turn to adverbial subordinate clauses. Some of these, such as the clauses of time and purpose, occur early and frequently in children's speech and are unlikely to cause particular difficulty in reading. Others, such as clauses introduced by *unless*, *provided that* and *although*, may cause comprehension problems for some children until the age of thirteen or so. The intrinsic difficulty of 'although' clauses (which was illustrated on pp. 143–4 above) is sometimes compounded by writers who use them rather imprecisely. Typically, 'although' clauses express a contrast, but in the next example that contrast is not made explicit:

50 Although they worked hard they were not beaten. (Junior)

This sentence comes from a passage about boys working in a nineteenth-century cotton mill. The author means something like, 'Although they had to work hard, they were fortunate in that, unlike other apprentices, they were not beaten.' As it stands, (50) can more naturally be interpreted as if it were introduced by *because* rather than *although*. It is obviously unfortunate to reinforce in this way an error of comprehension that children are inclined to make anyway when they first meet clauses of concession. Failure to make the contrast explicit is also evident in this adult example:

51 The tape is packed in rounded edge boxes although the white area on the label could be made bigger. (Adult)

In this assessment of the packaging of a cassette tape, the unstated assumption is that rounded edge boxes are a good feature, which can be contrasted with the bad feature of a small label.

Straightforward clauses of condition are mastered by children at quite an early age. Nevertheless, there are some literary varieties that are less familiar and may cause problems. First, there are inferential 'if' clauses, e.g.:

52 If, towards the end of his reign, he let Earl Godwin and Harold rule the kingdom, they were men of first-class ability. (Junior)

Here, there is none of the uncertainty usually associated with 'if' clauses because the author has already stated that the King did allow Godwin and Harold to rule the kingdom. Therefore, the first clause, despite its appearance, is expressing a fact and not a condition. The sentence could be laboriously paraphrased: 'If it is true that he let Earl Godwin and

Harold rule the kingdom (and it is true because I have just said so), then it is also true that they were men of first-class ability.' Clauses of this type are quite common in adult reading material but they also appear in books written for junior children more frequently than might be expected. Here is another example:

> 53 If our ancestors are said to have lived in the 'Stone Age', perhaps the present time will one day be known as the 'Plastics Age'.
>
> (Junior)

Second, clauses of condition may be signalled not by *if* but by inversion of the subject and auxiliary, e.g.:

> 54 Had their journey been made in years gone by, they would have found the downs far more open.   (Secondary)
> 55 Had they not done so, the Old Testament stories, which we read today and which were not written down for at least 1,200 years after Abraham's death, would have been lost.   (Secondary)

This pattern is much more likely to occur in writing than in speech.

Third, conditional clauses may be introduced by an imperative verb, e.g.:

> 56 Jump off a high wall, and you will land with a thump that may make you sprain an ankle.   (Secondary)

Despite appearances, the author is not instructing his readers to make reckless leaps; rather, he is describing the consequences of a hypothetical action. Children are familiar with this structure in the context of parental warnings – 'Do that again and I'll smack you!' – but they may not recognize it when more academic ideas are being expressed.

Like conditional clauses, clauses of cause (or reason) appear early in children's speech. But, again, there are some types that may not be fully understood during the junior school years. Studies described on pp. 140–2 above suggest that 'because' clauses expressing logical relations (rather than physical consequences) in reversible sentences may be particularly demanding. It is also worth noticing that there is always a potential ambiguity, in writing, when a negative main clause is followed by a 'because' clause, e.g.:

57a Andrea didn't go abroad because she was unhappy.

This sentence has two clearly different meanings, either:

> i) Andrea didn't go abroad and the reason she didn't go was that she was unhappy.

or:

> ii) Andrea went abroad but not because she was unhappy.

If the 'because' clause appears at the beginning of the sentence, then only the first interpretation is possible:

57b Because she was unhappy, Andrea didn't go abroad.

Most often, common sense and the context make the meaning clear; however, when the subject matter is difficult or unfamiliar, this construction can make processing more effortful, e.g.:

58 The children did not use more two-constituent relations than three-constituent relations because it was difficult for them to say more than two words at a time.   (Adult)

Superficially, this looks as if the children did not use more two-constituent relations than three-constituent relations. Only a close reading reveals that the sentence means the opposite: that the children DID use more two-constituent relations – but not because it was difficult for them to say more than two words at a time.

The last type of finite subordinate clause to consider is the relative. In chapter 5, I hypothesized a developmental sequence in the acquisition of relative clauses, suggesting that the kinds grouped in Stages III and IV generally do not appear until the secondary years. These more advanced types are clauses introduced by *whom, whose,* or a preposition plus a relative pronoun; and series of relatives within one sentence. They may present problems for a young reader, particularly if they occur in a sentence which is already difficult, e.g.:

59 'From his cradle, he was filled with the love of wisdom above all things' wrote a friend, the Welsh monk Asser, whom, like many others, he brought to Wessex to restore learning.   (Junior)

Here, the relative clause introduced by *whom* is interrupted by *like many others*; and the subject of the clause, *he,* refers back to *Alfred,* which is forty-two words away in the previous sentence. In addition, the main clause provides an example of object fronting, with the quotation preceding the verb and subject. But apparently simple sentences may cause difficulties too, e.g.:

60 Polythene is a tough solid material. Ethylene, from which it is made, is a gas.   (Junior)

It takes a moment to sort out that polythene is made from ethylene, and not the other way round. In non-fiction, it is quite common for several relative clauses to occur in one sentence, as in the following example which contains three – the first interrupted and the last unmarked by a relative pronoun (I shall suggest below that the absence of a relative pronoun may make 'chunking' harder):

61 The ethylene contained a very small amount of oxygen which, it has since been discovered, assists the reaction which turns ethylene into polythene at the temperatures and pressures the scientists were using. (Junior)

Any type of complex sentence can become especially difficult if it contains more than one negative, e.g.:

62 Of the million or so different kinds of animals there is hardly one that doesn't astonish us with a special characteristic, evolved through millions of years. (Junior)

In this example, the concealed negative *hardly* in the main clause and the explicit negative in the relative clause combine to produce a positive meaning – 'they almost all astonish us'. When two negatives occur in a sentence that has a nominal clause as object of such verbs as *say, think* and *pretend*, comprehension may falter (see pp. 118–19), e.g.:

63 It's no good pretending I did not expect to find some Medusa or Lady Macbeth. (Adult)

It may break down altogether in the face of a rare triple negative like this:

64 The reason they haven't stopped glue-sniffing is not because they have not been offered enough enlightenment. (Adult)

Apart from object nominal clauses and adverbial clauses of purpose, non-finite and verbless clauses are later acquisitions in children's language than finite subordinate clauses. In books for young readers there are occasional examples of non-finite subject nominal clauses, e.g.:

65 *Hearing the tales about Vinland* inspired Thorfinn to fit out the largest expedition yet. (Junior)

More frequent are non-finite adverbials, e.g.:

66 *Returning from its feeding sojourn in the Antarctic Ocean*, the emperor penguin leaps to a height twice its own length. (Junior)
67 Hot air, *being lighter than cool air*, always rises above the cool air. (Junior)

In sentences like (66) and (67), the subordinate clause is not introduced by a subordinator so its semantic role is not made explicit. If finite clauses were used instead in these examples, there would be a subordinator such as *while* or *when* in (66) and *because* in (67), and the meaning would be immediately obvious. Verbless adverbial clauses usually have subordinators but (obviously) no verbs, e.g.:

68 *When quite close* they spring on it.   (Junior)
69 *Though more like a monk than a king,* he was crafty enough to survive the bitter rivalry between his Norman friends and the English nobles.   (Junior)

Such clauses can only be interpreted if the missing subject and verb are mentally inserted, i.e. *they are* in (68) and *he was* in (69). When the subordinate clause precedes the main clause, as in these examples, this replacement operation cannot be performed until the subject and verb of the main clause have been read.

Like these adverbial constructions, non-finite relative clauses modifying the subject are characteristically written forms and are very late to appear in children's own writing. They are not uncommon in books written for junior children, e.g.:

70 The area *lived in by a pride of lions* is called a territory.   (Junior)
71 The nutritious salts of these waters, *brought down by rivers,* are beneficial to the fish.   (Junior)

Finite versions of these clauses would require *which is* in (70) and *which are* in (71).

On the whole, non-finite clauses are not only less familiar but also less informative than their finite counterparts as they never indicate tense or number and, when they do not begin with a subordinate clause marker (e.g. *because, which*), the most obvious signal of the grammatical and semantic relationship between the subordinate and main clause has been lost.

'Open-ended' structures

Late-acquired constructions are not the only ones that may be hard to predict. It is also the case that, even when the clause pattern is a straightforward and frequent one like SVA or SVO, some sentences are structurally less predictable than others. This variability derives from the differing extent to which individual verbs constrain what can follow them. The determining role of the verb becomes clear if we consider the structure of the most common English clauses: they can all be summarized like this – SV (+ complementation). From this it is apparent that on reading a subject we can predict that it will be followed by a verb, which may or may not be succeeded by some type of complementation. The type of complementation is governed by the class of the verb: transitive verbs accept objects, copular verbs accept complements, and intransitive verbs cannot take either. Transitive verbs can be further sub-divided into **monotransitives**, which allow only a direct object, **di-transitives**, which can take both a direct and an indirect object, and **complex transitives**, which can be followed by an object and an object complement. Some verbs belong to just one of these classes, others to several. The more classes a verb belongs to, the less possible it is to predict the clause elements that will follow it. So prediction is likely to be more accurate when a verb is relatively constraining rather than relatively 'open-ended' in terms of the complementation it allows.

To illustrate 'open-ended' and constraining verbs we can take *call* and *lift*. The verb *call* can be intransitive or any of the three types of transitive so there are four different possibilities for its complementation:

72a	Margaret called (loudly).	SV(A) (intransitive)
72b	Margaret called Robert.	SVO (monotransitive)
72c	Margaret called Ian a taxi.	SVOO (di-transitive)
72d	Margaret called the dog a nuisance.	SVOC (complex transitive)

In contrast, the verb *lift* is nearly always monotransitive, e.g.:

73	Gareth lifted the suitcase.	SVO (monotransitive)

(Very rarely it can be intransitive, e.g. *The fog lifted*.)

Although recognizing the class that a verb belongs to may enable the type of complementation to be predicted, there can still be considerable variety in the grammatical structure of any particular clause element. For example, if we consider the monotransitive class of verbs, we know that they are followed by a direct object but also that the object may be expressed by (among other things) a noun phrase, a 'that' finite clause and a non-finite clause. Some monotransitive verbs can be followed by all three of these structures, others by two or only one, e.g.:

74a Bernard expected the message.
74b Bernard expected that the message would arrive.
74c Bernard expected the message to arrive.

75a Bernard accepted the message.
75b Bernard accepted that the message would arrive.
75c *Bernard accepted the message to arrive.

76a Bernard took the message.
76b *Bernard took that the message would arrive.
76c *Bernard took the message to arrive.

There is some evidence (Bever, 1970, p. 301; Foss & Hakes, 1978, p. 127; Holmes & Forster, 1972, p. 152) that, when a transitive verb can potentially be followed by objects with a range of structures, the clause will be more demanding to read than one with a transitive verb that can accept only limited types of object. If this research finding is correct, then sentence (76a) should be easier than (74a), when they are both surrounded by other sentences.

Unusual placement of information focus

A third possible source of problems in predicting sentence structure is the placement of the focus of information. Normally, we expect this to fall on the last lexical word in the clause. In an unpublished study by Zollinger (reported by Levin, 1979, p. 143), subjects were given pairs of sentences to read and their eye-voice spans were measured. When the information focus in the second sentence was not in its characteristic position, eye-voice spans were significantly decreased, suggesting that the reading task was harder. Here are some examples where the focus does not fall on the last word of the clause and where, I believe, comprehension is momentarily impeded:

77 It may spring on its prey from trees, though it also tracks animals.
(Junior)

At first reading it is easy to think that *animals* is the information focus; in fact, of course, it is *tracks* that needs to be emphasized, to highlight its contrast with *spring . . . from trees.*

78 She would try dancing, acting – anything. She was incredibly ambitious. On the other hand, you couldn't make her do anything. Everything had to be talked over and she had to be guided gently.
(Adult)

In the third sentence in (78) it looks as though the focus is on *anything* but the rest of the passage shows that it is actually on *make.*

79a You should make this potato gratin with Swedish anchovies, which are really spiced, cured sprats. I have tried them but much prefer the true anchovies that come in little cans.   (Adult)

If (79a) were read aloud, the first sentence would have to be spoken like this:

79b you shŏuld make this po'tato 'gratin/ with Swĕdish anchovies/

but the need for the unusual placement of the nucleus on *should* (and for the contrastive fall-rise tone) does not become apparent until the second sentence. This is because it looks at first as if readers are being told to use Swedish anchovies, whereas the second sentence makes it clear that they are, in fact, being advised against it.

Structures that are difficult to segment

The second major source of grammatical difficulty in reading is a lack of certainty about the most fruitful division of a line of text into segments for processing. There is some evidence that, for younger and weaker readers, this difficulty may be compounded by unhelpful line endings. Many teachers are familiar with the way that young children, reading aloud, will strive to complete a sentence at the end of a line if possible. Crystal (1975, p. 30) gives this example:

80 They went for a ride
   on a pony. The next day . . .

Here, young readers have a tendency to give a falling intonation to *ride* and to start a new sentence, 'On a pony the next day . . .' Another characteristic of the immature reader is to read across punctuation in the middle of the line, in the attempt to match the sentence boundary to the line ending. Moon (1979, p. 38) illustrates this behaviour with the following example:

81 Saul listened. He did
   not know that David had been chosen
   by God.

He reports that some children read this as, 'Saul listened, he did.' He describes a study in which the oral reading miscues of children aged five to eleven were analysed, and notes that, although those with reading ages up to 8;11 made errors related to line endings, as reading ability improved such mistakes disappeared.

Nevertheless, W. Cromer (1970) found that even some eighteen-year-olds were apparently affected by the layout of a text. His subjects read stories in four different formats: normal sentence layout; one word at a time; meaningful phrases; random word groups. For example, when the text was divided into meaningful phrases it was presented like this:

82a The cow jumped   over the moon.

In contrast, a random grouping looked like this:

82b The cow   jumped over the   moon.

The male subjects, matched for age and intelligence, were divided into three groups according to reading ability. There were good readers, and two groups of poor readers whose reading ages were approximately three years behind their chronological age. One group of poor readers had inadequate vocabulary skills – they were labelled 'Deficit' readers. The other poor group, who had no measurable oral language deficit, were assumed to have a problem in organizing a written text into meaningful chunks – they were called 'Difference' readers. The idea behind the experiment was that arranging the text into meaningful phrases should help the Difference group, while having no effect on the others; presenting the text in random groups should have a deleterious effect on the good and Deficit readers but not trouble the Difference readers, who were assumed to read in a fragmented manner anyway. After reading the various formats the subjects were tested for comprehension and the results generally supported Cromer's prediction: taking the normal text as a base measure, the good readers showed impaired comprehension when the layout was randomly broken up but the Difference readers' scores did not decrease; on the other hand, when the text was organized into meaningful phrases, the good and Deficit readers showed no enhancement of comprehension but the Difference readers' scores were increased so that they did as well as the good readers. Cromer (p. 483) concludes:

> Readers who have not adequately learnt to deal with written material in terms of meaningful units can be encouraged to do so ... by ... grouping the material for them.

This raises the question of what the most helpful form of presentation is for young readers. Crystal (1979c) argues for a principled relationship between line-breaks and grammatical constituents, with the break coinciding with either a sentence, a clause or a phrase boundary. It is probably not maximally helpful for line-breaks in early reading materials ALWAYS to correspond with a sentence boundary. This is because there are two problems associated with this type of layout: first, it can encourage children to establish a reading habit they will soon have to break; and secondly, it results in an undifferentiated column of capital letters down the left-hand margin, providing no visual signpost for the reader's eyes as they sweep back across the page from the end of the previous line. A study by Raban (1982), with children aged 5;9 to 8;2, shows that such a layout produces a higher incidence of 'line-slips' (omitted lines) than one where some lines begin with capitals and some with lower-case letters. Her study also suggests that line-breaks are helpful when they encourage the reader to predict what will follow on the next line. Therefore, generally, it is better for *and* to end a line than to begin the following one. Also, surprisingly perhaps, a break within a phrase need not be difficult so long as it occurs towards the end of a sentence, where the chances of accurate prediction are high. So she reports that the division in (83a) is relatively easy, whereas the one in (83b) is particularly difficult:

83a The dog bit the man on the
    leg.
83b   The
    dog bit the man on the leg.

To summarize: children with a reading age below nine may be hampered by unhelpful layout and misleading line divisions. Drawing their attention to punctuation marks may help them to break the bad habit of reading to line endings and assist them in reading to full stops and question marks instead. In addition, there may be older readers who have overlearned word-by-word reading and who can be encouraged to read in longer units if the words are grouped on the page into major grammatical constituents, three or four words in length. But even skilful readers may occasionally be caught out by a particularly misleading line division, e.g.:

84 It is a very rare animal and only seventeen live
    pandas have ever left China to go to zoos in other
    countries.   (Junior)

Now we can consider constructions which, regardless of their layout on the page, may make the task of segmentation harder.

Visually odd constructions

The most obvious example of a visually odd construction occurs when the same word is repeated more than twice in succession, e.g.:

85a Sarah said that a bike she had had had had its tyres slashed.

This looks extraordinary and would not usually occur in writing. It is perfectly acceptable in speech, though, because the first and third instances of *had* are reduced to weak forms so we do not get a sequence of four words that sound the same:

85b . . . / 'baɪk ʃid 'hæd əd hæd ɪts 'taɪəz 'slæʃt/

The fact that we do not write such a sentence although we are quite happy to say it – and although there is nothing inherently colloquial about its grammatical structure – provides evidence that we are, unconsciously at least, aware that there are constructions that are straightforward for the listener which may not be easy for the reader.

A similar but less startling phenomenon occurs when three or more words belonging to the same word class are adjacent, while belonging to different constituents, e.g.:

86a The idea that children who rebelled failed flourished.

The tendency here is to treat the three verbs as if they were part of a conjoined list (e.g. '. . . children who sang, danced, skipped and jumped'). It is possible to demonstrate that it is the occurrence of three unconjoined verbs in a sequence that causes the difficulty (rather than the presence of two subordinate clauses) by expanding each clause, so that the verbs are separated from each other while the overall construction remains the same:

86b The idea that children who rebelled against authority failed at
     academic tasks flourished in the nineteenth century.

Admittedly, a string of unconjoined verbs is rare. It is more common for a string of nouns to cause momentary hesitation about the placing of constituent boundaries, e.g.:

87 On hill sheep farms land cannot provide winter feed for animals.
                                                                  (Junior)

The four nouns, *hill sheep farms land*, have to be divided between two constituents. It would be easier to make this division if there was a comma after *farms*, but it is very common for writers not to put a punctuation mark after an introductory adverbial, even when the omission causes considerable segmentation problems, as in this example:

> 88 When the TWA began farming the land used for sewage losses grew from £4,000 in the early years to £232,000 in 1977.   (Adult)

As the reader moves from left to right through this sentence, it is easy to think erroneously that the adverbial clause has ended at *farming*, or *land*, or *losses* (at first, *sewage losses* looks like one constituent), rather than recognizing the clause boundary between *sewage* and *losses*. Even if punctuation after initial adverbials was used more extensively, it could assist young readers only if they took notice of it and were aware of its function.

Constructions without function words

Function words are useful for the reader because they help to identify both the grammatical role of constituents and the boundaries between them. This can be illustrated by means of the following ambiguous sentence:

> 89a The dentist had frightened patients in his waiting room.

The ambiguity arises because *frightened* can either be a lexical verb, functioning as part of the VP *had frightened*, or it can be an adjective, functioning as part of the NP *frightened patients*. Thus, in the two different readings of the sentence, *frightened* has a different grammatical role, and the boundary between the VP and the object NP falls in different places. By adding a determiner – which has to occur at the beginning of an NP – the two possible structures are clearly revealed:

> 89b The dentist had frightened *some patients* in his waiting room.
> 89c The dentist had *some frightened patients* in his waiting room.

The most frequently occurring function words are determiners, auxiliaries, prepositions, conjunctions and pronouns. Pronouns are rather different from the others in that they frequently stand alone as clause elements – subject, object or complement. The other function words signal the kind of structure that will follow: determiners introduce NPs; auxiliaries mark the beginning of VPs; prepositions begin phrases which can function either as adverbials or as post-modification of nouns; and subordinating conjunctions mark the onset of subordinate clauses. The omission of these function words is commonest in telegrams and newspaper headlines, e.g.:

> 90 Scottish Labour Party plans home rule option.

But there are also examples in ordinary language, particularly in subordinate clauses. In object nominal clauses the clause marker *that* can be omitted; in restrictive relative clauses the relative pronoun can be left out whenever it is functioning as object of the clause; and in non-finite clauses there can be omission of pronouns and auxiliaries as well as clause markers.

Various psycholinguists have suggested that language processing is harder when words which signal structural relationships are omitted. For instance, Slobin (1973b, p. 203) says, 'It is easier to understand a complex sentence in which optionally deletable material appears in its full form.' Several studies have been carried out which provide support for this view. Hakes (1972), using a listening task with adult subjects, found that sentences with object nominal clauses were easier to process when the optional clause marker *that* was present. He gave his subjects tape-recorded sentences like this:

91 The world-famous physicist forgot (that) his old professor had been the first to suggest the crucial experiment to him.

When *that* is not included, it is easy to interpret *his old professor* as object of *forgot* rather than as subject of the following clause. This segmentation error is especially likely to occur after verbs like *forget, accept, know* and *believe*, which can equally naturally be followed by either an NP or a clause. If the NP is a long one, then the difficulty is increased, e.g.:

92 Peter knew *James Fitzpatrick, the captain of the old boys' cricket team*, would never agree.

We can note at this point that pronouns are more informative than nouns; even without a clause marker it is possible to tell whether the pronoun is object of the main clause or subject of the subordinate clause:

93a Peter knew him (very well indeed).
93b Peter knew he (would never agree).

A series of studies by Fodor and Garrett (1967), Hakes and Cairns (1970) and Hakes and Foss (1970) have indicated that, both in reading and listening, adults find that finite relative clauses modifying the subject are easier to process when relative pronouns are present; similarly, Beaumont (1982) has found that including relative pronouns improves the reading comprehension of seven-year-old children. The absence of the relative pronoun can lead to a confusing sequence of unconjoined NPs, e.g.:

94 The cat the dog chased escaped up a tree.

(The sequence of VPs will occur whenever a relative clause modifying the subject has the structure SV; to make the sentence easier it might be helpful to add an adverbial so that the two verbs are separated – as well as including a relative pronoun to separate the nouns, e.g. 'The cat that the dog chased round the garden escaped up a tree'.) Occasionally the segmentation problem can be quite severe when there is no guidance from a relative pronoun, e.g.:

> 95 Toby lies on his stomach on his bunk and focuses his telescope on the beach, where a girl in a green cardigan – *the green children paint grass* until they learn better – walks on the beach against the sea. (Adult)

As *green* is more often an adjective than a noun, it is easy at first to chunk *the green children* as a single NP rather than to recognize *children* as the subject of an unmarked relative clause.

Non-finite clauses may lack subordinators and auxiliaries – examples (65) to (71) showed that such omissions make these clauses less informative than their finite counterparts. Bever (1970, pp. 315–16) provides a constructed example of a sentence which is hard to segment because the non-finite verb *raced* in the relative clause looks at first like the main verb:

> 96 The horse raced past the barn fell.

The problem arises because all regular verbs in English have only one form for both the non-finite past participle and the finite simple past. If the regular verb *race* is replaced by an irregular verb that has two past forms, then it is clear straightaway that only the non-finite past participle can occur in this structure:

> 97a The horse ridden past the barn fell.
> 97b *The horse rode past the barn fell.

The first, mistaken, segmentation of (96), that makes readers stumble, cannot happen in (97a). If the difficulty illustrated in (96) were confined to constructed examples, it would not be important, but there are many instances in children's books of non-finite relative clauses where the verb can be misinterpreted as the main verb, e.g.:

> 98 The Bridgewater Canal opened in 1776, joining Manchester with the Mersey at Runcorn, could only take small barges. (Secondary)

It is worth considering briefly how function words make segmentation easier for the reader. First, they are to a certain extent visually distinctive, so it seems likely that skilled readers are able to recognize them very quickly. They are distinctive partly because they tend to be shorter than lexical words. For instance, apart from a few exceptions, it is only function words that can consist of just one or two letters, e.g. *a*, *me*. (Exceptions include *ox*, *go* and lexical *do*; abbreviations like *ma*, *pa*, *ta*; and technical terms, e.g. *pi*, *re*, *fa*.) This principle of the writing system can be demonstrated by comparing pairs of words that sound the same, but are spelt differently, so that the lexical word always has at least three letters: *be, bee*; *by, buy*; *I, eye*; *in, inn*; *or, oar*; *so, sew*. Then there are many thousands of lexical words that are polysyllabic but there is only a handful of function words that have more than one syllable, e.g. *although, whenever*. As well as length, another factor which helps to make function words visually distinctive is their spelling structure. Many function words begin with either *th-* or *wh-*, e.g. *than, that, the, their, them, there, these, they, this, those, though, through*; *what, when, where, whether, which, while, who, whose, whom, why*. There are also lexical words that begin like this, of course (*thank, thunder*; *whale, whistle*), but they occur very much less frequently than the function words.

Secondly, it is a characteristic of English that function words tend to occur at the beginning of phrases. This means that recognition of a function word generally leads the eyes helpfully to the start of a new constituent. In sentence (99), each of the three clause elements is introduced by a function word that contrasts markedly in length with the lexical words that follow it.

99 *A* technological revolution *is* taking place *in* manufacturing industries.

We have already seen that the eye-voice span of mature readers tends to coincide with phrase boundaries and that the span expands and contracts according to the grammatical structure of the sentence. It seems likely that one of the means by which this happens is the recognition of the visually distinctive function words as likely markers of new constituents.

Constructions with ambiguous function words

Although function words generally help to demarcate and identify constituents, some can themselves occasionally be misleading because they have a number of different functions. For example, *that* can be a pronoun, a determiner and a clause marker. Sentences (100) and (101) illustrate two of these uses:

100 It really is all a question of how you know where to apply your attention and with that emphasis and largeness or smallness of headlines has little to do. (Adult)

Here, *that* looks as if it is a determiner in the NP *that emphasis* but, in fact, it is a pronoun referring back to the noun *question*. The structure would be clearer if normal word order was used – 'and emphasis . . . has little to do *with that*'.

101 That wine is very good value for money although it is expensive is generally accepted these days. (Adult)

On first reading, *that* again looks like a determiner, this time modifying the noun *wine*, but it is actually a clause marker introducing the subject nominal clause. The structure would be unambiguous if the fuller clause marker *the fact that* replaced the simple *that*. Another word with several functions is *what*, which can be a determiner, a clause marker and a question word. *Her* can be either a determiner or a pronoun and in the following sentence it is not possible to tell which it is intended to be:

102 He read her poetry.   (Adult)

In contrast, the masculine forms are unambiguous, e.g.:

103a She read him poetry.
103b She read his poetry.

Then there are several words that can function as both prepositions and subordinators, e.g. *after, as, before, since, until.* It is possible that words which belong solely to one class or the other cause a reader less uncertainty, e.g.:

104a He left *during* the interval.
104b He left *when* the interval was over.
104c He left *after* the interval (was over).

In these examples, *during* can only be a preposition so has to be followed by a phrase; *when* can only be a subordinator so has to be followed by a clause; but *after* can be a preposition or a subordinator so it can take either a phrase or a clause. Sentences (105) and (106), which are taken from school textbooks, both contain subordinators (*as* and *before*) that look at first like prepositions:

105 The air is driven out as steam from the water fills the bottle.
                                                                     (Junior)
106 The towns of Galloway are small and reflect the importance of the sea in communications before the coming of the railway in the second half of the nineteenth century made the region a little less isolated.   (Secondary)

Constructions with grammatically uninformative lexical words

The role of function words in identifying grammatical structures is important because very many of the most frequently used lexical words in English provide little information about their own grammatical identity. This is most clearly seen in the words that belong to more than one word-class, for example, *iron*, which can be a noun, a verb and an adjective. Multiple class membership is so widespread among English lexical words partly because a very frequent way of augmenting the vocabulary is by **converting** an item from one word-class to another without adding any affixes. For instance, fairly recently the word *mothball*, originally a noun, has also been used as a verb, e.g.:

107 The Navy has had to mothball several frigates.

Quirk *et al.* (1972, p. 1009) point out that, 'In the English language, conversion is unusually prominent as a word-formation process.'

Not only are there a great many words which may be noun and/or adjective and/or verb but, in addition, the morphology of each of these classes is so limited that there are very few distinctions between them. Nouns have singular, plural and possessive forms – *girl, girls, girl's, girls'* – verbs in the present tense have just two forms – *like, likes*. (Here we can contrast French where regular verbs have five forms in the present tense alone: *aime, aimes, aiment, aimons, aimez*. The first three have the same pronunciation although they are spelt differently so, in French, the written forms are more informative than the spoken ones.) As the third person singular ending of English verbs is the same as the plural ending of nouns, it is sometimes not clear immediately, particularly in newspaper headlines, which word-class is being used, e.g.:

108 BR hopes rest with rebel drivers.

As *hope* and *rest* can both be either nouns or verbs it takes a moment to recognize that *hopes* is the plural subject noun – and that *BR* is being used adjectivally. Because of the sparseness of morphological marking in English it is very easy to make up sentences where one string of words has two different grammatical analyses, e.g.:

109a <u>Steel</u> <u>supports</u> a greater load than wood.
     s   v

109b <u>Steel supports</u> are stronger than wooden ones.
         s

   <u>   </u> <u>   </u>
   adj   n

In reading, if the first analysis turns out to be a mistaken one, then the reader has to backtrack and start again. In the following sentence, *produce* looks at first like a verb:

110 Refrigeration opened up the British market to produce from Australia and New Zealand.   (Secondary)

It is possible, very roughly, to divide lexical words into three groups according to their level of 'grammatical informativeness'. In the first group belong the least informative words – those that provide no clues as to their word-class and are regularly used as different parts of speech, e.g. *walk, shop, watch, dream*. The second group consists of words which are not morphologically distinctive but which are most frequently used as just one part of speech, for example, the verbs *bring, come, sing* and the nouns *tree, horse* and *game*. The third group contains the most informative words – those that are regularly used as one part of speech and that have suffixes which generally signal membership of a particular word-class. Some examples of such suffixes and the classes they denote are given in table 23. The presence of these class-specifying suffixes

TABLE 23   Some class-specifying suffixes

Suffix	Most usual word-class	Examples
-ful	adjective	careful, successful
-less	adjective	careless, hopeless
-ly	adverb	carelessly, quickly
-ness	noun	carelessness, happiness
-ation	noun	exploration, organization
-ism	noun	racism, idealism
-ment	noun	entertainment, arrangement
-ify	verb	simplify, diversify
-ize	verb	modernize, criticize

means that, even if a word is unfamiliar, e.g. *frumentation*, it is possible to be fairly sure of its part of speech.

I made a small test of this notion of grammatical informativeness by giving strings of seven nonsense words to twenty undergraduate linguistics students and asking them to arrange them in sentences, taking account of the function words and the morphological markers. Some strings had lexical nonsense words that could have belonged to any of the four classes, noun, verb, adjective, adverb, e.g.:

111 soat the will tays pell the dork

Others had lexical words with suffixes that signalled a particular grammatical class, e.g.:

112a by bondment the danted those was blins

There were far fewer versions of the informative strings than the uninformative ones. For example, the students produced only one grammatical arrangement for (112a):

112b The bondment was danted by those blins

but there were seventeen different acceptable versions of (111), and there could have been more. All four nonsense words appeared as several parts of speech; for instance, *soat* was used as an adjective, an adverb, a noun and a verb. This result shows that the syntactic possibilities for grammatically informative words are much more tightly constrained than for those that are uninformative.

It seems reasonable to hypothesize that when we, as readers, move through a text, striving to group the words into the most helpful units, we are aided in the process of segmentation not only by function words but also by those lexical words that are unequivocal in their grammatical role. This suggests that a text with lexical words that all belonged to the third, highly informative, group would be easier to segment than one where they belonged to the first group. However, a problem with this is that, on the whole, it is the rarer, more scholarly words in the vocabulary that have extensive morphological marking, so any gain in structural explicitness would probably be offset by a loss in lexical familiarity. Therefore, the words in group two would seem to have much to commend them as far as the young reader is concerned, since many of them are frequently used and, in addition, they are grammatically unambiguous. In order to test the hypothesis that differences in grammatical informativeness affect reading ease, it would be possible to prepare two texts, with word familiarity and grammatical structure held constant but with one using group one words and the other group two words. These passages could then be given to young readers to see whether they led to differences in reading performance.

Ambiguous strings

The last type of segmentation difficulty to mention is one that arises from intrinsic structural ambiguity. There are various sentence patterns that fall into this category: I shall illustrate just three of them. First, when a sentence has the structure *subordinate clause – adverbial – main clause*, it may not be clear which clause the adverbial belongs to, e.g.:

113 Because the baby was coughing a lot in the morning Diana called the doctor.

Here, *in the morning* could refer either to the time when the baby was coughing or to the time when Diana called the doctor. A comma at the end of the subordinate clause would disambiguate the sentence. Punctuation cannot solve the problem, however, when the subordinate clause is a restrictive relative modifying the subject (because of the convention that commas do not separate the subject from the rest of the sentence), e.g.:

114 People who play squash often like to take part in competitions.

In speech, it will be clear whether *often* is part of the relative clause or the main clause but the only way to achieve that clarity in writing is by moving *often* away from the boundary between the two clauses.

Another group of potentially ambiguous structures consists of those that contain a present participle. This is because the *-ing* form of the verb can function as an adjective, a noun, and as the verb of a non-finite clause. In (115a), *eating* could be either an adjective (contrasting with *cooking*) or a verb, with *apples* as its object:

115a Eating apples can be expensive.

The two structures are revealed by replacing the modal auxiliary, which is uninformative about the number of the subject:

115b Eating apples are expensive.
115c Eating apples is expensive.

In (116), *drinking* could be either the subject of the sentence – in which case, *quickly* belongs with the main clause – or the non-finite verb of the subject nominal clause *drinking quickly*:

116 Drinking quickly becomes a habit.

The third type of ambiguous string contains the conjunction *and* without it being clear what units are being joined, e.g.:

117 Science has given us a much wider range of materials to use when constructing our homes *and* the machines which today do so much of the hard work.   (Junior)

Here the structure could be either, 'Science has given us materials . . . and machines' or, 'Science has given us materials to use when constructing our homes and machines'.

Very often the sense of the passage will override any potential structural ambiguity but it is worth being alert to these constructions when writing for children, so that the task of language processing is not made any harder than necessary.

Structures that place a heavy burden on short-term memory

After structures that are hard to predict or to segment, the third major source of grammatical difficulty in reading lies in structures that overload the capacity of short-term memory. We have seen that verbatim memory, even in adult readers, is not likely to be accurate after about ten words. This suggests that any construction that entails holding an exact word or phrase in mind while the structure is completed will cause difficulties if the 'hold phase' exceeds ten words. If such constructions occur frequently in a text, reading with comprehension is likely to be particularly effortful.

An obvious candidate for this group is the interrupting construction between subject and verb, where the subject has to be held in memory during the interruption. This has already been illustrated in the section on late-acquired structures but here is a further example, which is startling because the thirty-three-word interruption so heavily outweighs the four-word main clause:

118 These sonatas, *owing much to the structural methods of C.P.E.*
Bach, Haydn, and Mozart and to the distinctive and influential
piano style of Muzio Clementi (1752–1832), an Italian who made
his home in England, are familiar.   (Secondary)

Long subject noun phrases, also previously illustrated, similarly place a
burden on memory until the verb is reached.

Wanner and Maratsos (1978) have suggested that some types of relative clause may be difficult to process because of the strain they impose
on short-term memory. Using adult subjects, they tested this hypothesis
by displaying sentences like (119) and (120) word by word on a television
screen:

119 The customer that the broker persuaded to cancel the illegal /
transaction had often engineered some shady deals.
120 The customer that the broker planned to cancel the illegal /
transaction for had often engineered some shady deals.

At the slash, the display was interrupted while the subjects read and
memorized a list of five Christian names. Then the sentence was completed and subjects were asked to recall what they had read. Sentences
like (119) were remembered significantly better than those like (120).
Wanner and Maratsos argue that this is because, in (120), the structure
of the relative clause does not become clear until the reader reaches *for*.
Therefore, as it cannot be grammatically processed until then, it has to
be held verbatim in short-term memory. Memorizing the list of names is
quite enough to eradicate much of the vulnerable, unprocessed material
from its temporary storage. In contrast, in (119), the structure of the
relative clause is largely revealed by *persuaded*, so grammatical processing can begin earlier and short-term memory does not get overloaded.

The last construction I shall mention that characteristically depends
on exact memory is ellipsis. Here, a word or phrase is omitted that is
recoverable from elsewhere in the text, e.g.:

121 Alice showed the girls which thread to use for the silk dresses
that had been given to them and [   ] taught the girls how to use
it.   (Richek, 1977, p. 156)

The correct mental replacement of the missing subject of the co-ordinate
clause can only be made if the reader remembers the subject of the first
clause. The more words there are between the ellipsis and its referent –
and especially the more intervening NPs there are that could sensibly fill
the slot – the more likely it is that misunderstanding will occur.

I shall now try to draw together the main points that have been made in
this section on reading difficulty at sentence level. First, it is possible

simply to list the main constructions that have been identified as being potential sources of difficulty in reading. They are: concealed negatives, literary negatives, multiple negatives, fronted constructions, interrupting constructions, long subject noun phrases, nominalizations, noun phrases in apposition, subject nominal clauses, adverbial clauses introduced by *although, unless* and *provided that*, inferential *if* clauses, literary conditional clauses, relative clauses introduced by *whom, whose*, or a preposition plus a relative pronoun, series of relatives within one sentence, non-finite and verbless clauses (apart from object nominals and adverbial clauses of purpose), and some kinds of ellipsis. However, if this list is to have any practical application – for example, if it is to be used to compile guidelines for writing workcards, or to make checklists for use in assessing the grammatical difficulty of textbooks – then it must be reduced to manageable proportions. This involves pinpointing those constructions that are likely to have the most noticeable effect on children's ease of reading.

As a first step in making this selection, I have chosen constructions that occur quite frequently in children's reading material. So, although multiple negatives, for example, are particularly demanding to read, they probably do not need to figure on a general checklist because they only occur very rarely. Next, from the fairly frequent constructions, I have selected those that have featured under more than one heading in this section. That is to say, constructions have been identified as being either difficult to predict, or difficult to segment, or as imposing a heavy burden on short-term memory; the following have appeared in two or all three of these categories: interrupting constructions, long subject NPs, subject nominal clauses, the 'advanced' relative clauses, non-finite and verbless clauses, and elliptical constructions.

In a small-scale study (Perera, forthcoming), I have noted that several of these constructions occur with much greater frequency in school textbooks than in fiction written for children. I believe that when there is a density of such structures in a piece of writing, they contribute very significantly to the difficulty that so many children experience in reading academic texts. This point can be illustrated by means of the extract at (122), which is taken from a science book in a series very widely bought by junior schools:

122 The fact that the monomers, and similar chemicals that are the starting materials for the manufacture of plastics, can now be made fairly cheaply, and in large quantities, is a result of all the research and development that has been carried out in recent years.

The conversion of the products obtained from the *crackers* of the oil refineries into the basic raw materials of the plastics industry occupies a large section of the world's chemical industry.

Some of the products of the oil refineries (such as ethylene,

propylene, butadiene – all known as *petrochemicals*) can be poly-
merised directly into plastics, but sometimes several steps are
needed to convert the petrochemicals into the chemicals needed
by the plastics industry.

The three sentences in this extract have subject NPs that are twenty-
eight, twenty-two and eight words long. In addition, the first sentence
has a subject nominal clause and two relative clauses; the second sentence has a non-finite clause; and the third sentence has a nine-word
interrupting construction and two non-finite clauses. Quite apart from
the difficulty of the vocabulary, such language is markedly different from
the language that junior school children meet in their reading of fiction.

6.3 READING DIFFICULTY AT DISCOURSE LEVEL

It is possible for young readers to understand individual sentences perfectly and yet not be able to gain an overall meaning from the whole
discourse. This may be because they do not recognize the connections
between the ideas in successive sentences for some reason, or it may be
because they find the organization of the text as a whole rather difficult.
Taking up the distinction that was made in chapter 5, we can consider
these two different aspects of discourse structure under the headings of
local and global discourse organization.

Local discourse organization

The most obvious way in which adjacent sentences in a discourse are
linguistically tied together is by the repetition of nouns, e.g.:

123 (i) When the temperature reaches 1,000,000°C, the STAR settles
down to a steady and much slower process of MIDDLE AGE.

(ii) During the *middle age* of a *star*, atoms of HYDROGEN are
continually combining to form ATOMS of a heavier gas –
HELIUM.

(iii) Each time an *atom* of *helium* is formed from *hydrogen*, a little
energy is released in the form of light and heat.   (Junior)

In this extract, the first appearance of each repeated noun has been
capitalized and the second italicized to show clearly that each sentence
takes up at least one noun from the sentence before.

Instead of nominal repetition, writers often use pronominal substitution. A danger is that, in careless writing, the reference of a pronoun can
sometimes be either misleading or ambiguous. In the following example,

the pronoun *this* (which here refers not to a noun but to a whole sentence) is misleading because it looks as if it relates to the immediately preceding sentence when, in fact, it must refer to the one before that:

124 Correct breathing involves becoming aware of breathing and trying to use the diaphragm and lower ribs while slowing the rhythm. When tense, the tendency is to breathe only with the upper chest or to hold the breath. *This* is often helpful at times of known stress.   (Adult)

Ambiguity may arise if there are two (or more) possible antecedents for the pronoun in the text, e.g.:

125 The sponsors spent some time talking to the divers about their expedition and its amazing finds. *They* were very excited about it all.   (Adult)

Here, *they* could refer to either the sponsors or the divers. Very often, even if the pronoun is potentially ambiguous, common sense identifies the antecedent, e.g.:

126 Mike picked up his son and carried him up to bed.
    He was looking very sleepy.

Although it could conceivably be Mike who was looking sleepy, the son seems a more likely referent. Unfortunately, it can sometimes happen that a pronoun is unambiguous in its reference and yet is still not easy to relate to its antecedent noun. Kantor (1977), in a revealing phrase, describes this phenomenon as an example of 'inconsiderate discourse'. One factor that can contribute to it is the distance of the pronoun from its antecedent; Sanford and Garrod (1981, p. 138) provide evidence that an increase in this distance increases the reader's processing time. In the following example, it is not immediately obvious which noun the final *it* refers to:

127 The logical conclusion, as the committee's two dissenting Labour MP's, Mr Alf Dubs and Mr Robert Kilroy-Silk, pointed out, can only be that 'any solution falling short of an independent system of investigation will be regarded as little more than cosmetic and will do nothing to restore public confidence.' Alas, the committee as a whole shrank back from drawing *it*.   (Adult)

The singular, non-animate noun phrases that are candidates for the role of antecedent are, working back from the pronoun: *confidence, system of investigation, solution, conclusion*. In fact, only *conclusion* can be the antecedent since it is the only noun that fits the frame, 'The committee shrank back from drawing this _____.' There seems no doubt that the distance between noun and pronoun and the number of intervening nouns that compete for consideration both contribute to the difficulty of this passage.

A number of factors influence the assignment of reference to a pronoun. The most straightforward are syntactic cues. Pronouns have to agree with their antecedent in number, animacy, and gender. When only one noun in the preceding discourse shares all the grammatical features of the pronoun, then making the connection is simple. In the following pair of examples, the first is easier than the second in this regard:

128 John gave Jane a gold watch. She was very _____.
129 John gave Bill a gold watch. He was very _____.

In (128) *she* has to refer to Jane, so even before we reach the complement we can predict the occurrence of adjectives like *pleased, surprised, delighted*. On the other hand, in (129) we cannot tell UNTIL we get to the complement whether *he* refers to Bill or John. If the sentence ends with *generous*, or *impulsive*, we will assume *he* refers to John, while *grateful* or *pleased* will be interpreted as describing Bill. An unpublished study by K. Ehrlich (1979) (cited in Sanford & Garrod, 1981, p. 143) concludes that sentences are processed faster when pronominal reference can be established by grammatical cues.

When there are several nouns that could qualify as the antecedent of a pronoun, then various preferences become apparent (Carpenter & Just, 1977; Sanford & Garrod, 1981). Generally, subject nouns are favoured over object nouns and close nouns take precedence over distant ones; in addition, nouns in main clauses are selected as antecedents more often than those in subordinate clauses, and nouns with several occurrences in the text are preferred to those that have appeared only once. In connection with this question of the identification of pronominal reference, Chafe (1972) has developed the notion of **foregrounding**. He suggests that a foregrounded element is one that can be 'assumed to be in the . . . reader's consciousness' (p. 50). A foregrounded noun will always be easier to recover than one that is no longer activated in this way. All the factors listed above contribute to foregrounding, and so can temporal and spatial features of the discourse. For example, in a text describing an episode in a restaurant, once a waiter has been introduced he can remain foregrounded for as long as the setting stays the same. If the location changes, however, then the waiter is no longer foregrounded (unless he leaves the restaurant too) and pronominal reference to him is likely to be odd or even incomprehensible.

Some types of writing have more nominal repetition and pronominal substitution than others. In a small sample of books written for children aged roughly nine to twelve, I found generally higher levels in fiction than non-fiction (Perera, forthcoming). This difference follows naturally from the fact that the primary function of non-fiction is to inform, which means there is a steady introduction of new material. It seems likely that texts which have a very low level of these most obvious types of cohesive device will be rather demanding to read. Indeed, Kieras (1978) has shown that paragraphs where sentences lack such connections with their predecessors are harder to read than those where each sentence takes up a noun from an earlier one; and Sanford and Garrod (1981, p. 183) believe that texts with some repetition are easier to remember: 'oft-mentioned entities reside in focus longer and therefore their representations will give rise to stronger representations in long-term memory.'

Another type of cohesive device – less obvious than nominal repetition or pronominal substitution – is the use of synonymy, which allows a writer to repeat an idea in different words. A problem arises if the reader does not recognize this lexical relation and assumes that a new entity has been introduced. In (130), young readers have to be able to identify three sets of synonyms:

> 130 Gaius Julius Caesar had conquered Gaul. In a bitter campaign the general had defeated the warrior-tribesmen of France and Belgium. (Junior)

Unless children realize that 'Caesar' and 'the general' are the same man; that 'Gaul' is the same place as 'France and Belgium'; and that 'conquered' and 'defeated' describe the same action, then they may think they are reading about two events rather than one. At (131), there is an adult example:

> 131 Existing UN case lore drops on the Malvinas side of sovereignty arguments. The great glass box on the East River is entirely capable . . . of demanding a simple ceasefire. (Adult)

This makes sense only if 'the great glass box on the East River' is understood to be a synonym for the UN.

Connections can also be made between sentences by means of ellipsis, e.g.:

> 132 Europe is divided into many countries, each with its own government. The largest [   ], in area and population, is the USSR. (Secondary)

Here, the mental insertion of *country* is unlikely to cause problems, at least for secondary children, because the ellipsis follows closely after its antecedent noun and, in any case, the meaning of the two sentences is quite straightforward. However, if there are several possibilities for the antecedent, or if it is a long way away, then ellipsis may make the reader's task harder, e.g.:

> 133 From the most pitiful of scavengers of London, the collectors of dogs' dung, or 'pure', to the municipal companies which boasted of their patented processes for sewage disposal, the concern for economic gain was a priority. In relation to the ends in view both worked on a slim budget. (Secondary)

In this extract, it seems rather difficult to interpret *both* correctly. To get it right, the reader has to select 'the collectors of dogs' dung' and 'the municipal companies' from six complex noun phrases in the first sentence. As far as distance is concerned, Moberly (1978), in a study with nine- to eleven-year-olds, has shown that replacing an ellipted item becomes harder when the antecedent noun is not in the immediately preceding sentence. The following is a particularly awkward adult example:

134 The second scores that happy experience some of us are currently having when an experiment supports a strongly-held intuition.

(Adult)

To understand this, it is necessary first to recognize that there is ellipsis after *The second* and then to remember the opening of the passage, three long paragraphs away, 'What insights to highlight? With difficulty I select two.' Only then can the reader make the interpretation, 'The second insight scores . . . .' (In passing, it is worth noting that the difficulty of this example is compounded by the fact that *scores* looks at first like a noun rather than a verb.)

Finally, cohesion between sentences can be explicitly marked by the adverbials and conjunctions that function as sentence connectives, and by a number of lexical words that serve as structural signposts in a text. We have seen that children do not begin to use the more formal connectives, like *nevertheless, therefore* and *similarly*, either in speech or writing until the teenage years. These words are particularly important for the understanding of academic writing because they signal the relationships between ideas. Rodgers (1974) has examined thirty-five school textbooks, covering geography, history and science, to see which connectives are used and with what frequency. By sampling 20 per cent of the pages of these books, he collected a total of 11,356 uses of 128 different connectives. Some of the ones he found to occur frequently are familiar to children, e.g. *but, if, because, then,* but others have been shown to cause considerable difficulty. Studies by Gardner (1977), Henderson (1979), and Robertson (1968) (see pp. 155–6 above) have identified the following as particularly liable to misunderstanding: *consequently, hence, instead, moreover, similarly, that is, thus.* In Rodgers' sample they occurred with these frequencies:

thus:	more than 1000 times
that is:	500–999 times
consequently:	250–499 times
hence, instead moreover similarly:	100–249 times

If Rodgers' figures typify usage in a wider sample of academic books, then children are rather often meeting and failing to understand words which are intended to make clear the relationships between ideas in the text.

The role of lexical items as structural signposts has been illustrated by Winter (1977). If, for example, a writer says, 'There are two reasons . . .', or 'Several suggestions have been made . . .', or 'There are three key features . . .' we expect the reasons, suggestions or features to follow. Sometimes they may be separated in the text; in this case, it is necessary for the reader to hold in mind the structure that the writer signalled at the outset.

Where sentences in a paragraph are not explicitly linked in some way, the reader has to make inferences to work out the connection between them. Sanford and Garrod (1981) describe several studies which provide evidence that paragraphs that require inferences to be made are more demanding than those that do not. Irwin (1980a) comments on the high level of implicit causal relationships in social studies texts and, having found that they cause reading difficulty both for ten-year-olds and college students, she concludes, 'One might speculate that whenever critical concepts are made implicit in order to reduce sentence length, comprehension may be impaired rather than facilitated' (p. 487). Marshall and Glock (1978, pp. 29–30) tested college students' ability to make inferences by giving them contrasted types of paragraph, like these:

135 If no more than one distribution is to be represented, bar graphs are the easiest to understand and are usually best. If two or more distributions are to be compared, line graphs are usually better since the superimposing of bar graphs can result in their lines coinciding, thus making the picture confusing.

136 Suppose that no more than one distribution is to be represented. Bar graphs are easy to understand and are usually good. Suppose that two or more distributions are to be compared. The superimposing of bar graphs can result in their lines coinciding. This makes the picture confusing. Line graphs are usually good.

They found that, although able students could understand both types of passage, weaker students performed less well on those like (136) where the relations of condition, comparison, contrast and result – explicitly stated in (135) – are largely implicit. Both passages contain 51 words but the first has an average sentence length of 25.5 words and the second of 8.5 words. Clearly, shorter sentences do not facilitate comprehension in this case.

There is an unfortunate tendency for writers of non-fiction books for the youngest readers to produce discourses that are really just collections of unconnected sentences on a single topic. This style of composition is even reflected in the layout, which frequently gives a new line to each sentence. It is possible that the writers are so concerned to avoid unfamiliar vocabulary and long sentences that they are reluctant to use extra words to make the links between sentences explicit. The following extract, taken from a book written and marketed for six- to eight-year-olds, constitutes the whole section on Grizzly Bears (sentences are numbered here for ease of reference):

137 *Grizzly Bears*
  (1) Huge brown bears living in North America are called Grizzlies.
  (2) Once they were thought to belong to a separate species.
  (3) Now they are quite rare.
  (4) Grizzlies used to prey upon the herds of bison.
  (5) When the bison became scarce the Grizzlies became fewer too.
  (6) In some places the forests where they lived have been cut down.

There are two words in (137) that appear to be marking discourse links: *once* in (2) and *now* in (3). These lead us to expect some kind of contrast between the two sentences but, in fact, there is no obvious semantic relationship at all. Then turning to sentences (4) to (6), as adult readers we can see that they explain why grizzlies are now rare. The reasons are that their food and habitat have been destroyed. But there is nothing in the text to help young readers to make these connections.

Global discourse organization

Generally, readers seem to be helped in their interpretation of a discourse if, near the beginning, there is a statement of the overall theme or gist. This may be in the form of a title or of an introductory sentence (Kieras, 1978; Marshall & Glock, 1978; Sanford & Garrod, 1981). When an author places a thematic statement at the end of a passage instead, it does not appear to have the same beneficial effect on comprehension.

The discourse structure that children seem to find most straightforward is one with a strong sense of sequential ordering. Birnbaum (1981, p. 277), for example, recognized that, in order to be able to read with ease, several of her nine- to twelve-year-old subjects needed texts with 'forward chronological ordering and explicit sequencing of events'. An awareness of some of the different possible ways of organizing story material seems to develop rather slowly during the school years. In a study by McClure *et al.* (1979), children aged eight to fifteen were given scrambled stories to arrange in the correct order. Each story was six sentences long and there were three different kinds of organization: one type conformed to canonical story order, with characters in a setting, event episodes, and a conclusion; another began with an orienting question; and the third had the conclusion at the beginning. The intended order was always signalled by grammatical cues in the text, such as tense, pronominal reference, ellipsis, definite noun phrases and sentence connectives. A highly significant finding was that scores were substantially higher for the canonical story order. The youngest children did very badly on the task as a whole, scoring on average only 6 per cent, and their results did not improve with practice. The fourteen- to fifteen-year-olds scored 51 per cent, and they gave some evidence of learning on the task. McClure *et al.* (p. 231) comment, 'The strategy most strikingly used by children was to order sentences such that the propositions they expressed appeared in a natural sequence of events.' They frequently did this even when it meant violating the grammar of the discourse. So they would start their stories with sentences that included substitution or a connective, e.g.:

138 Cliff Judkins *did*, when his airplane burst into flames and he had to leap out.

Or, in a different story:

139 *But* how could blind men climb this mountain?

The desire for stories to match the chronological order of events was also found by Baker (1978), whose subjects were college students. Using a video display, she presented simple stories in which the order of sentences either matched the order of events in real time, or ran counter to it by means of a flashback sequence. The subjects were then presented with two events from the story and asked to say whether they had actually taken place in that order. Their responses were consistently faster and more accurate on the passages that did not contain a flashback sequence.

The structure of a story does not derive simply from the links between successive events. There has to be an overall shape which holds together the characters, the time and place of the action, the development of the plot, the outcome, and so on. The term **frame** is commonly used to refer to this global organization of structure. (Another term sometimes used is **schema**.) A frame is a kind of idealized discourse outline; it has slots which are filled by various structural elements. Some slots are obligatorily filled while others have an optional status. To take the story frame as an example, the following slots are usually listed (the labels vary slightly from one researcher to another): Setting, Character(s), Theme, Episode(s), Outcome, Evaluation. The Character slot is an example of one that always has to be filled; the Evaluation slot can be left empty. This kind of theoretical apparatus, sometimes called a 'story grammar', enables researchers to make comparisons between texts that are superficially dissimilar and to make generalized observations of readers' responses.

It seems to be the case that the story frame is the easiest kind of discourse structure for young children to read. Applebee (1978) has shown that children become aware of the essential structural elements of this frame at a very early age. This means that, when a story conforms closely to the idealized frame, it should be relatively easy to process because, although the characters and events are new to the reader, the overall structure in which they occur is familiar. Sanford and Garrod (1981, p. 79) suggest that the reader's (implicit) knowledge of the story frame aids the storage and retrieval of information: 'From the memory point of view, the story frame is seen as a better retrieval structure than local links, because the frame holds everything together in a way which relies upon pre-established rather than arbitrary connections.'

A considerable amount of research has been done on story frames and story grammars. Much less has been done on frames for other kinds of writing. Davies *et al.* (1980) have identified seven different frames in scientific writing: Instruction, Classification, Structure, Mechanism, Process, Concept-Principle, and Hypothesis-Theory. Their Structure frame has the following slots: names of parts, properties of parts, location of parts, function of parts. In the reading of texts based on these frames (and of any others that do not conform to a story frame), there are perhaps two problems as far as young readers are concerned. First, children do not have any experience of non-story frames. Unlike stories, they are not part of our oral culture – no-one describes a structure in the way that they tell an anecdote – nor are they commonly read aloud. This means that children cannot bring to them the structural predictions that they are able to bring to their reading of stories. Second, non-story frames are harder for the writer. (This was mentioned briefly in chapter 5.) For this reason, such texts may be badly written, with a structure that is difficult to follow. Davies *et al.* (pp. 60–3) note that sometimes writers mix two or more frames within a short passage, without any clear signal to the reader; the result is 'an untidy text' which is particularly hard to read.

To sum up: discourses that conform to a story frame will generally be easier than those that do not; and stories that have strong chronological sequencing will be more straightforward than those that have 'out of order' episodes. Links between sentences are easier when they are explicit than when they have to be inferred. Difficulties may arise if pronominal reference is ambiguous or inconsiderate; if synonyms are not obviously related to their antecedents; if ellipsis occurs across too great a distance; and if the organization of the discourse rests heavily on unfamiliar connectives.

6.4 IMPLICATIONS FOR THE CLASSROOM

An awareness of some of the linguistic difficulties of written language can have implications for the writing and selecting of books, workcards and so on, and for the teaching of reading.

Writing and selecting books and workcards

Authors who want to make complex subject matter as accessible as possible need first of all to think about the overall structure of the discourse. A clear, well-ordered system of organization will help the reader. If a chronologically sequenced structure is appropriate, so much the better. For example, for young readers, facts about the characteristics, behaviour and habitat of a particular animal might be marshalled within a chronological account of its life from birth to maturity. Next, movement within the text from one section to another needs to be explicitly signalled. For instance, a sentence (or group of sentences) might have any of the following semantic relationships to the preceding text: chronological sequence, logical consequence, enumeration, exemplification, exception, comparison, contrast, condition, conclusion. The problem for the author is to recognize that, although HE knows why he has juxtaposed the two sections and is clear about the link between them, the reader might not make the connection unless the relationship is overtly marked in some way. As a general rule, in a well-constructed discourse it is not usually possible to carry out any substantial rearrangement of either sentences or paragraphs without some loss or distortion of meaning. Therefore, if a passage can tolerate considerable re-ordering, it suggests that either the overall structure has not been well enough conceived at the planning stage or the necessary connections have not been made explicit at the writing stage.

At sentence level, first, it is worth trying to arrange the material so that the grammatical subjects of sentences are also, whenever possible, the agents that perform the action of the verb. Second, links between ideas need to be made explicit; frequently this can be achieved more successfully by using a main clause plus a subordinate clause than by baldly juxtaposing two simple sentences. Third, the text will be more readable if there is not too great a density of difficult structures – for example, interrupting constructions, long subject noun phrases, subject nominal clauses, ellipsis, non-finite and verbless clauses, and Stage III and IV relative clauses.

All these linguistic features can be borne in mind – together with considerations of layout, subject matter, interest level and so on – by teachers who are selecting books for use in school. As well as trying to form a general impression of a book as a whole, it is useful to focus on two or three passages of a hundred words or so, and to examine them in some detail in order to assess the nature and frequency of the difficult constructions that are characteristic of the author's style. If a few pupils of the appropriate age read these passages aloud, then any errors they make may help in pinpointing potential sources of difficulty.

Writing instructions and examination questions

There are some kinds of writing where it is essential to avoid any possibilities of misunderstanding. These include examination questions, instructions for the use of dangerous or valuable equipment, and safety notices. The writer of such materials needs to be aware not only of the difficult constructions referred to above but also of a number of other structures that can impede comprehension. As they have already been discussed and exemplified earlier, here I shall simply list them:

- i) concealed negatives
- ii) two or more negatives in one sentence
- iii) fronted constructions
- iv) nominalizations
- v) reversible passives
- vi) adverbial clauses introduced by *although*, *unless* and *provided that*
- vii) inferential *if* clauses
- viii) misleading, ambiguous or inconsiderate pronominal reference
- ix) difficult connectives, e.g. *consequently*, *hence*, *moreover*, *similarly*, *that is*, *thus*.

Grammatical structure and the teaching of reading

Although there will be occasions when teachers feel it is appropriate to present their pupils with written material that is as clear and straightforward as possible, there will be other times when it is more constructive to provide the support that will enable them to read more demanding texts. The simplest and most obvious method (which I have advocated before) is for the teacher to read aloud to the class. In this way, children become familiar with some of the more literary discourse structures and sentence patterns before they meet them in their own reading. It is sometimes suggested that, rather than reading, infant teachers should TELL stories to their pupils, so that they can maintain eye contact with them and adapt the details of the story to the children's own experiences. I feel it would be unfortunate if this were the only kind of story-time that infant children were offered, since the social advantages have to be weighed against the diminished exposure to the forms of written language that results from this technique. Further up the age-range, teachers of lower secondary pupils may feel that it is indulgent or even babyish to read aloud to their classes. This is to underestimate the value to those pupils who have not yet reached the 'differentiation' stage in reading development of hearing language which they can understand aurally but which is nevertheless still too difficult for them to comprehend when they read silently.

As well as reading aloud, teachers might, from time to time, prepare activities to help children master a particular construction. (It might be a structure used with great frequency by the author of a textbook that they have to use, for example.) When working with extracts from books, it is useful either to have short passages duplicated, so that the pupils can write on them, or to provide reusable acetate sheets that can be placed on top of the text and marked with felt-tip pens, without damage to the original. Although the following activities all focus on structural aspects of language, it is not necessary for pupils to learn grammatical terminology in order to be able to carry them out – practical demonstration by the teacher should suffice.

To learn more about the structure of discourse, pupils can underline the sentence connectives and structural signposts that serve to guide the reader through the text; or they can number the events in the sequence in which they occurred; or they can join together in a paragraph all the words (nouns and pronouns) that refer to the same person or thing. It is probably also worth devising activities to develop the understanding of connectives, since they figure so prominently in school textbooks. Examples might include rearranging jumbled sentences using the connectives as a guide, and filling in gaps, perhaps from a multiple-choice list, where connectives have been omitted. To come to terms with sentence-level difficulty, pupils can circle the head noun of a long subject and then join it to the verb phrase, so that the structure of the sentence becomes visually apparent. If they underline interrupting constructions they can then make a note of the punctuation marks, the paired commas, dashes or brackets, that signal such interruptions. After all, in a difficult text a good author generally provides support of some kind for the reader, but young children, unaided, may not be aware of this support and, therefore, are not always able to make the best use of it.

Although this chapter has focused on constructions that might cause difficulty in reading, and although I have given some suggestions for writing more simply, I do not believe that the writer's or teacher's objective should be to eradicate all linguistic complexity from written language. One aim of this book has been to highlight the interrelationships among speaking, reading and writing. If, rather than avoiding difficult constructions, teachers provide specific support to enable their pupils to read them with understanding, then not only do the children gain access to a wider range of books – and the knowledge that they contain – but they also receive an important stimulus to the development of their own oral and written language.

Bibliography

Abercrombie, D. (1965) *Studies in phonetics and linguistics*. London: Oxford University Press.

Amidon, A. (1976) Children's understanding of sentences with contingent relations. *Journal of Experimental Child Psychology*, **22**, 423–37.

Applebee, A. N. (1978) *The child's concept of story: ages two to seventeen*. Chicago: University of Chicago Press.

Ardery, G. (1980) On co-ordination in child language. *Journal of Child Language*, **7**, 305–20.

Atwell, M. A. (1981) *The evolution of text: the interrelationship of reading and writing in the composing process*. Ed. D. thesis, Indiana University.

Baker, L. (1978) Processing temporal relationships in simple stories: effects of input sequence. *Journal of Verbal Learning and Verbal Behaviour*, **17**, 559–72.

Baldie, B. J. (1976) The acquisition of the passive voice. *Journal of Child Language*, **3**, 331–48.

Barnitz, J. G. (1980) Syntactic effects on the reading comprehension of pronoun-referent structures by children in grades two, four and six. *Reading Research Quarterly*, **15**, 268–89.

Beaumont, C. (1982) Reading relative clauses. *Journal of Research in Reading*, **5**, 29–41.

Bellugi, U. & Brown, R. (eds) (1964) *The acquisition of language*. Chicago: University of Chicago Press.

Bereiter, C. (1980) Development in writing. In Gregg & Steinberg (eds) (1980), 73–93.

Berko, J. (1958) The child's learning of English morphology. *Word*, **14**, 150–77.

Berkovits, R. & Wigodsky, M. (1979) On interpreting non-coreferent pronouns: a longitudinal study. *Journal of Child Language*, **6**, 585–92.

Berninger, G. & Garvey, C. (1982) Tag constructions: structure and function in child discourse. *Journal of Child Language*, **9**, 151–68.

Berry, M. (1975) *An introduction to systemic linguistics: 1 Structures and systems*. London: Batsford.

Bever, T. G. (1970) The cognitive basis for linguistic structures. In Hayes (ed.) (1970), 279–362.

Birnbaum, J. C. (1981) *A study of reading and writing behaviours of selected 4th grade and 7th grade students*. D.Ed. thesis, Rutgers, University of New Jersey.

Bloom, L. (1971) Why not pivot grammar? *Journal of Speech and Hearing Disorders*, **36**, 40–50.

Bloom, L., Miller, P. & Hood, L. (1975) Variation and reduction as aspects of competence in language development. In Pick (ed.) (1975), 3–55.

Bloom, L., Lahey, M., Hood, L., Lifter, K. & Fiess, K. (1980) Complex sentences: acquisition of syntactic connectives and the semantic relations they encode. *Journal of Child Language*, **7**, 235–61.

Bormuth, J. R., Manning, J., Carr, J. & Pearson, D. (1970) Children's comprehension of between- and within-sentence syntactic structures. *Journal of Educational Psychology*, **61**, 349–57.

Bowerman, M. (1979) The acquisition of complex sentences. In Fletcher & Garman (eds) (1979), 285–305.

Braine, M. D. S. (1976) Children's first word combinations. *Monographs of the Society for Research in Child Development*, **41**, no. 1.

Britton, J. (1970) *Language and learning*. Harmondsworth: Penguin.

(1975) Teaching writing. In Davies (ed.) (1975), 113–26.

Britton, J., Burgess, T., Martin, N., McLeod, A. & Rosen, H. (1975) *The development of writing abilities (11–18)*. Basingstoke: Macmillan Education.

Brown, H. D. (1971) Children's comprehension of relativized English sentences. *Child Development*, **42**, 1923–36.

Brown, R. (1957) Linguistic determinism and the part of speech. *Journal of Abnormal and Social Psychology*, **55**, 1–5.

(1968) The development of *Wh* questions in child speech. *Journal of Verbal Learning and Verbal Behaviour*, **7**, 279–90.

(1973) *A first language*. London: George Allen & Unwin.

Brown, R., Cazden, C. & Bellugi, U. (1969) The child's grammar from I to III. In Hill (ed.) (1969), 28–73.

Burgess, C. *et al.* (1973) *Understanding children writing*. Harmondsworth: Penguin.

Burgess, T. (1971) Kinds of writing. *English in Education*, **5**, 2, 36–47.

Burroughs, G. E. R. (1957) *A study of the vocabulary of young children*. University of Birmingham School of Education.

Cairns, H. S. & Hsu, J. R. (1978) *Who, why, when* and *how*: a development study. *Journal of Child Language*, **5**, 477–88.

Calkins, L. M. (1980) Children learn the writer's craft. *Language Arts*, **57**, 207–13.

Caplan, D. (1972) Clause boundaries and recognition latencies for words in sentences. *Perception and Psychophysics*, **12**, 73–6.

Carpenter, P. A. & Just, M. A. (1977) Reading comprehension as eyes see it. In Just & Carpenter (eds) (1977), 109–39.

Carrell, P. L. (1981) Children's understanding of indirect requests: comparing child and adult comprehension. *Journal of Child Language*, **8**, 329–45.

Carroll, J. B. & Freedle, R. O. (eds) (1972) *Language comprehension and the acquisition of knowledge*. Washington, DC: V. H. Winston & Sons.

Cashdan, A. (ed.) (1979) *Language, reading and learning*. Oxford: Basil Blackwell.

Chafe, W. L. (1972) Discourse structure and human knowledge. In Carroll & Freedle (eds) (1972), 41–69.

Cheshire, J. (1982) Dialect features and linguistic conflict in schools. *Educational Review*, **34**, 53–67.

Chomsky, C. (1969) *The acquisition of syntax in children from 5 to 10*. Cambridge, Mass.: MIT Press.

Clancy, P., Jacobsen, T. & Silva, M. (1976) The acquisition of conjunction: a cross-linguistic study. *Stanford Papers and Reports on Child Language Development*, **12**, 71–80.

Clark, E. V. (1971) On the acquisition of the meaning of *before* and *after*. *Journal of Verbal Learning and Verbal Behaviour*, **10**, 266–75.

Clay, M. M. (1969) Reading errors and self-correction behaviour. *British Journal of Educational Psychology*, **39**, 47–56.

Clegg, A. B. (ed.) (1964) *The excitement of writing*. London: Chatto & Windus.

Coker, P. L. (1978) Syntactic and semantic factors in the acquisition of *before* and *after*. *Journal of Child Language*, **5**, 261–77.

Coleman, E. B. (1962) Improving comprehensibility by shortening sentences. *Journal of Applied Psychology*, **46**, 131–4.

Collins, A. & Gentner, D. (1980) A framework for a cognitive theory of writing. In Gregg & Steinberg (eds) (1980), 51–72.

Cook, V. J. (1976) A note on indirect objects. *Journal of Child Language*, **3**, 435–7.

Corrigan, R. (1975) A scalogram analysis of the development of the use and comprehension of *because* in children. *Child Development*, **46**, 195–201.

Cotton, E. G. (1978) Noun-pronoun pleonasms: the role of age and situation. *Journal of Child Language*, **5**, 489–99.

Cromer, R. F. (1970) 'Children are nice to understand': surface structure clues for the recovery of a deep structure. *British Journal of Psychology*, **61**, 397–408.

Cromer, W. (1970) The difference model: a new explanation for some reading difficulties. *Journal of Educational Psychology*, **61**, 471–83.

Cruttenden, A. (1979) *Language in infancy and childhood*. Manchester: Manchester University Press.

Crystal, D. (1975) Neglected linguistic principles in the study of reading. In Moyle (ed.) (1975), 26–34.

(1979a) *Working with LARSP*. London: Edward Arnold.

(1979b) Language in education – a linguistic perspective. In Cashdan (ed.) (1979), 13–28.

(1979c) Reading, grammar and the line. In Thackray (ed.) (1979), 26–38.

(1980) Neglected grammatical factors in conversational English. In Greenbaum *et al.* (eds) (1980), 153–66.

Crystal, D. & Davy, D. (1969) *Investigating English style*. London: Longman.

Crystal, D. & Foster, J. L. (1979) *Databank*. London: Edward Arnold.

Crystal, D., Fletcher, P. & Garman, M. (1976) *The grammatical analysis of language disability*. London: Edward Arnold.

Curtiss, S. (1977) *Genie: a psycholinguistic study of a modern-day 'wild child'*. New York: Academic Press.

Cutts, M. & Maher, C. (1980) *Writing plain English*. Salford: Plain English Campaign.

Dale, P. S. (1976, 2nd ed.) *Language development: structure and function*. New York: Holt Rinehart and Winston.

Davies, A. (ed.) (1975) *Problems of language and learning*. London: Heinemann.

Davies, F., Greene, T. & Lunzer, E. (1980) *Reading for learning in science*. A discussion paper from the Schools Council Project, 'Reading for learning in the secondary school'. University of Nottingham.

DES (Department of Education and Science) (1975) *A language for life* [The Bullock Report]. London: HMSO.

de Villiers, J. G. & de Villiers, P. A. (1978) *Language acquisition.* Cambridge, Mass.: Harvard University Press.

de Villiers, J. G., Tager-Flusberg, H. & Hakuta, K. (1977) Deciding among theories of the development of co-ordination in child speech. *Stanford Papers and Reports on Child Language Development,* **13**, 118–25.

de Villiers, J. G., Tager-Flusberg, H., Hakuta, K. & Cohen, M. (1979) *Journal of Psycholinguistic Research,* **8**, 499–518.

de Villiers, P. A. & de Villiers, J. G. (1979) *Early language.* London: Fontana/ Open Books.

Dolan, T., Harrison, C. & Gardner, K. (1979) The incidence and context of reading in the classroom. In Lunzer & Gardner (eds) (1979), 108–38.

Dressler, W. U. (ed.) (1978) *Current trends in textlinguistics.* Berlin: Walter de Gruyter.

Durrell, D. D. (1969) Listening comprehension versus reading comprehension. *Journal of Reading,* **12**, 455–60.

Edwards, A. (1969) *The comprehension of written sentences containing relative clauses.* Ed.D. thesis, University of Harvard.

Edwards, J. R. (1979) *Language and disadvantage.* London: Edward Arnold.

Edwards, R. P. A. & Gibbon, V. (1964) *Words your children use.* London: Burke Books.

Ehrlich, K. (1979) *Comprehension and anaphora.* Unpublished Ph.D. thesis, University of Sussex. (Cited in Sanford, A. J. & Garrod, S. C. (1981).)

Eisenberg, A. R. (1981) The emergence of markers of current relevance. *Stanford Papers and Reports on Child Language Development,* **20**, 44–51.

Emerson, H. F. (1979) Children's comprehension of *because* in reversible and non-reversible sentences. *Journal of Child Language,* **6**, 279–300.

(1980) Children's judgments of correct and reversed sentences with *if. Journal of Child Language,* 7, 137–55.

Emslie, H. C. & Stevenson, R. J. (1981) Pre-school children's use of the articles in definite and indefinite referring expressions. *Journal of Child Language,* **8**, 313–28.

Ervin-Tripp, S. (1970) Discourse agreement: how children answer questions. In Hayes (ed.) (1970), 79–107.

Fawcett, R. P. & Perkins, M. R. (1980) *Child language transcripts 6-12,* Vols I–IV. Pontypridd: Polytechnic of Wales.

Ferguson, C. A. & Slobin, D. I. (eds) (1973) *Studies of child language development.* New York: Holt, Rinehart and Winston.

Fletcher, P. (1979) The development of the verb phrase. In Fletcher & Garman (eds) (1979), 261–84.

Fletcher, P. & Garman, M. (eds) (1979) *Language acquisition.* Cambridge: Cambridge University Press.

Flores d'Arcais, G. B. (1978) Levels of semantic knowledge in children's use of connectives. In Sinclair *et al.* (eds) (1978), 133–53.

Fluck, M. J. (1978) Comprehension of relative clauses by children aged five to nine years. *Language and Speech,* **21**, 190–201.

Fodor, J. & Garrett, M. (1967) Some syntactic determinants of sentential complexity. *Perception and Psychophysics,* **2**, 289–96.

Foss, D. J. & Hakes, D. T. (1978) *Psycholinguistics: an introduction to the psychology of language.* Englewood Cliffs, New Jersey: Prentice-Hall.

Foulke, E. & Sticht, T. G. (1969) Review of research on the intelligibility and comprehension of accelerated speech. *Psychological Bulletin,* **72**, 50–62.

French, L. A. & Brown, A. L. (1977) Comprehension of *before* and *after* in logical and arbitrary sequences. *Journal of Child Language*, **4**, 247–56.

Fries, C. C. (1952) *The Structure of English*. London: Longman.

Gamlin, P. J. (1971) Sentence processing as a function of syntax, short term memory capacity, the meaningfulness of the stimulus and age. *Language and Speech*, **14**, 115–34.

Gannon, P. & Czerniewska, P. (1980) *Using linguistics: an educational focus*. London: Edward Arnold.

Garber, M. D. (1979) *An examination and comparison of selected cohesive features found in child-produced texts and beginning reading materials*. Ph.D. thesis, Georgia State University College of Education.

Gardner, P. L. (1977) *Logical connectives in science: a summary of the findings*. Mimeographed report to the Australian Education Research and Development Committee.

Garman, M. (1979) Early grammatical development. In Fletcher & Garman (eds) (1979), 177–208.

Garrett, M., Bever, T. G. & Fodor, J. (1966) The active use of grammar in speech perception. *Perception and Psychophysics*, **1**, 30–2.

Givon, T. (1979) From discourse to syntax: grammar as a processing strategy. In Givon (ed.) (1979), 81–112.

(ed.) (1979) *Syntax and Semantics, Vol. 12: Discourse and Syntax*. New York: Academic Press.

Goldman-Eisler, F. (1961) The significance of changes in the rate of articulation. *Language and Speech*, **4**, 171–4.

(1964) Discussion and further comments. In Lenneberg (ed.) (1964), 109–30.

Goodluck, H. & Solan, L. (eds) (1978) *Papers in the structure and development of child language*. Occasional Papers in Linguistics, University of Massachusetts.

Goody, J. (1977) *The domestication of the savage mind*. London: Cambridge University Press.

Gourley, J. W. & Catlin, J. (1978) Children's comprehension of grammatical structures in context. *Journal of Psycholinguistic Research*, **7**, 419–34.

Graves, D. H. (1979) What children show us about revision. *Language Arts*, **56**, 312–9.

Greenbaum, S. (1980) The treatment of clause and sentence in *A Grammar of Contemporary English*. In Greenbaum *et al.* (eds) (1980), 17–29.

Greenbaum, S., Leech, G. & Svartvik, J. (eds) (1980) *Studies in English Linguistics for Randolph Quirk*. London: Longman.

Greenfield, P. M. (1972) Oral or written language: the consequences for cognitive development in Africa, the United States and England. *Language and Speech*, **15**, 169–78.

Gregg, L. W. & Steinberg, E. R. (eds) (1980) *Cognitive processes in writing*. Hillsdale, New Jersey: Lawrence Erlbaum Associates.

Hakes, D. T. (1972) Effects of reducing complement constructions on sentence comprehension. *Journal of Verbal Learning and Verbal Behaviour*, **11**, 278–86.

Hakes, D. T. & Cairns, H. S. (1970) Sentence comprehension and relative pronouns. *Perception and Psychophysics*, **8**, 5–8.

Hakes, D. T. & Foss, D. J. (1970) Decision processes during sentence comprehension: effects of surface structure reconsidered. *Perception and Psychophysics*, **8**, 413–16.

Hakuta, K., de Villiers, J. & Tager-Flusberg, H. (1982) Sentence co-ordination in Japanese and English. *Journal of Child Language*, **9**, 193–207.

Halle, M., Bresnan, J. & Miller, G. A. (eds) (1978) *Linguistic theory and psychological reality*. Cambridge, Mass.: MIT Press.

Halliday, M. A. K. (n.d.) Differences between spoken and written language. Mimeo.

Halliday, M. A. K. & Hasan, R. (1976) *Cohesion in English*. London: Longman.

Harpin, W. (1976) *The second 'R'*. London: George Allen and Unwin.

Harris, J. B. N. (1980) *Suprasentential organization in written discourse with particular reference to writing by children in the lower secondary age-range.* Unpublished M.A. thesis, University of Birmingham.

Harris, J. B. N. & Kay, S. (1981) *Writing development: suggestions for a policy 8–13.* Metropolitan Borough of Rotherham Education Committee.

Harris, R. J. (1975) Children's comprehension of complex sentences. *Journal of Experimental Child Psychology*, **19**, 420–33.

Harrison, C. (1980) *Readability in the classroom*. Cambridge: Cambridge University Press.

Hayes, J. R. (ed.) (1970) *Cognition and the development of language*. New York: John Wiley.

Henderson, I. (1979) *The use of connectives by fluent and not-so-fluent readers.* D.Ed. thesis, Columbia University Teachers College.

Hill, J. P. (ed.) (1969) *Minnesota Symposia on Child Psychology, vol. 2.* Minneapolis: University of Minnesota Press.

Hoey, M. P. (1979) *Signalling in discourse*. Birmingham: English Language Research, University of Birmingham.

Holbrook, D. (1961) *English for maturity*. London: Cambridge University Press.

Holmes, V. M. & Forster, K. I. (1972) Perceptual complexity and underlying sentence structure. *Journal of Verbal Learning and Verbal Behaviour*, **11**, 148–56.

Hopman, M. R. & Maratsos, M. P. (1978) A developmental study of factivity and negation in complex syntax. *Journal of Child Language*, **5**, 295–309.

Horgan, D. (1978) The development of the full passive. *Journal of Child Language*, **5**, 65–80.

Horowitz, M. W. & Newman, J. B. (1964) Spoken and written expression: an experimental analysis. *Journal of Abnormal and Social Psychology*, **68**, 640–7.

Hughes, A. & Trudgill, P. (1979) *English accents and dialects*. London: Edward Arnold.

Hunt, K. W. (1965) *Grammatical structures written at three grade levels.* Champaign, Illinois: National Council of Teachers of English.

(1966) Recent measures in syntactic development. *Elementary English*, **43**, 732–9.

(1970) Syntactic maturity in school children and adults. *Monographs of the Society for Research in Child Development*, **35**, no. 1.

Hutson, B. A. & Shub, J. (1975) Developmental study of factors involved in choice of conjunctions. *Child Development*, **46**, 46–52.

Irwin, J. W. (1980a) The effects of explicitness and clause order on the comprehension of reversible causal relationships. *Reading Research Quarterly*, **15**, 477–88.

(1980b) Implicit connectives and comprehension. *The Reading Teacher*, **33**, 527–9.

Isakson, R. L. (1979) Cognitive processing in sentence comprehension. *Journal of Educational Research*, **72**, 160–5.

Jarvella, R. J. (1971) Syntactic processing of connected speech. *Journal of Verbal Learning and Verbal Behaviour*, **10**, 409–16.

Johnstone, A. (1978) What's in a word? *New Scientist*, 18 May, 432–4.

Just, M. A. & Carpenter, P. A. (1971) Comprehension of negation with quantification. *Journal of Verbal Learning and Verbal Behaviour*, **10**, 244–53.

Just, M. A. & Carpenter, P. A. (eds) (1977) *Cognitive processes in comprehension*. Hillsdale, New Jersey: Lawrence Erlbaum Associates.

Kantor, K. J. & Rubin, D. L. (1981) Between speaking and writing: processes of differentiation. In Kroll & Vann (eds) (1981), 55–81.

Kantor, R. N. (1977) *The management and comprehension of discourse connection by pronouns in English*. Ph.D. dissertation, Ohio State University.

Karmiloff-Smith, A. (1979) Language development after five. In Fletcher & Garman (eds) (1979), 307–23.

Katz, E. W. & Brent, S. B. (1968) Understanding connectives. *Journal of Verbal Learning and Verbal Behaviour*, **7**, 501–9.

Keen, J. (1978) *Teaching English: a linguistic approach*. London: Methuen.

Kessel, F. S. (1970) The role of syntax in children's comprehension from ages six to twelve. *Monographs of the Society for Research in Child Development*, **35**, no. 6.

Kieras, D. E. (1978) Good and bad structure in simple paragraphs: effects on apparent theme, reading time, and recall. *Journal of Verbal Learning and Verbal Behaviour*, **17**, 13–28.

Kimball, J. (1973) Seven principles of surface structure parsing in natural language. *Cognition*, **2**, 15–47.

King, M. L. & Rentel, V. M. (1981) *How children learn to write: a longitudinal study*. Project report mimeo, Ohio State University.

Klima, E. S. & Bellugi, U. (1966) Syntactic regularities in the speech of children. In Lyons & Wales (eds) (1966), 183–219.

Kolers, P. A. (1970) Three stages of reading. In Levin & Williams (eds) (1970), 90–118.

Kramer, P. E., Koff, E. & Luria, Z. (1972) The development of competence in an exceptional language structure in older children and young adults. *Child Development*, **43**, 121–30.

Kress, G. (1982) *Learning to write*. London: Routledge and Kegan Paul.

Kroll, B. M. (1981) Developmental relationships between speaking and writing. In Kroll & Vann (eds) (1981), 32–54.

Kroll, B. M. & Vann, R. J. (eds) (1981) *Exploring speaking-writing relationships: connections and contrasts*. Urbana, Illinois: National Council of Teachers of English.

Kroll, B. M. & Wells, C. G. (eds) (1983) *Explorations in the development of writing*. Chichester: John Wiley.

Kroll, B. M., Kroll, D. L. & Wells, C. G. (1980) Researching children's writing development: the 'Children Learning to Write' Project. *Language for Learning*, **2**, 53–81.

Kuczaj, S. A. & Daly, M. J. (1979) The development of hypothetical reference in the speech of young children. *Journal of Child Language*, **6**, 563–79.

Lahey, M. (1974) Use of prosody and syntactic markers in children's comprehension of spoken sentences. *Journal of Speech and Hearing Research*, **17**, 656–68.

Leech, G. N. (1966) *English in advertising: a linguistic study of advertising in Great Britain*. London: Longman.

Leech, G. N. & Svartvik, J. (1975) *A communicative grammar of English*. London: Longman.

Lenneberg, E. H. (ed.) (1964) *New directions in the study of language*. Cambridge, Mass.: MIT Press.

Lesgold, A. M. (1974) Variability in children's comprehension of syntactic structures. *Journal of Educational Psychology*, **66**, 333–8.

Levin, H. (1979) *The eye-voice span*. Cambridge, Mass.: MIT Press.

Levin, H. & Kaplan, E. L. (1970) Grammatical structure and reading. In Levin & Williams (eds) (1970), 119–33.

Levin, H. & Williams, J. P. (eds) (1970) *Basic studies on reading*. New York: Basic Books.

Limber, J. (1973) The genesis of complex sentences. In Moore (ed.) (1973), 169–185.

Loban, W. D. (1963) *The language of elementary school children*. Champaign, Illinois: National Council of Teachers of English.

Longacre, R. & Levinsohn, S. (1978) Field analysis of discourse. In Dressler (ed.) (1978), 103–22.

Lunzer, E. & Gardner, K. (eds) (1979) *The effective use of reading*. London: Heinemann Educational.

Lyons, J. & Wales, R. J. (eds) (1966) *Psycholinguistics papers*. Edinburgh: Edinburgh University Press.

Major, D. (1974) *The acquisition of modal auxiliaries in the language of children*. The Hague: Mouton.

Maratsos, M. P. (1976) *The use of definite and indefinite reference in young children*. Cambridge: Cambridge University Press.

(1979) Learning how and when to use pronouns and determiners. In Fletcher & Garman (eds) (1979), 225–40.

Marshall, N. & Glock, M. D. (1978) Comprehension of connected discourse: a study into the relationships between the structure of text and information recalled. *Reading Research Quarterly*, **14**, 10–56.

Marsland, C. G. (1980) Early development of complex sentences. Paper presented at the Child Language Seminar, Manchester.

Massaro, D. W. (ed.) (1975) *Understanding language*. New York: Academic Press.

McClure, E., Mason, J. & Barnitz, J. (1979) An exploratory study of story structure and age effects on children's ability to sequence stories. *Discourse Processes*, **2**, 213–49.

Menyuk, P. (1969) *Sentences children use*. Cambridge, Mass.: MIT Press.

(1971) *The acquisition and development of language*. Englewood Cliffs, New Jersey: Prentice-Hall.

Miller, G. A. (1956) The magical number seven, plus or minus two: some limits on our capacity for processing information. *Psychological Review*, **63**, 81–96.

Miller, W. R. (1973) The acquisition of grammatical rules by children. In Ferguson & Slobin (eds) (1973), 380–91.

Miller, W. R. & Ervin, S. (1964) The development of grammar in child language. In Bellugi & Brown (eds) (1964), 9–34.

Mills, A. E. (1981) It's easier in German isn't it? The acquisition of tag questions in a bilingual child. *Journal of Child Language*, **8**, 641–7.

Milroy, L. & Milroy, J. (forthcoming) *Authority in language: a sociolinguistic study of prescriptivism*. London: Routledge & Kegan Paul.

Mittins, W. H., Salu, M., Edminson, M. & Coyne, S. (1970) *Attitudes to English usage*. London: Oxford University Press.

Moberly, P. G. C. (1978) *Elementary children's understanding of anaphoric relationships in connected discourse*. Ph.D. dissertation, Northwestern University, Evanston, Illinois.

Moffett, J. (1968) *Teaching the universe of discourse*. Boston: Houghton Mifflin.

Moon, C. (1979) Categorization of miscues arising from textual weakness. In Thackray (ed.) (1979), 135–46.

Moore, T. E. (ed.) (1973) *Cognitive development and the acquisition of language*. New York: Academic Press.

Moyle, D. (ed.) (1975) *Reading: what of the future?* London: Ward Lock Educational.

Nuttall, W. (1982) *The relationship between the phonology and spellings of southeast London children: a study of some consonants*. Unpublished M.A. dissertation, University of Manchester.

Oakan, R., Wiener, M. & Cromer, W. (1971) Identification, organization and reading comprehension for good and poor readers. *Journal of Educational Psychology*, **62**, 71–8.

Ochs, E. (1979) Planned and unplanned discourse. In Givon (ed.) (1979), 51–80.

O'Connor, J. D. & Arnold, G. F. (1961, 1973) *Intonation of colloquial English*. London: Longman.

O'Donnell, R. C., Griffin, W. J. & Norris, R. C. (1967) *Syntax of kindergarten and elementary school children: a transformational analysis*. Champaign, Illinois: National Council of Teachers of English.

Olds, H. F., Jr. (1968) *An experimental study of syntactic factors influencing children's comprehension of certain complex relationships*. (Center for Research and Development of Educational Difficulties Rep. No. 4) Cambridge, Mass.: Harvard University Press. (Cited in Palermo, D. S. & Molfese, D. L. (1972).)

Olson, D. R. (1977) From utterance to text: the bias of language in speech and writing. *Harvard Educational Review*, **47**, 257–81.

Osgood, C. E. & Zehler, A. M. (1981) Acquisition of bi-transitive sentences: pre-linguistic determinants of language acquisition. *Journal of Child Language*, **8**, 367–83.

Palermo, D. S. & Molfese, D. L. (1972) Language acquisition from age five onward. *Psychological Bulletin*, **78**, 409–28.

Palmer, F. R. (1974) *The English verb*. London: Longman.

Pearson, D. (1975) The effects of grammatical complexity on children's comprehension, recall and conception of certain semantic relations. *Reading Research Quarterly*, **10**, 155–92.

Peltz, F. K. (1974) The effect upon comprehension of repatterning based on students' writing patterns. *Reading Research Quarterly*, **9**, 603–21.

Perera, K. (1979) Reading and writing. In Cruttenden, A. (1979), 130–60.

(1980) The assessment of linguistic difficulty in reading material. *Educational Review*, **32**, 151–61.

(forthcoming) Some linguistic difficulties in school textbooks. In Gillham, B. A. (ed.) *The language of school subjects*. London: Heinemann Educational.

Perl, S. (1979) The composing processes of unskilled college writers. *Research in the Teaching of English*, **13**, 317–36.

Phinney, M. (1981) Children's interpretation of negation in complex sentences. In Tavakolian (ed.) (1981), 116–38.

Piaget, J. (1926) *The language and thought of the child*. London: Kegan Paul, Trench, Trubner.

Pick, A. D. (ed.) (1975) *Minnesota Symposia on Child Psychology, vol. 9*. Minneapolis: University of Minnesota Press.

Quirk, R. (1972) *The English language and images of matter*. London: Oxford University Press.

Quirk, R. & Greenbaum, S. (1973) *A university grammar of English*. London: Longman.

Quirk, R., Greenbaum, S., Leech, G. N. & Svartvik, J. (1972) *A grammar of contemporary English*. London: Longman.

Raban, B. (1982) Text display effects on the fluency of young readers. *Journal of Research in Reading*, **5**, 7–28.

Reid, J. F. (1966) Learning to think about reading. *Educational Research*, **9**, 56–62.

(1972) Children's comprehension of syntactic features found in some extension readers. In Reid (ed.) (1972), 394–403.

(ed.) (1972) *Reading: problems and practices*. London: Ward Lock Educational.

Richek, M. A. (1976) Effect of sentence complexity on the reading comprehension of syntactic structures. *Journal of Educational Psychology*, **68**, 800–6.

(1977) Reading comprehension of anaphoric forms in varying linguistic contexts. *Reading Research Quarterly*, **12**, 145–65.

Richmond, J. (1979) Dialect features in children's writing. *Language development, PE 232, Block 2, Supplementary readings*, 41–55. Milton Keynes: Open University Press.

Robertson, J. E. (1968) Pupil understanding of connectives in reading. *Reading Research Quarterly*, **3**, 387–417.

Rode, S. S. (1974) Development of phrase and clause boundary reading in children. *Reading Research Quarterly*, **10**, 124–42.

Rodgers, D. (1974) Which connectives? Signals to enhance comprehension. *Journal of Reading*, **17**, 462–6.

Rosen, C. & Rosen, H. (1973) *The language of primary school children*. Harmondsworth: Penguin.

Rosenberg, S. & Koplin, J. H. (1968) *Developments in applied psycholinguistics research*. New York: Macmillan.

Rubin, D. L. (1982) Adapting syntax in writing to varying audiences as a function of age and social cognitive ability. *Journal of Child Language*, **9**, 497–510.

Ruddell, R. B. (1965) The effect of oral and written patterns of language structure on reading comprehension. *The Reading Teacher*, **18**, 270–5.

Sachs, J. S. (1967) Recognition memory for syntactic and semantic aspects of connected discourse. *Perception and Psychophysics*, **2**, 437–42.

(1974) Memory in reading and listening to discourse. *Memory and Cognition*, **2**, 95–100.

Sanford, A. J. & Garrod, S. C. (1981) *Understanding written language*. Chichester: John Wiley.

Saukkonen, P. (1977) Spoken and written language. *Folia Linguistica*, **11**, 207–15.

Scholnick, E. K. & Wing, C. S. (1982) The pragmatics of subordinating conjunctions: a second look. *Journal of Child Language*, **9**, 461–79.

Schools Council (1976) *From talking to writing*. Writing Across the Curriculum 11–16 Project. London: Ward Lock Educational.

Schwartz, M. (1977) Rewriting or recopying: what are we teaching? *Language Arts*, **54**, 756–66.

Scinto, L. F. (1977) Textual competence: a preliminary analysis of orally generated texts. *Linguistics*, **194**, 5–34.

Scoville, R. P. & Gordon, A. M. (1980) Children's understanding of factive presuppositions: an experiment and a review. *Journal of Child Language*, **7**, 381–99.

Self, D. (1980) Radio newspeak. *Times Educational Supplement*, 20/6/1980, 21.

Shaughnessy, M. P. (1977) *Errors and expectations: a guide for the teacher of basic writing*. New York: Oxford University Press.

Sheldon, A. (1974) The role of parallel function in the acquisition of relative clauses in English. *Journal of Verbal Learning and Verbal Behaviour*, **13**, 272–81.

Siler, E. R. (1974) The effects of syntactic and semantic constraints on the oral reading performance of second and fourth graders. *Reading Research Quarterly*, **9**, 583–602.

Sinclair, A., Jarvella, R. J. & Levelt, W. J. M. (eds) (1978) *The child's conception of language*. Berlin: Springer.

Singer, H. & Ruddell, R. B. (eds) (1976, 2nd ed.) *Theoretical models and processes of reading*. Newark, Delaware: International Reading Association.

Slobin, D. I. (1966) Grammatical transformations and sentence comprehension in childhood and adulthood. *Journal of Verbal Learning and Verbal Behaviour*, **5**, 219–27.

(1971) *Psycholinguistics*. Glenview, Illinois: Scott, Foresman and Co.

(1973a) Introductory notes. In Ferguson & Slobin (eds) (1973), 333–4, 462–5.

(1973b) Cognitive pre-requisites for the development of grammar. In Ferguson & Slobin (eds) (1973), 175–208.

Slobin, D. I. & Welsh, C. A. (1973) Elicited imitation as a research tool in developmental psycholinguistics. In Ferguson & Slobin (eds) (1973), 485–97.

Strickland, R. G. (1962) The language of elementary school children: its relationship to the language of reading textbooks and the quality of reading of selected children. *Bulletin of the School of Education*, **38**, no. 4. Bloomington, Indiana: University of Indiana.

Stubbs, M. (1980) *Language and literacy: the sociolinguistics of reading and writing*. London: Routledge & Kegan Paul.

Sutton, C. (ed.) (1981) *Communicating in the classroom*. London: Hodder and Stoughton.

Tatham, S. M. (1970) Reading comprehension of materials written with select oral language patterns. *Reading Research Quarterly*, **5**, 402–26.

Tavakolian, S. L. (1976) Children's comprehension of pronominal subjects and missing subjects in complicated sentences. In Goodluck & Solan (eds) (1978), 146–52.

(1978) The conjoined-clause analysis of relative clauses and other structures. In Goodluck & Solan (eds) (1978), 38–83.

(ed.) (1981) *Language acquisition and linguistic theory*. Cambridge, Mass.: MIT Press.

Thackray, D. (ed.) (1979) *Growth in reading*. London: Ward Lock Educational.

Thieman, T. J. (1975) Imitation and recall of optionally deletable sentences by young children. *Journal of Child Language*, **2**, 261–9.

Thornton, G. (1980) *Teaching writing: the development of written language skills.* London: Edward Arnold.

Todd, P. (1982) Tagging after red herrings: evidence against the processing capacity explanation in child language. *Journal of Child Language,* **9**, 99–114.

Trudgill, P. (1975) *Accent, dialect and the school.* London: Edward Arnold.

Turner, E. A. & Rommetveit, R. (1967) The acquisition of sentence voice and reversibility. *Child Development,* **38**, 649–60.

Tyack, D. & Ingram, D. (1977) Children's production and comprehension of questions. *Journal of Child Language,* **4**, 211–24.

Umiker-Sebeok, D. J. (1979) Pre-school children's intraconversational narratives. *Journal of Child Language,* **6**, 91–109.

Vygotsky, L. S. (1962) *Thought and language.* Cambridge, Mass.: MIT Press.

Walker, L. (1976) Comprehending writing and spontaneous speech. *Reading Research Quarterly,* **11**, 144–67.

Wanat, S. F. (1976) Relations between language and visual processing. In Singer & Ruddell (eds) (1976), 108–36.

Wanner, E. (1974) *On remembering, forgetting and understanding sentences.* The Hague: Mouton.

Wanner, E. & Maratsos, M. P. (1978) An ATN approach to comprehension. In Halle *et al.* (eds) (1978), 119–61.

Warden, D. A. (1976) The influence of context on children's use of identifying expressions and references. *British Journal of Psychology,* **67**, 101–12.

Watkins, O. (1981) Writing: how it is set. In Sutton (ed.) (1981), 29–46.

Watts, A. F. (1944) *The language and mental development of children.* London: Harrap.

Weber, R. M. (1970) A linguistic analysis of first-grade reading errors. *Reading Research Quarterly,* **5**, 427–51.

Wells, C. G. (1974) School of Education, University of Bristol: Language development in pre-school children. *Journal of Child Language,* **1**, 158–62.

Wells, J. C. & Colson, G. (1971) *Practical phonetics.* London: Pitman.

Whitcombe, V. (1973) Every teacher a teacher of English. *English in Education,* **7**, 43–56.

Whitehall, H. (1951) *Structural essentials of English.* London: Longman.

Whitford, H. C. (1966) *A dictionary of American homophones and homographs.* New York: Teachers College Press.

Wilkinson, A. (1971) *The foundations of language.* London: Oxford University Press.

Wilkinson, A., Barnsley, G., Hanna, P. & Swan, M. (1979) Assessing language development: the Crediton Project. *Language for Learning,* **1**, 59–76.

Wilkinson, J. (1980) *A piranha in the sewers: narrative structure in children's writing, and its implications for primary education.* Unpublished M.A. thesis, University of Birmingham.

　(1981) Children's writing: composing or decomposing? *Nottingham Linguistic Circular,* **10**, 72–108.

Williams, J. M. (1979) Defining complexity. *College English,* **40**, 595–609.

Wing, C. S. & Scholnick, E. K. (1981) Children's comprehension of pragmatic concepts expressed in *because, although, if* and *unless. Journal of Child Language,* **8**, 347–65.

Winter, E. O. (1977) A clause-relational approach to English texts. *Instructional Science,* **6**, 1–92.

Wren, C. T. (1981) Identifying patterns of syntactic disorder in six-year-old children. *British Journal of Disorders of Communication*, **16**, 101–9.

Yerrill, K. A. J. (1977) *A consideration of the later development of children's syntax in speech and writing: a study of parenthetical, appositional and related items.* Unpublished Ph.D. thesis, University of Newcastle upon Tyne.

Index